Dow Alexander

History of Hindoostan, translated from the persian

Vol.1

Dow Alexander

History of Hindoostan, translated from the persian
Vol.1

ISBN/EAN: 9783337955540

Printed in Europe, USA, Canada, Australia, Japan

Cover: Foto ©ninafisch / pixelio.de

More available books at **www.hansebooks.com**

THE
HISTORY
OF
HINDOSTAN.

Frontispiece to Vol. I.

H. Brocas Sculp.

Shaw Allum the present Emperor of Hindostan.

THE HISTORY OF HINDOSTAN,

TRANSLATED FROM THE PERSIAN.

THE THIRD EDITION.

IN THREE VOLUMES.

VOL. I.

By ALEXANDER DOW, Esq.

Lieutenant-Colonel in the Company's Service.

DUBLIN:

LUKE WHITE.

M.DCC.XCII.

TO THE

KING.

SIR,

THE Hiſtory of India is laid, with great humility, at the foot of the throne. As no inconſiderable part of Hindoſtan is now in a manner comprehended within the circle of the Britiſh empire, there is a propriety in addreſſing the hiſtory of that country to the Sovereign.

The ſucceſs of your Majeſty's arms has laid open the Eaſt to the reſearches of the curious; and your gracious acceptance of this firſt, though ſmall ſpecimen of the literature of Aſia, will excite men of greater abilities than the preſent tranſlator poſſeſſes, to ſtudy the annals of a people, remarkable for their antiquity, civilization, and the ſingular character of their religion and manners.

In the hiſtory of Hindoſtan, now offered to your Majeſty, the people of Great-Britain may ſee a ſtriking contraſt of their own condition; and, whilſt they feel for human

nature

nature ſuffering under deſpotiſm, exult at the ſame time, in that happy liberty, which they enjoy under the government of a Prince who delights in augmenting the ſecurity and felicity of his ſubjects.

That your Majeſty may long remain a public bleſſing, and reign for a ſeries of many years over this happy nation, is the ſincere prayer of

Your Majeſty's
most dutiful,
moſt humble,
and moſt devoted
ſubject and ſervant,

ALEXANDER DOW.

ADVERTISEMENT.

THE favourable reception, which the Public have been pleaſed to give to the Firſt Edition, has encouraged the Tranſlator to offer another to the World, much leſs unworthy, than the former, of the attention of the curious in the affairs of Aſia. The objections made to the work are now removed; the number of proper Names, which made ſome parts of it harſh and uncouth, is very much reduced, and the diction, in general, is rendered more connected, clear, elegant, and ſmooth.

Feriſhta's account of the ancient Indians, and the invaſions of the Mahommedans, before the commencement of the Ghiznian Empire, is omitted, and an Introduction ſubſtituted in its place, more ſatisfactory, ſuccinct, and agreeable. To throw more light on the affairs of India, there is given at the concluſion of the different reigns, a ſummary review of the affairs of the reſt of Aſia; and, in ſhort, nothing has been neglected, that could be thought to contribute to render the work a compleat Hiſtory

Hiſtory of Hindoſtan, to the death of the Emperor AKBAR, the third of the Mogul race.

The Tranſlator was induced to review the whole, with the utmoſt attention and care, in order to render it a proper Introduction to the Hiſtory of the imperial houſe of Timur in Hindoſtan; which, if ſufficient materials ſhall come to his hands in Aſia, he intends to give to the Public, after his return.

CONTENTS

OF THE

FIRST VOLUME.

A DISSERTATION CONCERNING THE CUSTOMS, MANNERS, LANGUAGE, RELIGION, and PHILOSOPHY of the HINDOOS.

Divided

THE HISTORY OF HINDOSTAN.

A DISSERTATION CONCERNING THE ANTIENT HISTORY of the INDIANS.

MAHOM-

CONTENTS.

MAHOMMEDAN CONQUERERS of INDIA.

SUBUCTAGI.

ISMAIEL.

MAMOOD I.

Comes

C O N T E N T S.

Reduces

MAHOMMED I.

MUSAOOD I.

MODOOD.

Invasion

MUSAOOD II.

ALI.

RESHID.

FEROCH-ZAAD.

IBRAHIM I.

MUSAOOD III.

ARSILLA.

BYRAM.

CONTENTS.

BYRAM.

CHUSERO I.

CHUSERO II.

MAHOMMED GHORI.

Marches

CUTTUB.

ELDOZE.

ARAM.

ALTUMSH.

FEROSE I.

SULTANA RIZIA.

The

BYRAM II.

MUSAOOD IV.

MAMOOD II.

BALIN.

A gallant

KEI KOBAD.

FEROSE II.

The

ALLA I.

Alip,

OMAR.

MUBARICK I.

TUGLICK I.

MAHOMMED III.

FEROSE III.

TUGLICK II.

ABU BICKER.

MAHOMMED IV.

MAMOOD

MAMOOD III.

THOUGH, in an advanced ſtage of ſociety, the human mind is, in ſome reſpects, enlarged, a ruinous kind of ſelf-conceit frequently circumſcribes its reſearches after knowledge. In love with our own times, country and government, we are apt to conſider diſtant ages and nations, as objects unworthy of the page of the Hiſtorian. Theſe prejudices are not confined to the vulgar and illiterate: Some men of genius and reputation for Philoſophy, have entertained ſentiments upon that ſubject, too narrow and confined for the Goths of a much darker age.

Had the tranſlator of the following hiſtory thought ſo meanly of the affairs of the eaſt, as theſe men affect to do, he might have ſaved a great deal of time and labour. To unlock the ſprings, from which he has derived his knowledge was not ſo eaſy a taſk, that he would have undertaken it, without an opinion, that the domeſtic affairs of India were, in ſome degree, worthy of being related.

He has the satisfaction to find, from the encouragement given to the former edition, notwithstanding the uncouth form in which it appeared, that the history of Hindostan is an object of attention to many in Great Britain; and this has not been his least inducement to render it, now much less unworthy of the public eye. To translate from the Persian, was not the primary view of the publisher of Ferishta's Epitome of the History of the Mahommedan princes of India. To qualify himself for negotiation, was his first object in learning the language. As he proceeded in his studies, other motives for his continuing them arose. Though the manner of eastern composition differs from the correct taste of Europe, there are many things in the writings of Asiatic authors worthy of the attention of literary men. Their poetry it must be confessed, is too turgid and full of conceits to please, and the diction of their historians very diffuse and verbose: yet amidst the redundancy of the latter, we find that scrupulous attention to truth, and that manliness of sentiment, which constitute the very essence of good history.

The works of Mahommed Casim Ferishta of Delhi, who flourished in the reign of Jehangire, about the beginning of the seventeenth century, were put into the translator's hands, by his teachers. As he advanced, a new field gradually opened before him. He found, with some degree of astonishment, the authentic history

history of a great empire, the name of which had scarcely ever travelled to Europe. Being, at the same time, honoured with the particular friendship of the emperor, at whose court he had for some time lived, he was induced to listen to that prince's solicitations, for giving to the English some idea of his predecessors on the throne of India.

Though our author has given the title of the History of Hindostan to his work, yet it is rather that of the Mahommedan empire in India, than a general account of the affairs of the Hindoos. What he says concerning India, prior to the first invasion of the Afgan Mussulmen, is very far from being satisfactory. He collected his accounts from Persian authors, being altogether unacquinted with the Shanscrita or learned language of the Brahmins, in which the internal history of India is comprehended. We must not therefore, with Ferishta, consider the Hindoos as destitute of genuine domestic annals, or that those voluminous records they possess are mere legends framed by the Brahmins.

The prejudices of the Mahommedans against the followers of the Brahmin religion, seldom permit them to speak with common candour of the Hindoos. It swayed very much with Ferishta when he affirmed, that there is no history among the Hindoos of better authority than the Mahabarit. That work is a poem and not a history: It was translated into Persian by the brother of the great Abul Fazil, rather as a performance of fancy, than as an authentic account of the ancient dynaſties of the Kings of India. But that there are many hundred volumes in proſe in the Shanſcrita language, which treat of the ancient Indians, the tranſlator can, from his own knowledge, aver, and he has great reaſon to believe, that the Hindoos carry their authentic hiſtory farther back into antiquity, than any other nation now exiſting.

The Mahommedans know nothing of the Hindoo learning: and had they even any knowledge of the hiſtory of the followers of Brimha, their prejudices in favour of the jewiſh fictions contained in the Koran, would make them reject accounts, which tend to ſubvert the ſyſtem of their own faith. The Shanſcrita records contain accounts of the affairs of the weſtern Aſia, very different from what any tribe of the Arabians have tranſmitted to poſterity: and it is more than probable, that upon examination, the former will appear to bear the marks of more authenticity, and of greater antiquity than the latter.

But whether the Hindoos poſſeſs any true hiſtory of greater antiquity than other nations, muſt altogether reſt upon the authority of the Brahmins, till we ſhall become better acquainted with their records. Their pretenſions however are very high, and they confidently affirm, that the Jewiſh and Mahommedan religions are hereſies, from what

is

is contained in the Bedas. They give a very particular account of the origin of the Jewiſh religion in records of undoubted antiquity. Raja Tura, ſay they, who is placed in the firſt ages of the Cal Jug, had a ſon who apoſtatized from the Hindoo faith, for which he was baniſhed by his father to the Weſt. The apoſtate fixed his reſidence in a country called Mohgod, and propagated the Jewiſh religion, which the impoſtor Mahommed further corrupted. The Cal Jug commenced about 4887 years ago, and whether the whole ſtory may not relate to Terah and his ſon Abraham, is a point not worthy of being minutely diſcuſſed.

Feizi, the brother of Abul Fazil the hiſtorian, was the only Muſſulman we ever heard of, who underſtood the Shanſcrita. The fraudulent means by which he acquired it, will be ſhewn in another place. He never tranſlated any of the Indian hiſtories, excepting the Mahabarit, which, at beſt, is but an hiſtorical poem, in which a great deal of fable is blended with a little truth. We, upon the whole, cannot much depend upon the accounts which the followers of Mahommed give of the religion and ancient hiſtory of the Hindoos: Their prejudice makes them miſrepreſent the former, and their ignorance in the Shanſcrita language, has totally excluded them from any knowledge of the latter.

The hiſtory of Feriſhta being an abridgment of a variety of authors, who wrote diſ-

tinct

tinct accounts of the different reigns of the Mahommedan Emperors of Hindostan, he, with a view to comprehend in a small compass, every material transaction, has crowded the events too much together, without interspersing them with those reflections which give spirit and elegance to works of this kind: This defect seems however to have proceeded more from a studied brevity, than from a narrowness of genius in Ferishta. Upon some occasions, especially in the characters of the princes, he shews a strength of judgment, and a nervousness and conciseness of expression which would do no dishonour to the best writers in the west. What is really remarkable in this writer is, that he seems as much divested of religious prejudices, as he is of political flattery or fear. He never passes a good action without conferring upon it its due reward of praise, nor a bad one, let the villainous actor be never so high, without stigmatizing it with infamy. In short, if he does not arrive at the character of a good writer, he certainly deserves that of a good man.

The brevity which we censure in Ferishta, is by no means a common fault in the writers of Asia. Redundant and verbose in their diction, they often regard more the cadence and turn of their sentiments,. than the propriety and elegance of their thoughts; leading frequently the reader into a labyrinth to which he can find no end. This is too much the manner of the learned Abul Fazil himself.

He

He wrote the hiſtory of the reign of Akbar in two large volumes in folio. The intrigues of the court, and all the ſecret motives to action are inveſtigated with the utmoſt exactneſs; but the diction is too diffuſe, and the language too florid for the correct taſte of Europe.

It ought here to be remarked, that all the oriental hiſtorians write, in what they call in Europe, poetical proſe. This falſe taſte only commenced about five centuries ago, when literature declined in Aſia, with the power of the Caliphs. The tranſlator has now in his poſſeſſion, books written in the Perſian before that period, the diction of which is as conciſe and manly, as that which deſcended from Greece and Rome, to the writers of modern Europe. The learned and celebrated Abul Fazil, inſtead of correcting this vicious taſte, encouraged it greatly by his florid manner, in his hiſtory of the reign of Akbar. But this great writer has, notwithſtanding his circumlocutions, cloathed his expreſſions with ſuch beauty and pomp of eloquence, that he ſeems to come down upon the aſtoniſhed reader, like Ganges when it overflows its banks.

The ſmall progreſs which correctneſs and elegance of ſentiment and diction has made in the Eaſt, did not proceed from a want of encouragement to literature. We ſhall find in the courſe of this hiſtory, that no princes in the world patroniſed men of letters with more generoſity and reſpect, than the Mahommedan

Emperors

Emperors of Hindoſtan. A literary genius was not only the certain means to acquire a degree of wealth which muſt aſtoniſh Europeans, but an infallible road for riſing to the firſt offices of the ſtate. The character of the learned, was at the ſame time ſo ſacred, that tyrants, who made a paſtime of imbruing their hands in the blood of their other ſubjects, not only abſtained from offering violence to men of genius, but ſtood in fear of their pens. It is a proverb in the Eaſt, that the Monarchs of Aſia were more afraid of the pen of Abul Fazil, than they were of the ſword of Akbār; and, however amazing it may ſeem in abſolute governments, it is certain that the hiſtorians of that diviſion of the world, have wrote with more freedom concerning perſons and things, than writers have ever dared to do in the Weſt.

The tranſlator, however, being ſenſible of the impropriety of poetical diction, in the grave narration of hiſtorical facts, has, in many places, clipped the wings of Feriſhta's turgid expreſſions, and reduced his metaphors into common language, without however ſwerving in the leaſt from the original meaning of the author.

A frequent repetition of proper names is unavoidable in a work of ſuch brevity, and ſo much crowded with action. This defect is, in a great meaſure, remedied in this edition; the titles of the great men are, for the moſt part, omitted; and the pronouns are

more

more frequently ufed. The tranflator, in fhort, has given as few as poffible of the faults of his author; but he has been cautious enough, not wittingly at leaft, to fubftitute any of his own in their place.

Ferifhta with great propriety begins the hiftory of the Patan empire in Hindoftan, from the commencement of the kingdom of Ghizni. The Mahommedan government, which afterwards extended itfelf to India, rofe originally from very fmall beginnings among the mountains which divide Perfia from India. The Afgans or Patans, a warlike race of men, who had been fubjects to the imperial family of Samania, who, having revolted from the Caliphat, reigned, for a feries of many years, in Bochara, rebelled under their governor Abiftagi, in the fourth century of the Higera, and laid the foundation of the empire of Ghizni, known commonly in Europe by the name of Gazna. Under a fucceffion of warlike princes, this empire rofe to a furprifing magnitude. We find that in the reign of Mufaood I. in the beginning of the fifth century of the Higera, it extended from Ifpahan to Bengal, and from the mouths of the Indus to the banks of the Jaxartes, which comprehends near half of the great continent of Afia.

In lefs than a century after the death of Mufaood, the Charizmian empire arofe upon the ruins of the dynafty of the Siljokides, on the confines of Perfia and great Tartary.

It

It extended itſelf over Tartary and the greateſt part of the Perſian provinces; the Kings of the Ghiznian Patans were obliged to relinquiſh their dominions in the north, and to transfer the ſeat of their empire to Lahore, and afterwards to Delhi.

When the great conqueror of Aſia Zingis Chan, invaded and ſubverted the Charizmian empire under Mahommed, the Patan dominions were entirely confined within the limits of Hindoſtan. They poſſeſſed however power ſufficient to repel the generals of that great man, though fluſhed with victory and the ſpoils of the Eaſt. The whole force of Zingis, it is true, was never bent againſt Hindoſtan, otherwiſe it is probable it would have ſhared the fate of the weſtern Aſia, which was almoſt depopulated by his ſword.

The uncommon ſtrength of the Patan empire in Hindoſtan at this period, may be eaſily accounted for: It was the policy of the adopted Turkiſh ſlaves of the family of Ghor, who then held the kingdom of Delhi, to keep ſtanding armies of the mountain Afgans, under their reſpective chiefs, who were invariably created Omrahs of the empire. This hardy race, whatever domeſtic confuſions and revolutions they might occaſion in India, were, to uſe Feriſhta's words, a wall of iron againſt foreign enemies.

Our author has not been careful to mark the extent of the Empire in every reign. We can only form a general idea of it, from the tranſactions

tranſactions which he records. The Empire we find ſometimes reduced to a few diſtricts round the capital, and at other times, extending itſelf from the bay of Bengal to Perſia, and from the Carnatic to the great mountains of Sewalic. In ſhort, the boundaries of the Patan imperial dominions, varied in proportion to the abilities of thoſe princes who poſſeſſed the throne. When the monarchs diſcovered great parts, the governors of provinces ſhrunk back from their independance into their former ſubmiſſion; but when a weak Prince ſat on the Muſnud, his lieutenants ſtarted up into Kings around him.

The hiſtory now given to the public, preſents us with a ſtriking picture of the deplorable condition of a people ſubjected to arbitrary ſway; and of the inſtability of empire itſelf, when it is founded neither upon laws, nor upon the opinions and attachments of mankind. Hindoſtan, in every age, was an ample field for private ambition, and for public tyranny. At one time we ſee a petty Omrah ſtarting forth, and wading through an ocean of blood to the crown, or involving many thouſands of indigent adventurers in the ruin which he draws upon his own head. At another time we met with Kings, from a luſt of power which defeats itſelf, deſtroying thoſe ſubjects over whom they only wiſhed to tyrannize.

In a government like that of India, public ſpirit is never ſeen, and loyalty is a thing unknown.

unknown. The people permit themſelves to be transferred from one tyrant to another, without murmuring; and individuals look with unconcern upon the miſeries of others, if they are capable to ſcreen themſelves from the general misfortune. This, however, is a picture of Hindoſtan in bad times, and under the worſt Kings. As arbitrary government can inflict the moſt ſudden miſeries, ſo, when in the hand of good men, it can adminiſter the moſt expeditious relief to the ſubject. We accordingly find in this hiſtory, that the misfortunes of half an age of tyranny, are removed in a few years, under the mild adminiſtration of a virtuous prince.

It may not be improper in this place, to lay before the public, a ſhort ſketch of the conſtitution of Hindoſtan. The Emperor is abſolute and ſole arbiter in every thing, and is controlled by no law. The lives and properties of the greateſt Omrahs are as much at his diſpoſal, as thoſe of the meaneſt ſubjects. The former however are often too powerful to be puniſhed, while the latter are not only ſlaves to the King, but to the provincial governors. Theſe governors, diſtinguiſhed by the name of Nabobs, have in their reſpective juriſdictions, the power of life and death, and are, in every particular, inveſted with regal authority.

All the lands in India are conſidered as the property of the King, except ſome hereditary diſtricts poſſeſſed by Hindoo Princes, for which, when the Empire was in its vigour, they paid annual tributes, but retained an absolute jurisdiction in their own hands. The King is the general heir of all his subjects; but when there are children to inherit, they are seldom deprived of their father's estate, without the fortune is enormous, and has been amassed in the oppressive government of a province. In a case of this kind, the children, or nearest relations, are allowed a certain proportion for their subsistence, at the discretion of the Casy or Judge. The fortunes of merchants, tradesmen, and mechanics, are never confiscated by the crown, if any children or relations remain.

The King has the extraordinary power of nominating his successor by will. This part of royal prerogative is not peculiar to the monarchs of Hindostan. We find that our own nation, so remarkable for their political freedom, were, not above two centuries ago, made over like a private estate, and that without asking their consent, by the will of a Prince, who neither deserved to be beloved or admired. According to the opinion of the Indians, the right of succession is vested in the male heir, but the last will of the King very often supersedes this idea of justice. Notwithstanding this prejudice in favour of the first born, there is no distinction made between natural children and those born in lawful wedlock; for every child brought forth in the Haram, whether by wives or concubines, are equally legitimate.

The vizier is generally first minister of state. All edicts and public deeds must pass under his seal, after the royal signet is affixed to them. The Vizier's office consists of various departments, in every one of which all commissions, patents for honorary titles, and grants for Jagiers, are carefully registered. He superintends the royal exchequer, and, in that capacity, keeps accounts with the Dewans of the several provinces, in every thing which regards the finances.

A Vakiel Mutuluck is sometimes appointed by the King. The power of this officer is superior to that of the Vizier, for he not only has the superintendency of civil, but also of all military affairs. This last is never any part of the Vizier's office; the Amir ul Omrah, or Buxshi, being independent captain-general, and paymaster of the forces. It is not easy to explain to Europeans the full extent of authority conferred upon the Vakiel Mutuluck; he seems to be an officer to whom the King for a time delegates his whole power, reserving only for himself the imperial title, and ensigns of royalty.

The Emperor of Hindostan gives public audience twice a day from the throne. All petitioners, without distinction, are after having gone through the usual ceremonies, admitted. They are permitted to present their

written

written complaints to the Ariz Beg, or lord of the requeſts, who attends, in order to preſent them to the King. The King reads them all himſelf, and ſuperſcribes his pleaſure in a few words, with his own hand. Should any thing in the petition appear doubtful, it is immediately referred to the Sidder ul Sudder*, whoſe office anſwers to that of our chief juſtice, to be examined and determined according to law.

The Mahommedans of Hindoſtan have no written laws, but thoſe contained in the Koran. There are certain uſages founded upon reaſon, and immemorial cuſtom, which are alſo committed to writing. By the latter ſome cauſes are determined, and there are officers appointed by the crown, under the name of Canongoes, who, for a certain fee, explain the written uſages to the people. In every diſtrict or pergunna, there is a cutchery, or court of juſtice eſtabliſhed. Theſe courts are extremely venal, and even the legal fees for determining a cauſe concerning property, is one fourth of the value of the matter in diſpute. Their deciſions were, however, very expeditious; and through fear of the diſpleaſure of the King, who invariably puniſhed with the utmoſt ſeverity corrupt judges, the Caſys were pretty equitable in their determinations.

* Judge of Judges.

In

In the declining ſtate of the Empire, the provinces were ſubmitted to the management of Nabobs, or military governors, who farmed the revenues at a certain ſum, and reſerved the overplus for their own uſe. Originally the Nabobs were only commanders of the forces, who receiving their orders from court, through the medium of the Dewan, a civil officer who collected all the revenues for the King, paid the juſt expences of the government of the province, and remitted the ſurplus to the exchequer. But the Nabobs having the military power in their hands, deſpiſed the authority of the Dewans, and purpoſely fomented diviſions, factions, and inſurrections, that they might be indulged with great ſtanding armies, to make more money paſs through their own hands, and to favour their ſchemes of independence.

The imbecility of the Empire daily increaſing, the nominal authority veſted in the Dewan, was not ſufficient to contend with the real force in the hands of the Nabob. Continual altercations ſubſiſted between theſe officers in the province, and frequent complaints were tranſmitted to court. Miniſters who preferred preſent eaſe to the future intereſt of the empire, curtailed the power of the Dewan, and, from being in a manner the commander in chief of the province, he fell into the ſimple ſuperintendency of the collections. He had, it is true, the power to prevent new impoſts, and innovations in the law.

When

When the King took the field, the provincial Nabobs, with their troops, were obliged to repair to the imperial ſtandard. Each Nabob erected his own ſtandard, and formed a ſeparate camp, ſubject only to his own orders. The Nabobs every morning attended at the royal pavilion, and received their orders from the Amir ul Omrah *, who received his immediately from the King himſelf. If we except the army of the great Sultan Baber, there are few traces of real diſcipline to be met with among thoſe myriads, with whom the Emperors of Hindoſtan often took the field. The forces of Baber were formed on a very regular and maſterly plan. The diſpoſitions of his battles were excellent; and the ſurprizing victories he obtained with a handful of men, over immenſe armies, are ſufficient to convince us, that military diſcipline has not always been unknown in Aſia.

It may to an European, furniſh matter of ſome ſurprize, how Eaſtern armies of two or three hundred thouſand horſe, and triple that number of ſoldiers and followers, could be ſupplied with proviſions and forage upon their march, and in their ſtanding camps. To account for this it is to be obſerved, that every provincial Nabob, upon his taking the field, appoints an officer called the Cutwal, whoſe buſineſs it is to ſuperintend the Bazars

* The captain-general.

or markets, which may belong to his camp. Every commander of a body of troops obtains, at the ſame time, permiſſion to hoiſt a flag for a Bazar, and to appoint a Cutwal of his own, under the direction of the Cutwal-general. Theſe Cutwals grant licences to chapmen, ſutlers, and corn dealers, who gladly pay a certain tax for permiſſion to diſpoſe of their various commodities, under the protection of the different flags.

The ſutlers and dealers in corn, being provided with a ſufficient number of camels and oxen, collect proviſions from all the countries in their rear, and ſupply the wants of the camp. The pay of ſoldiers in Hindoſtan is very great, being from 60 to 200 rupees per month, to every ſingle trooper. This enables them to give ſuch high prices for proviſions, that the countries round run all hazards for ſuch a great proſpect of gain. The fertility of Hindoſtan itſelf, is the great ſource of this ready and plentiful ſupply to the armies; for that country produces, in moſt parts, two and ſometimes three crops of corn every year.

A

DISSERTATION

CONCERNING THE

CUSTOMS, MANNERS, LANGUAGE, RELIGION AND PHILOSOPHY

OF THE

HINDOOS.

THE learned of modern Europe have, with reaſon, complained that the writers of Greece and Rome did not extend their enquiries to the religion and philoſophy of the Druids. Poſterity will perhaps, in the ſame manner, find fault with the Britiſh for not inveſtigating the learning and religious opinions, which prevail in thoſe countries in Aſia, into which either their commerce or their arms have penetrated. The Brahmins of the Eaſt poſſeſſed in ancient times, ſome reputation for knowledge, but we have never had the curioſity to examine whether there was any truth in the reports of antiquity upon that head. Learning of the Brahmins

Excuſes, however, may be formed for our ignorance concerning the learning, religion and philoſophy of the Brahmins. Literary inquiries are by no means a capital object to many of our adventurers in Aſia. The few who have a turn for re- Neglected by the moderns.

ſearches of that kind, are diſcouraged by the very great difficulty in acquiring that language, in which the learning of the Hindoos is contained; or by that impenetrable veil of myſtery with which the Brahmins induſtriouſly cover their religious tenets and philoſophy.

Inaccuracies of travellers.

These circumſtances combining together, have opened an ample field for fiction. Modern travellers have accordingly indulged their talent for fable, upon the myſterious religion of Hindoſtan. Whether the ridiculous tales they relate, proceed from that common partiality which Europeans, as well as leſs enlightened nations, entertain for the religion and philoſophy of their own country, or from a judgment formed upon ſome external ceremonies of the Hindoos, is very difficult to determine; but they have prejudiced Europe againſt the Brahmins, and by a very unfair account, have thrown diſgrace upon a ſyſtem of religion and philoſophy, which they did by no means inveſtigate.

Cauſe of the author's enquiry.

The author of this diſſertation muſt own, that he for a long time, ſuffered himſelf to be carried down in this ſtream of popular prejudice. The preſent decline of literature in Hindoſtan, ſerved to confirm him in his belief of thoſe legends which he read in Europe, concerning the Brahmins. But converſing by accident, one day, with a noble and learned Brahmin, he was not a little ſurprized to find him perfectly acquainted with thoſe opinions, which, both in ancient and modern Europe, have employed the pens of the moſt celebrated moraliſts. This circumſtance did not fail to excite his curioſity, and in the courſe of many ſubſequent converſations, he found that philoſophy and the ſciences had, in former ages, made a very conſiderable progreſs in the Eaſt.

Studies the Shanſcrita.

Having then no intention to quit India for ſome time, he reſolved to acquire ſome knowledge in the

the Shanſcrita language; the grand repoſitory of the religion, philoſophy and hiſtory of the Hindoos. With this view, he prevailed upon his noble friend the Brahmin, to procure for him a Pundit, from the univerſity of Benaris, well verſed in the Shanſcrita, and maſter of all the knowledge of that learned body. But before he had made any conſiderable progreſs in his ſtudies, an unexpected change of affairs in Bengal, broke off all his literary ſchemes. He found that the time he had to remain in India would be too ſhort to acquire the Shanſcrita. He determined therefore, through the medium of the Perſian language, and through the vulgar tongue of the Hindoos, to inform himſelf as much as poſſible, concerning the mythology and philoſophy of the Brahmins. He, for this purpoſe, procured ſome of the principal SHASTERS, and his Pundit explained to him, as many paſſages of thoſe curious books, as ſerved to give him a general idea of the doctrine which they contain.

It is but juſtice to the Brahmins to confeſs that the author of this diſſertation is very ſenſible of his own inability to illuſtrate, with that fullneſs and perſpicuity which it deſerves, that ſymbolical religion, which they are at ſo much pains to conceal from foreigners. He however can aver, that he has not miſrepreſented one ſingle circumſtance or tenet, though many may have eſcaped his obſervation.

The books which contain the religion and philoſophy of the Hindoos, are diſtinguiſhed by the name of Bedas. They are four in number, and like the ſacred writings of other nations, are ſaid to have been penned by the divinity. Beda in the Shanſcrita, literally ſignifies SCIENCE: for theſe books not only treat of religious and moral duties, but of every branch of philoſophical knowledge. The Bedas.

The Bedas are, by the Brahmins, held ſo ſacred, that they permit no other ſect to read them; and ſuch Sacred Books.

ſuch is the influence of ſuperſtition and prieſtcraft over the minds of the other CASTS in India, that they would deem it an unpardonable ſin to ſatisfy their curioſity in that reſpect, were it even within the compaſs of their power. The Brahmins themſelves are bound by ſuch ſtrong ties of religion, to confine thoſe writings to their own tribe, that were any of them known to read them to others, he would be immediately excommunicated. This puniſhment is worſe than even death itſelf among the Hindoos. The offender is not only thrown down from the nobleſt order to the moſt polluted CAST, but his poſterity are rendered for ever incapable of being received into his former dignity.

Little known. All theſe things conſidered, we are not to wonder that the doctrine of the Bedas is ſo little known in Europe. Even the literary part of the Mahommedans of Aſia, reckon it an abſtruſe and myſterious ſubject, and candidly confeſs, that it is covered with a veil of darkneſs, which they could never penetrate. Some have indeed ſuppoſed, that the learned Feizi, brother to the celebrated Abul Fazil, chief ſecretary to the Emperor Akbar, had read the Bedas, and diſcovered the religious tenets contained in them to that renowned Prince. As the ſtory of Feizi made a good deal of noiſe in the eaſt, it may not be improper to give the particulars of it in this place.

Scheme of the Emperor Akbar. Mahommed Akbar being a prince of elevated and extenſive ideas, was totally diveſted of thoſe prejudices for his own religion, which men of inferior parts not only imbibe with their mother's milk, but retain throughout their lives. Though bred in all the ſtrictneſs of the Mahommedan faith, his great ſoul in his riper years broke thoſe chains of ſuperſtition and credulity, with which his tutors had, in his early youth, fettered his mind. With a deſign to chuſe his own religion, or rather from curioſity,

curioſity, he made it his buſineſs to enquire minutely into all the ſyſtems of divinity, which prevailed among mankind. The ſtory of his being inſtructed in the chriſtian tenets, by a miſſionary from Portugal, is too well known in Europe to require a place in this diſſertation. As almoſt all religions admit of proſelytes, Akbar had good ſucceſs in his enquiries, till he came to his own ſubjects the Hindoos. Contrary to the practice of all other religious ſects, they admit of no converts; but they allow that every one may go to heaven his own way, though they perhaps ſuppoſe, that theirs is the moſt expeditious method to obtain that important end. They chuſe rather to make a myſtery of their religion, than impoſe it upon the world, like the Mahommedans, with the ſword, or by means of the ſtake, after the manner of ſome pious chriſtians.

Impoſes Feizi upon a Brahmin.

Not all the authority of Akbar could prevail with the Brahmins to reveal the principles of their faith. He was therefore obliged to have recourſe to artifice to obtain the information which he ſo much deſired. The Emperor, for this purpoſe, concerted a plan with his chief ſecretary, Abul Fazil, to impoſe Feizi, then a boy, upon the Brahmins, in the character of a poor orphan of their tribe. Feizi being inſtructed in his part, was privately ſent to Benaris, the principal ſeat of learning among the Hindoos. In that city the fraud was practiſed on a learned Brahmin, who received the boy into his houſe, and educated him as his own ſon.

Story of Feizi.

When Feizi, after ten years ſtudy, had acquired the Shanſcrita language, and all the knowledge of which the learned of Benaris were poſſeſſed, proper meaſures were taken by the Emperor to ſecure his ſafe return. Feizi it ſeems, during his reſidence with his patron the Brahmin, was ſmitten with the beauty

beauty of his only daughter; and indeed the ladies of the Brahmin race are the handſomeſt in Hindoſtan. The old Brahmin ſaw the mutual paſſion of the young pair with pleaſure, and as he loved Feizi for his uncommon abilities, he offered him his daughter in marriage. Feizi, perplexed between love and gratitude, at length diſcovered himſelf to the good old man, fell down at his feet, and graſping his knees, ſolicited with tears forgiveneſs for the great crime he had committed againſt his indulgent benefactor. The Brahmin, ſtruck dumb with aſtoniſhment, uttered not one word of reproach. He drew a dagger, which he always carried on his girdle, and prepared to plunge it in his own breaſt; Feizi ſeized his hand, and conjured him, that if yet any atonement could be made for the injury he had done him, he himſelf would ſwear to deny him nothing. The Brahmin, burſting into tears, told him, that if Feizi ſhould grant him two requeſts, he would forgive him, and conſent to live. Feizi, without any heſitation, conſented, and the Brahmin's requeſts were, that he ſhould never tranſlate the Bedas, nor repeat the creed of the Hindoos.

How far Feizi was bound by his oath not to reveal the doctrine of the Bedas to Akbar is uncertain; but that neither he, nor any other perſon, ever tranſlated thoſe books, is a truth beyond any diſpute. It is however well known, that the Emperor afterwards greatly favoured the Hindoo faith, and gave much offence to zealous Mahommedans, by practiſing ſome Indian cuſtoms which they thought ſavoured of idolatry. But the diſpaſſionate part of mankind have always allowed, that Akbar was equally diveſted of all the follies of both the religious ſuperſtitions, which prevailed among his ſubjects.

Bedas ſaid to be coeval with the world.

To return from this digreſſion, the Brahmins maintain, that the Bedas are the divine laws, which Brimha, at the creation of the world, delivered

The Ganges.

ed for the inſtruction of mankind. But they affirm, that their meaning was perverted in the firſt period of time, by the ignorance and wickedneſs of ſome princes, whom they repreſent as evil ſpirits who then haunted the earth. They call thoſe evil genii Dewtas, and tell many ſtrange allegorical legends concerning them; ſuch as, that the Bedas being loſt, were afterwards recovered by Biſhen, in the form of a fiſh, who brought them up from the bottom of the ocean, into which they were thrown by a Deo, or Demon.

True æra of the Bedas.

The firſt credible account we have of the Bedas, is, that about the commencement of the period called the Cal Jug, of which æra the preſent year 1769 is the 4887th year, they were written, or rather collected by a great philoſopher, and reputed prophet, called Beäſs Muni, or Beäſs the inſpired. This learned man is otherwiſe called Kriſhen Basdeo, and is ſaid to have lived in the reign of Judiſhter, in the city of Hiſtanapore, upon the river Jumna, near the preſent city of Delhi.

Beäſs Muni.

The Brahmins do not give to Beäſs Muni the merit of being the author of the Bedas. They however acknowledge, that he reduced them into the preſent form, dividing them into four diſtinct books, after having collected the detached pieces of which they are compoſed, from every part of India. It is, upon the whole, probable, that they are not the work of one man, on account of their immenſe bulk.

Brimha not an allegorical perſon.

The Mahommedans of Aſia, as well as ſome of the learned of Europe, have miſtaken Brimha, an allegorical perſon, for ſome philoſopher of repute in India, whom they diſtinguiſh by the disfigured names of Bruma, Burma, and Bramha, whom they ſuppoſe to have been the writer of the religious books of the Hindoos. Feriſhta, in the hiſtory now given to the public, affirms, that Brimha was of the

the race of Bang, and flouriſhed in the reign of Kriſhen, firſt monarch of Hindoſtan. But the Brahmins deny, that any ſuch perſon ever exiſted, which we have reaſon to believe is the truth; as Brimha in the Shanſcrita language allegorically ſignifies WISDOM, one of the principal attributes of the ſupreme divinity.

Subject of the Bedas. The four Bedas contain 100,000 aſhiogues or ſtanzas in verſe, each of which conſiſts of four lines. The firſt Beda is called RUG BEDA, which ſignifies the ſcience of divination, concerning which it principally treats. It alſo contains aſtrology, aſtronomy, natural philoſophy, and a very particular account of the creation of matter, and the formation of the world.

Sheham Beda. The ſecond Beda is diſtinguiſhed by the name of SHEHAM. That word ſignifies piety or devotion, and this book accordingly treats of all religious and moral duties. It alſo contains many hymns in praiſe of the ſupreme being, as well as verſes in honour of ſubaltern intelligences.

Judger Beda. The third is the JUDGER BEDA, which, as the word implies, comprehends the whole ſcience of religious rites and ceremonies; ſuch as faſts, feſtivals, purifications, penances, pilgrimages, ſacrifices, prayers, and offerings. They give the appellation of OBATAR BAH to the fourth Beda. OBATAR ſignifies in the Shanſcrita, the being, or the eſſence, and BAH good; ſo that the Obatar Bah is literally the knowledge of the good being, and accordingly this book comprehends the whole ſcience of theology and metaphyſical philoſophy.

Obatar-Bah Beda. The language of the Obatar Bah Beda is now become obſolete; ſo that very few Brahmins pretend to read it with propriety. Whether this proceeds from its great antiquity, or from its being wrote in an uncommon dialect of the Shanſcrita, is hard to determine. We are inclined to believe that the firſt is the truth; for we can by no means

agree

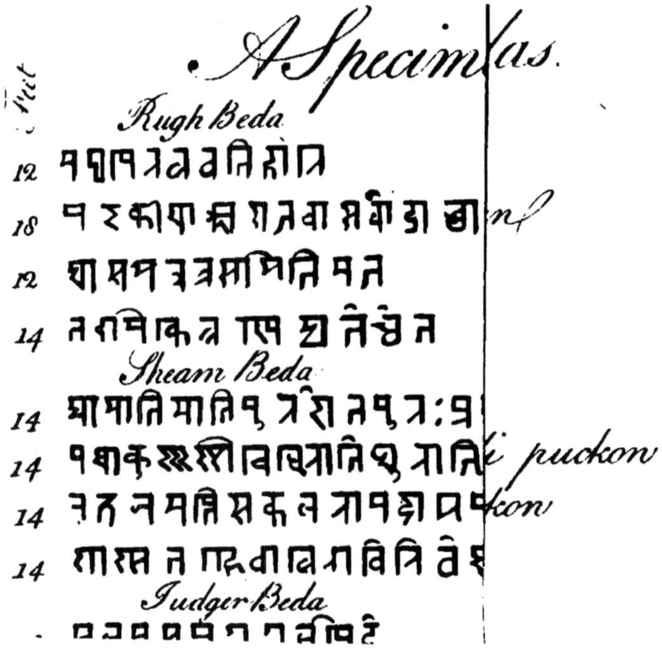

A Specim... as.

Rugh Beda

12 [illegible]

18 [illegible] n...

12 [illegible]

14 [illegible]

Sheam Beda

14 [illegible]

14 [illegible] ...i puckon

14 [illegible] ...kon

14 [illegible]

Judger Beda

[illegible]

agree with a late ingenious writer*, who affirms, that the Obatar Bah was written in a period pofterior to the reft of the Bedas.

It has been already obferved, that the Bedas are written in the Shanfcrita tongue. Whether the Shanfcrita was, in any period of antiquity, the vulgar language of Hindoftan, or was invented by the Brahmins, to be a myfterious repofitory for their religion and philofophy, is difficult to determine. All other languages, it is true, were cafually invented by mankind, to exprefs their ideas and wants; but the aftonifhing formation of the Shanfcrita feems to be beyond the power of chance. In regularity of etymology and grammatical order, it far exceeds the Arabic. It, in fhort, bears evident marks, that it has been fixed upon rational principles, by a body of learned men, who ftudied regularity, harmony, and a wonderful fimplicity and energy of expreffion. Shanfcrita language.

Though the Shanfcrita is amazingly copious, a very fmall grammar and vocabulary ferve to illuftrate the principles of the whole. In a treatife of a few pages, the roots and primitives are all comprehended, and fo uniform are the rules for derivations and inflections, that the etymon of every word is, with facility, at once inveftigated. The pronunciation is the greateft difficulty that attends the acquirement of the language to perfection. This is fo quick and forcible, that a perfon, even before the years of puberty, muft labour a long time before he can pronounce it with propriety; but when once the pronunciation is attained to perfection, it ftrikes the ear with amazing boldnefs and harmony. The alphabet of the Shanfcrita con- Very copious and regular.

* Mr. Holwell: The author of the differtation finds himfelf obliged to differ almoft in every particular concerning the religion of the Hindoos, from that gentleman.

fifts

ſiſts of fifty letters, but one half of theſe convey combined ſounds, ſo that its characters in fact, do not exceed ours in number. Some ſmall idea of the Shanſcrita may be conveyed by the annexed plate, which contains the alphabet, and the meaſure of the four Bedas.

Characteriſtical cuſtoms of the Indians.

Before we ſhall proceed to the religion and philoſophy of the Brahmins, it may not be improper to premiſe ſomething concerning the moſt characteriſtical manners and cuſtoms of the Hindoos in general. The Hindoos are ſo called from Indoo or Hindoo, which, in the Shanſcrita language, ſignifies the Moon; for from that luminary, and the ſun, they deduce their fabulous origin. The author of the diſſertation has in his poſſeſſion, a long liſt of a dynaſty of Kings, called Hindoo-buns or Chunder-buns, both of which words mean, the Children of the Moon. He alſo has a catalogue of the Surage-buns, or the Children of the Sun, from whom many of the Princes of India pretend to derive their blood. Hindoſtan, the domeſtic appellation of India; is a compoſition of Hindoo, and Stan, a region; and the great river Indus takes its name from the people, and not the people from the river, as has been erroneouſly ſuppoſed in Europe.

Divided into four tribes.

The Hindoos have, from all antiquity, been divided into four great tribes, each of which comprehends a variety of inferior caſts. Theſe tribes do not intermarry, eat, drink, or in any manner aſſociate with one another, except when they worſhip at the temple of Jagga-nat* in Oriſſa, where it is held a crime

* Jagga-nat, ſignifies Lord of the creation. This is one of the names of Biſhen and the Obatar, or Being, who is ſaid to preſide over the preſent period. He is repreſented under the figure of a fat man, ſitting croſs-legged, with his arms hanging

a crime to make any diſtinction. The firſt, and moſt noble tribe, are the Brahmins, who alone can officiate in the prieſthood like the Levites among the Jews. They are not however excluded from government, trade, or agriculture, though they are ſtrictly prohibited from all menial offices by their laws. They derive their name from Brimha, who they allegorically ſay, produced the Brahmins from his head, when he created the world. Brahmins.

The ſecond in order is the Sittri tribe, who are ſometimes diſtinguiſhed by the name of Kittri or Koytri. They, according to their original inſtitution, ought to be all military men; but they frequently follow other profeſſions. Brimha is ſaid to have produced the Kittri from his heart, as an emblem of that courage which warriors ſhould poſſeſs. Sittri.

The name of Beiſe or Biſe is given to the third tribe. They are for the moſt part, merchants, bankers, and bunias or ſhop-keepers. Theſe are figuratively ſaid to have ſprung from the belly of Brimha; the word Beiſh ſignifying a provider or nouriſher. The fourth tribe is that of Sudder. They ought to be menial ſervants, and they are incapable to raiſe themſelves to any ſuperior rank. They are ſaid to have proceeded from the feet of Brimha, in alluſion to their low degree. But indeed it is contrary to the inviolable laws of the Hindoos, that any perſon ſhould riſe from an inferior caſt into a higher tribe. If any therefore ſhould be excommunicated from any of the four tribes, he and his poſterity are for ever ſhut out from the ſociety of every body in the nation, excepting that of the Harri caſt, who are held in utter deteſtation by all the other tribes, and are

Biſe. Sudder.

hanging down by his ſide as if they had no ſtrength. This laſt circumſtance alludes to the imbecility of this age. His temple is in the greateſt repute of any now in India.

employed

employed only in the meaneſt and vileſt offices. This circumſtance renders excommunication ſo dreadful, that any Hindoo will ſuffer the torture and even death itſelf, rather than deviate from one article of his faith. This ſeverity prevented all intermixture of blood between the tribes, ſo that, in their appearance, they ſeem rather four different nations, than members of the ſame community.

Indians admit no proſelytes.

It is, as we have already obſerved, a principle peculiar to the Hindoo religion, not to admit of proſelytes. Inſtead of being ſolicitous about gaining converts, they always make a myſtery of their faith. Heaven, ſay they, is like a palace with many doors, and every one may enter in his own way. But this charitable diſpoſition never encouraged other ſects to ſettle among them, as they muſt have been excluded entirely from all the benefits of ſociety.

Aſtrology.

When a child is born, ſome of the Brahmins are called. They pretend, from the horoſcope of his nativity, to foretel his future fortune, by means of ſome aſtrological tables, of which they are poſſeſſed. When this ceremony is over, they burn incenſe, and make an offering according to the circumſtances of the parent; and without ever conſulting them, tie the zinar * round the infant's neck, and impoſe a name upon him, according to their own fancy.

Marriages.

Between the age of ſeven and ten, the children are by their parents, given away in marriage. The young pair are brought together, in order to contract an intimacy with one another. But when they approach to the years of puberty, they carefully ſeparate them, till the female produces ſigns of womanhood. She then is taken from her

* A ſtring which all the Hindoos wear, by way of charm or amulet.

parents

parents to cohabit with her husband: nor is she ever after permitted to visit them. It is not lawful anong the Hindoos to marry nearer than the eighth degree of kindred. Polygamy is permitted, but seldom practised; for they very rationally think that one wife is sufficient for one man.

The extraordinary custom of the women burning themselves with their deceased husbands, has, for the most part, fallen into desuetude in India; nor was it ever reckoned a religious duty, as has been very erroneously supposed in the West. This species of barbarity, like many others, rose originally from the foolish enthusiasm of feeble minds. In a text in the Bedas, conjugal affection and fidelity are thus figuratively inculcated; "The woman, in short, who dies with her husband, shall enjoy life eternal with him in heaven." From this source the Brahmins themselves deduce this ridiculous custom, which is a more rational solution of it, than the story which prevails in Europe; that it was a political institution, made by one of the Emperors, to prevent wives from poisoning their husbands, a practice, in those days, common in Hindostan. Burning of Widows.

People of rank and those of the higher casts, burn their dead and throw some incense into the pile. Some throw the bodies of their friends into the Ganges, while others expose them on the high ways, as a prey to vultures and wild beasts. There is one cast in the kingdom of Bengal, who barbarously expose their sick by the river's side to die there. They even sometimes choak them with mud, when they think them past hopes of recovery. They defend this inhuman custom by saying, that life is not an adequate recompence for the tortures of a lingering disease. Burials.

The Hindoos have a code of laws in the NEA SHASTER. Treason, incest, sacrilege, murder, adultery Laws.

dultery with the wife of a Brahmin, and theft, are capital crimes. Though the Brahmins were the authors of thofe laws, we do not find that they have exempted themfelves from the punifhment of death, when guilty of thofe crimes. This is one of thofe numerous fables, which modern travellers imported from the Eaft. It is however certain, that the influence of the Brahmins is fo great, and their characters as priefts fo facred, that they efcape in cafes where no mercy would be fhewn to the other tribes.

Punifhments.

Petty offences are punifhed by temporary excommunications, pilgrimages, penances and fines, according to the degree of the crime, and the wealth of the guilty perfon. But as the Hindoos are now for the moft part fubject to the Mahommedans, they are governed by the laws of the Koran, or by the arbitrary will of the prince.

Senaffeys or Fakiers.

The Senaffeys are a fect of mendicant philofophers, commonly known by the name of Fakiers, which literally fignifies poor people. Thefe idle and pretended devotees, affemble fometimes in armies of ten or twelve thoufand, and, under a pretext of making pilgrimages to certain temples, lay whole countries under contribution. Thefe faints wear no clothes, are generally very robuft, and convert the wives of the lefs holy part of mankind to their own ufe, upon their religious progreffes. They admit any man of parts into their number, and they take great care to inftruct their difciples in every branch of knowledge, to make the order the more revered among the vulgar.

Their pilgrimages.

When this naked army of robuft faints direct their march to any temple, the men of the provinces through which their road lies, very often fly before them, notwithftanding the fanctified character of the Fakiers. But the woman are in general more refolute, and not only remain in their dwellings

ings, but apply frequently for the prayers of thoſe holy perſons, which are found to be moſt effectual in caſes of ſterility. When a Fakier is at prayers with the lady of the houſe, he leaves either his ſlipper or his ſtaff at the door, which if ſeen by the huſband, effectually prevents him from diſturbing their devotion. But ſhould he be ſo unfortunate as not to mind thoſe ſignals, a ſound drubbing is the inevitable conſequence of his intruſion.

Though the Fakiers inforce with their arms, that reverence which the people of Hindoſtan have naturally for their order, they inflict voluntary penances of very extraordinary kinds upon themſelves, to gain more reſpect. Theſe fellows ſometimes hold up one arm in a fixed poſition, till it becomes ſtiff, and remains in that ſituation during the reſt of their lives. Some clench their fiſts very hard, and keep them ſo till nails grow into their palms, and appear through the back of their hands. Others turn their faces over one ſhoulder, and keep them in that ſituation, till they fix for ever their heads looking backward. Many turn their eyes to the point of their noſe, till they have loſt the power of looking in any other direction. Theſe laſt pretend ſometimes to ſee what they call the ſacred fire, which viſion, no doubt, proceeds from ſome diſorder ariſing from the diſtortion of the optic nerves. Penances.

It often appears to Europeans in India, a matter of ſome ridicule to converſe with thoſe diſtorted and naked philoſophers; though their knowledge and external appearance, exhibit a very ſtriking contraſt. Some are really what they ſeem, enthuſiaſts; but others put on the character of ſanctity, as a cloak for their pleaſures. But what actually makes them a public nuiſance, and the averſion of poor huſbands, is, that the woman think they derive Learning.

ſome holineſs to themſelves, from an intimacy with a Fakier.

Penances among the vulgar.

Many other fooliſh cuſtoms, beſides thoſe we have mentioned, are peculiar to thoſe religious mendicants. But enthuſiaſtic penances are not confined to them alone. Some of the vulgar on the faſt of Oppoſs, ſuſpend themſelves on iron hooks, by the fleſh of the ſhoulder-blade, to the end of a beam. This beam turns round with great velocity, upon a pivot, on the head of a high pole. The enthuſiaſt not only ſeems inſenſible of pain, but very often blows a trumpet as he is whirled round above, and, at certain intervals, ſings a ſong to the gaping multitude below; who very much admire his fortitude and devotion. This ridiculous cuſtom is kept up to commemorate the ſufferings of a martyr, who was in that manner tortured for his faith.

The religion of the Indians miſrepreſented in Europe.

To dwell longer upon the characteriſtical cuſtom and manners of the Hindoos, would extend this diſſertation too far. Some more particulars concerning that nation, will naturally ariſe from an inveſtigation of their religion and philoſophy. This laſt was the capital deſign of this introductory diſcourſe; and we hope to be able to throw a new, if not a compleat light, on a ſubject hitherto little underſtood in the Weſt. Some writers have very lately given to the world an unintelligible ſyſtem of the Brahmin religion; and they affirm, that they derived their information from the Hindoos themſelves. This may be the caſe, but they certainly converſed upon that ſubject only with the inferior tribes, or with the unlearned part of the Brahmins: and it would be as ridiculous to hope for a true ſtate of the religion and philoſophy of the Hindoos from the illiterate caſts, as it would be in a Mahommedan in London, to rely upon the accounts of a pariſh beadle, concerning the moſt abſtruſe point of the

the Christian faith; or, to form his opinion of the principles of the Newtonian philosophy, from a conversation with an English carman.

Divided into two sects.

The Hindoos are divided into two great religious sects: the followers of the doctrine of the BEDANG; and those who adhere to the principles of the NEADIRZIN. As the first are esteemed the most orthodox, as well as the most ancient, we shall begin to explain their opinions, by extracts literally translated from the original SHASTER *, which goes by the name of Bedang.

The Bedang Shaster.

Bedang, the title of the Shaster, or commentary upon the Bedas, concerning which we are about to treat, is a word compounded of Beda, *science*, and Ang, *body*. The name of this Shaster therefore, may be literally translated, the Body of science. This book has, in Europe, been erroneously called Vedam; and it is an exposition of the doctrine of the Bedas, by that great philosopher and prophet Beâss Muni, who, according to the Brahmins, flourished about four thousand years ago. The Bedang is said to have been revised some ages after Beâss Muni, by one Sirrider Swami, since which it has been reckoned sacred, and not subject to any further alterations. Almost all the Hindoos of the Decan, and those of the Malabar and Coromandel coasts, are of the sect of the Bedang.

* Shaster, literally signifies Knowledge: but it is commonly understood to mean a book which treats of divinity and the sciences. There are many Shasters among the Hindoos; so that those writers who affirmed, that there was but one Shaster in India, which, like the Bible of the Christians, or Koran of the followers of Mahommed, contained the first principles of the Brahmin faith, have deceived themselves and the public.

Principal tenets.

This commentary opens with a dialogue between Brimha*, the Wiſdom of the Divinity; and Narud† or Reaſon, who is repreſented as the ſon of Brimha. Narud deſires to be inſtructed by his father, and for that purpoſe, puts the following queſtions to him.

NARUD.

O father! thou firſt of God[1], thou art ſaid to have created the world, and thy ſon Narud, aſtoniſhed at what he beholds, is deſirous to be inſtructed how all theſe things were made.

BRIMHA.

Idea of God.

Be not deceived, my ſon! do not imagine that I was the creator of the world, independent of the divine mover[2], who is the great original eſſence[3],

* Brimha is the genitive caſe of BRIMH, which is a primitive ſignifying God. He is called Brimha or WISDOM, the firſt attribute of the ſupreme divinity. The divine wiſdom, under the name of Brimha, is figuratively repreſented with one head, having four faces, looking to the four quarters, alluding to his ſeeing all things. Upon the head of this figure is a crown, an emblem of power and dominion. He has four hands, implying, the omnipotence of divine wiſdom. In the firſt hand he holds the four Bedas, as a ſymbol of knowledge; in the ſecond a ſcepter, as a token of authority; and in the third a ring, or complete circle, as an emblem of eternity. Brimha holds nothing in the fourth hand, which implies, that THE WISDOM OF GOD is always ready to lend his aid to his creatures. He is repreſented riding upon a gooſe, the emblem of ſimplicity among the Hindoos. The latter circumſtance is intended to imply the ſimplicity of the operations of nature, which is but another name for the wiſdom of the divinity. Theſe explications, of the inſignia of Brimha, were given by the Brahmin, and are, by no means, conjectures of the author of this diſſertation,

† Narud literally ſignifies REASON, emphatically called the ſon of THE WISDOM OF GOD. He is ſaid to be the firſt-born of the MUNIS, of whom hereafter.

[1] Brimh. [2] The ſupreme divinity. [3] Pirrim Purrus; from PIR firſt, and PURRUS eſſence or being.

and

and creator of all things, Look, therefore, only upon me as the inſtrument of the great WILL[4], and a part of his being, whom he called forth to execute his eternal deſigns.

NARUD.

What ſhall we think of God?

BRIMHA.

Being immaterial[5], he is above all conception; being inviſible[6], he can have no form[7]; but, from what we behold in his works, we may conclude that he is eternal[8], omnipotent[9], knowing all things[1], and preſent every where[2]. Definition.

NARUD.

How did God create the world?

BRIMHA.

Affection[3] dwelt with God, from all eternity. It was of three different kinds, the creative[4], the preſerving[5], and the deſtructive[6]. This firſt is repreſented by Brimha, the ſecond by Biſhen[7], and the third by Shibah[8]. You, O Narud! are taught to worſhip all the three, in various ſhapes Manner of creation.

[4] ISH-BUR; from ISH will, and BUR great: commonly pronounced ISHUR. This is one of the thouſand names of GOD, which have ſo much perplexed the writers of Europe. In the anſwer of Brimha, mention is made of the firſt three great deities of the Hindoos; which three, however, they by no means worſhip as diſtinct beings from God, but only as his principal attributes.

[5] Nid-akar. [6] Oderiſſa. [7] Sirba-Sirrup. [8] Nitteh. [9] Ge-itch. [1] Subbittera-dirſi. [2] Surba-Birſi. Theſe are the very terms uſed in the Bedang, in the definition of God, which we have literally tranſlated in the text. Whether we, who profeſs Chriſtianity, and call the Hindoos by the deteſtable names of Pagans and Idolaters, have higher ideas of the ſupreme divinity, we ſhall leave to the unprejudiced reader to determine.

[3] Maiah, which ſignifies either affection or paſſion. [4] Redjo-goon, the creative quality. [5] Sittohgoon, the preſerving quality. [6] Timmugoon, the deſtructive quality. [7] The preſerver; Providence is perſonified under the name of Biſhen. [8] Shibah, the foe of good.

and

and likenesses, as the creator[9], the preserver[1], and the destroyer[2]. The affection of God then produced power[3], and power at a proper conjunction of time[4] and fate[5], embraced goodness[6], and produced matter[7]. The three qualities then acting upon matter, produced the universe in the following manner. From the opposite actions of the creative and destructive quality in matter, self-motion[8] first arose. Self-motion was of three kinds; the first inclining to plasticity[9], the second to discord[1], and the third to rest[2]. The discordant actions then produced the Akash[3], which invisible element possessed the quality of conveying sound; it produced air[4], a palpable element, fire[5], a visible element, water[6], a fluid element, and earth[7], a solid element.

The Akash dispersed itself abroad. Air formed the atmosphere; fire, collecting itself, blazed forth in

[9] Naat. [1] Bishen. [2] Shibah. The Hindoos worship the destructive attribute of the divinity, under the name of Shibah; but they do not mean evil by Shibah, for they affirm, that there is no such thing but what proceeds from the free agency of man.

[3] Jotna. [4] Kaal. [5] Addaristo. [6] Pirkirti, from *Pir* good, and *Kirti* action. God's attribute of goodness, is worshipped as a Goddess, under the name of Pirkirti, and many other appellations, which comprehend all the virtues. It has been ridiculously supposed in Europe, that PURRUS and PIRKIRTI were the first man and woman, according to the system of the Hindoos; whereas by Purrus is meant God, or emphatically, *the Being*; and by Pirkirti, his attribute of goodness.

[7] Mohat. In other places of the Bedang, matter is distinguished by the name of Maha-tit, *the great substance*. [8] Ahankar. The word literally signifies self-action. [9] Rajas. [1] Tamas. [2] Satig. [3] A kind of celestial element. The Bedang in another place, speaks of akash as a pure impalpable element, through which the planets move. This element, says the philosopher, makes no resistance, and therefore the planets continue their motion, from the first impulse which they received from the hand of Brimha or God; nor will they stop, says he, till he shall seize them the midst of their course.

[4] Baiow. [5] Tege. [6] Joal. [7] Prittavi.

the

the hoſt of heaven[8]; water roſe to the ſurface of the earth, being forced from beneath by the gravity of the latter element. Thus broke forth the world from the veil of darkneſs, in which it was formerly comprehended by God. Order roſe over the universe. The ſeven heavens were formed[9], and the ſeven worlds were fixed in their places; there to remain till the great diſſolution[1], when all things ſhall be abſorbed[2] into God.

God ſeeing the earth in full bloom, and that vegetation[3] was ſtrong from its ſeeds, called forth for the firſt time, Intellect[4], which he endued with various organs and ſhapes, to form a diverſity of animals[5] upon the earth. He endued the animals with five ſenſes, feeling, ſeeing, ſmelling, taſting, and hearing[6]. But to man he gave reflexion[7] to raiſe him above the beaſts of the field.

The creatures were created male and female[8], that they might propagate their ſpecies upon the earth. Every herb bore the ſeed of its kind, that the world might be cloathed with verdure, and all animals provided with food.

NARUD.

What doſt thou mean, O Father! by intellect?

BRIMHA.

It is a portion of the GREAT SOUL[9] of the universe,

[8] Dewta; of which Surage the Sun is firſt in rank. [9] The names of the ſeven heavens are, Bu, Buba, Surg, Moha, Junnoh, Tapu, and Sutteh. The ſeven worlds are, Ottal, Bittal, Suttal, Joal, Tallattal, Riſſatal and Pattal. The author of the diſſertation, by a negligence which he very much regrets, forgot to get the proper explanation of thoſe names, or the uſes to which the ſeven heavens were converted.

[1] Mah-pirly. [2] Mucht. [3] Birgalotta. [4] Mun. [5] Jount. [6] The five ſenſes are, Suppurſina, Chowkowna, Naſiga, Riſſina, Kurnowa. [7] Manus. [8] Nir and Madda ſignifies male and female. [9] Purmattima literally ſignifies the *great ſoul.*

verſe, breathed into all creatures, to animate them for a certain time.

NARUD.

What becomes of it after death?

BRIMHA.

Fate of the ſoul after death.

It animates other bodies, or returns like a drop into that unbounded ocean from which it firſt aroſe.

NARUD.

Shall not then the ſouls of good men receive rewards? Nor the ſouls of the bad meet with puniſhment?

BRIMHA.

Difference in the ſtate of the dead.

The ſouls of men are diſtinguiſhed from thoſe of other animals; for the firſt are endued with reaſon [1] and with a conſciouſneſs of right and wrong. If therefore man ſhall adhere to the firſt, as far as his powers ſhall extend, his ſoul, when diſengaged from the body by death, ſhall be abſorbed into the divine eſſence, and ſhall never more re-animate fleſh. But the ſouls of thoſe who do evil[2], are not, at death, diſengaged from all the elements. They are immediately cloathed with a body of fire, air, and akaſh, in which they are, for a time, puniſhed in hell[3]. After the ſeaſon of their grief is over, they re-animate other bodies; but till they ſhall arrive at a ſtate of purity, they can never be abſorbed into God.

NARUD.

What is the nature of that abſorbed ſtate [4] which the ſouls of good men enjoy after death?

[1] Upiman. [2] Mund [3] Nirick. The Hindoos reckon above eighty kinds of hells, each proportioned to the degree of the wickedneſs of the perſons puniſhed there. The Brahmins have no idea that all the ſins that a man can commit in the ſhort period of his life, can deſerve eternal puniſhment; nor that all the virtues he can exerciſe, can merit perpetual felicity in heaven. [4] Muchti.

BRIMHA.

BRIMHA.

It is a participation of the divine nature, where all passions are utterly unknown, and where consciousness is lost in bliss[5]. State of the blessed.

NARUD.

Thou sayst, O Father! that unless the soul is perfectly pure, it cannot be absorbed into God: Now, as the actions of the generality of men are partly good, and partly bad, whither are their spirits sent immediately after death?

BRIMHA.

They must atone for their crimes in hell, where they must remain for a space proportioned to the degree of their iniquities; then they rise to heaven to be rewarded for a time for their virtues; and from thence they will return to the world, to reanimate other bodies. Transmigration.

NARUD.

What is time[6]?

BRIMHA.

Time existed from all eternity with God; but it can only be estimated since motion was produced, and Of time.

[5] It is somewhat surprising, that a state of unconsciousness, which in fact is the same with annihilation, should be esteemed by the Hindoos as the supreme good; yet so it is, that they always represent the *absorbed state*, as a situation of perfect insensibility, equally destitute of pleasure and of pain. But Brimha seems here to imply, that it is a kind of delirium of joy.

[6] Kaal. It may not be improper, in this place, to say something concerning the Hindoo method of computing time. Their least subdivision of time is, the Nemish or twinkling of an eye. Three Nemish's make one Kaan, fifty Kana one Ligger, ten Liggers one Dind, two Dinds one Gurry, equal to forty-five of our minutes; four Gurries one Pâr, eight Pârs one Dien or day, fifteen Diens one Packa, two Packas one Mâsh, four Mâshes one Ribbi, three Ribbis one Aioon or year, which only consists of 360 days, but when the odd days, hours

and can only be conceived by the mind, from its own conſtant progreſs.

NARUD.

How long ſhall this world remain?

BRIMHA.

Diſſolution of the world

Until the four jugs ſhall have revolved. Then Rudder[7] with the ten ſpirits of diſſolution ſhall roll a comet under the moon, that ſhall involve all things in fire, and reduce the world into aſhes. God ſhall then exiſt alone, for matter will be totally annihilated[8].

Contents of the ſecond chapter of the Bedang.

Here ends the firſt chapter of the Bedang. The ſecond treats of providence and free will; a ſubject ſo abſtruſe, that it was impoſſible to underſtand it, without a compleat knowledge of the Shanſcrita. The author of the Bedang, thinking perhaps, that the philoſophical catechiſm which we have tranſlated above, was too pure for narrow and ſuperſtitious minds, has inſerted into his work, a ſtrange allegorical account of the creation, for the purpoſes of vulgar theology. In this tale, the attributes of God, the human paſſions and faculties of the mind are perſonified, and introduced upon the ſtage. As this allegory

hours and minutes, wanting of a ſolar year, amount to one revolution of the moon, an additional month is made to that year to adjuſt the Calendar. A year of 360 days, they reckon but one day to the Dewtas or hoſt of Heaven; and they ſay, that twelve thouſand of thoſe planetary years, make one revolution of the four Jugs or periods, into which they divide the ages of the world. The Sittoh Jug or age of truth contained, according to them, four thouſand planetary years. The Treta Jug, or age of three, contained three thouſand years. The Duapur Jug, or *age of two*, contained two thouſand; and the Kalle Jug, or age of pollution, conſiſts of only one thouſand. To theſe they add two other periods, between the diſſolution and renovation of the world, which they call Sundeh, and Sundaſs, each of a thouſand planetary years; ſo that from one Maperly, or great diſſolution of all things, to another, there are 3,720,000 of our years.

[7] The ſame with Shibah, the deſtroying quality of God.

[8] Niſht.

gory may afford matter of ſome curioſity to the public, we ſhall here tranſlate it.

" Brimh exiſted from all eternity, in a form of infinite dimenſions. When it pleaſed him to create the world, he ſaid, *Riſe up, O Brimha*[1]. Immediately a ſpirit of the colour of flame iſſued from his navel, having four heads and four hands. Brimha gazing round, and ſeeing nothing but the immenſe image, out of which he had proceeded, he travelled a thouſand years, to endeavour to comprehend its dimenſions. But after all his toil, he found himſelf as much at a loſs as before.

An allegory.

" Loſt in amazement, Brimha gave over his journey. He fell proſtrate and praiſed what he ſaw, with his four mouths. The Almighty. then, with a voice like ten thouſand thunders, was pleaſed to ſay; Thou haſt done well, O Brimha, for thou canſt not comprehend me!——Go and create the world!——How can I create it?——Aſk of me, and power ſhall be given unto thee.——O God, ſaid Brimha, thou art almighty in power!—

" Brimha forthwith perceived the idea of things, as if floating before his eyes. He ſaid, Let them be, and all that he ſaw became real before him. Then fear ſtruck the frame of Brimha, leſt thoſe things ſhould be annihilated. O immortal Brihm! he cried, who ſhall preſerve thoſe things which I behold. In the inſtant a ſpirit of a blue colour iſſued from Brimha's mouth, and ſaid aloud, I will. Then ſhall thy name be Biſhen[2], becauſe thou haſt undertaken to preſerve all things.

" Brimha then commanded Biſhen to go and create all animals, with vegetables for their ſubſiſtance, to poſſeſs that earth which he himſelf had made. Biſhen forthwith created all manner of beaſts, fiſh,

[1] The wiſdom of God. [2] The providence of God.

fowl,

fowl, insects and reptiles. Trees and grass rose also beneath his hands, for Brimha had invested him with power. But man was still wanting to rule the whole: and Brimha commanded Bishen to form him. Bishen began the work, but the men he made were idiots with great bellies, for he could not inspire them with knowledge; so that in every thing but in shape, they resembled the beasts of the field. They had no passion but to satisfy their carnal appetites.

" Brimha, offended at the men, destroyed them, and produced four persons from his own breath, whom he called by four different names. The name of the first was Sinnoc[3], of the second, Sinnunda[4], of the third Sonnatin[5], and of the fourth, Sonninkunar[6]. These four persons were ordered by Brimha, to rule over the creatures, and to possess for ever the world. But they refused to do any thing but to praise God, having nothing of the destructive quality[7] in their composition.

" Brimha, for this contempt of his orders, became angry, and lo! a brown spirit started from between his eyes. He sat down before Brimha, and began to weep: then lifting up his eyes, he asked him, " Who am I, and where shall be the place of my abode." Thy name shall be Rudder[8], said Brimha, and all nature shall be the place of thine abode. But rise up, O Rudder! and form man to govern the world.

" Rudder immediately obeyed the orders of Brimha. He began the work, but the men he made were fiercer than tigers, having nothing but the destructive quality in their compositions. They, however, soon destroyed one another, for anger

[3] Body. [4] Life. [5] Permanency. [6] Intellectual existence. [7] Timmu-goon. [8] The weeper; because he was produced in tears. One of the names of Sibah, the destructive attribute of the Divinity.

was

was their only paſſion. Brimha, Biſhen, and Rudder then joined their different powers. They created ten men, whoſe names were, Narud, Dico, Bashiſta, Birga, Kirku, Pulla, Puliſta, Ongira, Otteri and Murichi[9]: The general appellation of the whole, was the Munies[1]. Brimha then produced Dirmo[2] from his breaſt, Adirmo[3] from his back, Loab[4] from his lip, and Kâm[5] from his heart. This laſt being a beautiful female, Brimha looked upon her with amorous eyes. But the Munies told him, that ſhe was his own daughter; upon which he ſhrunk back, and produced a bluſhing virgin called Ludja[6]. Brimha thinking his body defiled by throwing his eyes upon Kâm, changed it, and produced ten women, one of which was given to each of the Munies."

In this diviſion of the Bedang Shaſter, there is a long liſt of the Surage Buns, or children of the ſun, who, it is ſaid, ruled the world in the firſt periods. But as the whole is a mere dream of imagination, and ſcarcely the belief of the Hindoo children and women, we ſhall not treſpaſs farther on the patience of the public with theſe allegories. The Brahmins of former ages wrote many volumes of romances upon the lives and actions of thoſe pretended Kings, inculcating, after their manner, morality by fable. This was the grand fountain from which the religion of the vulgar in India was corrupted; if the vulgar of any country require any adventitious aid to corrupt their ideas, upon ſo myſterious a ſubject.

Further account of the Bedang.

Upon the whole, the opinions of the author of the Bedang, upon the ſubject of religion, are not

Not unphiloſophical.

[9] The ſignifications of theſe ten names are in order, theſe: Reaſon, Ingenuity, Emulation, Humility, Piety, Pride, Patience, Charity, Deceit, Mortality.

[1] The Inſpired. [2] Fortune. [3] Misfortune. [4] Appetite. [5] Love. [6] Shame.

unphilo-

unphiloſophical. He maintains that the world was created out of nothing by God, and that it will be again annihilated. The unity, infinity and omnipotence of the ſupreme divinity are inculcated by him: for though he preſents us with a long liſt of inferior beings, it is plain that they are merely allegorical; and neither he nor the ſenſible part of his followers believe their actual exiſtence. The more ignorant Hindoos, it cannot be denied, think that theſe ſubaltern divinities do exiſt, in the ſame manner, that Chriſtians believe in Angels: but the unity of God was always a fundamental tenet of the uncorrupted faith of the more learned Brahmins.

Doctrine of tranſmigration of ſouls.

The opinion of this philoſopher, that the ſoul, after death, aſſumes a body of the purer elements, is not peculiar to the Brahmins. It deſcended from the Druids of Europe, to the Greeks, and was the ſame with the εἴδωλον of Homer. His idea of the manner of the tranſmigration of the human ſoul into various bodies, is peculiar to himſelf. As he holds it as a maxim that a portion of the GREAT SOUL or God, animates every living thing; he thinks it no ways inconſiſtent, that the ſame portion that gave life to man, ſhould afterwards paſs into the body of any other animal. This tranſmigration does not, in his opinion, debaſe the quality of the ſoul: for when it extricates itſelf from the fetters of the fleſh, it reaſſumes its original nature.

No phyſical evil exiſts.

The followers of the BEDANG SHASTER do not allow that any phyſical evil exiſts. They maintain that God created all things perfectly good, but that man, being a free agent, may be guilty of moral evil: which, however, only reſpects himſelf and ſociety, but is of no detriment to the general ſyſtem of nature. God, ſay they, has no paſſion but benevolence: and being poſſeſſed of no wrath, he never puniſhes the wicked, but by the pain and affliction which are the natural conſequences of evil actions. The more

learned

learned Brahmins therefore affirm, that the hell which is mentioned in the Bedang, was only intended as a mere bugbear to the vulgar, to inforce upon their minds, the duties of morality: for that hell is no other than a conſciouſneſs of evil, and thoſe bad conſequences which invariably follow wicked deeds.

Tenets of the Neadirſen Shaſter.

Before we ſhall proceed to the doctrine of the NEADIRSEN SHASTER, it may not be improper to give a tranſlation of the firſt chapter of the DIRM SHASTER, which throws a clear light upon the religious tenets, common to both the grand ſects of the Hindoos. It is a dialogue between Brimha, or the wiſdom of God; and Narud, or human reaſon.

NARUD.

[7] O thou firſt of God! Who is the greateſt of all Beings.

BRIMHA.

BRIMHA; who is infinite and almighty.

NARUD.

Is he exempted from death?

BRIMHA.

He is: being eternal and incorporeal.

NARUD.

Who created the world?

BRIMHA.

GOD, by his power.

NARUD.

Who is the giver of bliſs?

BRIMHA.

KRISHEN: and whoſoever worſhippeth him, ſhall enjoy heaven[8].

[7] Brimha, as we have already obſerved, is the genitive caſe of BRIMH; as WISDOM is, by the Brahmins, reckoned the chief attribute of God.

[8] Kriſhen is derived from *Kriſh* giving, and *Ana* joy. It is one of the thouſand names of God.

NARUD.

NARUD.

What is his likeneſs?

BRIMHA.

God has no likeneſs.

He hath no likeneſs: but to ſtamp ſome idea of him upon the minds of men, who cannot believe in an immaterial being, he is repreſented under various ſymbolical forms.

NARUD.

What image ſhall we conceive of him?

BRIMHA.

Allegorical deſcription of him

If your imagination cannot riſe to devotion without an image; ſuppoſe with yourſelf, that his eyes are like the Lotos, his complexion like a cloud, his cloathing of the lightning of heaven, and that he hath four hands.

NARUD.

Why ſhould we think of the almighty in this form?

BRIMHA.

explained.

His eyes may be compared to the Lotos, to ſhew that they are always open, like that flower which the greateſt depth of water cannot ſurmount. His complexion being like that of a cloud, is an emblem of that darkneſs with which he veils himſelf from mortal eyes. His cloathing is of lightning, to expreſs that awful majeſty which ſurrounds him: and his four hands are ſymbols of his ſtrength and almighty power.

NARUD.

What things are proper to be offered unto him?

BRIMHA.

Reaſon of offerings.

Thoſe things which are clean, and offered with a grateful heart. But all things which by the law are reckoned impure, or have been defiled by the touch of a woman in her times; things which have been coveted by your own ſoul, ſeized by oppreſ-

ſion,

ſion, or obtained by deceit, or that have any natural blemiſh, are offerings unworthy of God.

NARUD.

We are commanded then to make offerings to God of ſuch things as are pure and without blemiſh, by which it would appear that God eateth and drinketh, like mortal man, or if he doth not, for what purpoſe are our offerings?

BRIMHA.

God neither eats nor drinks like mortal men. But if you love not God, your offerings will be unworthy of him; for as all men covet the good things of this world, God requires a free offering of their ſubſtance, as the ſtrongeſt teſtimony of their gratitude and inclinations towards him. explained.

NARUD.

How is God to be worſhipped?

BRIMHA.

With no ſelfiſh view; but for love of his beauties, gratitude for his favours, and for admiration of his greatneſs. God how to be worſhipped.

NARUD.

How can the human mind fix itſelf upon God, being, that it is in its nature changeable, and perpetually running from one object to another?

BRIMHA.

True: The mind is ſtronger than an elephant, whom men have found means to ſubdue, though they have never been able entirely to ſubdue their own inclinations. But the ankuſh[9] of the mind is true wiſdom, which ſees into the vanity of all worldly things. Self-denial neceſſary.

[9] Ankuſh is an iron inſtrument uſed for driving elephants.

NARUD.

Where ſhall we find true wiſdom?

BRIMHA.

In the ſociety of good and wiſe men.

NARUD.

But the mind, in ſpite of reſtraint, covets riches, women, and all worldly pleaſures. How are theſe appetites to be ſubdued?

BRIMHA.

Penance. If they cannot be overcome by reaſon, let them be mortified by penance. For this purpoſe it will be neceſſary to make a public and ſolemn vow, leſt your reſolution ſhould be ſhaken by the pain which attends it.

NARUD.

We ſee that all men are mortal, what ſtate is there after death?

BRIMHA.

State of the dead. The ſouls of ſuch good men as retain a ſmall degree of worldly inclinations, will enjoy Surg[1] for a time; but the ſouls of thoſe who are holy, ſhall be abſorbed into God, never more to reanimate fleſh. The wicked ſhall be puniſhed in Nirick[2] for a certain ſpace, and afterwards their ſouls are permitted to wander in ſearch of new habitations of fleſh.

NARUD.

Thou, O father, doſt mention God as one; yet we are told, that Râm, whom we are taught to call God, was born in the houſe of Jeſſarit: That Kiſhen, whom we call God, was born in the houſe of Baſdeo, and many others in the ſame manner. In what light are we to take this myſtery?

[1] Heaven. [2] Hell.

BRIMHA.

BRIMHA.

You are to look upon these as particular manifestations of the providence of God, for certain great ends, as in the case of the sixteen hundred women, called Gopi, when all the men of Sirendiep[3] were destroyed in war. The women prayed for husbands, and they had all their desires gratified in one night, and became with child. But you are not to suppose, that God, who is in this case introduced as the actor, is liable to human passions or frailties, being in himself, pure and incorporeal. At the same time he may appear in a thousand places, by a thousand names, and in a thousand forms; yet continue the same unchangeable, in his divine nature.——

Allegorical appearances of God explained.

Without making any reflections upon this chapter of the DIRM SHASTER, it appears evident, that the religion of the Hindoos has hitherto been very much misrepresented in Europe. The followers of the NEADIRSEN SHASTER, differ greatly in their philosophy, from the sect of the BEDANG, though both agree about the unity of the supreme being. To give some idea of the Neadirsen philosophy, we shall in this place give some extracts from that Shaster.

NEADIRSEN is a compound from NEA, signifying right, and DIRSEN, to teach or explain; so that the word may be translated an *exhibition of truth*. Though it is not reckoned so antient as the Bedang, yet it is said to have been written by a philosopher called Goutam, near four thousand years ago. The philosophy contained in this Shaster, is very abstruse and metaphysical; and therefore it is but justice to Goutam to confess, that the author of the dissertation, notwithstanding the great pains he took to

Etymon of Neadirsen

[3] The island of Ceylon.

have proper definitions of the terms, is by no means certain, whether he has fully attained his end. In this ſtate of uncertainty he choſe to adhere to the literal meaning of words, rather than by a free tranſlation, to deviate perhaps from the ſenſe of his author.

Indians of Bengal of that Sect.

The generality of the Hindoos of Bengal, and all the northern provinces of Hindoſtan, eſteem the NEADIRSEN a ſacred Shaſter; but thoſe of the Decan, Coromandel, and Malabar, totally reject it. It conſiſts of ſeven volumes. The firſt only came to the hands of the author of the Diſſertation, and he has, ſince his arrival in England, depoſited it in the Britiſh Muſeum. He can ſay nothing for certain, concerning the contents of the ſubſequent volumes; only that they contain a compleat ſyſtem of the theology and philoſophy of the Brahmins of the Neadirſen ſect.

Goutam's philoſophy.

Goutam does not begin to reaſon, *a priori*, like the writer of the Bedang. He conſiders the preſent ſtate of nature, and the intellectual faculties, as far as they can be inveſtigated by human reaſon; and from thence he draws all his concluſions. He reduces all things under ſix principal heads; ſubſtance, quality, motion, ſpecies, aſſimulation, and conſtruction[4]. In ſubſtance, beſides time, ſpace, life, and ſpirit, he comprehends earth, water, fire, air, and akaſh. The four groſſer elements, he ſays, come under the immediate comprehenſion of our bodily ſenſes; and akaſh, time, ſpace, ſoul, and ſpirit, come under mental perception.

Diviſion of things.

A Materialiſt.

He maintains, that all objects of perception are equally real, as we cannot comprehend the nature of a folid cubit, any more than the ſame extent of ſpace. He affirms, that diſtance in point of time

[4] Theſe are in the original Shanſcrita, Dirba, Goon, Kirmo, Summania, Biſheſh, Sammabae.

and

and ſpace, are equally incomprehenſible; ſo that if we ſhall admit, that ſpace is a real exiſtence, time muſt be ſo too That the ſoul, or vital principle, is a ſubtile element, which pervades all things; for that intellect, which, according to experience in animals, cannot proceed from organization and vital motion only, muſt be a principle totally diſtinct from them.

" The author of the Bedang[5], ſays Goutam, finding the impoſſibility of forming an idea of ſubſtance, aſſerts that all nature is a mere deluſion. But as imagination muſt be acted upon by ſome real exiſtence, as we cannot conceive that it can act upon itſelf, we muſt conclude, that there is ſomething real, otherwiſe philoſophy is at an end."

Diviſion of the properties of things.

He then proceeds to explain what he means by his ſecond principle, or Goon, which, ſays he, comprehends twenty-four things; form, taſte, ſmell, touch, ſound, number, quantity, gravity, ſolidity, fluidity, elaſticity, conjunction, ſeparation, priority, poſteriority, diviſibility, indiviſibility, accident, perception, eaſe, pain, deſire, averſion and power[6]. Kirmo or motion is, according to him, of two kinds, direct and crooked. Sammania, or ſpecies, which is his third principle, includes all animals and natural productions. Biſheſh he defines to be a tendency in matter towards productions; and Sammabae, or the laſt principle, is the artificial conſtruction or formation of things, as a ſtatue from a block of marble, a houſe from ſtones, or cloth from cotton.

[5] A ſyſtem of ſceptical philoſophy, to which many of the Brahmins adhere.

[6] The twenty-four things are, in the Shanſcrita, in order theſe; Rup, Ris, Gund, Supurſa, Shubardo Sirica, Purriman, Gurritte, Dirbitte, Sinniha, Shanſkan, Sangoog, Bibag, Pirrible,, Particca, Apporticta, Addariſto, Bud, Suc, Duc, Itcha, Deſh, Jotna.

Under

Eternal principles.

Under these six heads, as we have already observed, Goutam comprehends all things which fall under our comprehension; and after having reasoned about their nature and origin in a very philosophical manner, he concludes with asserting, that five things must of necessity be eternal. The first of these is Pirrum Attima, or the GREAT SOUL, who, says he, is immaterial, one, invisible, eternal, and indivisible, possessing omniscience, rest, will and power[7].

The great soul or God.

The vital soul.

The second eternal principle is the Jive Attima, or the vital soul, which he supposes is material, by giving it the following properties; number, quantity, motion, contraction, extension, divisibility, perception, pleasure, pain, desire, aversion, accident, and power. His reasons for maintaining, that the *vital soul* is different from the *great soul*, are very numerous, and it is upon this head that the followers of the Bedang and Neadirsen are principally divided. The first affirm that there is no soul in the universe but God, and the second strenuously hold that there is, as they cannot conceive, that God can be subject to such affections and passions as they feel in their own minds; or that he can possibly have a propensity to evil. Evil, according to the author of the Neadirsen Shaster, proceeds entirely from Jive Attima, or the vital soul. It is a selfish craving principle, never to be satisfied; whereas GOD remains in eternal rest, without any desire but benevolence.

Time.

Goutam's third eternal principle is time or duration, which, says he, must of necessity have existed, while any thing did exist; and is therefore infinite. The fourth principle is space or extension, without

[7] These properties of the divinity, are the following in order; Nidakaar, Akitta, Oderisa, Nitte, Appartičta, Budtirha, Suck, Itcha, Jotna.

which

which nothing could have been; and as it comprehends all quantity, or rather is infinite, he maintains that it is indivisible and eternal. The fifth eternal principle is Akash, a subtile and pure element, which fills up the vacuum of space, and is compounded of purmans or quantities, infinitely small, indivisible and perpetual. "God," says he, "can neither make nor annihilate these atoms, on account of the love which he bears to them, and the necessity of their existence; but they are, in other respects, totally subservient to his pleasure." Celestial element.

"God," says Goutam, "at a certain season, endued these atoms, as we may call them, with Bishesh or plasticity, by virtue of which they arranged themselves into four gross elements, fire, air, water, and earth. These atoms being, from the beginning, formed by God into the *seeds* of all productions, Jive Attima, or the vital soul, associated with them, so that animals, and plants of various kinds, were produced upon the face of the earth." Of the creation of matter.

"The same vital soul," continues Goutam, "which before associated with the Purman of an animal, may afterwards associate with the Purman of a man." This transmigration is distinguished by three names, Mirt, Mirren, and Pirra-purra-purvesh which last literally signifies *the change of abode*. The superiority of man, according to the philosophy of the Neadirsen, consists only in the finer organization of his parts, from which proceed reason, reflexion, and memory, which the brutes only possess in an inferior degree, on account of their less refined organs. Of the transmigration of souls.

Goutam supposes, with the author of the Bedang, that the soul after death, assumes a body of fire, air, and akash, unless in the carnal body, it has been so purified by piety and virtue, that it retains no selfish inclinations. In that case it is absorbed into the State after death.

the GREAT SOUL OF NATURE, never more to reanimate fleſh. Such, ſays the philoſopher, ſhall be the reward of all thoſe who worſhip God from pure love and admiration, without any ſelfiſh views. Thoſe that ſhall worſhip God from motives of future happineſs, ſhall be indulged with their deſires in heaven, for a certain time. But they muſt alſo expiate their crimes, by ſuffering adequate puniſhments: and afterwards their ſouls will return to the earth, and wander about for new habitations. Upon their return to the earth, they ſhall caſually aſſociate with the firſt organized Purman they ſhall meet. They ſhall not retain any conſciouſneſs of their former ſtate, unleſs it is revealed to them by God. But thoſe favoured perſons are very few, and are diſtinguiſhed by the name of Jates Summon[8].

Sins of the parents deſcend to the children.

The author of the Neadirſen teaches, for the purpoſes of morality, that the ſins of the parents will deſcend to their poſterity; and that, on the other hand, the virtues of the children will mitigate the puniſhments of the parents in Nirick, and haſten their return to the earth. Of all ſins he holds ingratitude[9] to be the greateſt. Souls guilty of that black crime, ſays he, will remain in hell, while the ſun remains in heaven, or to the general diſſolution of all things.

Intellect.

Intellect, ſays Goutam, is formed by the combined action of the ſenſes. He reckons ſix ſenſes: five external[1], and one internal. The laſt he calls Manus, by which he ſeems to mean conſcience. In the latter he comprehends reaſon, perception[2] and memory: and he concludes, that by their means only, mankind may poſſible acquire knowledge.

[8] The acquainted with their former ſtate. [9] Mitterdro.
[1] Onnuman, reaſon. Upimen, perception. [2] Chakous, Shraban, Raſan, Granap, Tawaſs.

ledge. He then proceeds to explain the manner by which theſe ſenſes act.

Sight.

Sight, ſays he, ariſes from the Shanſkar or repulſive qualities of bodies, by which the particles of light which fall upon them, are reflected back upon the eyes from all parts of their ſurfaces. Thus the object is painted in a perfect manner upon the organ of ſeeing, whither the ſoul repairs to receive the image. He affirms that, unleſs the ſoul fixes its attention upon the figure in the eye, nothing can be perceived by the mind; for a man in a profound reverie, though his eyes are open to the light, perceives nothing. Colours, ſays Goutam, are particular feelings in the eye, which are proportioned to the quantity of light reflected from any ſolid body[3]

Hearing.

Goutam defines hearing in the ſame manner with the European philoſophers, with this difference only, that he ſuppoſes, that the ſound which affects the ear, is conveyed through the purer element of akaſh, and not by the air; an error which is not very ſurprizing, in a ſpeculative philoſopher. Taſte, he defines to be a ſenſation of the tongue and palate, occaſioned by the particular form of thoſe particles which compoſe food. Smell, ſays he, proceeds from the effluvia which ariſes from bodies to the noſtrils. The feeling, which ariſes from touching, is occaſioned by the contact of denſe bodies with the ſkin, which, as well as the whole body, excepting the bones, the hair and the nails, is the organ of that ſenſe. There run, ſays he, from all parts of the ſkin, very ſmall nerves to a great nerve, which he diſtinguiſhes by the name of

Taſting. Smelling. Touching.

[3] To ſave the credit of Goutam, in this place, it is neceſſary to obſerve, that anatomy is not at all known among the Hindoos, being ſtrictly prohibited from touching a dead body, by the ſevereſt ties of religion.

Medda.

Medda. This nerve is compoſed of two different coats, the one ſenſitive, and the other inſenſitive. It extends from the crown of the head, down the right ſide of the vertebræ to the right foot.[1] When the body becomes languid, the ſoul, fatigued with action, retires within the inſenſible coat, which checks the operation of the ſenſes, and occaſions ſound ſleep. But ſhould there remain in the ſoul, a ſmall inclination to action, it ſtarts into the ſenſitive part of the nerve, and dreams immediately ariſe before it. Theſe dreams, ſays he, invariably relate to ſomething perceived before by the ſenſes, though the mind may combine the ideas together at pleaſure.

Conſcience. Manus, or conſcience, is the internal feeling of the mind, when it is no way affected by external objects. Onnuman, or reaſon, ſays Goutam, is that faculty of the ſoul which enables us to conclude that things and circumſtances exiſt, from an analogy to things, which had before fallen under the conception of our bodily ſenſes: for inſtance, when we ſee ſmoak, we conclude that it proceeds from a fire; when we ſee one end of a rope, we are perſuaded that it muſt have another.

Reaſon. By reaſon, continues Goutam, men perceive the exiſtence of God; which the Boad or Atheiſts deny, becauſe his exiſtence does not come within the comprehenſion of the ſenſes. Theſe atheiſts, ſays he, maintain that there is no God but the univerſe; that there is neither good nor evil in the world; that there is no ſuch thing as a ſoul; that all animals exiſt, by a mere mechaniſm of the organs, or by a fermentation of the elements; and that all natural productions are but the fortuitous concourſe of things.

Goutam refutes Atheiſts. The philoſopher refutes theſe atheiſtical opinions, by a long train of arguments, ſuch as have been often urged by European divines. Though ſuperſtition,

ſtition and cuſtom may biaſs reaſon to different ends, in various countries, we find a ſurpriſing ſimilarity in the arguments uſed by all nations, againſt the Boad, thoſe common enemies of every ſyſtem of religion.

Of Atheiſm.

" Another ſect of the Boad, ſays Goutam, are of opinion that all things were produced by chance*." This doctrine he thus refutes. Chance is ſo far from being the origin of all things, that it has but a momentary exiſtence of its own; being alternately created and annihilated, at periods infinitely ſmall, as it depends entirely on the action of real eſſences. This action is not accidental, for it muſt inevitably proceed from ſome natural cauſe. Let the dice be rattled eternally in the box, they are determined in their motion, by certain invariable laws. What therefore we call chance, is but an effect proceeding from cauſes which we do not perceive.

Perception.

" Perception," continues Goutam, " is that faculty by which we inſtantaneouſly know things without the help of reaſon. This is perceived by means of relation, or ſome diſtinguiſhing property in things, ſuch as high and low, long and ſhort, great and ſmall, hard and ſoft, cold and hot, black and white."

Memory.

Memory, according to Goutam, is the elaſticity of the mind, and is employed in three different ways; on things preſent as to time, but abſent as to place; on things paſt, and on things to come. It would appear from the latter part of the diſtinction, that the philoſopher comprehends imagination in memory. He then proceeds to define all the original properties of matter, and all the paſſions and faculties of the mind. He then deſcants on the nature of generation.

* Addariſto.

" Generation,

Generation. "Generation, ſays he, may be divided into two kinds; Jonidge, or generation by copulation; and adjonidge, generation without copulation. All animals are produced by the firſt, and all plants by the latter. The purman or ſeed of things, was formed from the beginning, with all its parts. When it happens to be depoſited in a matrix ſuitable to its nature, a ſoul aſſociates with it; and, by aſſimulating more matter, it gradually becomes a creature or plant; for plants, as well as animals, are poſſeſſed of a portion of the *vital ſoul* of the world.

Free will. Goutam, in another place, treats diffuſely of providence and free will. He divides the action of man under three heads: The will of God, the power of man, and caſual or accidental events. In explaining the firſt, he maintains a particular providence; in the ſecond, the freedom of will in man; and in the third, the common courſe of things, according to the general laws of nature. With reſpect to providence, though he cannot deny the poſſibility of its exiſtence, without diveſting God of his omnipotence, he ſuppoſes that the deity never exerts that power, but that he remains in eternal reſt, taking no concern, neither in human affairs, nor in the courſe of the operations of nature.

World ſubject to ſucceſſive diſſolutions and renovations. The author of the Neadirſen maintains, that the world is ſubject to ſucceſſive diſſolutions and renovations at certain ſtated periods. He divides theſe diſſolutions into the leſſer and the greater. The leſſer diſſolution will happen at the end of a revolution of the Jugs. The world will be then conſumed by fire, and the elements ſhall be jumbled together, and after a certain ſpace of time, they will again reſume their former order. When a thouſand of thoſe ſmaller diſſolutions ſhall have happened, a Mahperley or great diſſolution will take

take place. All the elements will then be reduced to their original Purmans or atoms, in which ſtate they ſhall long remain. God will then, from his mere goodneſs and pleaſure, reſtore Biſheſh or plaſticity. A new creation will ariſe; and thus things have revolved in ſucceſſion, from the beginning, and will continue to do ſo to eternity.

Allegories on that ſubject.

Theſe repeated diſſolutions and renovations have furniſhed an ample field for the inventions of the Brahmins. Many allegorical ſyſtems of creation are upon that account contained in the Shaſters. It was for this reaſon, that ſo many different accounts of the coſmogony of the Hindoos have been promulgated in Europe; ſome travellers adopting one ſyſtem, and ſome another. Without deviating from the good manners due to thoſe writers, we may venture to affirm, that their tales, upon this ſubject, are extremely puerile, if not abſurd. They took their accounts from any common Brahmin, with whom they chanced to meet, and never had the curioſity or induſtry to go to the fountain head.

In ſome of the renovations of the world, Brimha, or the wiſdom of God, is repreſented in the form of an infant with his toe in his mouth, floating on a comala or water flower, or ſometimes upon a leaf of that plant, upon the watery abyſs. The Brahmins mean no more by this allegory, than that at that time, the wiſdom and deſigns of God will appear, as in their infant ſtate. Brimha floating upon a leaf, ſhews the inſtability of things at that period. The toe which he ſucks in his mouth, implies that infinite wiſdom ſubſiſts of itſelf; and the poſition of Brimha's body, is an emblem of the endleſs circle of eternity.

We ſee Brimha ſometimes creeping forth from a winding ſhell. This is an emblem of the untraceable way by which divine wiſdom iſſues forth from

from the *imfinite ocean of God.* He, at other times, blows up the world with a pipe, which implies, that the earth is but a bubble of vanity, which the breath of his mouth can deſtroy. Brimha, in one of the renovations, is repreſented in the form of a ſnake, one end of which, is upon a tortoiſe which floats upon the vaſt abyſs, and upon the other, he ſupports the world. The ſnake is the emblem of wiſdom, the tortoiſe is a ſymbol of ſecurity, which figuratively ſignifies providence, and the vaſt abyſs is the eternity and infinitude of God.

Brahmins believe in the unity of God.

What has been already ſaid has, it is hoped, thrown a new light on the opinions of the Hindoos, upon the ſubject of religion and philoſophical inquiry. We find that the Brahmins, contrary to the ideas formed of them in the weſt, invariably believe in the unity, eternity, omniſcience and omnipotence of God: that the polytheiſm of which they have been accuſed, is no more than a ſymbolical worſhip of the divine attributes, which they divide into three principal claſſes. Under the name of BRIMHA, they worſhip the wiſdom and creative power of God; under the appellation of BISHEN, his providential and preſerving quality; and under that of SAIBAH, that attribute which tends to reduce matter to its original principles.

Of images.

This ſyſtem of worſhip, ſay the Brahmins, ariſes from two opinions. The firſt is, that as God is immaterial, and conſequently inviſible, it is impoſſible to raiſe a proper idea of him, by any image in the human mind. The ſecond is, that it is neceſſary to ſtrike the groſs ideas of man, with ſome emblems of God's attributes, otherwiſe, that all ſenſe of religion will naturally vaniſh from the mind. They, for this purpoſe, have made ſymbolical repreſentations of the three claſſes of the divine attributes; but they aver, that they do not believe them to be ſeparate intelligences. BRIMH,

or

or the ſupreme divinity, has a thouſand names; but the Hindoos would think it the groſſeſt impiety to repreſent him under any form. "The human mind, ſay they, may form ſome conception of his attributes ſeparately, but who can graſp the whole, within the circle of finite ideas."

That in any age or country, human reaſon was ever ſo depraved as to worſhip the work of hands, for the creator of the univerſe, we believe to be an abſolute deception, which aroſe from the vanity of the abettors of particular ſyſtems of religion. To attentive inquirers into the human mind, it will appear, that common ſenſe, upon the affairs of religion, is pretty equally divided among all nations. Revelation and philoſophy have, it is confeſſed, lopped off ſome of thoſe ſuperſtitious excreſcences and abſurdities that naturally ariſe in weak minds, upon a ſubject ſo myſterious: but it is much to be doubted, whether the want of thoſe neceſſary purifiers of religion, ever involved any nation in groſs idolatry, as many ignorant zealots have pretended. No idolaters.

In India, as well as in many other countries, there are two religious ſects; the one look up to the divinity, through the medium of reaſon and philoſophy; while the others receive, as an article of their belief, every holy legend and allegory which have been tranſmitted down from antiquity. From a fundamental article in the Hindoo faith, that God is *the ſoul of the world*, and is conſequently diffuſed through all nature, the vulgar revere all the elements, and conſequently every great natural object, as containing a portion of God; nor is the infinity of the ſupreme being, eaſily comprehended by weak minds, without falling into this error. This veneration for different objects, has, no doubt, given riſe among the common Indians, to an idea of ſubaltern intelligences; Different opinions in religion in India.

telligences; but the learned Brahmins, with one voice, deny the exiſtence of inferior divinities; and, indeed, all their religious books of any antiquity, confirm that aſſertion.

END OF THE DISSERTATION.

A
GENERAL MAP
of
HINDOSTAN,
with the
ADJACENT COUNTRIES.
HINDOSTAN
TURAN
TARTARY
PERSIA
TIBET or BUDTAN
KOBI or GREAT SANDY DESERT
K.m of TANGUT
K.m of ASAM
EYGUR
MOGULISTAN
THE CASPIAN SEA OR BEHR MAZINDERAN
TURKESTAN
CHARIZM
AGIM or IRAN
FARSISTAN
TELLINGANA
BAY OF BENGAL
ARACAN
K.m of TIPPRA
MALDIVES

A
CATALOGUE
OF THE
GODS OF THE HINDOOS.

To prevent future writers from confounding themſelves and others, by miſtaking ſynonimous names of the Gods of the Hindoos, for different intelligences, we here preſent the public with a catalogue of them, as taken from an original book of the Brahmins. A liſt of proper names, eſpecially in a foreign language, is ſo very dry of itſelf, that it is ſuperfluous to adviſe ſuch as are not particularly inquiſitive upon this ſubject, to paſs entirely over this liſt, as it can afford very little amuſement.

Brimh, or the ſupreme being, is diſtinguiſhed by a thouſand names, in the Shanſcrita, according to the Brahmins; but it is to be obſerved, that in that number they include the names of all thoſe powers, properties, and attributes, which they conceive to be inherent in the divine nature, as well as the names of all thoſe ſymbols and material eſſences, under which God is worſhipped. Thoſe commonly uſed are, Iſhbur, the great will; Bagubaan, the receptacle of goodneſs; Narrain, the giver of motion; Pirrimpurrous, the firſt eſſence; Niringen, the diſpaſſionate; Nidakar, the immaterial.

Brimha, or God, in his attribute of wiſdom, is worſhipped under the following names. Attimabah, the good ſpirit. Beda, ſcience. Beddatta, the giver of knowledge. Biſheſhrick, the flower of the creation. Surrajiſt, Purmiſti, Pittamah, Hirinagirba, Lokeſſa, Saimbu, Chottranun, Datta, Objajoni, Birrinchi, Commalaſein, Biddi.

Bishen, or God in his providential quality, is worſhipped under the following names. Kriſhana, the giver of joy; Biſhana, the nouriſher. Baycanta, Bitara-ſirba, Dammudar, Biſhi-keſh, Keſeba, Mahdob, Subduh, Deitari, Pundericack, Gurrud-idaja, Pittamber, Otchuta, Saringi, Biſſickſon, Jannardan, Uppindera, Indrabah-raja, Suckerpani, Chullerbudge, Puttanab, Mudcripu, Baſdebo, Tribickerma, Deibuckinindan, Suri, Sirriputti, Purruſittam, Bunnumali, Billidinſi, Kangſarratti, Oddu-kego, Biſſimber, Koitabagit, Sirbaſſa, Lanchana.

Shibah, or as it is generally pronounced, Shieb, and ſometimes Shiew, emblematically, the deſtructive power of God, is known by the names of Mahoiſſur, the great Demon; Mahdebo, the great ſpirit; Bamdebo, the frightful ſpirit; Mohilla, the deſtroyer; Khaal, time; Sumbu, Iſh, Puſhuputti, Shuli, Surboh, Iſhan, Shawkacarrah, Sandraſeikar, Butcheſſa, Candapurſu, Giriſſa, Merrurah, Mittinja, Kirtibaſh, Pinnaki, Pirmatadippo, Ugur, Choppurdi, Scricant, Sitticant, Copalbrit, Birrupacka, Trilochuna, Kerſanwreta, Sirbugah, Durjutti, Neloloito, Harra, Sarraharra, Trimbick, Tripurantacka, Gangadir, Undukorripu, Kirtudanſi, Birſadija, Bumkeſa, Babah, Bimeh, Stanu, Rudder, Ummaputti.

In the ſame manner as the power of God is figuratively ſaid to have taken upon itſelf three maſculine forms at the creation; ſo Pirkitti, or the goodneſs of God, is ſaid to have taken three feminine forms. The firſt of theſe was *Drugah*, or or Virtue, who, ſay they, was married to Shibah; to intimate that good and evil are ſo blended together, that they could not have exiſted ſeparately: for had there been no ſuch thing as evil, in conſequence there could be no good. She is worſhipped in this character under the names of Bowani, courage; Maiah, love; Homibutti, Iſhura, Shibae, Rudderani, Sirbani, Surba-mungula, Appurna, Parbutti, Kattaini Gouri, and a variety of other names.

As the conſort of Biſhen, ſhe is worſhipped under the names of Litchmi, which ſignifies fortune; Puddamah, Leich, Commala, Siri Horripria.

As the conſort of Brimha, ſhe is generally known by the names of Surſitti, which means the beſtower of wiſdom; Giandah, the giver of reaſon; Gire, Baak, Bani, Sardah, Brimhapira.

Beſides the above ſix capital diviſions of the divine attributes, they raiſe temples to Granesh, or policy, whom they worſhip at the commencement of any deſign, by the names of Biggenrage, Binnauck, Deimatar, Gunnadebo, Eckdant, Herrumboo, Lumbodre, Gunjanund. This divinity is feigned to be the firſt born ſon of Shibah; and is repreſented with the head of an elephant, with one tooth only.

Kartick, or Fame, is alſo worſhipped under various names as follows; Farruck-gite, Mahaſin, Surjunmah, Surranonno, Parbutti-nundun, Skunda Sonnani, Agnibu, Guha, Bahulliha, Biſhaka, Shuckibahin, Shanmattara, Shuckliddir, Cummar, Corimchidarna. He is ſaid to be the ſecond ſon of Sibah.

Cam-debo, the ſpirit of love, is alſo known by the names of Muddun, Mannumut, Maro, Purrudumun, Minckatin, Kundurp, Durpako, Annungah, Panſuſur, Shwaro, Sumberari, Munnuſigah, Kusſhumeſha, Ommenidja, *Paſsbadinna*,

Kulliputti, Nackera-dija, Ratimoboo: he is ſaid to be the firſt born of Biſhen.

Cobere, or wealth, is known by the following names; Trumbuca-ſuca, Juckrage, Gudja-keſſera, Monnuſa-dirma, Dunnedo, Raja Raja, Donnadippa, Kinareſſo, Borſſerbunnu, Polluſta, Narru-bahin, Joikaika, Ellabilla, Srida Punejaniſherah. Nill Cobere, the ſon of wealth, is alſo repreſented in the emblems of luxury, but is ſeldom worſhipped.

Soorage, or the Sun, is worſhipped under the names of Inder, or the King of the Stars; Mohruttan, Mugubah, Biraja, Packſaſen, Birdirſiſba, Sonnaſir, Purruhutta, Purrinder, Giſtnow, Likkerſubba, Sockor, Sukamunneh, Depasputti, Suttrama, Gottrabit, Budgeri, Baſub, Bitterha, Baſtoſputti, Suraputti, Ballaratti, Satchiputti, Jambubedi, Horriheia, Surat, Nomiſinundun, Sonkrindana, Duſſibina, Turraſat, Negabahina, Akindilla, Sorakah, Ribukah.

Chunder, or the Moon, is woſhipped under the names of Hindoo, Himmanchu, Chundermah, Kumuda-bandibah, Biddu, Sudduns, Subranſu, Oſſadiſſa, Niſhaputti, Objoja, Soom, Gullow, Merkanku, Kollandi, Dirjarage, Seſudirra, Nuhtitreſſa, Kepakina.

Beſides all the above, they have divinities which they ſuppoſe to preſide over the elements, rivers, mountains, &c. or rather worſhip all theſe as parts of the divinity, or on a ſuppoſition of his exiſtence in all things.

Agunni, or the God of fire, hath thirty-five names. Birren, or the God of water, ten names. Baiow, or the God of air, twenty-three names: all which are too tedious to mention.

The Jum are fourteen in number, and are ſuppoſed to be ſpirits who diſpoſe of the ſouls of the dead.

The

The Ussera are beautiful women, who are feigned to reside in heaven, and to sing the praises of God.

The Gundirp are boys who have the same office.

The Rakiss are ghosts or spectres who walk about the earth.

The Deints or Oissurs are evil spirits or demons, who were expelled from heaven, and are now said to live under ground.

The Deos or Debos are spirits whose bodies are supposed to be of the element of fire; they are sometimes represented beautiful as angels, and at other times in horrible forms; they are supposed to inhabit the air.

Such is the strange system of religion which priestcraft has imposed on the vulgar, ever ready in all climes and ages to take advantage of superstitious minds. There is one thing however to be said in favour of the Hindoo doctrine, that while it teaches the purest morals, it is systematically formed on philosophical opinions. Let us therefore no longer imagine half the world more ignorant than the stones which they seem to worship, but rest assured, that whatever the external ceremonies of religion may be, the self-same infinite Being is the object of universal adoration.

THE

THE
HISTORY
OF
HINDOSTAN.

A Dissertation concerning the ancient Hiſtory of the Indians.

The ancient hiſtory of India little known.

THE accounts of the ancients concerning India are extremely unſatisfactory, and the induſtry of the moderns has not ſupplied that defect, by an inquiry into the domeſtic literature of that part of the world. The Greeks and Romans ſcarcely ever extended their informations beyond the limits of their conqueſts; and the Arabians, though minute in the detail of their own tranſactions, are very imperfect, in the hiſtory of thoſe nations whom they ſubdued.

A few facts from an Indian hiſtorical poem.

The averſion of the Indians themſelves to diſcloſe the annals of their hiſtory, which are interſperſed with their religious tenets, to ſtrangers, has, in a manner, involved their tranſactions, in ancient times, in impenetrable darkneſs. The only light to conduct us, through the obſcure paths of their antiquities, we derive from a hiſtorical poem, founded upon real facts, tranſlated into the Perſian language in the reign of Mahommed Akbar, who died

died in the 1605th of the Chriſtian æra. The author of the Hiſtory of India, now tranſlated from the Perſian, has extracted ſome facts from the poem, which we ſhall arrange into order, in a more ſuccinct, and, perhaps, in a more agreeable manner, than they were delivered down by him.

The Indians divide the age of the world into four grand periods, each of which conſiſts of an incredible number of years. The laſt of theſe, called the CAL period, comprehends thirty thouſand years, near five thouſand of which have already elapſed. The Brahmins relate many fictions concerning the former three, but their authentic accounts extend not further than the commencement of the CAL period.

Dynaſty of the Kriſhens.

According to the Maha-Barit, or the Great War, the name of the poem we have already mentioned, India, ſome time after the commencement of the CAL æra, was formed into one empire. The founder of the firſt dynaſty of its Kings was Kriſhen, who, and his poſterity, reigned over the Indians for the ſpace of four hundred years. Very little concerning this race of monarchs has come to our knowledge, except that they held their court in the city of Oud, the capital of a province of the ſame name, to the north-eaſt of the kingdom of Bengal.

Of the Marajas.

Maraja, who was deſcended by a female of the royal houſe of Kriſhen, ſucceeded to the throne after the extinction of the male line. He is ſaid to have been a good and great prince, devoting his whole time to the juſt adminiſtration of public affairs. Under him the governments of provinces became hereditary, for the firſt time in particular families; and he is ſaid, though perhaps erroneouſly, to have been the firſt who divided the Indians into thoſe four diſtinct tribes, which we have mentioned

mentioned in the dissertation concerning their religion and philosophy. Learning is said to have flourished under Maraja, and little else is recorded concerning his reign. His family, who all bore the name of Maraja, enjoyed the throne of India for seven hundred years.

Towards the close of the æra of the royal dynasty of the Marajas, the first invasions of India by the Persians is placed. One of the blood-royal of India, disgusted with the reigning prince fled into Persia, whose king was called Feredon. That monarch espousing the cause of the fugitive, sent an army into Hindostan, and carried on a war with that empire for the space of ten years. The country, during so long a series of hostilities, suffered exceedingly, and the Maraja, who sat on the throne, was obliged to cede part of his dominions to the fugitive prince, who it seems, was his nephew. A tribute, at the same time, was sent to the king of Persia, and the empire of India seems ever after to depend, in some measure, upon that of Persia. First invasion of the Persians.

During the Persian war, the imperial governors of Ceylon and the Carnatic rebelled. The eldest son of the Emperor was killed in battle, and his army defeated, by the rebels. Maraja was, at the same time, threatened with a second Persian invasion, but some presents well applied diverted the storm from India, though not without ceding to the Persians all the provinces upon the Indus. The imperial general, who opposed the invasion from the north, turning his arms against the Decan, recovered that extensive country to the empire, together with the revolted islands. That species of music, which still subsists in the eastern provinces, is said to have been introduced, during this expedition, from the Tellenganians of the Decan. We have The Decan revolts from the empire.

have no further particulars concerning this long line of kings.

Dynasty of Kesro-raja. When the family of the Marajas became extinct, one Kesro-raja mounted the throne of India, as near as we can compute the time, about 1429 years before the Christian æra. This prince was descended, by the mother's side, from the royal house of the Marajas. He is said, at his accession, to have had fourteen brothers, whom he made governors of different provinces. It appears that the island of Ceylon, was not thoroughly reduced till the reign of Kesro-raja, who went in person to that country, and subdued the rebels. The Decan revolted in his time, and to reduce it Kesro-raja solicited the aid of his Lord Paramount, the king of Persia. An army from that country, in conjunction with the imperial forces of India, soon reduced the Decan, and the customary tribute was continued to the Persian. Kesro-raja, and his posterity after him, reigned in peace over India, in the capital of Oud, for the space of two hundred and twenty years.

Of Feros-ra. In the 1209 before the commencement of the Christian æra, we find one Feros-ra on the throne of India. He is said to have been versed in the Indian sciences of the Shaster, to have taken great delight in the society of learned men, and to have entirely neglected the art of war. He expended the public revenue upon devotees and enthusiasts, and in building temples for worship in every province of his dominions. Nothwithstanding this outward shew of religion, Feros-ra did not hesitate to take the opportunity of a Tartar invasion of Persia, to wrest from that empire the provinces upon the Indus, which had been ceded, by his predecessors, for the assistance received from the King of Persia in the reduction of the Decan.

It is related, by ſome authors, that Punjâb, or the province lying upon the five branches which compoſe the Indus, were in poſſeſſion of the empire of Hindoſtan till the reign of Kei Kobad, King of Perſia. In his time, Ruſtum Diſta, King of the Perſian province of Seiſtan, who, for his great exploits is ſtiled the Hercules of the Eaſt, invaded the Northern provinces of India; and the prince of the family of Feros-ra, who ſat on the throne, unable to oppoſe the progreſs of that hero's arms, retired to the mountains of Turhat. Ruſtum ſoon diſpoſſeſſed him of that faſtneſs, and it is ſaid that the King of India died, a fugitive, in the mountains on the confines of Bengal and Oriſſa. The dynaſty of Feros-ra comprehends one hundred and thirty-ſeven years. A Perſian invaſion.

The whole empire of India fell into the hands of the victory, by the death of the King. Ruſtum, however, was not willing to retain it as a dependent of Perſia, on account of its diſtance, and he placed a new family on the throne. The name of the prince raiſed to the empire, by Ruſtum, was Suraja, who was a man of abilities, and reſtored the power of the empire. This dynaſty commenced about 1072 before the Chriſtian æra; and it laſted two hundred and eight-ſix years. The dynaſty of Suraja.

It is affirmed, by the Brahmins, that it was in the time of this dynaſty that the worſhip of emblematical figures of the divine attributes, was firſt eſtabliſhed in India. The Perſians, in their invaſions, ſay they, introduced the worſhip of the Sun, and other heavenly bodies, together with the proper ſymbol of God, the element of fire; but the mental adoration of the Divinity, as one Supreme Being, was ſtill followed by many. The great city of Kinoge, ſo long the capital of Hindoſtan, was built by one of the Surajas, on the banks of the Ganges. Idolatry introduced.

The

The circumference of its walls are ſaid to have been one hundred miles.

Baraja. After the extinction or depoſition of the royal houſe of Suraja, Baraja acceded to the throne of Hindoſtan, which he poſſeſſed thirty-ſix years. We know little concerning him, but that he built the city of Barage, ſtill remaining in India. He had a genius for muſic, and wrote ſome books upon that ſubject, which were long in high repute. He, at laſt, grew diſordered in his ſenſes, bacame tyrannical, and was depoſed by Keidar, a Brahmin, who aſſumed the empire.

Keidar. Keidar, being a man of learning and genius, became an excellent prince. He paid the cuſtomary tribute to the King of Perſia, and ſo ſecured his Kingdom from foreign invaſion. A domeſtic enemy, however, aroſe, that at length deprived him, in the nineteenth year of his reign, of his life and empire. This was Sinkol, a native of Kinoge, who breaking out into open rebellion, in Bengal and Behâr, defeated, in ſeveral battles, the imperial army, and mounted the throne.

Sinkol. Sinkol was a warlike and magnificent prince. He rebuilt the capital of Bengal, famous under the names of Lucknouti and Goura, and adorned it with many noble ſtructures. Goura is ſaid to have been the chief city of Bengal for two thouſand years; and the ruins that ſtill remain, prove that it has been an amazingly magnificient place. The unwholeſomneſs of the air prevailed upon the imperial family of Timur to order its being abandoned, and Tanda became the ſeat of government two hundred and fifty years ago.

Perſian invaſion. Sinkol, keeping an immenſe army in pay, was induced to withhold the tribute from the King of Perſia, and to turn the ambaſſador of that Monarch, with diſgrace, from his court. Fifty thouſand Perſian horſe, under their general, Peiran, invaded

invaded India, and advanced without much oppoſition to the confines of Bengal, where they came to battle with the imperial army, under Sinkol. Though the bravery of the Perſians was much ſuperior to that of the Hindoos, they were, at laſt, by the mere weight of numbers, driven from the field, and obliged to take ſhelter, in a ſtrong poſt, in the neighbouring mountains, from whence the victors found it impoſſible to diſlodge them. They continued to ravage the country, from their ſtrong hold, and diſpatched letters to Perſia, to inform the King of their ſituation.

Sinkol defeated.

Affraſiab, for that, ſay the Brahmins, was the name of the monarch who reigned, in the days of Sinkol, over Perſia and a great part of Tartary, was at the city of Gindis, near the borders of China, when he received intelligence of the misfortune of his army in India. He haſtened to their relief with one hundred thouſand horſe, came to battle with the Emperor Sinkol, whom he totally defeated, and purſued to the capital of Bengal. Sinkol did not think it ſafe to remain long at that place, and therefore took refuge in the inacceſſible mountains of Turhat. Affraſiab, in the mean time, laid waſte the country with fire and ſword. Sinkol thought it prudent to beg peace and forgiveneſs of Affraſiab, and he accordingly came, in the character of a ſuppliant, to the Perſian camp, with a ſword and a coffin carried before him, to ſignify that his life was in the diſpoſal of the King. Sinkol was carried priſoner to Tartary, as an hoſtage for the obedience of his ſon Rohata, who was placed upon the throne of Hindoſtan.

Rohata.

Sinkol died in the 731 year before the Chriſtian æra, and Rohata continued his reign over India. He was a wiſe, religious, and affable prince. The revenues of the empire, which extended from Kirmi to Molava, he divided into three parts; one he expended

expended in charities, another he ſent to Perſia, by way of tribute, and to ſupport his father, and a third he appropriated to the neceſſary expences of government. The ſtanding army of the empire was, upon this account, ſmall, which encouraged the prince of Malava to revolt, and to ſupport himſelf in his rebellion. Rohata built the famous fort of Rhotas, and left what remained to him of the empire, in peace, to his ſon. The race of Sinkol held the ſcepter of India 81 years after his death, and then became extinct.

Maraja

After a long diſpute about the ſucceſſion, a chief of the Raja-put tribe of Cutſwa, aſſumed the dignities of the empire, under the name of Maraja. The firſt act of the reign of Maraja, was the reduction of Guzerat, where ſome diſturbances had happened in the time of his predeceſſor. He built a port in that country, where he conſtructed veſſels, and carried on commerce with all the ſtates of Aſia. He mounted the throne, according to the annals of India, in the 586 year before the birth of Chriſt, and reigned forty years. He is ſaid to have been cotemporary with Guſtaſp, or Hyſtaſpes, the father of Darius, who mounted the throne of Perſia after the death of Smerdis. It is worthy of being remarked in this place, that the chronology of the Hindoos agrees, almoſt exactly, with that eſtabliſhed by Sir Iſaac Newton. Newton fixes the commencement of the reign of Darius in the 521 year before the Chriſtian æra; ſo that, if we ſuppoſe that Hyſtaſpes, who was governor of Turkeſtan, or Tranſoxiana, made a figure in Tartary twenty-five years before the acceſſion of his ſon to the throne of Perſia, which is no way improbable, the chronology of India agrees perfectly with that of Sir Iſaac Newton.

Keda-

Keda-raja, who was nephew, by a ſiſter, to the former emperor, was nominated by him to the throne. Ruſtum Diſta, the Perſian governor of the ceded Indian provinces, being dead, Keda-raja turned his arms that way, reduced the countries upon the Indus, and fixed his reſidence in the city of Bera. The mountaineers of Cabul and Candahar, who are now called Afgans, or Patans, advanced againſt Keda-raja, and recovered all the provinces of which he had poſſeſſed himſelf upon the Indus. We know no more of the Tranſactions of Keda-raja. He died after a reign of forty-three years. Keda-raja.

Jei-chund, the commander in chief of Keda-raja's armies, found no great difficulty in mounting the throne after the death of his ſovereign. We know little of the tranſactions of the reign of Jei-chund. A peſtilence and famine happened in his time, and he himſelf was addicted to indolence and pleaſure. He reigned ſixty years, and his ſon ſucceeded him in the empire, but was diſpoſſeſſed by Delu, the brother of Jei-chund. Bemin and Darâb, or Darius, ſay the Indians, were two ſucceſſive Kings of Perſia in the days of Jei-chund, and he punctually paid to them the ſtipulated tribute. Jei-chund.

Delu is ſaid to have been a prince of uncommon bravery and generoſity; benevolent towards men, and devoted to the ſervice of God. The moſt remarkable tranſaction of his reign is the building of the city of Delhi, which derives its name from its founder, Delu. In the fortieth year of his reign, Phoor, a prince of his own family, who was governor of Cumaoon, rebelled againſt the Emperor, and marched to Kinoge, the capital. Delu was defeated, taken, and confined in the impregnable fort of Rhotas. Delu.

Phoor immediately mounted the throne of India, reduced Bengal, extended his power from ſea to Phoor.

ſea,

ſea, and reſtored the empire to its priſtine dignity. He died after a long reign, and left the kingdom to his ſon, who was alſo called Phoor, and was the ſame with the famous Porus, who fought againſt Alexander.

Phoor or Porus.

The ſecond Phoor, taking advantage of the diſturbances in Perſia, occaſioned by the Greek invaſion of that empire under Alexander, neglected to remit the cuſtomary tribute, which drew upon him the arms of that conqueror. The approach of Alexander did not intimidate Phoor. He, with a numerous army, met him at Sirhind, about one hundred and ſixty miles to the north-weſt of Delhi, and in a furious battle, ſay the Indian hiſtorians, loſt many thouſands of his ſubjects, the victory, and his life. The moſt powerful prince of the Decan, who paid an unwilling homage to Phoor, or Porus, hearing of that monarch's overthrow, ſubmitted himſelf to Alexander, and ſent him rich preſents by his ſon. Soon after, upon a mutiny ariſing in the Macedonian army, Alexander returned by the way of Perſia.

Sinſarchund.

Sinſarchund, the ſame whom the Greeks call Sandrocottus, aſſumed the imperial dignity after the death of Phoor, and in a ſhort time regulated the diſcompoſed concerns of the empire. He neglected not, in the mean time, to remit the cuſtomary tribute to the Grecian captains, who poſſeſſed Perſia under, and after the death of, Alexander. Sinſarchund, and his ſon after him, poſſeſſed the empire of India ſeventy years. When the grandſon of Sinſarchund acceded to the throne, a prince named Jona, who is ſaid to have been a grandnephew of Phoor, though that circumſtance is not well atteſted, aſpiring to the throne, roſe in arms againſt the reigning prince, and depoſed him.

Jona

Jona was an excellent prince, endued with many and great good qualities. He took great pains in peopling and in cultivating the waste parts of Hindostan, and his indefatigable attention to the police of the country established to him a lasting reputation for justice and benevolence. Jona acceded to the throne of India little more than two hundred and sixty years before the commencement of the Christian æra; and, not many years after, Aridshere, whom the Greeks call Arsaces, possessing himself of the Eastern provinces of Persia, expelled the successors of Alexander, and founded the Parthian, or second Persian empire. Arsaces assumed the name of King about two hundred and fifty-six years before Christ, according to the writers of Greece, which perfectly agrees with the accounts of the Brahmins. Aridshere, or Arsaces, claimed and established the right of Persia to a tribute from the empire of India; and Jona, fearing his arms, made him a present of elephants and a vast quantity of gold and jewels. Jona reigned long after this transaction, in great tranquillity, at Kinoge; and he and his posterity together possessed the throne peaceably, during the space of ninety years.

Callian-chund, by what means is not certain, was in possession of the empire of Hindostan about one hundred and seventy years before the commencement of our æra. He was of an evil disposition, oppressive, tyrannical and cruel. Many of the best families in Hindostan, to avoid his tyrannies, fled beyond the verge of the empire; so that, say the Brahmin writers, the lustre of the court, and the beauty of the country, were greatly diminished. The dependent princes at length took arms, and Callian-chund, being deserted by his troops, fled and died in obscurity.

Callian-chund.

The empire in a manner dissolved.

With him the empire of India may be said to have fallen. The princes and governors assumed independence, and though some great men, by their valour and conduct, raised themselves afterwards to the title of Emperors, there never was regular succession of Kings. From the time of Callian-chund, the scanty records we have, give very little light in the affairs of India, to the time of Bicker-Majit, King of Malava, who made a great figure in that part of the world.

Bicker-Majit.

Bicker-Majit is one of the most renowned characters in Indian history. In policy, justice and wisdom, they affirm that he had no equal. He is said to have travelled over a great part of the East, in the habit of a Mendicant devotee, in order to acquire the learning, arts and policy of foreign nations. It was not till after he was fifty years of age that he made a great figure in the field; and his uncommon success justified, in some measure, a notion, that he was impelled to take arms by divine command. In a few months he reduced the kingdoms of Malava and Guzerat, securing with acts of justice and sound policy what his arms obtained. The poets of those days praise his justice, by affirming that the magnet, without his permission, durst not exert its power upon iron, nor amber upon the chaff of the field; and such was his temperance and contempt of grandeur, that he slept upon a mat, and reduced the furniture of his apartment to an earthen pot, filled with water from the spring. To engage the attention of the vulgar to religion, he set up the great image of Ma-câl, or Time, in the city of Ugein, which he built, while he himself worshipped only the infinite and invisible God.

The Hindoos retain such a respect for the memory of Bicker-Majit, that the most of them, to this day, reckon their time from his death, which happened

happened in the 89th year of the Christian æra. Shawpoor, or the famous Sapor, king of Persia, is placed, in the Indian chronology, as cotemporary with this renowned king of Malava. He was slain in his old age, in a battle against a confederacy of the princes of the Decan.

The empire of Malava, after the demise of Bicker-Majit, who had raised it to the highest dignity, fell into anarchy and confusion. The great vassals of the crown assumed independence in their respective governments, and the name of Emperor was, in a great measure, obliterated from the minds of the people. One Raja-Boga, of the same tribe with Bicker-Majit, drew, by his valour, the reins of general government into his hands. He was a luxurious, though otherwise an excellent prince. His passion for architecture produced many magnificent fabrics, and several fine cities in Hindostan own him for their founder. He reigned in all the pomp of luxury, about fifty years, over a great part of India. Raja-Boga.

The ancient empire of Kinoge was in some measure revived by Basdeo, who, after having reduced Bengal and Behâr, assumed the imperial titles. He mounted the throne at Kinoge about 330 years after the birth of Christ, and reigned with great reputation. Byram-gore, king of Persia, came, in the time of Basdeo, to India, under the character of a merchant, to inform himself of the power, policy, manners and government of that vast empire. This circumstance is corroborated by the joint testimonies of the Persian writers; and we must observe upon the whole, that, in every point, the accounts extracted from the Maha-barit agree with those of foreign writers, when they happen to treat upon the same subject; which is a strong proof, that the short detail it gives of the affairs of India is founded upon real Basdeo.

facts. An accident which redounded much to the honour of Byram-gore brought about his being discovered. A wild elephant, in rutting-time, if that expression may be used, attacked him in the neighbourhood of Kinoge, and he pierced the animal's forehead with an arrow, which acquired to him such reputation, that the Emperor Basdeo ordered the merchant into his presence; where Byram-gore was known by an Indian nobleman, who had carried the tribute, some years before, to the court of Persia. Basdeo, being certainly assured of the truth, descended from his throne, and embraced the royal stranger.

Byram-gore being constrained to assume his proper character, was treated with the utmost magnificence and respect while he remained at the Indian court, where he married the daughter of Basdeo, and returned, after some time, into Persia. Basdeo and the princes, his posterity, ruled the empire in tranquillity for the space of eighty years.

Ramdeo. Upon the accession of a prince of the race of Basdeo in his non-age, civil disputes arose, and those soon gave birth to a civil war. The empire being torn to pieces by civil dissensions, an assembly of the nobles thought it prudent to exclude the royal line from the throne, and to raise to the supreme authority Ramdeo, general of the imperial forces. Ramdeo was of the tribe of Rhator, the same with the nation, well known in India, under the name of Mahrattors. He was a bold, wise, generous and good prince. He reduced into obedience the chiefs, who, during the distractions of the empire, had rendered themselves independent. He recovered the country of Marvar from the tribe of Cutswa, who had usurped the dominion of it, and planted it with his own tribe of Rhator, who remain in possession of Marvar to this day.

Ramdeo

Ramdeo was one of the greateſt princes that ever ſat upon the throne of Hindoſtan. In the courſe of many ſucceſsful expeditions, which took up ſeveral years, he reduced all India under his dominion, and divided the ſpoil of the vanquiſhed princes among his ſoldiers. After a glorious reign of fifty-four years he yielded to his fate, but the actions of his life, ſays our author, have rendered his name immortal. Notwithſtanding his great power, he thought it prudent to continue the payment of the uſual tribute to Feros-ſaſſa, the father of the great Kei-kobâd, king of Perſia. A great prince.

After the death of Ramdeo, a diſpute aroſe between his ſons concerning the ſucceſſion, which afterwards terminated in a civil war. Partab-chund, who was captain-general to the Emperor Ramdeo, taking advantage of the public confuſions, mounted the throne, and, to ſecure the poſſeſſion of it, extirpated the imperial family. Partab was cruel, treacherous and tyrannical. He drew by fair, but falſe promiſes, the princes of the empire from their reſpective governments, and, by cutting off the moſt formidable, rendered the reſt obedient to his commands. An uninterrupted courſe of ſucceſs made Partab too confident of his own power. He neglected, for ſome years, to ſend the uſual tribute to Perſia, returning, ſays our author, the ambaſſadors of the great Noſhirwan, with empty hands, and diſhonour, from his court. A Perſian invaſion, however, ſoon convinced Partab, that it was in vain to contend with the Lord Paramount of his empire. He was, in ſhort, forced to pay up his arrears, to advance the tribute of the enſuing year, and to give hoſtages for his future obedience. Partab-chund.

Partab mounted the imperial throne of India about the 500dth year of Chriſt; and though he left the empire in the poſſeſſion of his family, it ſoon The empire declines.

ſoon declined in their hands. The dependent princes rendered themſelves abſolute in their reſpective governments; and the titular Emperor became ſo inſignificant, with regard to power, that he gradually loſt the name of Raja, or Sovereign, and had that of Rana ſubſtituted in its place. The Ranas, however, poſſeſſed the mountainous country of Combilmere, and the adjacent provinces of Chitôr and Munduſir, till they were conquered by the Emperors of Hindoſtan of the Mogul race.

Soon after the death of Partab-chund, Annindeo, a chief of the tribe of Biſe, ſeized upon the extenſive kingdom of Malava, and, with rapidity of conqueſt, brought the peninſula of Guzerat, the country of the Mahrattors, and the whole province of Berâr, into the circle of his command. Annindeo was cotemporary with Chuſero Purveſe, king of Perſia; and he reigned over his conqueſts for ſixteen years. At the ſame time that Annindeo broke the power of the empire, by his uſurpation of the beſt of its provinces, one Maldeo, a man of an obſcure original, raiſed himſelf into great power, and took the city of Delhi and its territory, from the imperial family. He ſoon after reduced the imperial city of Kinoge, which was ſo populous, that there were, within the walls, thirty thouſand ſhops, in which arreca, a kind of nut, which the Indians uſe as Europeans do tobacco, was ſold. There were alſo in Kinoge, ſixty thouſand bands of muſicians and ſingers, who paid a tax to government. Maldeo, during the ſpace of forty years, kept poſſeſſion of his conqueſts, but he could not tranſmit them to his poſterity. Every petty governor and hereditary chief in Hindoſtan rendered themſelves independent, and the name of univerſal empire was loſt, till it was eſtabliſhed, by the Mahommedans, on the confines

confines of India and Perſia. The hiſtory of this latter empire comprehended the whole plan of Feriſhta's annals; but to underſtand them properly, it may be neceſſary to throw more light, than he furniſhes, upon the origin of that power which ſpread afterwards over all India.

MAHOMMEDAN Conquerors of INDIA.

Religion of Mahommed favourable to conqueſt.

SHOULD we judge of the truth of a religion from the ſucceſs of thoſe who profeſs it, the pretended revelation of Mahommed might be juſtly thought divine. By annexing judiciouſly a martial ſpirit to the enthuſiaſm which he inſpired by his religious tenets, he laid a ſolid foundation for that greatneſs at which his followers ſoon after arrived. The paſſive humility inculcated by Chriſtianity, is much more fit for philoſophical retirement than for thoſe active and daring enterprizes, which animate individuals, and render a nation powerful and glorious. We accordingly find that the ſpirit and power, and, we may ſay, even the virtue of the Romans, declined with the introduction of a new religion among them; whilſt the Arabians, in the ſpace of a few years after the promulgation of the faith of Mahommed, roſe to the ſummit of all human greatneſs.

State of the Greek empire.

The ſtate of the neighbouring nations, it muſt be acknowledged, was extremely favourable to conqueſt, when the invaſions of the Arabians happened. That part of the Roman empire, which ſurvived the deluge of Barbarians that overſpread the weſt, ſubſiſted in the Leſſer Aſia, Syria, and Egypt, more from the want of foreign enemies than by the bravery or wiſe conduct of its Emperor. Humanity never appeared in a more degrading light, than in the hiſtory of thoſe execrable princes who ruled the Eaſtern empire. Mean, cruel, and cowardly, they were enthuſiaſts, without religion; aſſaſſins, without boldneſs; averſe to war, though unfit for the arts of peace. The

character

character of the people took the colour of that of their Emperors; vice and immorality increaſed under the cloak of enthuſiaſm, all manly ſpirit was extinguiſhed by deſpotiſm, and exceſs of villainy was the only proof given of parts.

The empire of Perſia was upon the decline, in Of Perſia. its internal vigour and ſtrength, for two ages before the Arabian invaſion, after the death of Mahommed. The ſplendid figure it made under Noſhirwan, was the effect of the extraordinary abilities of that great man, and not of any ſpirit remaining in the nation. The ſucceſſors of Noſhirwan were generally men of weak parts; the governors of provinces, during public diſtractions, aſſumed the independence, though not the name of princes, and little more than the imperial title remained to the unfortunate Yeſdegert, who ſat upon the throne of Perſia, when the arms of the Arabs penetrated into that country.

It being the deſign of this Diſſertation to give a Conqueſt of ſuccinct account of the manner in which the em- Choraſſan. pire of Ghizni, which afterwards extended itſelf to India, was formed, it is foreign to our purpoſe to follow the Arabs through the progreſs of their conqueſts in Syria and Perſia. It is ſufficient to obſerve, that the extenſive province of Choraſſan, which comprehended the greateſt part of the original dominions of the imperial family of Ghizni, was conquered in the thirty-firſt year of the Higerah, by Abdulla the ſon of Amir, one of the generals of Oſman, who then was Calipha, or Emperor of the Arabians. Abdulla, being governor of Buſſora, on the Gulph of Perſia, by the command of Oſman, marched an army through Kirman, into Choraſſan, and made a complete conqueſt of that country, which had been ſcarcely viſited before by the arms of the Arabs. Choraſſan is bounded, on the ſouth, by a deſert, which ſeparates

ſeparates it from Pharis*, or Perſia, properly ſo called; on the north by Maver-ul-nere, or the ancient Tranſoxiana; on the eaſt by Seiſtan and India; and it terminates on the weſt, in a ſandy deſert towards the confines of Georgia. It is the moſt fruitful and populous, as well as the moſt extenſive province in Perſia, and comprehends the whole of the Bactria of the Antients. It forms a ſquare of almoſt four hundred miles every way†.

Maver-ul-nere, or Tranſoxiana.

The immenſe territory of Maver-ul-nere‡, diſtinguiſhed in antient times by the name of Tranſoxiana, though it was invaded by Abdulla, the ſon of the famous Zeiâd, governor of Buſſora, by the command of the Calipha, Mavia, in the fifty-third of the Higera, was not completely conquered by the Arabs, till the 88th year of that æra, when Katiba took the great cities of Bochara and Samercand. After the reduction of Bochara,

* Pharis is the name, from which Perſia is derived. It is alſo called Phariſtan, or the Country of Horſes.

† The Climate of Choraſſan is excellent, and the moſt temperate of all Perſia. Nothing can equal the fruitfulneſs of its ſoil. All ſorts of exquiſite fruits, cattle, corn, wine and ſilk, thrive there to a miracle: neither are there wanting mines of ſilver, gold, and precious ſtones. The province of Choraſſan, in ſhort, abounds with every thing that can contribute to make a country rich and agreeable. It was formerly amazingly populous. The whole face of the country was almoſt covered with great cities, when it was invaded and ruined by Zingis Chan.

‡ Maver-ul-nere is little more than a tranſlation of the Tranſoxiana of the Ancients. It ſignifies the country beyond the river. It is now more generally known by the name of Great Bucharia. Its ſituation is between the 34 and 44 degrees of latitude, and the 92 and 107 degrees of longitude, reckoning from Faro. The country of the Calmacs bounds it now, on the north; Little Bucharia, or kingdom of Caſgar, on the eaſt; the dominions of India and Perſia, on the ſouth; and Charizm on the weſt. This extenſive country is nearly 600 miles every way.

the

the Arabian governor of Maver-ul-nere resided in that city. During the dynasty of the imperial family of Mavia, the Arabian empire remained in full vigor; and it even seemed to increase in strength, stability and extent under several sovereigns of the house of Abbassi, who acceded to the Caliphat, in the 132d of the Higera, or 749th of the Christian æra.

After the death of the great Haroun Al Reshîd, the temporal power of the Caliphas began gradually to decline. Most of the governments of provinces, by the neglect or weakness of the imperial family, became hereditary; and the viceroys of the empire assumed every thing but the name of Kings. The revenues were retained, under a pretence of keeping a force to defend the provinces against foreign enemies, when they were actually designed to strengthen the hereditary governors against their lawful sovereign. When Al Radi mounted the throne, little more remained to the Calipha, beside Bagdad and its dependencies, and he was considered supreme only in matters of religion. The governors, however, who gradually grew into princes, retained a nominal respect for the empire, and the Calipha's name was inserted in all public writings.

The power of the Caliphas declines.

The most powerful of those princes, that became independent, under the Caliphat, was Ismael Samani, governor of Maver-ul-nere and Chorassan, who assumed royal titles, in the 263d of the Higera. He was the first of the dynasty of the Samanians, who reigned in Bochara, over Maver-ul-nere, Chorassan, and a great part of the Persian empire, with great reputation for justice and humanity. Their dominions also comprehended Candahar, Zabulistan, Cabul, the mountainous countries of the Afgans or Patans, who afterwards established a great empire in India.

Dynasty of Samania.

The

Of the Afgans. The Mahommedan government, which subsisted in India more than three centuries before the invasion of that country by Timur was called the Patan or Afgan empire, on account of its being governed by princes, descended of the mountaineers of that name, who possessed the confines of India and Persia. The Afgans, from the nature of the country they possessed, became divided into distinct tribes. Mountains intersected with a few vallies did not admit either of general cultivation or communication; yet mindful of their common origin, and united by a natural, though rude, policy, they, by their bravery, became extremely formidable to their neighbours. We shall have occasion to see, in the sequel, that they not only conquered, but retained, the empire of India for several centuries, and though the valour and conduct of the posterity of Timur wrested the government from them, they continued formidable, from the ferocity and hardiness peculiar to Mountaineers. As late as the beginning of the eighteenth century, they, under one of their chiefs, conquered Persia; and they now possess not only a great part of that empire by their bravery, but also bid fair to establish another dynasty of Kings in Hindostan.

Subject to the house of Samania. The power as well as conduct of the race of Samania, who reigned in Bochara, subjected a great part of the Afgans to their empire. They were governed in chief by the viceroy of Chorassan, who generally had a substitute in the city of Ghizni*, the capital of Zabulistan, to command the regions of the hills. It however appears, that

* Ghizni is known in Europe by the name of Gazna. It lies in the mountains between India and Persia, and was a considerable city even before it was made the imperial residence by the family of Subuctagi.

those

those who possessed the most inaccessible mountains towards India, remained independent, till they were reduced by Mahmood, the second prince of the imperial family of Ghizni.

The family of Samania enjoyed their extensive empire for ninety years, in tranquillity, accompanied with that renown, which naturally arises from a just and equitable administration. Abdul Malleck Noo, the fourth of that race, dying at Bochara * in the three hundred and fiftieth year of the Higera, left a son, a very young man, called Munsur. The great men about court were divided in their opinion about the succession, some favouring the brother of the late Emperor, and others declaring themselves for Munsur. To end the dispute, it was agreed to refer the whole to Abistagi, who governed for the empire, with great reputation, the extensive province of Chorassan. Abistagi returned for answer, that, Munsur being as yet but a child, it was prudent for the friends of the family of Samania to chuse his uncle king. Before Abistagi's messengers arrived at Bochara, the contending factions had settled matters together, and jointly raised Munsur to the throne: That young monarch, offended with Abistagi's advice, recalled him immediately to Bochara.

Munsur al Samani succeeds to the empire of Bochara.

The great abilities of Abistagi, and the reputation he had acquired in his government, created to him many enemies at the court of Bochara, and he was unwilling to trust his person in the hands of a young prince, who, in his present rage, might be easily instigated to his ruin. He sent an excuse to Munsur, and, says our Persian author, resolved to stand behind his disobedience with thirty thou-

Abistagi, governor of Chorassan, revolts.

* The city of Bochara is situated in 39° 30′ of lat. and is still a very considerable place, and the residence of the great Chan of Bucharia.

sand

ſand men. He marched, next year, from Neſſapoor, the capital of Choraſſan, to Ghizni; ſettled the affairs of that country, and aſſumed the enſigns of royalty.

Defeats the imperial army.

The young Emperor, Munſur, finding that Abiſtagi had, in a manner, left Choraſſan totally deſtitute of troops, ordered one of his generals, named Haſſen, to march an army into that province. Abiſtagi, apprized of Haſſen's march, left Ghizni ſuddenly, encountered the imperial army, and gave them two ſignal defeats. Theſe victories ſecured to Abiſtagi the peaceable and independent poſſeſſion of the provinces of Choraſſan and Zabuliſtan, over which he reigned in tranquillity fifteen years. He, in the mean time, employed his army, under his general Subuctagi, in ſucceſsful expeditions to India, by which he acquired great ſpoil.

The right of his family to their dominions ratified by treaty.

Abiſtagi dying in the 363d of the Higera, his ſon Abu Iſaac ſucceeded him in the kingdoms of Choraſſan and Ghizni. This young prince, by the advice of his experienced general Subuctagi, invaded the dominions of Bochara, in order to force the family of Samania to relinquiſh their title to Choraſſan. The Emperor, Munſur, being accordingly worſted in ſome engagements, by the valour and conduct of Subuctagi, agreed to a peace, by which it was ſtipulated that Iſaac, under the tuition of Subuctagi, ſhould enjoy his dominions as a nominal tenure from the empire. Iſaac did not long ſurvive this pacification, for being too much addicted to pleaſure, he ruined his conſtitution, and died two years after the demiſe of his father Abiſtagi. The army, who were much attached to Subuctagi, proclaimed him their king; and he mounted the throne of Ghizni in the 365th year of the Higera, which agrees with the 977th of the Chriſtian æra.

SUBUCTAGI.

SUBUCTAGI.

SUBUCTAGI, who, upon his acceſſion to the throne, aſſumed the title of Nazir-ul-dien, was a Tartar by extraction, and was educated in the family, and brought up to arms, under the command of Abiſtagi, governor of Choraſſan, for the houſe of Samania. His merit ſoon raiſed him to the firſt poſts in the army, which he commanded in chief during the latter years of Abiſtagi, and under his ſon Iſaac, who ſucceeded him in the government. When he became king, he married the daughter of his patron, Abiſtagi, and applied himſelf aſſiduouſly to an equal diſtribution of juſtice, which ſoon gained him the hearts of all his ſubjects. The court of Bochara perceiving, perhaps, that it was in vain to attempt to oppoſe Subuctagi, approved of his elevation, and he received letters of confirmation from the Emperor, Munſur Al Samania. A. D. 977. Higer. 367. Subuctagi mounts the throne of Ghizni.

Soon after Subuctagi had aſſumed the enſigns of royalty, he was very near being taken off by one Tigga, an independent chief, on the confines of the province of Ghizni. Subuctagi had reſtored Tigga to his eſtate, from which he had been expelled by one of his neighbours, upon condition that he ſhould hold it of the crown of Ghizni. Tigga broke his promiſe, and, ſoon after, making a circuit of his dominions, Subuctagi came to the territory of Tigga. He invited that chieftain to the chace, and when they were alone, he upbraided him for his breach of faith. Tigga, who was a daring and impetuous man, put his hand to his ſword; the king drew his; a combat enſued, and Is in danger.

Subuctagi

A. D. 977. Higer. 367. Subuctagi was wounded in the hand. The royal attendants interfered; the adherents of Tigga engaged them, but were defeated. The citadel of Bust*, whither Tigga fled, was taken, but he himself made his escape.

Abul-Fatti. In the fort of Bust the king found the famous Abul-Fatti, who, in the art of writing and in the knowledge of the sciences, had no equal in those days. He had been secretary to the chief, whom Subuctagi had expelled in favor of the ungrateful Tigga; and after the defeat of his patron, he had lived retired to enjoy his studies. The King called him into his presence, made him his own secretary, and dignified him with titles of honor. Abul Fatti continued in his office at Ghizni, till the accession of Mamood, when he retired in disgust to Turkestan.

Indian expedition. Subuctagi, after taking the fortress of Bust, returned towards the neighbouring district of Cusdâr, and annexing it to his dominions, conferred the government upon one Actas. Towards the close of the first year of his reign, the King, having resolved upon a war with the idolators of India, marched that way, and, having ravaged the provinces of Cabul and Punjâb, which last lies about the conflux of the five rivers which form the Indus, he returned with considerable spoil to Ghizni.

Second expedition. Jeipal, the son of Hispal, of the Brahmin race, reigned at that time over the country, extending, in length, from the mouth of the Indus to Limgan, and in breadth, from the kingdom of Cashmire to Moultan. This Prince, finding, by the reiterated invasions of the Mahommedans, that he was not

* Bust, which is at present the capital of Zabulistan, is a considerable and well-built city; the country round it is very pleasant and fertile; and by being situated in the confines of India and Persia, Bust drives a considerable trade. It lies in latitude 32.

likely

likely to enjoy any tranquillity, levied a great army, with a design to invade them in their own country. Subuctagi, upon receiving intelligence of Jeipal's motions, marched towards India, and the armies came in sight of each other on the confines of Limgan. Some skirmishes ensued, and Mamood, the son of Subuctagi, though then but a boy, gave signal proofs of his valour and conduct. A. D. 977. Higer. 367.

Historians, whose credulity exceeded their wisdom, have told us, that, on this occasion, a certain person informed Subuctagi, that in the camp of Jeipal there was a spring, into which, if a small quantity of a certain drug, called Casurat, should be thrown, the sky would immediately be overcast, and a dreadful storm of hail and wind arise. Subuctagi having accordingly ordered this to be done, the effects became visible, for immediately the sky loured, and thunder, lightning, wind and hail began, turning the day into darkness, and spreading horror and desolation around; insomuch that a great part of the cavalry were killed, and some thousands of both armies perished; but the troops of Ghizni, being more hardy than those of Hindostan, suffered not so much upon this occasion. Jeipal in the morning found his army in such weakness and dejection, by the effects of this storm, which was rather natural than the work of magic, that fearing Subuctagi would take advantage of his condition, he sent Heralds to treat of a peace: He offered to the King of Ghizni a certain tribute, and a considerable present in elephants and gold. A storm occasions a peace.

Subuctagi was not displeased with these terms, but his son, Mamood, who was an ambitious young man, fearing this would put an end to his expedition, prevailed with his father to reject the proposal. Jeipal, upon this, told him, that the customs of the Indian soldiers were of such a nature,

A. D. 977. Higer. 367. that if he persisted in distressing them, it must make him, in the end, pay very dear for his victories. Upon such occasions, and when reduced to extremity, said Jeipal, they murder their wives and children, set fire to their houses, let loose their hair, and rushing in despair among the enemy, drown themselves in the crimson torrent of revenge. Subuctagi hearing of this custom, he was afraid to reduce them to despair, and consented to let them retreat upon their paying a million of Dirms, and presenting him with fifty elephants. Jeipal not being able to discharge the whole of this sum in camp, he desired that some persons of trust, on the part of Subuctagi, should accompany him to Lahore, to receive the balance; for whose safety, Subuctagi took hostages.

Jeipal's perfidy.

Jeipal having arrived at Lahore, and finding Subuctagi had returned home, imprisoned his messengers, and refused to pay the money. It was then customary among the Rajas, in affairs of moment, to assemble the double council, which consisted of an equal number of the most respectable Brahmins, who sat on the right side of the throne; and of the noblest Kittries, who sat on the left. When they saw that Jeipal proceeded to such an impolitic measure, they intreated the King, saying, that the consequence of this step would bring ruin and distress upon the country; the troops, said they, have not yet forgot the terror of their enemy's arms; and Jeipal may rest assured, that a conqueror will never brook such an indignity: It was, therefore, the opinion of the double council, to comply strictly with the terms of the peace, that the people might enjoy the blessings of tranquillity; but the King was obstinate, and would not hearken to their advice.

Renews the war.

Intelligence of what was done, soon reached the ears of Subuctagi; like a foaming torrent he has-

tened

tened towards Hindoſtan with a numerous army, to take revenge upon Jeipal for his treacherous behaviour: Jeipal alſo collected his forces, and marched forth to meet him; for the neighbouring Rajas, conſidering themſelves intereſted in his ſucceſs, ſupplied him with troops and money. The Kings of Delhi, Ajmere, Callinger and Kinnoge, were now bound in his alliance, and Jeipal found himſelf at the head of an army of a hundred thouſand horſe, and two hundred thouſand foot; with which he marched with full aſſurance of victory. A. D. 978. Higer. 378.

When the moving armies approached each other, Subuctagi aſcended a hill, to view the forces of Jeipal, which he beheld like a ſhoreleſs ſea, and in number like the ants or the locuſts; but he looked upon himſelf as a wolf among a flock of goats: Calling therefore together his chiefs, he encouraged them to glory, and honoured them diſtinctly with his commands. His troops, though few in number, he divided into ſquadrons of five hundred each, which he ordered, one after another, to the attack in a circle, ſo that a continual round of freſh troops haraſſed the Indian army.

The Hindoos being worſe mounted than the cavalry of Subuctagi, could effect nothing againſt them; ſo that wearied out with this manner of fighting, confuſion became viſible amongſt them. Subuctagi, perceiving their diſorder, ſounded a general charge; ſo that they fell like corn before the hands of the reaper; and were purſued with great ſlaughter to the banks of the river Nilab*, one of the branches of the Indus; where many, who had eſcaped the edge of the ſword, periſhed by their fear in the waters. Subuctagi acquired in this action much glory and wealth; for, beſides the rich plunder of the Indian camp, he raiſed and is defeated.

* The blue river: the ancient *Hydaſpes.*

A. D. 978. Higer. 368. great contributions in the countries of Limgan and Peſhawir, and annexed them to his own dominions, joined them to his titles, and ſtamped their names, as was cuſtomary, upon his coins. One of his Omrahs, with three thouſand horſe, was appointed to the government of Peſhawir; and the Afghans, who reſided among the mountains, having promiſed allegiance, he entertained ſome thouſands of them in his army, and returned victorious to Ghizni.

Subuctagi ſolicited for aid by the King of Bochara.

Munſur, Emperor of Bochara, being dead, his ſon, Noo, the ſixth of the houſe of Samania, ſat upon the throne. Being at this time hard preſſed by the rebel Faeck, he ſent one Pharſi to Subuctagi, to beg his aſſiſtance. Subuctagi was moved by gratitude to the family of Bochara, and haſtened with his army towards Maver-ul-nere, while Noo advanced to the country of Sir-chuſh to meet him. Subuctagi, being not well in his health, ſent a meſſenger to Noo, to excuſe his lighting from his horſe; but when he advanced and recognized the features of his royal houſe, in the face of the young prince, he could not ſuppreſs the emotions of his heart. He leaped from his horſe and run to kiſs his ſtirrup, which the young King perceiving, prevented him, by diſmounting and receiving him in his embrace. At this happy interview the flower of joy bloomed in every face, and ſuch a knot of friendſhip was bound as can hardly be paralleled in any age. As the ſeaſon was now too far advanced for action, it was agreed, that Subuctagi ſhould return, during the winter, to Ghizni, and prepare his forces to act in conjunction with thoſe of the Emperor in the ſpring. But when Sumjure, who had ſeized part of Choraſſan, at whoſe court Faeck was then in treaty, heard of the alliance formed between Noo and Subuctagi, he began to fear the conſequence of his

engagement

engagement with Faeck. He asked his council, where he should take protection, in case fortune, which was seldom to be depended upon, should desert his standards in war. They replied, that the situation of affairs required he should endeavour to gain the alliance of Fuchir ul Dowla, prince of Jirja*. Jaffier was accordingly appointed ambassador to the court of Jirja, with presents of every thing that was valuable and curious: and in a short time a treaty of friendship and alliance was settled between the two powers.

A. D. 988. Higer. 378.

Subuctagi in the mean time put his troops in motion, and marched towards Balich†, where Noo joined him with his forces from Bochara. The rebels Faeck and Sumjure hearing of this junction, with consent of Dara, the general of Fuchir ul Dowla, marched out of Herat in great pomp and magnificence. Subuctagi pitched his camp in an extensive plain, where he waited for the enemy. They soon appeared in his front, he drew out his army in order of battle, and took post in the center, with his soon Mamood and the young Emperor.

The confederates join their armies.

In the first charge the troops of the enemy came forward with great violence and bravery, and pressed so hard upon the flanks of Subuctagi, that both wings began to give ground, and the whole army was upon the point of being defeated. But Dara, the general of Fuchir ul Dowla, charging the center where Subuctagi in person led on his troops with great bravery, as soon as he had got near, threw his shield upon his back, which was a signal of friendship, and riding up to the King,

* A small province to the North-East of Chorassan.

† An ancient and great city near the Oxus or Amu, situated at the end of great Bucharia, in latitude 37° 10′ and 92° 20′ East of Faro.

begged

A. D. 994. Higer. 384. begged he would accept of his ſervices. He then returned with the few who had accompanied him, and immediately brought over his troops to the ſide of Subuctagi, facing round on his deſerted friends, who were aſtoniſhed at this unexpected treachery. Subuctagi took immediate advantage of their confuſion, charged them home, and ſoon put their whole army to flight, purſuing them with great ſlaughter, and taking many priſoners. Thus the unfortunate man, who had exalted the ſpear of enmity againſt his ſovereign, loſt his honour and his wealth, a tenth of which might have maintained him and his family in ſplendor and happineſs.

Defeat the rebels.

Faeck and Sumjure took in their flight the way of Neſhapoor*, the capital of Choraſſan, with the ſcattered remains of their army. Noo and Subuctagi entered forthwith the city of Herat, where they remained a few days to refreſh their troops and divide the ſpoil. Subuctagi after this ſignal victory received the title of Naſir ul Dien, or the Supporter of the Faith; and his ſon Mamood was dignified with that of Seif al Dowla, or the Sword of Fortune, by the Emperor, who was ſtill acknowledged, though his power was greatly diminiſhed.

Noo, after theſe tranſactions, directed his march to Bochara, and Subuctagi, and his ſon Mamood, turned their faces towards Neſhapoor; the Emperor having confirmed the King of Ghizni in the government of Choraſſan. Faeck and Sumjure fled into Jirja, and took protection with Fuchir ul Dowla. The country being thus cleared of the enemy, Subuctagi returned to Ghizni, while his ſon Mamood remained at Neſhapoor with a ſmall

* Neſhapoor is ſtill a very conſiderable city, well peopled, and drives a great trade in all ſorts of ſilk, ſtuffs and carpets.

force.

force. Faeck and Sumjure, ſeizing upon this opportunity, collected all their forces, marched towards Mamood, and before he could receive any aſſiſtance from the Emperor, or his father, he was compelled to an engagement, in which he was defeated, and loſt all his baggage.

A. D. 997. Higer. 387.

Mamood, the ſon of Subuctagi, defeated.

Subuctagi hearing of the ſituation of his ſon, haſtened towards Neſhapoor, and in the diſtricts of Toos, meeting with the rebels, engaged them without delay. In the heat of the action a great duſt was ſeen to riſe in the rear of Sumjure, which proved to be the Prince Mamood; and Faeck and Sumjure, finding they would ſoon be attacked on both ſides, made a reſolute charge againſt Subuctagi, which was ſo well received that they were obliged to give ground. Mamood arriving at that inſtant attacked them like an angry lion, and they, unable to ſupport the conteſt, turned their face to flight, and took refuge in the fort of Killat.

Subuctagi comes to the aid of his ſon.

The rebels are again totally overthrown.

Subuctagi, after this victory, reſided at Balich, in peace and tranquillity. In leſs than a year after the defeat of the rebels, he fell into a languiſhing diſtemper, which would not yield to the power of medicine. He reſolved to try whether a change of air would not relieve him, and he accordingly reſolved upon a journey to Ghizni. He was ſo weak when he came to the town of Turmuz, not far from Balich, that he was obliged to ſtop at that place. He expired in the month of Shabân of the year 387, and his remains were carried to Ghizni.

Subuctagi dies.

Subuctagi was certainly a prince of great bravery, conduct, probity, and juſtice; and he governed his ſubjects with uncommon prudence, equity and moderation, for twenty years. He died in the fifty-ſixth year of his age. Fourteen Kings of his race reigned at Ghizni and Lahore. His Vizier was Abul Abas Fazil, a great miniſter

His character.

in

A. D. 997. Higer. 387. in the management of both civil and military affairs.

The Author of Jam ul Hickaiat relates, that Subuctagi was at firſt a private horſeman in the ſervice of Abiſtagi, and being of a vigorous and active diſpoſition, uſed to hunt every day in the foreſt. It happened one time as he employed himſelf in this amuſement, that he ſaw a deer grazing with her young fawn, upon which, ſpurring his horſe, he ſeized the fawn, and binding his legs, laid him acroſs his ſaddle, and turned his face towards his home. When he had rode a little way, he looked behind and beheld the mother of the fawn following him, and exhibiting every mark of extreme affliction. The ſoul of Subuctagi melted within him into pity, he untied the feet of the fawn, and generouſly reſtored him to his liberty. The happy mother turned her face to the wilderneſs, but often looked back upon Subuctagi, and the tears dropt faſt from her eyes. Subuctagi is ſaid to have ſeen that night a figure or apparition in his dream, who ſaid to him, That generoſity and compaſſion which you have this day ſhown to a diſtreſſed animal, has been approved of in the preſence of God: therefore, in the records of Providence, the kingdom of Ghizni is marked as a reward againſt thy name. But let not greatneſs deſtroy your virtue, but thus continue your benevolence to men.

It is ſaid in the Maſir ul Maluck, that Mamood his ſon, having built a pleaſure-houſe in an elegant garden near the city of Ghizni, he invited his father, when it was finiſhed, to a magnificent entertainment which he had prepared for him. The ſon, in the joy of his heart, deſired the opinion of Subuctagi concerning the houſe and garden, which were eſteemed admirable in taſte and ſtructure. The King, to the great diſappointment of Mamood,

mood, told him, that he looked upon the whole as a bauble, which any of his subjects might have raised by the means of wealth: But that it was the business of a prince to erect the more durable structure of good fame, which might stand for ever, to be imitated, but never to be equalled, by posterity. The great poet Nizami makes upon this saying the following reflection: Of all the magnificent palaces which we are told Mamood built, we now find not one stone upon another; but the edifice of his fame, as he was told by his father, still triumphs over time, and seems established on a lasting foundation. A. D. 997. Higer. 387.

Altay, the son of Al Moti, kept up the name of Emperor at Bagdâd, without any real power, during the greatest part of the reign of Subuctagi. Altay was deposed in the 381 of the Higera, and Al Kader Billa raised to the Caliphat. The provinces of the Arabian Empire, in the Western Persia, remained in the same condition as before, under the hereditary governors, who had assumed independence. Chorassan, and Zabulistan, Cabul, the provinces upon the Indus, and in general all the countries from the Oxus or Amu to Persia proper, and from the Caspian to the Indus, were secured to the house of Subuctagi. The power of the house of Samania was even declined in the province of Maver-ul-nere; and the middle and Eastern Tartary were subject to their native princes. State of Asia.

ISMAIEL.

I S M A I E L.

A. D. 997. Higer. 387. SUBUCTAGI dying ſuddenly, and his eldeſt ſon, Mamood, being at Neſhapoor, the capital of Choraſſan, which was a conſiderable diſtance from the place of the King's deceaſe, his ſecond ſon, Iſmaiel, prevailed with his father, in his laſt moments, to appoint him to ſucceed till the return of his brother. The reaſon aſſigned for this demand, was to prevent other uſurpations, which were then feared in the government. Iſmaiel therefore, immediately upon the demiſe of his father, was crowned with great ſolemnity at Balich. To gain popularity, he opened the treaſury, and diſtributed the greateſt part of his father's wealth in preſents to the nobility, and in expenſive ſhews and entertainments to the people. He alſo augmented the pay of the troops, and rewarded ſmall ſervices with the hand of prodigality. This policy being overacted, had not the deſired effect. The nobility, perceiving that all this generoſity proceeded from the fear of his brother, ungenerouſly increaſed their demands, while the troops, puffed up with pride by his indulgences, begun to be mutinous, diſorderly and debauched.

Iſmael ſucceeds his father Subuctagi.

When intelligence was brought to Mamood of the death of his father, and the acceſſion of his younger brother, he wrote to Iſmaiel by the hand of Abul Haſſen. In this letter he ſaid thus, That ſince the death of his royal father, he held none upon earth ſo dear as his beloved brother, the noble Iſmaiel, whom he would oblige to the full extent of his power: But that the art of government required years, experience, wiſdom and knowledge,

Mamood's behaviour upon his brother's acceſſion.

knowledge, in the affairs of ſtate, which Iſmaiel could not poſſibly pretend to poſſeſs, though Subuctagi had appointed him to ſucceed to the throne in the abſence of Mamood. He therefore adviſed Iſmaiel ſeriouſly to conſider the matter, to diſtinguiſh propriety from impropriety, and to give up his title to government without further diſpute, which would reſtore him to the love and generoſity of Mamood; for that it was his original intention to confer upon Iſmaiel the governments of the extenſive provinces of Balich and Choraſſan. A. D. 997. Higer. 387.

Iſmaiel ſhut his ears againſt all the propoſals of his brother, and prepared for his own ſecurity, turning the edge of the ſword of enmity againſt him. Mamood ſaw no remedy but in war, and attaching his uncle Bujerâc, and his brother Niſir, to his intereſt, advanced with his ſtandards towards Ghizni, while Iſmaiel haſtened alſo from Balich to oppoſe him. When the two armies approached towards one another, Mamood took great pains to avoid coming to extremities, and in vain tried to reconcile matters in an amicable manner. He was therefore forced to form his troops in order of battle, while Iſmaiel alſo extended the lines of war, which he ſupported by a chain of elephants. Both armies engaging with great violence, the action became extremely bloody, and the victory doubtful. Mamood at length charged the center of the enemy with ſuch fury, that they trembled as with an earthquake, and turned their faces to flight, taking refuge in the citadel of Ghizni. Thither the conqueror purſued them, and immediately inveſted the place. Such a prodigious number of the runaways had crouded into Ghizni, that for want of proviſions Iſmaiel was reduced to the neceſſity of treating about a ſurrender. Having therefore received promiſes of perſonal ſafety, he ſubmitted himſelf, and delivered

War between the brothers.

Iſmaiel defeated and taken.

A. D. 997. Higer. 387. livered up the keys of the garrifon and the treafury to his brother Mamood.

Mamood having appointed a new miniftry, and regulated the government of the country, proceeded with his army towards Balich. It is faid, that a few days after the fubmiffion of Ifmaiel, he was afked by his brother, What he intended to have done with him had his better fortune prevailed? To which Ifmaiel replied, That he intended to have imprifoned him for life in fome caftle, and to indulge him with every pleafure but his liberty. Upon which Mamood made no reflections at that time, but foon after confined Ifmaiel in the fort of Georghan, in the manner that he himfelf had intimated, where he remained till his death, which happened not long after his being depofed.

Is imprifoned, and dies.

MAMOOD

MAMOOD I.

WE are told by hiſtorians, that Mamood * was a King who conferred happineſs upon the world, and reflected glory upon the faith of Mahommed: that the day of his acceſſion illuminated the earth with the bright torch of juſtice, and cheriſhed it with the beams of beneficence. Others inform us, that in his diſpoſition, the ſordid vice of avarice found place, which however could not darken the other bright qualities of his mind. A certain poet ſays, that his wealth was like a pearl in the ſhell; but as poets hunt after wit rather than truth, we muſt judge of Mamood by his actions, from which it appears, that he was indeed a prince of great œconomy, but that he never withheld his generoſity upon a juſt and proper occaſion. We have the teſtimony of the Fatti Bilad, wrote by Abu Niſir Muſcati, and of the famous Abul Fazil, that no King had ever more learned men at his court, kept a finer army, or diſplayed more magnificence, than Mamood. All theſe things could not be done without expence; ſo that the ſtigma of avarice muſt have been owing to particular circumſtances of his life, which ought by no means to have ſtamped his general character with that ſordid vice.

A. D. 997. Higer. 387. Acceſſion of Mamood. His character.

It may not be improper to mention one circumſtance in the conduct of Mamood, which argued that too great love of money had taken poſſeſſion of the ſoul of that mighty prince. Having a great

* His titles at length, are Amin ul Muluck, Emin ul Dowla, Sultan Mamood Ghiznavi.

propenſity

A. D. 997. Higer. 387. propenſity to poetry, in which he made ſome tolerable progreſs himſelf, he promiſed to the celebrated Phirdoci a golden mher * for every verſe of an heroic poem which he was deſirous to patronize. Under the protection of this promiſe, that divine poet wrote the unparalleled poem called the Shaw Namma, which conſiſted of ſixty thouſand couplets. When it was preſented, Mamood repented of his promiſe, telling Phirdoci, that he thought ſixty thouſand rupees might ſatisfy him for a work which he ſeemed to have performed with ſo much eaſe and expedition. Phirdoci, juſtly offended at this indignity, could never be brought to accept of any reward, though the Emperor would, after reflection, have gladly paid him the ſum originally ſtipulated; the poet, however, took ample revenge in a ſatire of ſeven hundred couplets, which he wrote upon that occaſion.

His perſon. Mamood, who it is reported was defective in external appearance, ſaid one day, obſerving himſelf in a glaſs, "The ſight of a King ſhould brighten the eyes of the beholders, but nature has been ſo capricious to me, that my aſpect ſeems the picture of misfortune." The Vizier replied, It is not one of ten thouſand who are bleſſed with a ſight of your majeſty's countenance, but your virtues are diffuſed over all. But to proceed with our hiſtory.

We have already obſerved, that Mamood was the eldeſt ſon of Subuctagi. His mother was a princeſs of the houſe of Zabuliſtan, for which reaſon ſhe is known by the name of Zabuli. He was born in the year 357 of the Higerah, and as aſtrologers ſay, with many happy omens expreſſed

* A mher is about fourteen rupees: this coin was called mher from having a ſun ſtampt upon it. Mher ſignifies *the ſun*, in the Perſian.

in

in the horoscope of his fate. Subuctagi, being asleep at the time of his birth, dreamed, that he beheld a green tree springing forth from his chimney, which threw its shadow over the face of the earth, and screened from the storms of heaven the whole animal creation. This indeed was verified by the justice of Mamood; for, if we can believe the poet, in his reign the wolf and the sheep drank together at the same brook. In the first month of his reign, a vein of gold, resembling a tree of three cubits in circumference, was found in Seistan, which yielded pure gold till the reign of Musaood, when it was lost in consequence of an earthquake.

A. D. 997. Higer. 387.

His justice.

A golden mine.

When Mamood had settled his dispute with his brother, he hastened to Balich, from whence he sent an ambassador to Munsur, Emperor of Bochara, to whom the family of Ghizni still pretended to owe allegiance, complaining of the indignity which he met with in the appointment of Buctusin to the government of Chorassan, a country so long in possession of his father: it was returned to him for answer, that he was already in possession of the territories of Balich, Turmuz, and Herat*, which held of the empire; and that there was a necessity to divide the favours of Bochara among her friends. Buctusin, it was also insinuated, had been a faithful and good servant; which seemed to throw a reflection upon the family of Ghizni, who had rendered themselves independent in the governments they held of the royal house of Samania.

Mamood's complaint to Munsur, King of Bochara, is ill received.

* Herat is situated in the southern part of the province of Chorassan, in the 34th degree of latitude. It was always a great city, and is very much increased in splendor, since the ruin of the city of Meshed by the Usbecs, it is become the capital of Chorassan. It is the chief staple of all the commerce carried on between India and Persia.

Mamood,

A. D. 998. Higer. 389. Mamood, not diſcouraged by this anſwer, ſent Haſſen Jemmavi with rich preſents to the court of Bochara, and a letter in the following terms: "That he hoped the pure ſpring of friendſhip, which had flowed in the time of his father, ſhould not now be polluted with the aſhes of indignity, nor Mamood be reduced to the neceſſity of diveſting himſelf of that obedience, which he had hitherto paid to the imperial family of Samania." When Haſſen delivered his embaſſy, his capacity and elocution appeared ſo great to the Emperor, that, deſirous to gain him over to his intereſt by any means, he bribed him at laſt with the honours of the Vizarit*, but never returned an anſwer to Mamood. That prince having received information of this tranſaction, through neceſſity turned his face towards Neſhapoor; and Buctuſin, adviſed of his intention, abandoned the city, and ſent the Emperor intelligence of his ſituation. Munſur, upon this, exalted the imperial ſtandard, and in the raſhneſs of inexperienced youth, haſtened towards Choraſſan, and halted not till he arrived at Sirchus. Mamood, though he well knew that the Emperor was in no condition to oppoſe him, yet gratitude to the imperial family of Samania wrought ſo much upon his mind, that aſhamed of meaſuring ſpears with his Lord, he evacuated the diſtrict of Neſhapoor, and marched to Murghab. Buctuſin in the mean time treacherouſly entered into a confederacy with Faeck, and forming a conſpiracy in the camp of Munſur, ſeized upon the perſon of that prince, and cruelly put out his eyes. Abdul, the younger brother of Munſur, who was but a boy, was advanced by the traitors to the throne. Being however afraid of the reſentment of Mamood, the conſpirators haſtened

War between Mamood and the Emperor of Bochara; whoſe eyes are put out by his own officers.

* The office of Vizier.

to

to Murve*, whither they were purfued by the King with great expedition. Finding themfelves, upon their march, hard preffed in the rear by Mamood, they halted and gave him battle. But the fin of ingratitude had darkened the face of their fortune, fo that the gales of victory blew upon the ftandards of the King of Ghizni. Faeck carried off the young King, and fled to Bochara, and Buctufin was not heard of for fome time, but at length he found his way to his fellow in iniquity, and begun to collect his fcattered troops. Faeck in the mean time fell fick, and foon after vanifhed in the regions of death. Elich, the Ufbec King, feizing upon the opportunity offered him by that event, marched with an army from Kafhgar † to Bochara, and rooted Abdul Malleck and his adherents out of the empire and the foil of life. Thus the pofterity of the houfe of Samania, which had continued for the fpace of one hundred and twenty-feven years to illuminate the firmament of empire, fet for ever in the fhadows of death.

A. D. 999. Higer. 390.

They are overthrown by Mamood.

The royal family of Bochara extirpated.

The Emperor of Ghizni, at this juncture, employed himfelf in fettling the government of the provinces of Balich and Choraffan, which he regulated in fuch a manner, as to exalt the voice of his fame fo high, that it reached the ears of the Calipha of Bagdat, the illuftrious Al Kadir Billa, of the noble houfe of Abbaffi. The Calipha fent

* Murve, or Meru, ftands in a very fandy plain, in 37 degrees of latitude, and 88 degrees Eaft from Faro. It was formerly one of the richeft and moft beautiful towns of Perfia; but fince the grand invafion of the Tartars into the Southern Afia, it has fuffered fo much, that, at prefent, it is but the fhadow of its former magnificence.

† Little Bucharia. This kingdom extends from 38° 30′ of latitude to the 44° 30′ and from 105° to the 120° of longitude. It is populous and fertile, but, on account of its great elevation, it is much colder than one would expect from its advantageous fituation.

 him

A. D. 1000. Higer. 391. him a rich honorary dreſs, ſuch as he had never before beſtowed on any King, and dignified Mamood with the titles of The Protector of the State, and Treaſurer of Fortune. In the end of the month Zicada, in the year three hundred and ninety, Mamood haſtened from the city of Balich to Herat, and from Herat to Seiſtan, where he defeated Chiliph, the ſon of Amid, the governor of that province on the part of the extinguiſhed family of Bochara, and returned to Ghizni. He then turned his face to India, took many forts and provinces; in which having ſettled his own governors, he again returned to his dominions, where he ſpread the carpet of juſtice ſo ſmoothly upon the face of the earth, that the love of him, and loyalty gained place in every heart. Having at the ſame time ſet a treaty on foot with Elich the Uſbec, he had the province of Maver-ul-nere * ceded to him, for which he made an ample return in preſents of great value; and the ſtricteſt friendſhip, and greateſt familiarity, for a long time ſubſiſted between the Kings.

Mamood's firſt expedition to Hindoſtan.

His ſecond expedition to Hindoſtan.

Mamood having made a vow to Heaven, that if ever he ſhould be bleſſed with tranquillity in his own dominions, he would turn his arms againſt the idolators of Hindoſtan, marched in the year three hundred and ninety-one from Ghizni, with ten thouſand of his choſen horſe, and came to Peſhawir, where Jeipal the Indian prince of Lahore, with twelve thouſand horſe and thirty thouſand foot ſupported by three hundred chain-elephants, oppoſed him on Saturday the eighth of Mohirrim, in the three hundred and ninety-ſecond of the Higera. An obſtinate battle enſued, in which the Emperor was victorious; Jeipal, with fifteen of his principal friends, was taken priſoner, and

Jeipal defeated and taken.

* Tranſoxiana.

five

five thousand of his troops lay dead upon the field. Mamood in this action acquired great fame and wealth, for round the neck of Jeipal only, were found sixteen strings of jewels, each of which was valued at one hundred and eighty thousand rupees*.

A.D. 1002. Higer. 393.

After this victory, the Emperor marched from Peshawir, and investing the fort of Bitindi, reduced it, and releasing his prisoners upon the payment of a large ransom and a stipulation of an annual tribute, returned to Ghizni. It was in those ages a custom of the Hindoos, that whatever Raja was twice worsted by the Mussulmen, should be, by that disgrace, rendered unfit for further command. Jeipal in compliance to this custom, having raised his son to the government, ordered a funeral pile to be prepared, upon which he sacrificed himself to his Gods.

The death of Jeipal.

Mamood's third expedition to India.

In the Mohirrim of the year three hundred and ninety-three, Mamood again marched into Seistan†, and brought Chiliph, who had misbehaved in his government, prisoner to Ghizni. Finding that the tribute from Hindostan had not been paid in the year three hundred ninety-five, he directed his march towards the city of Battea; and leaving the boundaries of Moultan, arrived at Tahera, which was fortified with an exceeding high wall and a deep broad ditch. Tahera was at that time governed by a prince called Bachera, who had, in the pride of power and wealth, greatly molested the Mahommedan governors, whom the Emperor had established in Hindostan. Bachera had also refused to pay his proportion of the tribute to

* About 320,000l. of our money.

† A maritime province of Persia, lying between Kirman, or the ancient Carmania, and the mouths of the Indus.

A.D. 1004. Higer. 395. Annindpal, the ſon of Jeipal, of whom he held his authority.

When Mamood entered the territories of Bachera, that prince drew out his troops to receive him, and taking poſſeſſion of ſtrong poſts, continued to engage the Mahommedans for the ſpace of three days; in which time they ſuffered ſo much, that they were on the point of abandoning the attack: But on the fourth day, Mamood ſpoke at the head of his troops, and encouraged them to glory. He concluded with telling them, that this day he had devoted himſelf to conqueſt or to death. Bachera, on his part, invoked the Gods at the temple, and prepared with his former reſolution to repel the enemy. The Muſſulmen advanced with great impetuoſity, but were repulſed with ſlaughter; yet returning with freſh courage, and redoubled rage, the attack was continued till the evening, when Mamood turning his face to the holy Caaba*, invoked the aid of the prophet in the preſence of his army.—"Advance, advance, cried then the King, our prayers have found favour with God."—Immediately a great ſhout aroſe among the hoſt, and the Muſſulmen preſſing forward, as if they thirſted after death, obliged the enemy to give ground, and purſued them to the gates of the town.

Defeats Bachera, The Emperor having next morning inveſted the place, gave orders to make preparations for filling up the ditch; which in a few days was nearly compleated. Bachera, finding he could not long maintain the town, determined to leave only a ſmall garriſon for its defence; and accordingly one night, marched out with the reſt of his troops, and took poſt in a wood on the banks of the Indus. Mamood being informed of his retreat, detached part

* The temple of Mecca.

of

of his army to purſue him. Bachera by this time was deſerted by his fortune, and conſequently by the moſt of his friends; he found himſelf ſurrounded by the Muſſulmen, and he attempted, in vain, to force through them his way: Being juſt upon the point of being taken priſoner, he turned his ſword againſt his breaſt, and the moſt of his adherents were ſlaughtered in attempting revenge. Mamood had in the mean time taken Tahera by aſſault. He found there one hundred and twenty elephants, many ſlaves, and rich plunder, and annexing the town and its dependencies to his own dominions, he returned victorious to Ghizni.

A. D. 1005. Higer. 396.

who kills himſelf.

In the year three hundred and ninety-ſix, he formed the deſign of re-conquering Moultan, which had revolted from his obedience. Amid Lodi, the regent of Moultan, had formerly paid Mamood allegiance, and after him his grandſon Daood, till the expedition againſt Bachera, when he withdrew his loyalty. The King marched in the beginning of the ſpring, with a great army from Ghizni, and was met by Annindpal, the ſon of Jeipal prince of Lahore, in the hills of Peſhawir, whom he defeated, and obliged to fly into Caſhmire*. Annindpal had entered into an alliance

Mamood's fourth expedition into India.

Defeats Annindpal, Raja of Lahore.

* The kingdom of Caſhmire may be reckoned a terreſtrial paradiſe. It is entirely encloſed with high mountains, which ſeparate India from Tartary; in ſo much that there is no entrance, on any ſide, but over rocks of a prodigious height. It conſiſts, in a manner, of one valley of ſurprizing fertility and beauty. The air is temperate and charming; it is neither viſited with ſcorching heat, nor the viciſſitude of extreme cold. A thouſand little ſprings, which iſſue, on all ſides, from the mountains, form there a fine river, which, after watering the plains of this delightful country, falls down rocks of an aſtoniſhing height into the great river Indus. The inhabitants are aſtoniſhingly handſome, and the women eſpecially enchantingly beautiful. The Caſhmirians, moreover, are extremely ingenious, and carry the arts of civil life to high perfection. Their

A.D. 1006. Higer. 397. alliance with Daood, and as there were two paſſes only, by which the Mahommedans could enter Moultan, Annindpal had taken upon himſelf to ſecure that by the way of Peſhawir, which Mamood chanced to take. The Sultan returning from the purſuit, entered Moultan, by the way of Betinda, which was his firſt intention. When Daood received intelligence of the fate of Annindpal, thinking himſelf too weak to keep the field, he ſhut himſelf up in his fortified places, and ſubmiſſively ſolicited forgiveneſs for his faults, promiſed to pay a great tribute, and for the future to obey implicitly the Sultan's commands. Mamood received him again as a ſubject, and prepared to return to Ghizni, when news was brought to him from Arſilla, who commanded at Herat, that Elich the King of Caſgar had invaded his government with an army. The King haſtened to ſettle the affairs of Hindoſtan, which he put into the hands of Shockpal, an Hindoo prince, who had reſided with Abu Ali, governor of Peſhawir, and had turned Muſſulman by the name of Zab Sais.

Miſunderſtanding between Mamood and Elich, The particulars of the war of Mamood with Elich are theſe: We have already mentioned that an uncommon friendſhip had ſubſiſted between this Elich the Uſbec King of Kaſhgar, a kingdom in Tartary, and Mamood. The Emperor himſelf was married to the daughter of Elich, but ſome factious men about the two courts, by miſrepreſentations of the princes to one another, changed their former friendſhip into enmity. When Mamood therefore marched to Hindoſtan, and had left the fields of Choraſſan almoſt deſtitute of

who invades Choraſſan.

Their beauty, in ſhort, ſays a Perſian author, makes them appear to be of divine race, and their charming country furniſhes them with the life of Gods.

troops,

troops, Elich took that opportunity, and resolved to appropriate that province to himself. To accomplish his design, he ordered his chief general Sipistagi, with a great force, to enter Chorassan; and Jaffier Tighi, at the same time, was appointed to command in the territory of Balich. Arsilla, the governor of Herat, being informed of these motions, hastened to Ghizni, that he might secure the capital. In the mean time, the chiefs of Chorassan finding themselves deserted, and being in no condition to oppose the enemy, submitted themselves to Sipistagi, the general of Elich. A. D. 1006. Higer. 397.

But Mamood having by great marches reached Ghizni, he poured onward like a torrent, with his army towards Balich. Tighi, who had by this time possessed himself of the place, fled towards Turmuz at his approach. The Emperor then detached Arsilla with a great part of his army, to drive Sipistagi out of Chorassan; and he also, upon the approach of the troops of Ghizni, abandoned Herat, and marched towards Maver-ul-nere. Mamood marches against him.

The King of Kashgar, seeing the bad state of his affairs, solicited the aid of Kudir King of Chuton, a province of Tartary, on the confines of China, and that prince marched to join him with fifty thousand horse. Strengthened by this alliance, he crossed, with the confederate armies, the river Gion*, which was five pharsangs from Balich, and opposed himself to the camp of Mamood. That Monarch immediately drew up his army in order of battle, giving the command of the center to his brother the noble Nisir, supported by Abu Nisir, governor of Gorgan, and by Abdulla, a chief, of reputation in arms. The right wing he committed to the care of Alta Sash,

* The Oxus.

an

A.D. 1007. Higer. 398. an old experienced officer, while the left was the charge of the valiant Arſilla, a chief of the Afgans. The front of his line he ſtrengthened with five hundred chain-elephants, with intervals behind them, to facilitate their retreat, in caſe of a defeat.

Comes to battle with Elich, The King of Kaſhgar poſted himſelf in the center, the noble Kudir led the right, and Tighi the left. The armies advanced to the charge. The ſhouts of warriors, the neighing of horſes, and the claſhing of arms, reached the broad arch of heaven, while duſt obſcured the face of day. The flame of war might be ſaid to have been blown up to its height, and the clay of the field to be tempered with blood.

Elich advancing with ſome choſen ſquadrons, threw diſorder into the center of Mamood's army, and was buſy in the affairs of death. Mamood perceived the enemy's progreſs, leaped from his horſe, and kiſſing the ground, invoked the aid of the Almighty. He inſtantly mounted an elephant of war, encouraged his troops, and made a violent aſſault upon Elich. The elephant ſeizing the ſtandard-bearer of the enemy, folded round him his trunk, and toſſed him aloft into the ſky. He then preſſed forward like a mountain removed from its place by an earthquake, and trod the enemy like locuſts under his feet. When the troops of Ghizni ſaw their King forcing thus his way alone through the enemy's ranks, they ruſhed on with headlong impetuoſity, and drove the enemy with great ſlaughter before them. Elich, who is totally overthrown. abandoned by fortune and his army, turned his face to flight. He croſſed the river with a few of his ſurviving friends, never afterwards appearing in the field to diſpute glory with Mamood.

The King after this victory propoſed to purſue the enemy, which was thought unadviſeable by his generals,

generals, on account of the inclemency of the season, it being then winter, and the troops hardly capable of motion: But the King was positive in his resolution, and marched two days after the runaways. On the third night, a great storm of wind and snow overtook the Ghiznian army in the desart. The King's tents were with much difficulty pitched, while the army was obliged to lie in the snow. Mamood having ordered great fires to be kindled around his tents, they became so warm, that many of the courtiers began to turn off their upper garments; when a facetious chief, whose name was Dilk, came in shivering with cold. The King observing him, said, go out Dilk, and tell the Winter that he may burst his cheeks with blustering, for here we value not his resentment. Dilk went out accordingly, and returning in a short time, kissed the ground, and thus presented his address. "I have delivered the King's message to Winter, but the surly season replies, that if his hands cannot tear the skirts of royalty and hurt the attendants of the King, yet he will so execute his power to-night on his army, that in the morning Mamood will be obliged to saddle his own horses."

A.D. 1008. Higer. 399.

Mamood's army in distress.

Facetious answer of an officer to Mamood.

The King smiled at this reply, but it presently rendered him thoughtful, and he determined to proceed no further. In the morning some hundreds of men and horses were found to have perished with the cold. Mamood at the same time received advice from India, that Zab Sais the renegado Hindoo, had thrown off his allegiance, and, returning to his former religion, expelled all the officers, who had been appointed by the King, from their respective departments. The King immediately determined to punish this revolt, and with great expedition advanced towards India. He detached some part of his cavalry in front, who

Mamood defeats and takes Zab Sais.

A. D. 1008. Higer. 399. who coming unexpectedly upon Zab Sais, defeated him, and brought him prisoner to the King. The rebel was fined in four lacks of rupees, of which Mamood made a present to his treasurer, and kept Zab Sais a prisoner for life.

Annindpal raises disturbances. Mamood's fifth expedition into India. Mamood, having thus settled his affairs in India, returned in autumn to Ghizni, where he remained for the winter in peace. But in the spring of the year three hundred and ninety-nine, Annindpal, Sovereign of Lahore, began to raise disturbances in Moultan, so that the King was obliged to undertake another expedition into those parts, with a great army, to correct the Indians. Annindpal hearing of his intentions, sent ambassadors every where to request the assistance of the other princes of Hindostan; who considered the extirpation of the Mussulmen from India, as a meritorious and political, as well as a religious action.

The Rajas confederate against him. Accordingly the princes of Ugeïn, Gualiar, Callinger, Kinnoge, Delhi, and Ajmere, entered into a confederacy, and collecting their forces, advanced towards the heads of the Indus, with the greatest army that had been for some hundreds of years seen upon the field in India. The two armies came in sight of one another in a great plain near the confines of the provinces of Peshawir. They remained there encamped forty days without action: but the troops of the idolaters daily increased in number. They were joined by the Gickers and other tribes with numerous armies, and surrounded the Mussulmen, who fearing a general assault were obliged to entrench themselves.

They are overthrown. The King having thus secured himself, ordered a thousand archers to his front, to endeavour to provoke the enemy to advance to the entrenchments. The archers accordingly were attacked by the Gickers, who, notwithstanding all the King could

could do, purſued the runaways within the trenches, where a dreadful ſcene of ſlaughter enſued on both ſides, in which five thouſand Muſſulmen in a few minutes were ſlain. The enemy at length being cut off as faſt as they advanced, the attack became fainter and fainter, when on a ſudden the elephant upon which the Prince of Lahore, who commanded the Indians in chief, rode, took fright at the report of a gun*, and turned his face to flight. This circumſtance ſtruck the Hindoos with a panic, for thinking they were deſerted by their general, they immediately followed the example. Abdulla, with ſix thouſand Arabian horſe, and Arſilla, with ten thouſand Turks, Afghans, and Chilligis, purſued the enemy for two days and nights; ſo that twenty thouſand Hindoos were killed in their flight, together with the great multitude that fell on the field of battle. A. D. 1008. Higer. 399.

Thirty elephants with much rich plunder were brought to the King, who, to eſtabliſh the faith, marched againſt the Hindoos of Nagracot, breaking down their idols and ſubverting their temples. There was at that time in the territory of Nagracot a famous fort called Bimé, which Mamood inveſted, after having deſtroyed the country round with fire and ſword. Bimé was built by a prince of the ſame name, on the top of a ſteep mountain, and here the Hindoos, on account of its ſtrength, had depoſited the wealth conſecrated to their idols in all the neighbouring kingdoms; ſo that in this fort there was a greater quantity of gold, ſilver, precious ſtones and pearls, than had been ever collected into the royal treaſury of any

* According to our accounts there were no guns at this time, but many Eaſtern authors mention them, aſcribing the invention to one Lockman.

A.D. 1008. Higer. 399. Mamood invests Bimé. prince on earth. Mamood invested the place with such expedition, that the Hindoos had not time to throw troops into it for its defence, the greatest part of the garrison being before carried into the field. Those within consisted for the most part of priests, a race of men who, having little inclination to the bloody business of war, in a few days solicited to be permitted to capitulate. Their request being granted by Mamood, they opened the gates, and fell upon their faces before him; and, with a few of his officers and attendants, he immediately entered the place.

Bimé taken.

In Bimé were found seven hundred thousand golden dinars, seven hundred maunds * of gold and silver plate, forty maunds of pure gold in ingots, two thousand maunds of silver bullion, and twenty maunds of various jewels set, which had been collecting from the time of Bimé. With this immense treasure the King returned to Ghizni, and in the year 400 prepared a magnificent festival, where he displayed to the people his wealth in golden thrones, and in other rich ornaments, in a great plain without the city of Ghizni; and after the feast every individual received a princely present.

In the following year, Mamood led his army towards Ghor. The native prince of that country, Mahommed of the Soor Tribe of Afgans, a principality in the mountains famous for giving birth to the Ghorian Dynasty, who succeeded to the throne after the extirpation of the royal House of Ghizni, with ten thousand troops, opposed him. From morning to noon the fire of war flamed, and justice was done to valour on both sides. The King, finding that the troops of Ghor defended

* The least maund in India is about thirty-seven pounds avoirdupoise.

themselves

themſelves in their intrenchments with ſuch obſtinacy, commanded his army to make a feint of retreating, to allure the enemy out of their fortified camp, which accordingly ſucceeded. The Ghorians being deceived, purſued the army of Ghizni to the plain, where the King, facing round with his troops, attacked them with great impetuoſity and ſlaughter. Mahommed was taken priſoner and brought to the King; but in his deſpair he had taken poiſon, which he always kept under his ring, and died in a few hours. His country was annexed to the dominions of Ghizni. Some hiſtorians affirm, that neither the ſovereigns of Ghor, nor its inhabitants, were Muſſulmen, till after this victory, whilſt others of good credit aſſure us, that they were converted many years before, even ſo early as the time of the famous Ali, the ſon-in-law of the Prophet. A.D. 1009. Higer. 400. Mamood reduces Ghor.

Mamood, in the ſame year, was under the neceſſity of marching again to Moultan, which had revolted; but having ſoon reduced it, and cut off a great number of the chiefs, he brought Daood the ſon of Nazir, the rebellious governor, priſoner to Ghizni, and confined him in the fort of Gorci for life.

In the year 402, the paſſion of war fermenting in the mind of Mamood, he reſolved upon the conqueſt of Tannaſar*, in the kingdom of Hindoſtan. It had reached the ears of the King, that Tannaſar was held in the ſame veneration by idolators as Mecca was by the Muſſulmen; that there they had ſet up a whole tribe of rich idols, the principal of whom they called Jug Soom; that this Jug Soom, they pretended to ſay, exiſted when as yet the world exiſted not. When the King reached the country about the five branches His ſixth expedition to India.

* A city thirty miles to the Weſt of Delhi.

of

A.D. 1011. Higer. 402. of the Indus, he wanted that, according to the treaty that ſubſiſted between him and Annindpal, he ſhould not be diſturbed in his march through that country. He accordingly ſent an embaſſy to Annindpal, adviſing him of his intentions, and deſiring him to ſend guards for the protection of his towns and villages, which he would take care ſhould not be moleſted by the followers of his camp.

Sends an ambaſſador to Annindpal.

Annindpal agreed to this propoſal, and prepared an entertainment for the reception of the King, iſſuing out an order for all his ſubjects to ſupply the royal camp with every neceſſary of life. He, in the mean time, ſent his brother with two thouſand horſe to meet the King, and deliver this embaſſy to thoſe who approached the throne: "That he was the ſubject and ſlave of the King; but that he begged permiſſion to acquaint his majeſty, that Tannaſar was the principal place of worſhip of the inhabitants of that country: that if it was a virtue required by the religion of Mamood to deſtroy the religion of others, he had already acquitted himſelf of that duty to his God, in the deſtruction of the temple of Nagracot: But if he ſhould be pleaſed to alter his reſolution againſt Tannaſar, Annindpal would undertake that the amount of the revenues of that country ſhould be annually paid to Mamood, to reimburſe the expence of his expedition: that beſides, he, on his own part, would preſent him with fifty elephants, and jewels to a conſiderable amount."

Annindpal's requeſt to Mamood.

Is refuſed.

The King replied, "That in the Muſſulman religion it was an eſtabliſhed tenet, that the more the glory of the prophet was exalted, and the more his followers exerted themſelves in the ſubverſion of idolatry, the greater would be their reward in heaven. That therefore, it was his firm reſolution, with the aſſiſtance of God, to root out the

the abominable worship of idols from the face of the country of India. Why then should he spare Tannasar?" A.D. 1011. Higer. 402.

When this news reached the Indian king of Delhi, he prepared to oppose the invaders, sending messengers all over Hindostan to acquaint the Rajas that Mamood, without any reason or provocation, was marching with an innumerable army to destroy Tannasar, which was under his immediate protection: that if a mound was not expeditiously raised against this roaring torrent, the country of Hindostan would be soon overwhelmed in ruin, and the tree of prosperity rooted up: that therefore it was adviseable for them to join their forces at Tannasar, to oppose with united strength the impending danger.

Tannasar taken.

But Mamood reached Tannasar before they could take any measures for its defence, plundered the city, and broke down the idols, sending Jug Soom to Ghizni, where he was soon stripped of his ornaments. He then ordered his head to be struck off, and his body to be thrown on the highway. According to the account of the historian Hago Mahommed of Kandahar, there was a ruby found in one of the temples which weighed four hundred and fifty miskal*.

Delhi taken.

Mamood, after these transactions at Tannasar, proceeded to Delhi, which he also took, and wanted much to annex it to his dominions. But his nobles told him, that it was impossible to keep the Rajaship of Delhi, till he had entirely subjected Moultan under the Mussulman government, and exterminated the power and family of Annindpal prince of Lahore, who lay between Delhi

* A miskal is thirty-six rutty, and a rutty seven-eighths of a carat, so that the size of this ruby is too improbable to deserve any credit.

and

A. D. 1012. Higer. 403.

and the northern dominions of Mamood. The King approved of this counſel, and he immediately determined to proceed no farther againſt that country, till he had accompliſhed the reduction of Moultan and Annindpal. But that prince behaved with ſo much policy and hoſpitality, that he changed the purpoſe of the King, who returned to Ghizni. He brought to Ghizni forty thouſand captives and much wealth, ſo that that city could now be hardly diſtinguiſhed in riches from India itſelf.

In the 403d year of the Higerah, the next in command to the famous Arſilla, governor of Herat, reduced the province of Girgiſtan, and brought Niſir, the prince of that province, priſoner to Ghizni. Mamood at this time wrote to the Calipha of Bagdad, Al Kadir Billa, of the noble houſe of Abbaſſi, "That the greateſt part "of the kingdom of Choraſſan was under his ju-"riſdiction, and that he hoped he would order "his governors to give up the remainder." The Calipha, fearing his great power, which might fall upon his other dominions, conſented to this demand.

Mamood's embaſſy to the Caliph.

His ſeventh expedition into India.

The King, in the year 404, drew his army againſt the fort of Nindoona, which is ſituated upon the mountains of Belnat, and was in the poſſeſſion of the Indian prince of Lahore. Annindpal by this time was dead, and his ſon had acceded to his government. When Pitterugepal, for that was the young prince's name, ſaw that he could not ſtand againſt the King in the field, he drew off his army towards Caſhmire, leaving a good garriſon for the defence of the place. Mamood immediately inveſted it, and, with mining and other arts of attack, aſſiduouſly employed himſelf; ſo that, in a few weeks, the governor ſeeing his walls in ruins, was under the neceſſity

of

of begging to capitulate. The King granted his request, took every thing of value out of the place, appointed a governor, and set out without delay for Cashmire, upon which Pitterugepal abandoned that province, and fled to the hills. Mamood plundered Cashmire of all its great wealth, and having forced the inhabitants to acknowledge the Prophet, returned with the spoil to his capital of Ghizni. A.D. 1015. Higer. 406.

Returns to Cashmire.

Mamood, in the year 406, returned with an army to Cashmire, to punish some revolted chiefs, and to besiege some forts which he had not reduced in his former expedition. The first of those forts was Lokote, very famous for its height and strength, which entirely defeated the King's utmost efforts; for not being able to reduce it all the summer season, he was obliged, on the approach of winter, to abandon his enterprize, and return to Ghizni. On his way home, he was led astray by his guides, and fell into an extensive morass covered with water, from which he, for several days, could not extricate his army, so that many of his troops perished upon that occasion.

Abul Abas king of Charizm, demands Mamood's sister in marriage.

Abul Abas, king of Charizm, in the course of the same year, wrote to Mamood, to ask his sister in marriage. The King agreed to the match, and sent her to Charizm, according to the desire of Abas. In the year 407, a tribe of plunderers rising against Abul Abas, and defeating him, he fell into their hands, and was put to death. Mamood having had advice of this disaster, marched to Balich, and from thence to Charizm, and when he arrived at Hisserbund, on the frontiers of that country, he ordered his general, Mahommed Taï, to advance before him with a detachment. When the Mussulmen were at prayers in their camp, Himar Tash, the general of the Charizmians, rushed upon this detachment from a neighbouring

Is put to death.

 wood,

A. D. 1016. Higer. 407. wood, and making a great ſlaughter, put them to flight. Mamood having received intelligence of this affair, ſupported them with ſeveral ſquadrons of his beſt horſe. The runaways deriving courage from this reinforcement, returned to the charge, routed the enemy, and took their chief priſoner, whom they carried before the King.

Which is revenged by Mamood.

Mamood advancing to the fort of Hazar Aſp, perceived that the troops of Charizm were prepared to receive him in the field before it: But they were ſoon defeated, their general, Abiſtagi, a native of Bochara, taken priſoner, and the murderer of Abul Abas met the juſt vengeance due to his crime. Mamood ſpent ſome time in regulating the government, which he beſtowed upon the noble Hajib, with the title of King of Charizm: He annexed alſo to his government the province of Orgunge*. Returning to Balich, Mamood gave the government of Herat to his ſon the prince Muſaood, appointing Abu Sul his vizier; and the government of Gurgan he conferred upon his younger ſon, the Noble Mahommed, under the care of Abu Bicker. After the final ſettlement of the affairs of Charizm, the Ghiznian army were cantoned, for the winter, at Balich.

Mamood's eighth expedition into India.

In the beginning of the year 409, as ſoon as the ſun began to awake the children of the ſpring, Mamood, with a hundred thouſand choſen horſe and thirty thouſand foot, raiſed in the countries of Turkiſtan, Maver-ul-nere, Choraſſan, and the adjacent provinces, undertook an expedition againſt Kinnoge, which, from the time of † Guſtaſp, the father of Darab, to this period, had not been viſited by any foreign enemy. Kinnoge was diſtant from Ghizni three months march, and ſeven

* The famous city of Urgens, capital of Turkeſtan.

† Hyſtaſpes, the father of the firſt Darius, king of Perſia.

great

great rivers * rushed across the way. When Mamood reached the confines of Cashmire, the prince, whom he had established in that country, sent him presents of every thing curious and valuable in his kingdom, and waited to have the honour of expressing his loyalty. When the King, with much difficulty, had conducted his army through the mountains, he entered the plains of Hindostan, drove all opposition before him, and advanced to Kinnoge†. A.D. 1018. Higer. 408.

He there saw a city which raised its head to the skies, and which, in strength and structure, might justly boast to have no equal. The Indian prince of this rich city, whose name was Korra, and who affected great pomp and splendor, being thus unexpectedly invaded, had not had time to put himself in a posture of defence, or to collect his troops together. Terrified by the great force and warlike appearance of the King, he, in his embarrassment, resolved to sue for peace, and accordingly went out, with his family, to the camp, where he submitted himself to the mercy of Mamood. Some authors relate, that he even turned a true believer. The great city of Kinnoge submits.

The King of Ghizni tarried in Kinnoge only three nights, and then turned his face towards Merat, the prince of which place, by name Hirdit, retreated with his army, leaving only a garrison, which was obliged to capitulate in a few days. The terms were two hundred and fifty thousand rupees and fifty elephants, to be paid by the Raja, besides the plunder of the city. The Sultan marched from thence to invest the fort of Mamood takes Merat.

* These were the principal branches of which the Indus is composed.

† Mamood's route lay through the mountains behind Cashmire; and he must have entered Hindostan by the way of Tibet.

A. D. 1018. Higer. 409. Mavin, upon the banks of the river Gihon, now called the Jumna. The Prince of Mavin coming forth to make his ſubmiſſion, at the head of his troops, a quarrel accidentally enſued between ſome ſoldiers, and immediately the action became general. Calchunder, for that was the prince's name, and moſt of his troops, being driven into the river, he drew his ſword againſt his own wife and children, and having diſpatched them, turned it in deſpair upon himſelf. The fort immediately ſurrendered, where the conqueror found much treaſure and rich ſpoil, among which were ſeventy elephants of war.

Marches againſt and takes Muttra.

When Mamood had here refreſhed his troops, he was given to underſtand, that, at ſome diſtance, there was a rich city, called Muttra*, conſecrated to Kiſſen Baſdeo, which in buildings and extent yielded to none in Hindoſtan. The King directed his march towards the place, and entering it with very little oppoſition from the troops of the prince of Delhi, to whom it belonged, gave it up to plunder. He broke down or burnt all the idols, and amaſſed an immenſe quantity of gold and ſilver, of which theſe figures were moſtly made. He intended to deſtroy the temples, but he found that the labour exceeded his capacity; while ſome ſay that he was turned from his purpoſe, by the admirable beauty and ſtructure of thoſe edifices. He, it is certain, extravagantly extolled the magnificent beauty of the buildings and city, in a letter to the nobles of Ghizni, after this conqueſt.

Great ſpoil found in Muttra.

It is ſaid, that Mamood found in Muttra five great idols of pure gold, with eyes of rubies, each of which eyes were worth fifty thouſand dinars. Upon another idol he found a ſapphire,

* Muttra ſtands upon the Jumna 36 miles above Agra, and is ſtill a very conſiderable city.

weighing

weighing four hundred miſkal; and the image being melted down, produced ninety-eight thouſand three hundred miſkal of pure gold. Beſides theſe, there were above a hundred idols of ſilver, which loaded a hundred camels with bullion. The King, having tarried here twenty days, in which time the city ſuffered greatly from fire, beſides what it ſuffered from the hand of ravage and deſolation, he marched againſt the other fortified places in theſe diſtricts, ſome of which he took himſelf, while others fell into the hands of his chiefs. A.D. 1018. Higer. 409.

One of thoſe forts, called Munge, held out twenty-five days, being full of Rajaputs; but when they found the place no longer tenable, ſome ruſhed through the breaches among the enemy, and met that death which they no longer endeavoured to avoid. Some threw themſelves headlong from the walls, and were daſhed to pieces, while others burnt themſelves in their houſes, with their wives and children; ſo that not one of the garriſon ſurvived this fatal cataſtrophe. The Sultan having ſecured what was valuable, inveſted the fort of Chundpal. But Chundpal, for that alſo was the prince's name, had ſent off all his treaſure to the mountains, and, at the approach of the King, evacuated the place. There however ſtill remained much ſpoil and proviſions, which Mamood divided among his troops. Munge taken.

Mamood immediately marched againſt a proud and imperious Raja, whoſe name was Jundroy. This prince, after ſome ſkirmiſhes, finding himſelf unable to cope with the King, ſent off his treaſure and other valuable effects, and fled alſo to the mountains. Jundroy had an elephant of a moſt uncommon ſize, ſuch as had never before been ſeen in Hindoſtan; nor was he more remarkable for his enormous bulk, than for his docility Mamood marches againſt Jundroy.

A.D. 1018. Higer. 409. cility and courage. Mamood having heard much of this elephant, ſent to the Raja, offering him advantageous terms of peace, and a great ſum of money, for this animal. But the obſtinacy of Jandroy would never liſten to any terms with the Muſſulmen, ſo that Mamood, with regret, was obliged to deſiſt. The elephant however happened one night to break looſe from his keepers, and went into the Ghiznian camp, where he permitted himſelf to be mounted and brought before the King, who received him with great joy, and named him, The gift of God, becauſe he came, by accident, into his hands. Mamood, loaded with ſpoil and encumbered with captives, returned to Ghizni; where he enumerated the articles of his plunder. It conſiſted of twenty millions of dirms, fifty-three thouſand captives, three hundred and fifty elephants, beſides jewels, pearls, and precious effects, which could not be properly eſtimated. Nor was the private ſpoil of the army leſs than that which came into the public treaſury.

Returns to Ghizni.

Builds the Celeſtial Bride.

The King, upon his return to Ghizni, ordered a magnificent moſque to be built of marble and granite, of ſuch beauty and ſtructure as ſtruck every beholder with aſtoniſhment and pleaſure. This moſque he afterwards adorned with ſuch beautiful carpets, chandeliers, and other ornaments of ſilver and gold, that it became known by the name of the Celeſtial Bride. In the neighbourhood of this moſque he founded an univerſity, which he furniſhed with a vaſt collection of curious books, in various languages, and with natural and artificial curioſities. He appropriated a ſufficient fund for the maintenance of the ſtudents, and learned men, who were appointed to inſtruct the youth in the ſciences.

When

When the nobility of Ghizni ſaw that the taſte of their King began to run upon architecture, they alſo endeavoured to outvie each other in the magnificence of their private palaces, as well as in public buildings, which they raiſed for the embelliſhment of the city. Thus, in a ſhort ſpace of time, the capital was ornamented with moſques, porches, fountains, reſervoirs, aqueducts and ciſterns, in a degree ſuperior to any city at that time in the eaſt. Some authors affirm, that, among the curioſities which the Sultan poſſeſſed, there was a bird of the ſize of a cuckoo, which was poſſeſſed of this particular inſtinct or quality, that whenever poiſon was brought, however ſecretly, into the apartment in which he hung, he was affected with the ſmell in ſuch a manner, as to fly diſtractedly about his cage, while the tears ſtreamed involuntarily from his eyes. This bird, with other curioſities, was ſent as a preſent to the Calipha of Bagdat, Al Kadir Billa, of the noble houſe of Abbaſſi. We, however, believe, that this ſtory roſe from the policy of Mamood, and the credulity of mankind, rather than that it actually had any foundation in truth. Other authors mention a ſtone which he brought from Hindoſtan, as a great curioſity. This ſtone being dipped in water, and applied to a wound, proved a powerful and efficacious remedy. A.D. 1021. Higer. 412. Magnificence of the Ghiznians.

The Sultan, in the year 410, ordered a writing of victories * to be made out, which he ſent to the Calipha, who ordered it to be read to the people of Bagdat, making a great feſtival upon the occaſion, to expreſs his joy for the propagation of the faith, which now began to be ſpread over almoſt the whole face of the earth. Mamood writes to the Calipha.

* This was an account of Mamood's wars in verſe.

A.D. 1021. Higer. 412. In the year 412, Mamood was presented with a petition from his subjects, setting forth, that some tribes of the wild Arabs had, for many years, shut up the roads to Mecca, so that for fear of them, and on account of the weakness of the Calipha, who neglected to expel them, and whose power had long since declined, they had not been able to pay their devotions at the shrine of the prophet. The King immediately appointed Abu Mahommed, his chief justice, with a considerable force, to protect the Caffila*. But lest the enemy should be too strong for him, he sent thirty thousand dirms, to procure a safe journey to the pilgrims. Accordingly many thousands of all degrees prepared to go to Mecca.

Sends a convoy with the pilgrims to Mecca.

When they had reached the desert of Achmid, they beheld a great camp of Arabs pitched in their way. The banditti drew up in order to receive them. Abu Mahommed, being desirous of treating with the Arabs, sent a message to their chief, offering him five thousand dirms. The chief, instead of accepting the proposal, resented it so much, that, without delay, he advanced with intention to rob the Caffila. Mahommed, in the mean time, drew out his troops to receive the robbers, when fortunately, in the very beginning of the action, a Turkish slave, in the Caffila, who was master of the art of archery, lodged an arrow in the brain of Himad the son of Ali, the chief of the Arabs. The banditti immediately upon the fall of their chief turned their face to flight; and the Caffila, without further molestation, proceeded to Mecca; and having paid their devotions, returned the same way, and arrived safe at Ghizni.

Who defeat the wild Arabs.

* The Caravan of Pilgrims.

The

The Sultan received, this year, advices from India, that the neighbouring princes had, in his abſence, fallen upon Korra, the Raja of Kinnoge, for having entered into an alliance, and for putting himſelf under the protection of the King. Mamood immediately marched to the aid of his vaſſal; but before he could arrive, Nunda, prince of Callinger, had drawn his army upon Kinnoge, and had ſlain Korra, with a great many of his principal chiefs. Mamood arriving at the river Jumna, encamped on the bank oppoſite to the enemy.

A.D. 1021. Higer. 412. Mamood's ninth expedition into India.

Seven officers in his army, without orders, ſwam acroſs the river, and entering the enemy's camp in the morning by ſurprize, ſtruck ſuch a panic in their troops, that they all betook themſelves to flight. The King, notwithſtanding their ſucceſs, was greatly enraged, but paſſing with the remainder of his army, he immediately commenced the purſuit. When Nunda came to the frontiers of his own dominions, he halted with his army, and prepared to receive Mamood with thirty-ſix thouſand horſe, forty-five thouſand foot, and ſix hundred and fifty elephants. The King of Ghizni, after having reconnoitred the ſtrength of the enemy and their ſituation, from a riſing ground, proſtrated himſelf before God, and prayed that the ſtandard of Iſlamiſm might be exalted with glory and triumph. The day being far advanced, he determined to wait for the morning, which, in the event, diſappointed his hopes and ambition, for Nunda decamped in the night with the utmoſt diſorder, leaving his tents, equipage and baggage behind him.

Defeats the Hindoos.

Mamood, having next morning reconnoitred the woods and hollow grounds around, ordered his army to march into the enemy's camp, and to lengthen their hands upon the ſpoil, which proved

A.D. 1022. Higer. 413. proved to be very considerable, besides five hundred and eighty elephants, which were found in the neighbouring wood. He then laid waste, with fire and sword, the country, and returned to Ghizni, without prosecuting the war any further.

Mamood's expedition to Kiberat, which he reduces.

He had not remained there many days, before he heard that the inhabitants of Kiberat and Nardien, countries upon the boundaries of Hindostan, would not acknowledge the Mussulman faith, but continued the worship of Lions*. Mamood resolved to compel them, and accordingly marched towards their country, taking with him a great number of masons, carpenters, smiths, and labourers, that he might there build a fort, to overawe them after his departure. The Lord of the country of Kiberat, finding he could not pretend to oppose the King, submitted himself, acknowledging the faith of the Prophet. The Ghiznian general Ali was sent, with a division of the army, to reduce the dominion of Nardien, which he soon accomplished, pillaging the country, and carrying away many of the people captives. There was a temple in Nardien which Ali destroyed, and brought from thence a stone, upon which there was a curious inscription, that bore that it was forty thousand years old.

Mamood's tenth expedition to India.

The Sultan ordered a fort to be built in that place, and left it under the care of Ali, the son of Kudur. He himself, in the mean time, returned by the way of Lahore, and in his march invested the strong hold of Locote, in the province of Cashmire. He besieged the place for a whole month, but, finding it impregnable, he

* The Divinity is worshipped under the figure of a Lion by some of the Hindoos: That animal being, in their opinion, a proper emblem of almighty power and strength.

decamped;

decamped, and proceeding to Lahore, entered that city without much oppoſition, giving it up to be ſacked by his troops. Here wealth, and precious effects, beyond the power of eſtimation, fell into their hands. A. D. 1022. Higer. 413. Lahore reduced.

Patturugepal, the prince of Lahore, unable to contend with ſo powerful an adverſary, fled to Ajmere for protection; and Mamood immediately appointed one of his Omrahs to the government of Lahore, and ſent other commanders to various diſtricts in the territories of Hindoſtan. Mamood himſelf returned in the ſpring to Ghizni.

The martial diſpoſition of Mamood could not reſt long in peace. He marched again by the way of Lahore, in the 414th year of the Higerah, againſt Nunda, the prince of Callinger, with a great army. Paſſing by the fort of Guaher, he ordered it to be beſieged; but the prince of the province prevailed upon him to remove from before that place in a few days, by the means of rich preſents and thirty-five elephants: The King immediately directed his march to Callinger, inveſted that city, and Nunda offered him three hundred elephants and other preſents for peace. The King agreed to the terms propoſed; and the Raja, to try the bravery of the Sultan's troops, intoxicated the elephants with certain drugs, and let them looſe without riders into the camp; Mamood ſeeing the animals advancing, perceived the trick, by the wildneſs of their motions, and immediately ordered a party of his beſt horſe to ſeize, kill, and drive them from the camp: Some of the Turks, emulous to diſplay their bravery in the preſence of their King, and of both armies, mounted the greateſt part of the elephants, and drove the reſt into an adjacent wood, where they were ſoon reduced to obedience. Mamood's eleventh expedition to India. Nunda ſubmits.

The

A. D. 1024. Higer. 415. His panegyrick upon Mamood.

The enemy, upon feeing the refolution of the Ghiznians, were much intimidated, and Nunda, taking advantage of one of the foibles of Mamood, fent to him a panegyric, in the Indian tongue. The King was much pleafed with this elegant piece of flattery; for the poetry was much admired by the learned men of India, Arabia, and Perfia, who were at his court. To make a return for this compliment, Mamood conferred the government of fifteen forts upon Nunda, with many curious prefents; but the peace was principally ratified by means of many valuable prefents in jewels and gold, given on the part of Nunda. Mamood immediately returned to Ghizni.

Mamood mufters his forces.

Mamood, in the year 415, muftered all his forces. He found them, exclufive of his garrifons and thofe upon duty in various parts of his dominions, to confift of fifty-five thoufand chofen horfe, one thoufand three hundred elephants, and one hundred thoufand infantry. With this force, excepting a part of the infantry which he left at Ghizni, he marched to Balich to expel Tiggi from the government of Maver-ul-nere for oppreffing the people, who complained of his tyranny to the King. When the chiefs of Maver-ul-nere heard that the King had croffed the Jagetay, they came with prefents to meet him; Kudir, king of Turkiftan, paid him, at the fame time, the compliment of a vifit, and was received with joy and friendfhip. Mamood prepared a great feaft upon the occafion; and after having concluded a treaty, the monarchs took leave of each other, making an exchange of princely prefents. Tiggi, feizing this opportunity, betook himfelf to flight. But the King of Ghizni fending a party of horfe after him, he was, after a long fearch, difcovered

and

and brought to camp, and confined for life in one of the forts of India. A.D. 1022. Higer. 413.

Mamood underſtood, in the ſame year, that there was a famous temple called Sumnat, in the province of Guzerat, near the harbour of Deo*, very rich and greatly frequented by devotees from all parts of Hindoſtan. Theſe infidels believed that ſouls, after death, went before Sumnat, who transferred them into other bodies or animals, according to their merits in their former ſtate. The King was alſo informed, that the prieſts of this God gave out, that the ſins of the people of Delhi and Kinnoge had incenſed him ſo much, that he abandoned them to the vengeance of the Muſſulmen, otherwiſe that, in the twinkling of an eye, he could have blaſted the whole army of Mamood. The King, rather irritated than intimidated by this report, was determined to put the power of the God to a trial, by perſonally treating him ill. He therefore marched from Ghizni, with a numerous army, in the month Shaban. Mamood's twelfth expedition into India.

The temple of Sumnat, which alſo gave name to a great city, was ſituated upon the ſhore of the Ocean, and is at this time to be ſeen in the diſtricts of the harbour of Deo, under the dominion of the idolaters of Europe†. Some hiſtorians affirm, that Sumnat was brought from Mecca, where he ſtood before the time of the Prophet. But the Brahmins deny this tale, and ſay, that it ſtood near the harbour of Deo ſince the time of Kriſhen, who was concealed in that place about four thouſand years ago. Deſcription of the temple of Sumnat.

* This place is now called Diu, and is in the poſſeſſion of the Portugueſe.

† The Portugueſe.

The

A. D. 1022. Higer. 413. Mamood arrives at Moultan.

The King of Ghizni, about the middle of Ramzan, reached the city of Moultan, and as there was a great desart before him, he gave orders that all his troops should provide themselves with several days water and provisions, as also with provender for their horses; he besides loaded twenty thousand camels with necessaries for the army. When he had passed that terrible desart, he arrived at the city of Ajmere, and finding that the Raja and inhabitants had abandoned the place, and that he could not prevail with them to come and submit themselves, he ordered the city to be sacked, and the adjacent country to be laid waste with fire and sword. But as the reduction of the citadel would take up too much time, he left it, and proceeding upon his expedition, reduced some small forts in the way by assault. Having then arrived at Narwalla, a city of Guzerat, which was evacuated at his approach, another desart presented itself to the King beyond that place. Mamood, however, taking the same precautions as before, without any remarkable occurrence, reached Sumnat, which was a lofty castle, upon a narrow peninsula, washed on three sides by the sea. Upon the battlements of the place there appeared an innumerable multitude of people in arms. They immediately made a signal for a Herald to approach, and told him, that their great idol, Sumnat, had drawn the Mussulmen thither, that he might blast them in a moment, and avenge the destruction of the Gods of India. The Sultan only smiled at this vain threat, and commanded, that as soon as the morning should appear, his army should be ready for an assault.

Sacks Ajmere.

Arrives at Narwalla,

and at Sumnat,

which he assaults.

In the morning, the valiant troops of the sublime Mamood, advanced to the foot of the walls, and began the attack. The battlements were in a short time cleared, by the experience and valour of of the archers, and the dastardly Hindoos, astonished and dispirited, crouded into the temple, and prostrating themselves in tears before the idol, prayed for assistance. The Mussulmen seized the opportunity which the devotion of their enemies offered them, applied their scaling-ladders, and, mounting the wall, began to exclaim Alla Akber*. The Hindoos now reduced to despair, found they must fight for themselves or die; they collected their force together, and made so violent an attack upon the assailants, that, from the time that the King of day dispelled the darkness, till the Moon, fair bride of night, illuminated the court of heaven with paler rays, the flames of war were not quenched with blood†. The Mussulmen, wearied out with fatigue, were at length obliged to abandon all their advantages, and retire to rest. Next morning, the work of death was renewed, but as fast as they mounted the wall, so fast were they pushed headlong down by the spears of the defendants, who, weeping, had taken leave of their God, and now seemed wishing for death. And thus the labours of this day proved more unsuccessful than the first.

A.D. 1022. Higer. 413. Scales the wall, but is repulsed.

An army of idolaters, upon the third day, presented themselves in order of battle, in sight of the Ghiznian camp. Mamood immediately advanced, with an intention to raise the siege of Sumnat, and therefore ordered a party to amuse the besieged, while he himself prepared to engage the enemy in the field. He marched in order of battle towards the idolaters, who advanced with equal resolution. The battle began with great fury, and victory for some time seemed doubtful,

The army of the Hindoos appears, whom he engages,

* God is greatest.

† The original in this place has some poetical merit, and it is therefore translated verbatim.

till

A. D. 1022. Higer. 413. till two Indian princes, Byramdeo and Dabiſelima, in the middle of the action, joined the enemy with their troops, and inſpired them with ſuch freſh courage, that faintneſs became viſible in Mamood's army. Mamood, perceiving a languor ſpreading over his lines, leapt from his horſe, and proſtrating himſelf before God, implored his aſſiſtance. Then mounting with a noble aſſurance, he took Abul Haſſen Chirkani, one of his generals, by the hand, and inſpired him with hope and glory. He himſelf advanced upon the enemy, encouraging his troops with ſuch determined reſolution, that, aſhamed to abandon their king, with whom they had ſo often trod the path of renown, they, with one accord, gave a ſhout of victory, and ruſhed forward as for a prize. They bore the enemy before them upon the points of their ſpears, laying five thouſand of them dead at their feet.

and overthrows.

Sumnat ſurrenders.

When the garriſon of Sumnat beheld this defeat, they were ſtruck with confuſion and fear. They withdrew their hands from the fight, and iſſuing out at a gate towards the ſea, to the number of four thouſand, embarked in boats, intending to proceed to the iſland of Sirindiep*. But they did not eſcape the eyes of the King. He ſeized upon boats which were left in a neighbouring creek, and, manning them with rowers and ſome of his beſt troops, purſued the enemy, taking and ſinking ſome of their boats, while others eſcaped. Having then placed guards round the walls and at the gates, he entered Sumnat, with his ſon and a few of his nobles and principal attendants. When they advanced to the temple, they ſaw a great and antique ſtructure, built of ſtone, with a ſpacious court. They immediately

Mamood enters Sumnat.

* Ceylon.

entered

entered it, and discovered a great square hall, having it's lofty roof supported by fifty-six pillars, curiously turned and set with precious stones. In the center of the hall stood Sumnat, an idol of stone, five yards in height, two of which were sunk in the ground.

A.D. 1022. Higer. 413.

The King was enraged when he saw this idol, and raising his mace, struck off the nose from his face. He then ordered that two pieces of the image should be broke off, to be sent to Ghizni, there to be thrown at the threshold of the public mosque, and in the court of his palace. Two more fragments he reserved to be sent to Mecca and Medina. When Mamood was thus employed in breaking up Sumnat, a croud of Brahmins petitioned his attendants, and offered some crores * in gold, if the King should be pleased to proceed no further. The Omrahs endeavoured to persuade Mamood to accept of the money; for they said that breaking up the idol could not remove idolatry from the walls of Sumnat, that therefore it could serve no purpose to destroy the image, but that such a sum of money given in charity, among believers, would be a very meritorious action. The King acknowledged, that what they said was, in some measure, true; but should he consent to that bargain, he might justly be called a seller of idols; and that he looked upon a breaker of them as a more honourable title. He therefore ordered them to proceed. The next blow having broke up the belly of Sumnat, which had been made hollow, they discovered that it was full of diamonds, rubies, and pearls, of a much greater value than the amount of what the Brahmins had offered, so that a zeal for religion was not the sole cause of their application to Mamood.

Destroys the Idol of Sumnat.

Finds an immense treasure.

* Ten millions.

A. D. 1022. Higer. 413. Account of Sumnat. It is said, by some writers, that the name of this idol is a compound word of *Sum* and *Nat*; *Sum* being the name of the prince who erected it, and *Nat* the true name of the God, which, in the language of the Brahmins, signifies Creator. In the time of eclipses we are told, that there used to be forty or fifty thousand worshippers at this temple; and that the different princes of Hindostan had bestowed, in all, two thousand villages, with their territories, for the maintenance of its priests; besides the innumerable presents received from all parts of the empire. It was a custom among those idolaters, to wash Sumnat, every morning and evening, with fresh water from the Ganges, though that river is above one thousand miles distant.

Among the spoils of this temple was a chain of gold, weighing forty maunds, which hung from the top of the building by a ring. It supported a great bell, which warned the people to the worship of the God. Besides two thousand Brahmins, who officiated as priests, there belonged to the temple five hundred dancing girls, three hundred musicians, and three hundred barbers, to shave the devotees before they were admitted to the presence of Sumnat. The dancing girls were either remarkable for their beauty or their quality, the Rajas thinking it an honour to have their daughters admitted. The King of Ghizni found, in this temple, a greater quantity of jewels and gold, than, it is thought, any royal treasury ever contained before. In the history of Eben Assur, it is related that there was no light in the temple, but one pendant lamp, which, being reflected from the jewels, spread a strong and refulgent light over the whole place. Besides the great idol abovementioned, there were in the temple some thousands

ſands of ſmall images, in gold and ſilver, of various ſhapes and dimenſions. A.D. 1022. Higer. 413.

The Emperor having ſecured the wealth of Sumnat, prepared to chaſtiſe the Indian prince Byram Deo, from whom the harbour of Deo takes its name, for having endeavoured to diſtreſs him during the ſiege, and having cut off above three thouſand of the Muſſulmen. Byram Deo, after the taking of Sumnat, had fled from Narwalla, the capital of Guzerat, and ſhut himſelf up in the fort of Gundia, which was forty pharſangs from Sumnat. The King, without oppoſition, arrived before the fort, and ſaw that it was ſurrounded on all ſides by the ſea, which, in every place, appeared impaſſable. He ſent however to ſound the depth of the water, and received intelligence, that at one place it was fordable at low water; but if he ſhould be caught by the tide, in his paſſage, the troops muſt inevitably periſh. Mamood having ordered public prayers, and caſt his fortune in the Koran, turned his horſe into the ſea, at the head of his troops, and reaching in ſafety the oppoſite ſhore, immediately made an aſſault upon the place. Byram Deo, looking upon life preferable to every other conſideration, left his family and wealth, and, in the habit of a ſlave, ſtealing out of the fort, ran and concealed himſelf in a corner. The troops who defended the place, ſeeing themſelves thus ſhamefully deſerted, were alſo ſtruck with fear; and quitted their poſts upon the walls. The Muſſulmen mounted their ſcaling ladders, and commenced a dreadful havock among the unfortunate ſlaves, reſerving the women and children for captivity. The wealth of the Byram was lodged in the treaſury of the king.

The Emperor marches againſt Byram Deo.

Mamood being thus victorious, marched to Narwalla, the capital of all the peninſula of Guzerat. He found the ſoil of that place ſo fertile,

Marches to Narwalla.

 the

A. D. 1022. Higer. 413. the air ſo ſalubrious and pure, and the country ſo well cultivated and pleaſant, that he propoſed to take up his reſidence there for ſome years, and to make it his capital, conferring the government of Ghizni upon his ſon, the illuſtrious Muſaood. Some hiſtorians relate, that, in that age, there were gold mines in Guzerat; which occaſioned Mamood to incline to fix his reſidence in that country. But to this we cannot well give any credit, as there are now no traces of thoſe mines; but it is acknowledged, that the country was, at all times, one of the richeſt in Hindoſtan. In ſupport of their aſſertion, they however give many inſtances of the diſappearance of gold mines, ſuch as that in Seiſtan, which was ſwallowed up by an earthquake. There are other writers who pretend to ſay, that the King, having heard of gold and ruby mines upon the iſland of Sirendeip, and in the country of Pegu, intended to fit out a fleet for the conqueſt of thoſe parts, but that he was diverted by his council from this ſcheme, and alſo prevailed upon not to abandon his native kingdom and capital.

Is diverted from making it his capital. Mamood yielding to this latter advice, conſented to return, and at the ſame time begged of his nobles, to recommend a fit perſon to him for the government of the kingdom of Guzerat. After conſulting among themſelves, they told the King, that on account of the great diſtance of this country from his other dominions, and the number of troops it would require for its defence, they thought it adviſeable that ſome one of the natives ſhould receive that honour. The King then enquired among the chiefs of the natives, and was informed that the family of Dabiſſalima was the nobleſt in thoſe parts, and that then a man of parts and diſtinction, of that tribe, was in his camp, in the habit of a common Brahmin. That they knew no no perſon fitter to be exalted to royalty than him, though he had been obliged to chuſe that way of life, to conceal himſelf from the cruelty of a younger brother, who had uſurped his inheritance. A.D. 1022. Higer. 413.

Some authors, ſuſpecting the probability of this ſtory, have informed us, that Dabiſſalima was an unſubdued prince of a neighbouring country, famous as well for his policy and wiſdom, as for his great knowledge in the ſciences. To him the King ſent a friendly meſſage, inviting him to his preſence, to receive his allegiance for the government of Guzerat, which he intended to beſtow upon him. But as we have many authentic proofs of the truth of our firſt relation, it muſt be acknowledged that the King, upon having ſettled an annual tribute, beſtowed the kingdom of Guzerat upon Dabiſſalima, the poor Brahmin, and not upon the Raja of the ſame name, who lived at that period. We find, that when the King had beſtowed the regency upon the Brahmin, the latter petitioned him to leave ſome forces for his protection, for that the prince Dabiſſalima, as ſoon as Mamood ſhould evacuate the country, would undoubtedly invade him before his power was thoroughly eſtabliſhed, the conſequence of which might be eaſily foreſeen: But that, if the king would grant him his protection, he would annually give double the revenues of Cabuliſtan and Zabuliſtan. Theſe conſiderations prevailed with Mamood to form a deſign to reduce the prince Dabiſſalima before he left the country. He accordingly ſent a part of his army into the dominions of the prince, which, in a ſhort time, defeated him, and brought him priſoner to Mamood. He immediately delivered over the unfortunate Raja into the hands of his kinſman Dabiſſalima, the viceroy, to take away his life. Makes Dabiſſalima king of Guzerat.

Dabiſſalima

A. D. 1026. Higer. 417. Dabiſſalima addreſſed himſelf to the King after this manner; That, in his religion, the murder of a king was unlawful; but that it was cuſtomary, when one king got poſſeſſion of the perſon of another who was his enemy, to make a dark pit under his throne, where he ſhould remain impriſoned for life, or till the death of his conqueror. Dabiſſalima's clemency. That, for his own part, he eſteemed ſuch uſage a cruelty of which he could not be guilty; but that, on the other hand, if the Raja ſhould be confined by him in another priſon, his adherents would, upon the King's departure, attempt to releaſe him. He therefore earneſtly begged that the King might carry him to Ghizni. Mamood returns to Ghizni. Mamood complied with this laſt requeſt, and, after two years and ſix months abſence, turned homewards his victorious ſtandards. But having received intelligence, that Byram Deo, and the prince of Ajmere, with others, had collected a great army to oppoſe him in the deſart, he turned by the way of the Indus and Moultan. He there alſo met with deſarts in his march, wherein his army greatly ſuffered by want of water, and his cavalry by want of graſs; but in the year 417, he with much difficulty and toil reached Ghizni. During his march through the country on the banks of the Indus, he was led aſtray three days and nights, by one of his Hindoo guides, in a deſart of dry ſand, ſo that madneſs and thirſt began intolerably to rage through his periſhing troops. Mamood, ſuſpecting his guide, commanded him to be put to the torture, when he confeſſed that he was one of the prieſts of Sumnat, who, to revenge the injuries done to his God, had thus endeavoured to bring about the ruin of the Ghiznian army. The King then commanded him to be put to death; and it being towards evening, he fell proſtrate before God, imploring a ſpeedy deliverance. A meteor was

was immediately ſeen in the eaſt, to which he directed his march, and, before morning, found himſelf upon the banks of a lake. A.D. 1026. Higer. 417.

Dabiſſalima the devout, having eſtabliſhed himſelf upon the throne of Guzerat, as deputy to the King of Ghizni, continued to ſend his revenues punctually to the King, and ſome years after deſired the impriſoned Raja might be returned to him. But that prince had, by this time, gained upon the mind of the King, which made him unwilling to part with him. He however was overperſuaded by his counſellors, who were envious of the favour which the unfortunate Raja had acquired; and he was accordingly put into the hands of the perſon who brought the revenue to Ghizni. When they reached the dominions of Guzerat, Dabiſſalima the devout gave orders to dig a hole under his own throne, in which he intended to confine the unhappy Raja, according to the barbarous cuſtom of the Indians. To ſtretch his triumph ſtill further, he advanced to ſome diſtance from his capital, to meet the prince, that the unfortunate man might run before his horſe, with a baſon on his head and an ewer in his hand.

Dabiſſalima demands the impriſoned Raja.

His cruelty,

The King of Guzerat, it is ſaid, having overheated himſelf upon this occaſion, lay down, much diſordered, in a ſhade, drew a red handkerchief over his face, and ordered his attendants to withdraw. A Vulture, which was hovering over that place, miſtaking the red handkerchief for prey, ſouſed down upon Dabiſſalima, and fixing her talons about his eyes, rendered him totally blind; and therefore incapable to reign, according to the laws of the country. When the accident which befel the King became public, the whole camp and city were filled with confuſion and uproar. The impriſoned prince, arriving at that very inſtant, was received with univerſal acclamations, and immediately

and puniſhment.

A. D. 1026. Higer. 417. mediately elected King. He put the baſon upon the head of Dabiſſalima, and placed the ewer in his hand, and drove him before him into the dungeon which he himſelf had prepared, where he ſpent the remainder of his life. This barbarous action, however, ſhewed that his ſucceſſor was unworthy of what providence had, ſo miraculouſly, beſtowed upon him. The ſtory is a ſtriking inſtance of the juſt puniſhment of pride, and that he who digs a pit for another, will fall into it himſelf.

Story of an iron idol. The author of the Jam ul Hikaiat has related, that, when Mamood was at Guzerat, he ſaw a ſmall black idol under a circular arch, which, to all appearance, was ſuſpended in the air without ſupport. The King, amazed at this phenomenon, conſulted the philoſophers of his court concerning it. They told him that they believed the image to be iron, and the ſtones of the arch magnets. The King obſerved, that he thought the equilibrium of weight and attraction could not be ſo exactly found. He, however, by way of experiment, ordered a ſtone to be ſtruck out of the arch; which was no ſooner done, than the idol fell to the ground, and the ſtone was accordingly found to be a magnet; but philoſophers of latter days are of the King's opinion; and this ſtory may be ranked among the fabulous.

The Calipha writes to Mamood. The Calipha of Bagdat being informed of the expedition of the King of Ghizni, wrote him a congratulatory letter, in which he ſtiled him, The Guardian of Fortune, and the Faith of Mahommed. To his ſon, the illuſtrious Emir Muſaood, he gave the title of The Light of Poſterity, and the Beauty of Nations; and to his ſecond ſon, the noble Euſoph, the appellation of The Strength of the Arm of Fortune, and Eſtabliſher of the State. He at the ſame time aſſured Mamood, that whoever

ever he ſhould appoint to the ſucceſſion, he himſelf would confirm and ſupport. A.D. 1027. Higer. 418.

Mamood marched this year an army againſt the Jits, who had inſulted him in his way from Sumnat. This people inhabited the country on the borders of Moultan, near the banks of the river that runs by the mountains of Jude. When he arrived at Moultan, finding that the country of the Jits was defended by great rivers, he ordered fifteen hundred boats to be built, each of which he armed with ſix iron ſpikes projecting from their prows and ſides, to prevent their being boarded by the enemy, who were very expert in that kind of war. When he had launched this fleet, he ordered twenty archers into each boat, and five others, with fire-balls, to burn the craft of the Jits, and naphtha to ſet the whole river on fire. This force he commanded to extirpate the Jits, and remained with the remainder of his army at Moultan. The Jits having intelligence of this armament, ſent their wives and children, and moſt valuable effects, into an iſland, and launching, according to ſome, four thouſand, or, according to others, eight thouſand boats, manned and armed, prepared to receive the Ghiznians. They met, and a terrible conflict enſued; but the projected ſpikes from the imperial boats did ſuch execution, when they ran againſt the craft of the Jits, that many of them were overſet. The archers, at the ſame time, plied their bows to ſuch good purpoſe, that many of the enemy plunged overboard to avoid their galling arrows. Some of the Jitſiad boats being, in the mean time, ſet on fire, communicated their flames to others; ſome were ſunk, ſome boarded by the Ghiznians, and others endeavoured to make their eſcape. In this ſcene of confuſion and terror, very few of the Jits could ſhun their hard fate. All thoſe therefore, who

Mamood attacks the Jits; who are overthrown.

eſcaped

A.D. 1028. Higer. 419. escaped death, met with the more severe misfortune of captivity.

The King, after this victory, returned in triumph to Ghizni, and in the 418th year of the Higera, ordered Amir Toos, one of his generals, to the government of the Persian district of Badwird, that he might chastise the Turkumans of Siljoki*, who had crossed the river Amavia, and invaded that province. But Amir Toos, being defeated in a very bloody action, wrote to the King, that without his presence and fortune nothing could be done against the enemy. Mamood immediately put his army in motion, and having come up with them, gave them a total defeat, which entirely dispersed them, and cleared the country. Hearing, at this time, that one of his generals had conquered Irac†, he marched that way, and seized all the treasure that had been amassed by the race of Boia, who had possessed that country, and lived in the city of Rai‡. Having there enforced some laws respecting the religion of the inhabitants, who had adopted false tenets, he settled the government of Rai and Ispahan upon his son, the prince Musaood, and returned himself to Ghizni.

Amir Toos defeated by the Turkumans.

Mamood overthrows the Turkumans. Reduces Irac.

Returns to Ghizni.

Falls sick.

Mamood was soon after afflicted with the stone, which disorder daily increased. He went in this condition to Balich to settle some state affairs, and in the beginning of the spring he turned his face again to Ghizni; where, upon Friday the 23d of the second Ribbi, in the 419th of the Higera, and the sixty-third year of his age, this great conqueror,

Dies.

* These were the Tartar tribe who soon after conquered Persia, and whose prince, Togrul Bec, founded the dynasty of the Siljokides.

† This is the province of Persia, distinguished by the name of Irac Agemi, by the Arabians.

‡ A great city, capital of Irac, before Ispahan.

queror, amidſt the tears of his people, gave up his body to death, and his ſoul to immortality. A.D. 1028. Higer. 419.

He reigned thirty-five years, and he was buried by torch light, with great pomp and ſolemnity, in the palace of triumph at Ghizni. He was certainly a great man and an excellent prince, a good friend to his own people, a dreadful enemy to foreigners. Ambitious but ſeldom cruel; not religious but enthuſiaſtic, he did many bad things from a good principle. His perſon was of the middle ſize, not handſome, but without deformity or blemiſh. His character.

Two days before his death, he commanded that all the ſacks of gold and caſkets of precious ſtones, which were in the treaſury, ſhould be placed before him; when he beheld them as with regret, he wept, ordering them to be carried back to the treaſury, without exhibiting his generoſity at that time to any body, for which he has been accuſed of avarice. He ordered, the following day, a review of his Army, his Elephants, Camels, Horſes and Chariots, with which, having feaſted his eyes for ſome time, from his travelling throne, he again burſt into tears, and retired in grief to his palace. Inſtances of his avarice.

It is ſaid, that Mamood, upon hearing that a citizen of Neſhapoor was poſſeſſed of immenſe wealth, commanded him to be called into his preſence. The King began to reproach him for being an idolater and an apoſtate from the faith. The citizen replied, "O King, I am no idolater nor apoſtate, but it is true that I am poſſeſſed of much wealth; take it therefore, but do me not a double injuſtice, by robbing me of my money and my good name." The King, for this inſolence, as he termed it, ordered him to be puniſhed, and confiſcated his whole eſtate.

But

A. D. 1028. Higer. 419. But Mamood was, in other inſtances, famous for juſtice. A perſon one day, thruſting himſelf into the preſence, called loudly for juſtice. The King ordered him to explain his complaint, which he thus did: That, unfortunately having a handſome wife, the King's nephew had conceived a paſſion for her, and came to his houſe every night with armed attendants, beating him and turning him into the ſtreet, till he had gratified his adulterous paſſion. That he had frequently complained to thoſe who ought to have done him juſtice, but that the rank of the adulterer had ſhut their ears againſt him.

Of his juſtice. The King, upon hearing this, was ſo much enraged, that tears of reſentment and compaſſion ſtarted from his eyes; he reprimanded the poor man for not making ſooner his complaint to him. The man replied, That he often attempted it, but could not gain admittance, He was then commanded by the King, to return to his houſe, and to give him notice the firſt time that his nephew was guilty of the like violence; charging thoſe who were preſent, upon pain of death, to let nothing of this complaint tranſpire, ordering the poor man to be admitted at any hour. Accordingly the man returned to his houſe, and, upon the third night following, the King's nephew, as uſual, came, and having whipped the huſband ſeverely, turned him into the ſtreet. The poor man haſtened to the King; but the captain of the guards would not give him admittance, ſaying, that his Majeſty was in the Haram. The man immediately began to make a violent outcry, ſo that the porter fearing that the court might be diſturbed, and that the noiſe might reach the King, he was under the neceſſity to conduct him to the Eunuchs of the bedchamber, who immediately acquainted Mamood of the affair.

The

The King immediately rose, and drawing on a garment, followed the man to his house. He found his nephew and the man's wife sleeping together in one bed, with a candle standing on the carpet near them. Mamood, extinguishing the candle, drew his dagger and severed his nephew's head from his body: Then commanding the man to bring a light, he called out for some water, and having taken a deep draught, he told him, he might now go and sleep with safety, if he could trust his own wife. A.D. 1028. Higer. 419.

The poor man fell down at the King's feet, in gratitude to his justice and condescension, but begged him to tell why he put out the candle, and afterwards called out so vehemently for water. The King replied, That he put out the candle that pity might not arrest his hand in the execution of justice, on a youth whom he tenderly loved; and that he had made a vow to God, when he first heard the complaint, that he would neither eat nor drink till he had brought the criminal to justice, in so much that he was upon the point of dying of thirst.

The learned men who flourished under Mamood.

The learned men who lived at the court of Mamood were principally these; Ozaeri Rasi, a native of Rai in Persia, whose poetical performances as a panegyrist are esteemed very good, for one of which he received a present of 4000 Dirms from Mamood.—Assidi Toosi, a native of the province of Chorassan, a poet of great fame, whom the Sultan often entreated to undertake the Shaw Namma, but he excused himself on account of his age. He was the master of Phirdoci, who afterwards undertook that work; but Phirdoci falling sick, by too much application, before it was finished, he applied himself to his old master Assidi; telling him, that he was now at the point of death, and that his only regret for leaving this

vain

A. D. 1028. Higer. 419. vain world was, that his poem was unfiniſhed. The old man weeping replied, that, though he had often excuſed himſelf to the King from having any hand in that performance, yet, for the affection he bore to Phirdoci, he would undertake to finiſh his poem. The dying poet replied, that he was well aſſured no other man of the age had the genius to attempt it; but at the ſame time he was afraid, years and infirmities had damped the native fire of Aſſidi. The old man, warmed with friendſhip and emulation, collecting the force of his mind, made the attempt, and brought into the chains of rhime, in a few days, that part of the poem, between the Arabian conqueſt of the weſtern Perſia, to the end, which conſiſts of four thouſand couplets. He immediately brought it to Phirdoci, who was ſo rejoiced that he recovered from his diſorder. The Shaw Namma is eſteemed among the firſt of poetical productions, and Phirdoci the author, conſequently among the firſt of poets.

Minuchere was a noble of Balich, and famous for his poetry and wit. But Ali Unſuri is eſteemed to hold the firſt rank, as to genius, in that age; for, beſides being one of the beſt poets, he was a great philoſopher, verſed in all the known ſciences and all the learned languages of thoſe times. Four hundred poets and learned men, beſides all the ſtudents of the univerſity of Ghizni, acknowledged him for their maſter. He was therefore appointed by the King to ſuperintend literature, and it was ordered, that no performance ſhould be brought before Mamood, without being previouſly honoured with the approbation of Ali Unſuri.

Among the works of Unſuri there is an heroic poem, upon the actions of Mamood. The King having one night, in his cups, cut off the long treſſes

treſſes of his beloved*, he was much afflicted in the morning for what he had done. He ſat, he roſe, he walked by turns, and there was a terror round him, which kept the people at diſtance. Ali Unſuri accoſted him with ſome extempore lines†, which ſo pleaſed the King, that he ordered his mouth to be filled three times with jewels. Calling then for wine, he ſat with the poet, and waſhed down his grief, ſeaſoning ſociety with wit. A. D. 1028. Higer. 419.

Asjuddi was one of the ſcholars of Unſuri: He was a native of Hirvi, a poet bleſſed with the light of true genius, but his works are very ſcarce, and the greateſt part of them loſt. Firochi was alſo a pupil of Unſuri. He was of the antient royal race of the kings of Seiſtan; but reduced by fortune ſo low, that he was obliged to hire himſelf to a farmer for the yearly wages of a hundred Dirms. When he married, he found this ſmall ſum would not anſwer his expences, ſo he became deſirous of having his wages increaſed. The farmer told him, he certainly deſerved a great deal more, but that his capacity could not extend the allowance further. Firochi, in this ſtate of dependence, waited on the Sultan's nephew, Abul Muziffir, with a poem, for which he was honoured with a handſome reward, with a horſe and a dreſs. He was introduced to the King by Muziffir, who ſettled a penſion upon him, which enabled him to ride with a retinue of twenty well mounted ſlaves.

* His favourite miſtreſs.

† The beauty of the lines conſiſted chiefly in a happy chime of words, which cannot poſſibly be imitated in a tranſlation. The ſenſe runs thus: On this happy day, when the treſſes of your beloved are cut off, what place is there for grief? Let it be rather crowned with mirth and wine, for the taper form of the cypreſs is beſt ſeen from the pruning of its branches.

A. D. 1028. Higer. 419. State of Asia at the death of Mamood.

Al Kader Billa kept up the title of Calipha, without any power, excepting in the city of Bagdâd and its territory, during the whole reign of Mamood. Elich Chan, king of Kasgar, by the extinction of the imperial family of Samania, possessed himself of the city of Bochara, and became sovereign of Maver-ul-nere or Transoxiana. Mamood added to the empire of Ghizni, to the west and north, Seistan, the Persian Iraac, Georgia, and, in general, all Persia, to the east of the small territory of the Caliphat. He dethroned and extinguished the family of Boia, who had held out for so many years their best provinces against the Caliphas of the house of Abas. On the side of India, he conquered and possessed all the provinces to the north-west of Delhi, all Sindia and Guzerat; and, by spreading his ravages further into that vast empire, rendered almost all its Rajas dependent upon his power. Mamood, in short, possessed a greater empire than any Mahommedan prince before his time in Asia. Almost all Persia was subject to him, the Oxus bounded his empire on the north-east side, and the mountains of Ajmere and Malava seem to have been on his frontiers on the south.

MAHOMMED

WHEN the hand of Mamood was ſhortened from worldly labour, his ſon Mahommed * was in the province of Gourgan, and the prince Muſaood in Iſpahan. Ali, the ſon of the famous Arſilla, the father-in-law of Mamood, called the prince Mahommed to Ghizni, and according to the will of his father placed the crown upon his head. Mahommed, upon his acceſſion, beſtowed the dignity of captain general upon his uncle Euſoph, the ſon of Subuctagi, and the honour of Vizier upon Abu Seil Ahummud; then opening the treaſury, he gladdened his friends and the public with liberal donations; but the hearts of the ſoldiery and people ran chiefly in favour of his brother Muſaood. A.D. 1028. Higer. 419. Mahommed the ſon of Mamood ſucceeds to the throne of Ghizni.

About fifty days after the death of Mamood, one of the nobles, by name Abul Nigim, having, in confederacy with Ali Dia, gained over the ſlaves†, they broke into the royal ſtables, and mounting the King's beſt horſes, rode off towards Buſt. The Emperor Mahommed informed of The ſlaves revolt,

* His titles are, Jellal ul Dowla, Jemmal ul Muluc, Sultan Mahommed, ben Sultan Mamood Ghiznavi.

† By the ſlaves mentioned in this place, and in the ſequel of this hiſtory, are meant the captives and young children bought by kings, and educated for the offices of ſtate. They were often adopted by the emperors, and very frequently ſucceeded to the empire. A whole dynaſty of them poſſeſſed afterwards the throne in Hindoſtan. We muſt not therefore conſider the word ſlave, which often occurs in this hiſtory, in the mean ſenſe which it carries in our language.

A. D. 1028. Higer. 419. this, immediately dispatched Subundraï, an Indian chief of trust, with a numerous body of Hindoo cavalry, in pursuit of them. He came up with the slaves in a few days; a skirmish ensued, in which Subundraï with the greatest part of his troops were killed, and not a few of the slaves. The surviving part of the rebels, with their two chiefs, pursued their journey to the prince Musaood, whom they met at Neshapoor, a city of the province of Chorassan. Musaood having heard of his father's decease at Hammedan in Persia*, settled viceroys and governors of trust in the Persian provinces of Irac Agemi, and hastened towards Chorassan. From thence he wrote to his brother, that he had no inclination to take those countries from him, which his father, notwithstanding his preferable right, had been pleased to bequeath to the prince Mahommed. He moreover added, that the regions of the Hills, Tiberistan and Erac, which he had mostly acquired with his own sword, were ample enough dominions for him. He only insisted so far on his birthright, as to have his name first read in the Chutba†, over all his dominions. The Prince Musaood is allowed to have been very moderate in this case, for though he and Mahommed were twins, he was the elder by some hours, and consequently had the undoubted right of succession.

and declare for Musaood.

Musaood writes to his brother.

War between the brothers.

But enmity had subsisted between the brothers from their youth, and Mahommed returned his brother, upon this occasion, a very unfriendly an-

* Hammedan is situated in the province of Irac, towards the frontiers of Curdistan. It is one of the principal cities of Persia, because it is in a manner the door by which every thing goes from Bagdad to Ispahan.

† The genealogy and titles of their kings read from the pulpit on all public occasions of worship, after the praise of the prophet.

swer,

ſwer, and began to prepare for war, in ſpite of all that his council could do to oppoſe ſo raſh a meaſure. He accordingly put his army in motion, and leaving Ghizni, proceeded to meet Muſaood: It is ſaid, that at the feaſt, upon the concluſion of the Ramzan which Mahommed held at Tunganabad, his crown fell accidentally from his head when he ſat in ſtate. This was reckoned a very unfortunate omen, of which ſome diſaffected chiefs taking advantage, eſtranged the minds of the ſoldiery from their prince. Accordingly upon the third night after, there was a confederacy formed by the noble Ali, Euſoph, the ſon of Subuctagi, uncle to the King, and Haſſnic Mical, who ſounding the trumpets to arms, put themſelves at the head of the troops, ſurrounded the King's tents, and ſeizing upon his perſon, ſent him priſoner to the fort of Chilligie. They immediately marched with the army to Herat, to meet the prince Muſoood, to whom they ſwore allegiance.

A.D. 1028. Higer. 419.

Mahommed depoſed.

Muſaood directed immediately his march to Balich, where he ordered Haſſnic to be executed, for having deſerted him before, and fled to the King of Egypt. There was alſo, it is ſaid, a private pique, which haſtened the death of Haſſnic, for he was in publick heard to ſay, that if ever Muſaood ſhould be King, he would ſuffer himſelf to be hanged. The noble Ali had his head ſtruck off for his ingratitude to his prince; and Euſoph, the ſon of the Emperor Subuctagi, the other conſpirator, and the King's uncle, was impriſoned for life. The eyes of the unfortunate Mahommed were put out, and he himſelf confined; ſo that the reign of Mahommed ſcarcely laſted five months. But, as we ſhall hereafter ſee, he was, after nine years impriſonment, bleſſed with one more ray of bright fortune.

Muſaood ſucceeds.

The conſpirators puniſhed.

MUSAOOD I.

A. D. 1029. Higer. 419. Musaood's great strength.

MUSAOOD * was a man of a lofty spirit, and was honoured with the appellation of Rustum the second. His arrow could pierce the strongest mail, and sink into the body of an elephant, and his iron mace was so ponderous, that no man of his time could raise it with one hand. He was withal, of an obstinate and fierce disposition, contemptuous of all authority, and disdaining all obedience. This circumstance, in his youth, engaged him in many quarrels, and greatly disobliged his father; who, for that reason, fixed his affections upon his brother, the prince Mahommed, who was of a more mild and tractable disposition.

His fierce disposition.

Anecdote concerning Musaood.

Abu Niser Muscati relates, that when the name of Mahommed was inserted before that of Musaood in the Chutba, and read in public for the first time, that he himself followed Musaood to the door of the mosque, and told him, that what he had heard, gave him the utmost concern, for that his own, as well as the hearts of most of the nobles, burnt with affection for him. The prince replied with a smile, Give yourselves no concern about it; the world is for the longest sword. One of the King's spies, hearing this conversation, immediately gave information of it to his father. Mamood immediately calling Abu Niser, asked him what had passed between him and the prince

* His titles were Shahab ul Dowla, Jemmal ul Muluck, Sultan Musaood, ben Sultan Mamood Ghiznavi.

Musaood.

Muſaood. Abu Niſer, thinking that truth would be his beſt defence, related the particulars. Upon which the King ſaid, that he had always a high opinion of the ſuperior abilities of Muſaood, who, he foreſaw, would one day be King; but that the prince Mahommed had gained his heart, by filial duty and implicit obedience. A.D. 1031. Higer. 422.

Muſaood, upon his acceſſion, releaſed Ahummud, the ſon of Haſſen Mumundi, who, by the orders of the Emperor Mamood, had been impriſoned in the fort of Callinger, and again made him Vizier. He called the noble Ahummud, the ſon of Mealtagi, the treaſurer, to a ſtrict account, and after having obliged him to refund a great ſum for malpractices in his office, appointed him general of all his forces in Hindoſtan, and ordered him to proceed to Lahore. He, at the ſame time, releaſed Willamï, who had alſo been impriſoned in one of the forts of Hindoſtan, and called him to his court. Muſaood releaſes ſeveral priſoners of ſtate.

The King, in the year 422, having left Balich, came to Ghizni, and ſent an army to Kutch and Mackeran, the maritime provinces of Perſia, and the coin of both provinces was ſtruck in his name. The prince of thoſe countries died about that time, and left two ſons, Aſakir and Iſah.—Iſah, the younger brother, taking poſſeſſion of the government, Aſakir had recourſe for aid, to regain his inheritance, to the Emperor Muſaood, to whom the fugitive prince promiſed an annual tribute, and to hold his dominions, when recovered, of him. Muſaood agreeing to this propoſal, ſent a great army with Aſakir, with orders to his general, if poſſible, to reconcile the difference between the brothers, and to divide the country equally between them; but if this could not be done, to put the whole into the poſſeſſion of Aſakir. Aſakir arrived upon the frontiers, with this powerful army, Invades Kutch and Mackeran, which are reduced.

A.D. 1031. Higer. 422. army, but ſo obſtinate was his brother, and ſo much devoted to his own ruin, that he would not be brought to liſten to any accommodation; and though he was deſerted by many of his friends, who joined his brother, he determined to decide the affair with his ſword. He accordingly fought with great bravery, till he obtained that death he ſeemed ſo eagerly to purſue. The provinces fell into the hands of Aſakir, who paid tribute and allegiance to the empire.

Maſh made governor of Raï in Perſia. Muſaood, in the ſame year, beſtowed the vice-royſhip of Raï in Perſia, of Hammedan, and of all the regions of the hills, upon Maſh, a man who, though he had raiſed himſelf from the loweſt office in the camp, diſplayed uncommon abilities in reducing thoſe provinces to obedience. After the departure of the King, the countries which we have juſt mentioned revolted in part, but Maſh not only reduced them to their former dependence, but chaſtiſed Ali ul Dowla, the Ghiznian governor of Chorаſſan, who had been tampering with the rebels.

Unſucceſsful war with the Turkumans. Muſaood, after having ſettled affairs at Ghizni, intended to march to Iſpahan * and Raï. But when he arrived at Herat, the people of Sirchus and Badwird complained to him of the ravages of the famous Tartar tribe of Siljoki Turkumans. The King, moved by the injuries done to his ſubjects, was incenſed very much againſt the enemy, and therefore immediately ordered Abduſe, the ſon of Adiz, a brave general, with a great force, to chaſtiſe them. This officer, however,

* Iſpahan is not only the capital of Irac, but of all Perſia. It was, till the commotions after the death of Nadir Shaw in 1747, a very large town, ſurrounded with a brick wall, and drove a great trade in ſilks and other commodities. It ſuffered ſo much in the late troubles in Perſia, that Kerim Chan, the preſent Emperor, has removed his court to Schiraz.

was

was received by the Turkumans with ſo much bravery, that he could gain no advantages over them; and the King, for what reaſon is not known, returned to Ghizni. A.D. 1032. Higer. 424.

In the year 423, the King diſpatched Altaſaſh, who governed Charizm, under the regal title of Viceroy, with a great army, to oppoſe Ali Tiggi, the Uſbec Tartar, who had invaded and conquered Samarcand and Bochara. Altaſaſh marched to Maver-ul-nere, or the country beyond the Amu*, where fifteen thouſand horſe were ordered to join him from Ghizni. After this junction was effected, he croſſed the river Amavia, in the face of the enemy, and continued his rout to Bochara, which he reduced, and then proceeded to Samarcand. Ali Tiggi marched out of the city, and took poſſeſſion of a ſtrong poſt, having the river on one ſide and a high mountain on the other. When the battle begun, a party of Ali Tiggi's horſe, having turned the mountain, attacked the army of Altaſaſh in the rear. A great ſlaughter commenced, and the Ghiznian commander was wounded, in a part of the body in which he had formerly received a wound in taking one of the forts of Hindoſtan. He however concealed his blood from his army, and charged the enemy with ſuch vigour, in his front and rear, that, after an obſtinate and bloody conflict, they were at length put to flight. War with Ali Tiggi. Bochara reduced. Ali Tiggi overthrown by Altaſaſh,

When the battle was over, Altaſaſh called a council of his principal officers, and ſhewing his wound, told them his end was approaching, and that they muſt now manage affairs in the beſt manner they could, intimating at the ſame time, that he thought they could do nothing better than conclude a peace with the enemy. This motion who dies of his wounds.

* Tranſoxiana.

being

A.D. 1032. Higer. 424. being approved, a meſſenger was diſpatched to them, that very night, with propoſals, which were eagerly accepted. The conditions were, that Ali Tiggi ſhould keep poſſeſſion of Samarcand, and that Bochara ſhould remain to Muſaood. The two armies, immediately after this pacification, departed, the one for Samarcand, and the other for Chorasſan. The brave Altaſaſh died the ſecond day after, but his death was concealed from the army, and the chiefs conducted the troops to Charizm: And when theſe accounts came to the King, he conferred the government upon Haro, the ſon of Altaſaſh.

Muſaood invades Hindoſtan. The Vizier, Ahmed, the ſon of Haſſen Mumundi, dying this year, Muſaood appointed Abu Niſer Ahmid to ſucceed him in his office. In the 424th of the Higera, the King reſolved upon an expedition into India. Taking the route of Caſhmire, he inveſted the fort of Surſutti, which commanded the paſſes. The garriſon being intimidated, ſent meſſengers to the King, promiſing valuable preſents and an annual tribute, if he ſhould deſiſt from his enterprize. Muſaood began to liſten to the propoſals, when his ears were ſtunned with a grievous complaint from ſome Muſſulmen captives, who were then detained in the place. He immediately broke up the conference, and began to beſiege the fort, ordering the ditch to be filled up with Sugarcanes, from the adjacent plantations. This being done, he ordered ſcaling ladders to be applied to the walls, which, after a bloody conteſt, were mounted, and the garriſon, without diſtinction of age or ſex, barbarouſly put to the ſword, excepting a few women and children, who were protected by the ſoldiers for ſlaves. The King commanded, that what part of the ſpoil was ſaved from pillage, ſhould be given to the Muſſulmen who had been

ſlaves

ſlaves in Surſutti, and who had formerly loſt their effects. This year was remarkable for a great drought and famine, in many parts of the world. The famine was ſucceeded by a calamitous peſtilence, which ſwept many thouſands from the face of the earth; for in leſs than one month forty thouſand died in Iſpahan alone. Nor did it rage with leſs violence in Hindoſtan, where whole countries were entirely depopulated.

A. D. 1032. Higer. 424. A famine and peſtilence.

The King of Ghizni, in the mean time, was obliged to march back to quell ſome diſturbances in Tibiriſtan, one of the Perſian provinces, now forming a part of the Ghiznian empire. The inhabitants of Amaliſar oppoſed him in his progreſs, but they were diſperſed by the imperial troops with little oppoſition, and Callingar, prince of Tibiriſtan, ſent an ambaſſador, and ſubjected himſelf and his country to the King. He, at the ſame time, gave his ſon Bhamin, and his nephew Shirvi, as hoſtages, for his future good behaviour. Muſaood turned from thence his face towards Ghizni; and when he arrived at Neſhapoor, the capital of Choraſſan, the people of that place again complained of the incurſions of the Tartar tribe of Siljoki, and he immediately diſpatched Buctadi, and Huſſein the ſon of Ali, with a great force to chaſtiſe them. When the Ghiznian army reached the village of Seindenſauk, a meſſenger came from the Turkumans with a letter, to the following purpoſe: "That they were the King's ſervants, and not at all deſirous to diſturb any body but his enemies, if they ſhould be enabled, by any annual ſubſidy, to live at home without plunder, or led out to war, that they might exert their ſkill in what they reckoned their only profeſſion." The anſwer of Buctadi was very haughty. "There is no peace, ſays he, between us, but the ſword, unleſs you will give over your depredations, and

Diſturbances in Tibiriſtan.

War with the Turkumans,

who are defeated by Buctadi,

ſubmit

A.D. 1034. Higer. 426. submit yourselves implicitly to the laws and authority of the King." After the Tartars had heard this message from their ambassador, they advanced and made a violent assault upon the camp of Buctadi; but as they were conducted more by rage than conduct, they were repulsed, and obliged to turn their backs upon the honours of the field. Buctadi, pursuing them with great expedition, took all their baggage, and their wives and children.

whom in another battle, they overthrow. But when Buctadi was returning from the pursuit, while yet many of his troops were dispersed and intent upon the plunder, the Siljoki issued out from between two hills, and, rendered desperate by their former loss, made a dreadful slaughter among the troops, who could not be regularly brought up to the charge. The Ghiznians continued to fight and retreat for two days and nights, but Hussein, the son of Ali, could not be persuaded to quit the field, so that after the most of his men were killed, he himself fell a prisoner into the hands of the enemy. Buctadi fled, and carried advice of his own defeat to the King at Neshapoor.

Disturbances in Hindostan. Musaood was obliged for that time to restrain his resentment, upon account of some disturbances in India. He marched back to Ghizni, in the year 426; and thence sent an army under Ban, an Indian chief, against Ahmud, who had rebelled in his government. But, when the two armies met, The rebels defeated. Ban was defeated with great slaughter. Musaood being informed of this disaster, sent Touluck, another Indian chief, who, coming to battle with Ahmud, gave him a total overthrow. He fled in Their great distress. great haste towards Munsura, Tatta, and the country near the mouth of the Indus. Touluck pursued him so close, that many thousands of the runaways fell into his hands; whom he treated in the

the moſt inhuman manner, cutting off their noſes and ears. When Ahmud reached the banks of the Indus, he found himſelf, if poſſible, in greater diſtreſs than before; for collecting all the boats, which the preſſure of the enemy would permit, he endeavoured to croſs the river. But the ſoldiers, afraid of being abandoned, hurried into the boats with ſuch violence, and in ſuch numbers, that moſt of them were either overſet or ſunk. A ſudden ſtorm, and an inundation of the river, added to the confuſion of the vanquiſhed; ſo that very few of them eſcaped. The body of their chief was ſoon after found by the enemy, and his head ſent to Ghizni. A.D. 1035. Higer. 427.

A new palace being finiſhed in the year 427 at Ghizni, a golden throne, ſtudded with jewels, was erected in a magnificent hall, and a crown of gold, weighing ſeventy maunds*, darting luſtre from its precious ſtones, ſuſpended by a golden chain over it, by way of canopy, under which the King ſat in ſtate, and gave public audience. He in the ſame year conferred the enſigns and drums of royalty upon his ſon the prince Modood, and ſent him to the government of Balich, whilſt he himſelf marched with an army to India to reduce the ſtrong city of Haſſi. This city was the capital of Sewalic, a country towards the head of the Ganges, and was, by the Hindoos, reckoned impregnable; for they were taught to believe, by ſome of their prophets, that it ſhould never fall into the hands of the Muſſulmen. But the Indian prophets, like thoſe of other nations, deceived their followers; for the King, in the ſpace of ſix

A new palace built at Ghizni.

Muſaood invades Hindoſtan.

* The leaſt maund in India is that of Surat, which weighs thirty-ſeven pounds five ounces and ſeven drachms avoirdupoize; by which we may conjecture, that the value of this crown was immenſe.

days,

A.D. 1036. Higer. 428. days, though with a very conſiderable loſs on his ſide, ſcaled the place and took it. He found immenſe treaſures in Haſſi; and having put it into the hands of a truſty ſervant, he marched towards the fort of Sunput. Deipal, the governor of Sunput, evacuated the place, and fled into the woods; but he had no time to carry off his treaſure, which fell into the conqueror's hands. Muſaood ordered all the temples to be laid in ruins, and all the idols to be broke down.

Muſaood ſurpriſes Deipal.

Muſaood proceeded from thence in purſuit of Deipal, who began to ſhew himſelf in the field; but he was ſurprized by the King, and all his army taken priſoners, while he himſelf eſcaped in the habit of a ſlave. Muſaood marched from thence towards Ram, another prince of thoſe parts, who, upon receiving intelligence of the King's intentions, ſent immenſe preſents of gold and elephants, excuſing himſelf, on account of his age, from perſonally attending upon Muſaood. The King received his preſents and excuſe, and withheld his hand from giving him any farther moleſtation; then leaving a truſty chief in Sunput*, he took poſſeſſion of all the countries in his rear, intending to return to Ghizni. When he reached Lahore, he left there his ſon Mugdood, on whom he conferred the government of that famous city and province, and the drums and enſigns of ſtate, with Eur, his favourite, to be his counſellor in matters of importance.

Marches to Balich.

In the year 428 Muſaood again marched to Balich, to quell the tumults raiſed by the reſtleſs tribe of Siljoki Tartars, who, upon hearing of the King's approach, evacuated that country. The inhabitants of that province addreſſed Mu-

* Forty miles from Delhi, on the road to Lahore.

ſaood,

ſaood, and acquainted him that Tiggi the Tartar, after his departure, had made divers incurſions into their territories, and croſſing the river, had lengthened his hands upon the lives and effects of his ſubjects. The King determined therefore to chaſtiſe him that winter, and, in the beginning of the ſpring, to bring the other Siljoki to a better underſtanding. The Omrahs of his court, with one accord, adviſed him to march firſt againſt the Siljoki, becauſe they had, for two years, gained an aſcendancy over the inhabitants of Choraſſan, and were daily acquiring ſtrength. Muſaood, at that time, received alſo a letter from one of the nobles of that province, acquainting him, that his enemies, who were once but Ants, were now become little Snakes, and, if they were not ſoon deſtroyed, they might grow in a ſhort time to Serpents. A.D. 1038. Higer. 430.

But the ſtar of the King's fortune had now reached the houſe of adverſity, and he would not by any means hearken to their advice. In hopes to conquer the country before him, he laid a bridge over the Gion*, and croſſing his army without oppoſition, took poſſeſſion of the whole province of Maver-ul-nere†. But, during that winter, ſuch a quantity of ſnow fell, that it was with the greateſt difficulty he marched back his army towards Ghizni. In the mean time, Daood‡, prince of the Siljoki, marched with an army againſt Balich, from whence Amud, the governor, wrote to the King the particulars, begging, as he had not a ſufficient force to oppoſe the enemy, that he would take ſome meaſures to reinforce him. Muſaood upon this turned his army towards Balich. The good fortune of Muſaood declines.

* The Oxus. † Tranſoxiana.

‡ He was brother to the famous Torgril-Beg, firſt of the dynaſty of the Seljukedes of Perſia.

Tiggi,

A. D. 1038. Higer. 430. Ghizni pillaged.

Tiggi, the other moſt capital man among the Siljoki, taking this advantage, marched quickly to Ghizni, where he plundered the King's ſtables, and, after having greatly diſhonoured the capital, he was repulſed. When Muſaood reached the confines of Balich, Daood retreated towards Murve, upon which the King, in conjunction with his ſon Modood, ſet out in purſuit of him to Gurgan. When the Siljoki heard of the motion of the Ghiznians towards Murve, they ſent an ambaſſador, profeſſing obedience and loyalty, if the King would beſtow a track of country upon them, in which they might ſettle. He, conſenting to this propoſal, ſent a meſſenger to their reigning prince, whoſe name was Pugu, to come and ſettle the treaty, which accordingly he did, and the King, upon promiſe of their future good behaviour, alienated a large territory for their maintenance.

Peace with the Siljoki.

Their perfidy.

Muſaood, after this treaty, turned with his army towards Herat; but ſuch was the infidelity of thoſe ravagers, that they attacked the rear of the King's army, carrying off part of his baggage, and ſlaying a number of his attendants. Incenſed at this behaviour, he ſent a detachment in purſuit of them, who took a ſmall party of them priſoners, and brought them to his feet. He immediately ordered their heads to be cut off and ſent to Pugu, who excuſed himſelf, ſaying, that for his part he was glad they had met with their deſerts, for he had no knowledge of their proceedings.

Muſaood takes the rout of Herat;

Muſaood continued his march to Herat, from Herat to Neſhapoor, and from thence to Toos. At Toos he was attacked by another tribe of the Siljoki, whom he defeated with great ſlaughter. In the mean time he received intelligence, that the inhabitants of Badwird had given up their forts to the Siljoki. He marched immediately againſt

against them, retook the forts, and cleared that country of the enemy. He then returned to Neshapoor, the capital of Chorassan, where he spent the winter, and in the spring of the year 430, he again returned to Badwird, which had been infested in his absence by Toghril, a prince among the Siljoki; who fled upon the Sultan's approach towards Tizin. Musaood, after this exploit, returned by the way of Sirchus, whose inhabitants had refused to pay their taxes: But upon some of their chiefs being put to death, they became more tractable; and upon their submission the King continued his march to Dindaka. A.D. 1038. Higer. 430.

The Siljoki, collecting their forces at Dindaka, surrounded the King's army, securing the passes upon every side: Musaood, to bring them to an engagement, drew out his army in order of battle, which the enemy by no means declined, advancing upon all quarters with barbarous shouts and great impetuosity. This uncommon method of charging discouraged the Ghiznian troops; and whether thro' fear or perfidy, several generals, in the beginning of the action, rode off with their whole squadrons, and joined the enemy. The King, enraged at this treachery, and seeing his affairs in a desperate situation, addressed himself in a few words to his friends about him. He told them, that their own safety, their long acquired honour, the glory of their King, and the security of their native country, now depended upon one noble effort to revenge themselves upon their enemies, and those still greater enemies, who had so basely deserted their cause. His army surrounded by the Siljoki.

Musaood then turning his horse to where he beheld the torrent of gleaming arms rolling on, plunged singly to oppose the stream, bearing down all before him, and exhibiting such acts of gigantic force and valour, as never king had before displayed. His valour.

A.D. 1041. Higer. 433. played. A few of his friends, rouzed by his words and actions, and that innate honour which inspires the brave, seconded their Lord so well, that whithersoever he turned his fatal sword, the enemy were mowed down, or retreated before him. But now, when victory seemed to blow on his standard, misfortune was active behind it; for when he looked round he beheld almost his whole army, excepting that body he commanded in person, devouring the paths of flight. The King, seeing himself thus shamefully deserted, and that no hope from his single arm remained, turned his steed, and trampling down the enemy, opened to himself a clear passage with his own sword. When he reached the river near Murve, he met with a few of the fugitives, who now began to collect themselves from all quarters. He took from thence the way of Ghor, and proceeded to Ghizni. There he seized upon the generals who had so ingloriously deserted him. He ordered Ali Daia, Buctadi and Sab Sinai, to be conveyed to Hindostan, and confined in a certain fort for life.

His army deserts him.

He opens a passage for himself thro' the enemy;

punishes the deserters.

He retreats to India.

The King, finding himself, at this period, unable to withstand the enemy, resolved to withdraw to India, till he could collect his forces, and make another effort to retrieve his affairs. He left his son Modood, and his Vizier, with four thousand horse, to defend Balich, and ordered his other son the prince Mugdood, who had come from Lahore with two thousand horse, to secure Moultan. In the mean time Erid, another of his sons, was sent with a detachment to awe the mountain Afghans, near Ghizni, who were in arms. He then collected all his wealth from the different strong holds to Ghizni, and laying it upon camels, bent his way to Lahore, sending for his brother Mahommed, who had been dethroned and blinded from his confinement.

When

When Musaood arrived upon the banks of the Gelum, the water of which, on account of its purity, is called the water of Paradise, the slaves, who were very numerous in his camp, entered into a confederacy with the camel-keepers, and began to divide the treasure among them. The troops observing this, they were determined to partake of the spoil, so that in a moment nothing was to be seen but drawn swords, ravage, and confusion. Every one plundered his neighbour; some gained much wealth, while others, more weak or unfortunate, were robbed of all upon which they had laid their hands, and stripped of their own besides. The army, for this tumult, fearing the resentment of the King, and not chusing to refund the plunder, hastened in a mob to Mahommed the blind, who had been before king, and, exalting him upon their shoulders, proclaimed him Emperor.

A.D. 1041. Higer. 433. A tumult in the camp.

Mahommed proclaimed King.

Musaood was, during this time, collecting what friends he could to suppress the mutiny; but no sooner was it known that his brother was proclaimed King, than he found himself intirely deserted. The mob pressing round him, he was obliged to give himself up into their hands, and he was carried before the new King. Mahommed told him, he had no design to take his life, and desired he might pitch upon some fort, whiher he might retire with his family into confinement. Musaood, in this extremity, chose the fort of Kurri, but was even in distress for money to pay his few menial attendants. This obliged him to send a person to his brother to request him for some. Mahommed accordingly ordered the pitiful sum of five hundred dirms to be sent him; upon which Musaood, when it was brought him, exclaimed after the following manner: "O wonderful cast of Providence! O cruel reverse of fate! Yesterday was I not a mighty prince; three thousand

Musaood deposed

A. D. 1041. Higer. 433. camels bending under my treaſure? To-day I am forced to beg, and to receive but the mere mockery of my wants." With that he borrowed a thouſand dirms from his ſervants, and beſtowed it in a preſent upon his brother's meſſenger, who had brought the five hundred dirms, which he deſired he might again carry back to his maſter.

and aſſaſſinated. Mahommed, upon his acceſſion, advanced his ſon Ahmed to the government, reſerving for himſelf only the name, though Ahmed was, by many, ſuppoſed to have a tincture of madneſs in his diſpoſition. The firſt thing he did was, without conſulting his father, in conjunction with his couſin Soliman the ſon of Euſoph, and the ſon of Ali Cheſhawind, to go to the caſtle of Kurri, and aſſaſſinate Muſaood, in the year 433. But ſome affirm, that he buried him alive in a well. The reign of Muſaood was nine years and nine months.

His character. He was a prince of uncommon ſtrength and bravery; affable, of eaſy acceſs, and generous to prodigality; particularly to learned men, of whoſe company he was exceſſively fond, which drew many from all parts to his court.

Among the firſt of the learned in the court of Muſaood, we muſt reckon Abu Keihan of Chariſm, a great philoſopher and aſtrologer, who wrote one of the beſt treatiſes upon aſtronomy, called Canoon Muſaoodi, for which he was preſented with an elephant made of ſilver, the ſize of which we are not told. Abu Mahommed Naſahi was alſo a man of much reputation in this age. He wrote a book called Muſaoodi, in ſupport of the doctrine of Abu Hanifa, which he preſented to the King. The author of the Roſit ul Suffa tells us, that ſo extenſive was the King's charity, that ſome days, in the month of Ramzan, he beſtowed often a lack of dirms upon the poor. In the beginning of his reign, he built many noble

Charitable.

Magnificent.

moſques,

moſques, and endowed many colleges and ſchools, which he erected in different cities of his dominions. A.D. 1041. Higer. 433.

Muſaood was far from being ſo fortunate as his father Mamood. Al Kader Billa reigned with the title of Calipha in Bagdad and its territory: A branch of the family of Boia were ſovereigns of Perſia Proper, Kerman or the ancient Caramania, Meſopotamia, and the Arabian Irac. The Siljoki Tartars, having, in a courſe of depredatory expeditions, ravaged and conquered the vaſt country of Maver-ul-nere, or Tranſoxiana, paſſed the Oxus in the reign of Muſaood, defeated him in many battles, and ſtripping him of Choraſſan and all the Perſian conqueſts of his father, founded, under their chief, Trogrilbeg, the famous dynaſty of the Siljokies. The dominions of Ghizni became very much contracted to the north, conſiſting only of the provinces of Seiſtan, Zabuliſtan and Cabul, to the north-weſt of the Hydaſpes. The boundaries of the empire, on the ſide of India, ſuffered no change in this reign. State of Aſia at the death of Muſaood.

MODOOD.

A. D. 1041. Higer. 433. Mahommed grieves for the death of Musaood.

WHEN the news of the murder of Musaood came to Mahommed the blind, he wept bitterly, and severely reproached the assassins. He, at the same time, wrote to the prince Modood, who was then at Balich, that such and such people had killed his father; calling God to witness, that his hands were clear of the wicked deed. To this Modood* replied, sarcastically: May God lengthen the days of so good and so merciful a King, and grant that his mad son, Ahmed, may gain glory in the practice of regicide, till his reward be obtained from our hands. Modood was for marching immediately, to revenge the death of his father; but he was persuaded by his council, to go first to Ghizni; where the citizens, upon his approach, thronged out to meet him, and expressed their joy in acclamations and congratulations upon his accession.

Modood ascends the throne of Ghizni.

Marches to revenge the death of his father.

In the year 433, he marched from Ghizni; while Mahommed the blind, appointing his younger son Nami, governor of Peshawir and Moultan, marched in person to the banks of the Indus to receive Mamood, who was moving that way, and the two armies meeting in the forest of Diner, between the uncle and nephew, the flames of con-

* His titles are, Abul Fatte, Cuttub ul Muluc, Shahab ul Muluc, Shahâb ul Dowla, Amir Modood ben Musaood, ben Mamood Ghiznavi, the son of the Victorious, the Pole-star of the Empire, the Light of Fortune, the Lord MODOOD son of Musaood, the son of Mamood of Ghizni.

tention

tention began to arise. The gales of victory, at length, began to fan the standards of Modood, while Mahommed, with his sons, and Ali Chesha-wind, and Soliman the son of Eusoph, were taken prisoners. They were all put to death, except Abdul Rahim, the son of Mahommed, whom Modood pardoned for this reason; that during the time that his father Musaood was prisoner, Abdul Rahim went with his brother Reiman to see him. When, upon this occasion, the latter insultingly threw off Musaood's royal cap, Rahim took it up, and put it upon the King's head with much respect, chastising his brother for his mean and barbarous behaviour. A.D. 1041 Higer. 433. Totally defeats Mahommed.

Modood having thus revenged his father's murder, built a town on the spot upon which he had obtained the victory, and called it the victorious city*. He carried the remains of his father and family to be interred at Ghizni; whither he returned, and appointed Ahmed his Vizier. But he soon after discharged that chief from his high office, and conferred the dignity upon Chaja Tahir. He sent, at the same time, Ahmed with a force to Moultan, against Nami, the son of his uncle Mahommed, whom he slew, reducing the country under the obedience of Modood. The King had now nothing to fear but from his own brother, who was in possession of Lahore and its dependencies. This brother, upon the murder of his father, marched from Moultan, and by the counsel of Eas, possessed himself of all the country lying between the Indus, Hassi and Tannasar.

Modood finding that his brother refused to pay him allegiance, ordered an army against him. Mugdood being apprised of this expedition, marched from Hassi, where he then resided, with his whole Modood sends an army against his brother,

* Fatte-Abad.

force,

A.D. 1043. Higer. 435. force, to oppoſe the imperial troops. He came up with them before they reached Lahore, with an army ſo numerous, that the forces of Modood were upon the point of flying at their appearance, ſeveral of the chiefs deſerting their colours, and enliſting themſelves under the banners of Mugdood. But fortune here, or treachery, befriended Modood. In the morning of the ide of ſacrifice, Mugdood was found dead in his bed, without any previous complaint, or apparent cauſe of his diſeaſe. But what ſeemed to diſcover the hand of traitors, was, that next day, his counſellor and friend Eas was found dead in the ſame manner. Mugdood's army marched under the banners of Modood, ſo that the ſouthern countries ſubmitted in peace. Nor was Modood leſs fortunate towards the north. The province of Maver-ul-nere, which had for ſome time aſſerted its independance, ſubmitted. But the Siljokies, notwithſtanding the King had taken one of the daughters of their chief in marriage, began to make incurſions anew into his territories.

who is found dead in his bed.

Invaſion from Delhi.

In the year 435, the prince of Delhi, in alliance with others, raiſing an army, took Haſſi, Tannaſar, and their dependencies, from the governors to whom Modood had entruſted them. The Hindoos from thence marched towards the fort of Nagracut, which they beſieged for four months, and the garriſon being diſtreſſed for proviſions, and no ſuccours coming from Lahore, were under the neceſſity of capitulating. The Hindoos, according to the antient form, erected new idols, and recommenced the rites of idolatry. We are told that the prince of Delhi, obſerving a weakneſs in the empire of Ghizni, pretended to have ſeen a viſion, in which the great idol of Nagracut told him, that having now revenged himſelf upon Ghizni, he would meet him at Nagra-

A pretended viſion.

cut

cut in his former temple. This ſtory being propagated by the Brahmins, who probably were in the ſecret, it gained faith among the ſuperſtitious, by which means the Raja was joined by zealots from all parts, and ſoon ſaw himſelf at the head of a very numerous army. With this army, as we have already mentioned, he beſieged Nagracut, and when the place ſurrendered, he took care to have an idol, of the ſame ſhape and ſize with the former, which he had cauſed to be made at Delhi, introduced, in the night, into a garden in the center of the place. This image being diſcovered in the morning, there was a prodigious rejoicing among his deluded votaries, who exclaimed, that their God was returned from Ghizni. The Raja, and the Brahmins, taking the advantage of the credulity of the populace, with great pomp and feſtivity, carried him into the temple, where he received the worſhip and congratulations of his people. The ſtory raiſed ſo much the fame of the idol, that thouſands came daily to worſhip from all parts of Hindoſtan, as alſo to conſult him as an oracle, upon all important occaſions. The manner of conſultation was this: the perſons who came to inquire into futurity, ſlept on the floor of the temple before him, after drinking a doſe of ſomething which the Brahmins preſcribed, to create dreams, from which they predicted their fortune, in the morning, according to their own fancy.

A. D. 1043. Higer. 435.

A holy trick.

The ſucceſs of the prince of Delhi gave ſuch confidence to the Indian chiefs of Punjaab, or the province about the five branches of the Indus, and other places, that though before, like foxes, they durſt hardly creep from their holes, for fear of the Muſſulman arms, yet now they put on the aſpect of lions, and openly ſet their maſters at defiance. Three of thoſe Rajas, with ten thouſand

The ſiege of Lahore.

A.D. 1044. Higer. 436. ſand horſe, and an innumerable army of foot, advanced to Lahore, and inveſted it. The Muſſulmen, in defence of their laws, families, and effects, exerted all imaginable valour upon this occaſion, during the ſpace of ſeven months, defending the town, ſtreet by ſtreet; for the walls being bad, were ſoon laid in ruins. Finding, however, that in the end, they muſt be rooted out by this defenſive war, unleſs they had ſpeedy ſuccours, they bound themſelves by oath, to devote their lives to victory or martyrdom, and making a ſally out of the city, preſented themſelves, in order of battle, before the enemy's camp. The Hindoos, either ſtruck with their unexpected appearance, or intimidated by their reſolution, betook themſelves inſtantly to flight, and were purſued with great ſlaughter.

In the year preceding this event, the King ſent Artagi Hajib, with an army, to Tiberiſtan, againſt the ever-reſtleſs Siljoki. When he reached that place, he heard that the ſon of Daood had advanced to Arkin; but when the two armies drew up in order againſt one another, the chief of the Siljoki, who was a young man, without either experience or courage, ſhewed ſuch puſillanimity in arranging his troops, that the enemy had begun the charge before they were properly formed, which occaſioned an immediate confuſion, ſo that they abandoned the field, and were purſued with great ſlaughter. Artagi, having returned from the purſuit, marched directly to Balich, which the Siljoki had taken, and recovered that city out of their hands. Not long after, the Siljoki advanced again with a powerful force, and inveſted the ſame place. As it was not very defenſible, and Artagi was too weak to engage the enemy in the field, he wrote to Modood for ſuccours. The ſuccours not arriving, and the general finding his difficulties daily increaſing,

The Turkumans defeated.

increasing, and his force diminishing, determined to evacuate the place, which he accordingly did, and fled to Ghizni, with a few of his attendants. But the popular outcry was so great against the unfortunate Artagi, that Modood was obliged, in some measure, to silence the clamour by the death of his servant. About this time, another tribe of the Turkumans of Ghizizi made an incursion into the Ghiznian territories, by the way of Bust, against whom Modood sent an army, which gave them a signal defeat.

A.D. 1046. Higer. 438.

Artagi Hajib put to death.

In the year 436, Tahir the vizier was deposed, and Abdul Rysaac was exalted to that dignity; and, in the same year, Tughril was sent, with a force, towards Bust, from whence he proceeded to Seistan, and brought his own brother, and Ringi, who had rebelled against the King, prisoners to Ghizni. The Siljoki, in the year following, collected all their forces, and directed their march towards Ghizni, plundering the palace of Bust. Tughril was ordered against them, with the troops of Ghizni, and he defeated them with great slaughter, and pursued them out of the country. After this victory Tughril marched immediately against the Turkumans of Candahar, whom they called *red-caps*, and defeating them also, took many prisoners, whom he brought to Ghizni.

The Turkumans repeatedly defeated.

In the 438th year, Tughril was again ordered to Bust, with a numerous army; but when he came to Tiggiabad, he began to hatch treason against his sovereign. News of his revolt having reached Modood, he sent some persons to endeavour to reclaim him to his duty, with promises of pardon, and a removal of all the disgusts which he might have entertained. To this Tughril replied, that the reason of this step was to secure himself: That he had an information of a plot formed against his life, by those sycophants, whose only business was to

Tughril revolts.

A.D. 1046. Higer. 438. to ſtand by the throne, and to amuſe the too eaſy ears of the King with lies and flattery: That being once forced to diſobedience, he had, for a ſubject, gone too far to retreat. The King's emiſſaries however, though they had no effect upon Tughril, found that the moſt part of the chiefs were ſtill loyal to the King, and brought over others, who had changed, rather out of a deſire of innovation, than diſaffection to their ſovereign. Upon this they returned, and having told the King in what manner things were concerted with the other chiefs, he immediately ordered Ali the ſon of Ribbi, one of his generals, with two thouſand horſe, to favour the inſurrection: ſo that Tughril, finding himſelf deſerted by the army, upon the appearance of Ali, betook himſelf to flight, with a few of his adherents.

Willidingi Tiggi, another Omrah, was in the ſame year ſent to Ghor, to the aſſiſtance of Willidingi, who, joining him with his force, they both marched againſt Abu Ali, prince of Ghor, and having driven him into a fort, he was there beſieged, and taken priſoner. This place was reckoned ſo ſtrong, that, for ſeven hundred years before, the reduction of it had not been attempted by any body. When Tiggi found himſelf maſter of the fort, he treacherouſly laid hands upon Willidingi, whoſe right he came to ſupport, and carried him in basely put to death. chains, with Abu Ali, to Ghizni, where the King ſettled their diſpute, by cutting off both their heads. Tiggi was ſent, ſoon after, againſt Byram Neal, general of the Siljoki. He met the enemy in the diſtricts of Buſt, and engaged them, gaining, at length, the long diſputed field. He was again, in the year 439, ſent againſt Kiſdar, who refuſed to pay his tribute, whom he ſubdued, and obliged to comply with the King's commands, and returned

returned with his army to Ghizni the year following. A.D. 1047. Higer. 439.

Modood, the following year, in one day, conferred the royal drefs, drums and colours, upon his two eldeft fons, Mamood, whom he fent to Lahore, and upon Munfur, whom he fent to the province of Pefhawir. At the fame time Ali, chief magiftrate of Ghizni, was fent to command the other imperial conquefts in India. Ali firft marched to Pefhawir, and took the fort of Mahitila, from Ahin, who had rebelled againft the King's authority, then fent a letter of invitation to Higgi Rai, a general of the Hindoos, who had done much fervice in the time of Mamood, but, upon account of fome political matters, had fled from the court, and had taken up his abode in the mountains of Cafhmire. The invitation being complied with, the King defired his attendance at Ghizni. Modood confers the drums, &c. on two of his fons.

While Ali was fettling the countries about the Indus, fome malicious chiefs in his camp forwarded many complaints againft him to the King. He was called to Ghizni, and imprifoned, under the care of one Mirik the fon of Haffen. This man, out of former enmity, and with a defign to extort money from him, put him to the torture, and foon after to death itfelf. Fearing, however, that the King might fome day inquire for the prifoner, and order him to be produced, he himfelf being then a great favourite, endeavoured to divert Modood's mind to fome important affairs, till he fhould be able to frame fome excufe for the death of Ali. He at length prevailed upon the Sultan to form an expedition againft Choraffan, by the way of Cabul. When they reached Lowgur, they befieged the fort of Sancoot, where there was a confiderable treafure lodged. But there the King was feized with a diforder in his liver, which daily gaining ground, Ali put to death. Modood falls fick;

A.D. 1049. Higer. 441. ground, he was obliged to proceed to Ghizni in a litter; while his vizier, Abul Ryſac, with the army, marched back into Seiſtan, to oppoſe the Siljokies, who had invaded that country.

When the King arrived at Ghizni, he ordered Mirik to bring his priſoner Ali before him, in order to be diſcharged from confinement. Mirik, by plauſible excuſes, delayed the time for a week, Dies. before the expiration of which, the King took leave of the world, in the year four hundred and forty one, having reigned nine years, with ability, ſome clemency, and great reputation.

State of Aſia at the death of Modood. The ſtate of affairs in Aſia ſuffered very little change during the reign of Modood. Al Kayem ſucceeded Al Kadir in the Caliphat, and Togril Beg, King of the Siljoki Tartars, who was now in poſſeſſion of all Perſia and Tranſoxiana, payed a nominal allegiance to the Calipha, by the acceptance of the title of Captain-general of the forces. Modood kept poſſeſſion of all the territories left to him by his father Muſaood in the north, and there was very little alteration on the ſide of India.

MUSAOOD

MUSAOOD II.

WHEN Modood had taken his journey to the other world, Ali the ſon of Ribbi, who was then in great power, had formed a deſign to uſurp the throne; but concealing his intentions, he raiſed Muſaood, the ſon of Modood, who was then a child of four years, to the Muſnud. Tiggi, the next in power to Ali, not being made a partner in his meaſures, was highly offended, and drew off, with half the army, who were in his intereſt. The troops were thus ſplit into two factions, and came to action; in which Ali being worſted, the faction of Tiggi took Abul Haſſen Ali, one of the ſons of the Emperor Muſaood, who had eſcaped the reſentment of Ali the ſon of Ribbi, and proclaimed him King, depoſing Muſaood, after a nominal reign of ſix days.

A.D. 1049. Higer. 441. Muſaood, an infant, placed upon the throne.

He is depoſed.

A L I.

A.D. 1051. Higer. 443. Ali afcends the throne.

UPON Friday, the firft of Shaban, in the year four hundred and forty-one, Ali * afcended the throne of Ghizni, and took the wife of his brother Modood, the former King, in marriage. In the mean time, Ali the fon of Ribbi, in affociation with Mirik, broke open the treafury, and taking out a vaft quantity of gold and jewels, fled, with a company of the royal flaves, and fome of the chiefs, whom they had brought over to their intereft, to Pefhawir. At Pefhawir they were joined by the natives, raifed a great army, and reduced Moultan, and the countries near the mouth of the Indus, to their obedience, making a great flaughter of the Afghans or Patans, who had taken advantage of the public difturbances, to plunder thofe provinces.

Defeated and depofed by Abdul Refhid.

In the year four hundred and forty-three, Ali called his brothers, Murda Shaw, and Ezid Ear, from the fort of Naáláma, where they had been imprifoned, and treated them with affection and refpect. But, at this time, Abdul Refhid, the fon of the Emperor Mamood, began to form a faction in his own favour. To crufh Refhid, the King opened his treafury, and entertained a great army; notwithftanding which, his power began daily vifibly to decline. Refhid advanced in the mean time, with his army, to Ghizni, and, gaining a compleat victory, afcended the throne.

* Abul Haffen Ali.

RESHID.

RESHID.

ABDUL RESHID*, as we have already mentioned, was the ſon of the Emperor Mamood, and was, by the order of Modood, impriſoned in a caſtle near Buſt. When the Vizier, Abdul Ryſac, about the time of the death of Modood, marched with an army to ſettle the country of Seiſtan; he, upon hearing of the King's death, in confederacy with Abul Fazil, Reſid the ſon of the famous Altaſaſh, and Noſhtagi Hajib, in the year 443, releaſed Reſhid from his confinement, and, aſſerting his cauſe with vigour, raiſed him, as we have ſeen, to the throne. His predeceſſor Ali was ſeized by ſome of the Zemindars, in the country into which he had fled, brought priſoner before Reſhid, and confined in the fort of Didi. A.D. 1052. Higer. 444. Reſhid mounts the throne.

The King, by various means, prevailed upon Ali the ſon of Ribbi, who had uſurped the Ghiznian conqueſts in India, to ſubmit to his allegiance, and return to Ghizni. He appointed Noſhtagi Hajib to the command of thoſe provinces, created him an Omrah, and ſent him with a fine army to Lahore. Noſhtagi, upon his way, turning to Nagracot, laid ſiege to that place, and, on the ſixth day, ſcaling the walls, took it by aſſault. Brings over Ali the ſon of Ribbi.

Tughril, whom we have already mentioned, was, notwithſtanding his treachery to his former

* His titles at length are, Zein-ul-Muluck, Sultan Abdul Reſhid.

maſter,

A.D. 1052. Higer. 444. maſter, now again intruſted with the government of Seiſtan, which he ſoon brought under proper regulations. Being ſtirred up by the ſpirit of treachery and ambition, he conceived hopes of aſſuming royalty; and raiſing a great army, marched towards Ghizni; where Reſhid being almoſt deſtitute of troops, was forced to ſhut himſelf up; but the place being very extenſive, it was impoſſible for him to defend it long, which he however did to the laſt extremity. Ghizni was taken at length, and the King, with nine of the blood royal, were inhumanely put to death by the uſurper, who now aſcended the throne. But Tughril did not long enjoy the fruits of his villainy; having wrote to Noſhtagi, endeavouring to bring him over by fair means to acknowledge him, that chief anſwered him with the contempt he deſerved. Noſhtagi, at the ſame time, wrote private letters to the daughter of the Emperor Muſaood, whom the tyrant had compelled to marry him, as alſo to all the Omrahs who he knew had retained their loyalty for the imperial family, ſpiriting them up to conſpire againſt the uſurper's life. They were ſo far excited to reſentment, that a conſpiracy was forthwith formed amongſt them, and put in execution on new year's day, when Tughril was ſtepping up to the throne to give public audience. Thus the uſurper, at the end of forty days, arrived at his tragical end.

Tughril rebels.

Beſieges Ghizni. The King taken and ſlain.

The Uſurper aſſaſſinated.

After this important tranſaction, Noſhtagi arrived at Ghizni with his army, and calling a council of ſtate, enquired whether any yet remained of the royal race of Subuctagi. He was informed, that there were ſtill impriſoned in a certain fort, Firoch Zaad, Ibrahim and Suja. Theſe he ordered to be called, and it being agreed that fortune ſhould decide it by lot who ſhould reign; ſhe favoured Firoch Zaad, who was accordingly placed upon

Firoch Zaad made King.

upon the throne, and received the allegiance of the court: The reign of Reſhid comprehended only one year. A.D. 1052. Higer. 443.

A certain author tells us, that Tughril, being one day aſked by one of his intimate friends,—what induced him to think of aſpiring to the empire, replied, that when the Emperor Reſhid diſpatched him to take the government of Seiſtan, he found that his hand trembled, from which circumſtance he concluded, that he was deſtitute of that reſolution and fortitude which are neceſſary accompliſhments of a King. Anecdote of Tughril.

FEROCH-ZAAD.

A.D. 1052. Higer. 444. Noſhtagi manages the affairs of ſtate.

WHEN Feroch-Zaad*, the ſon of the Emperor Muſaood, placed the crown of fortune upon his head, he gave the reins of adminiſtration into the hands of Noſhtagi, who had called him from obſcurity. Daood†, chief of the Siljoki Turkumans, hearing of the commotions in the empire, ſeized upon that favourable opportunity to invade Ghizni. He advanced with a numerous army, while Noſhtagi, collecting all his forces, went forth to meet him. When the armies engaged, the battle was obſtinate and bloody; for, from the riſing to the ſetting of the ſun, the victory was extremely doubtful; and, though thouſands fell, the troops ſeemed inſenſible of their own mortality. Victory at length declared for Noſhtagi, while his enemies betook themſelves to flight, leaving all their camp, equipage, and baggage on the field to the conquerors, who immediately returned victorious to Ghizni.

This victory ſerved to eſtabliſh Feroch-Zaad without fear upon the throne. He now exalted the ſtandard of triumph, and inclined it towards Choraſſan, where, on the part of the Siljoki, he was met by Calliſarick, one of their principal

* Jemmal ul Dowla Feroch-Zaad, ben Muſaood Ghiznavi.

† Brother of the famous Togril Beg, the firſt of the dynaſty of the Siljokides of Perſia.

Omrahs,

Omrahs, with a numerous army. The action was extremely violent and bloody; at length victory declared for the King of Ghizni, and Callisarick and several other persons of note were taken prisoners. Intelligence of this defeat coming to Daood prince of the Siljoki, he collected all his forces, which he submitted to the command of his son Arsilla, a youth of great expectations. Arsilla advanced to oppose the King, and having engaged him with great resolution, recovered the honour of the Siljoki, and took many of the Omrahs of Ghizni prisoners in the pursuit. But he did not think proper, at that time, to make further use of his fortune, and he therefore returned with his victorious army.

A. D. 1058. Higer. 450 Feroch-Zaad overthrows the Turkumans. Defeated by Arsilla.

When Feroch-Zaad arrived at Ghizni, he called Callisarick and all the prisoners of the Siljoki into his presence, bestowed upon each of them the honour of a dress, and gave them their liberty. The Siljoki returning home, represented in so strong a light the humanity of the King, that Daood, ashamed to be outdone in a virtuous action, ordered the prisoners of Ghizni to be also released.

Prisoners released.

Feroch-Zaad, who, according to the best authorities, was the son of Musaood, though some say that the Emperor Reshid was his father, having extended his reign to six years, mostly in peace, in the year four hundred and fifty, turned his face to the regions of futurity. The year before his death, his slaves, having been instigated to a conspiracy against his life, made an attempt to assassinate him in the bath. Feroch-Zaad having wrested a sword out of the hand of one of them, killed many, and defended himself against the rest, till his guards, hearing the noise, came in to his assistance; upon which all the slaves were put to instant death. His first vizier was Hassen the son of

Feroch-Zaad dies.

A.D. 1058. Higer. 450. Mora, and, in the latter part of his reign, Abu Beker Sali. He was a good, though not a ſplendid prince. He was poſſeſſed of humanity, and not deſtitute of bravery.

State of Aſia. Very little change happened in the political ſtate of Aſia, during the ſhort reigns of Muſaood the ſecond, Ali, Reſhid and Feroch-Zaad. Al Kayam ſtill ſat upon the throne of the Caliphat, ſupported in his ſpiritualities by Togril Beg, the temporal Emperor of Perſia. The brother of Togril failed in an attempt upon the empire of Ghizni, and the reigning family poſſeſſed, in all their extent, the territories left to them by Modood.

IBRAHIM

WHEN Feroch-Zaad became the inhabitant of another world, his brother Ibrahim * afcended the throne of empire: A King remarkable for morality and devotion, having in the flower of his youth, amidft a paradife of pleafure, conquered all the fenfual appetites, and added two months more to the feaft of Ramzan, which he kept with the ftricteft feverity. He, at the fame time, gave proper attention to government and the due adminiftration of juftice, and opened the hand of charity to the poor. This prince excelled in the art of fine writing, and in the libraries of Mecca and Medina there are two copies of the Koran wrote with his own hand, which were fent as prefents to the Calipha.——In the firft year of his reign, he concluded a treaty of peace with the Siljoki, ceding to them all the countries they had feized, upon condition that they would not lengthen the hand of violence any further upon his dominions. He married, at the fame time, his fon Mufaood to the daughter of their king, Malleck Shaw, which opened the door of friendfhip and intercourfe between the two nations. A.D. 1058. Higer. 450. Ibrahim, a religious and good prince.

We are told, that before this peace was concluded, Malleck had collected a great army, with

* Zehir ul Dowla, Sultan Ibrahim, ben Mufaood Ghiznavi.

an

A.D. 1058. Higer. 450. an intention to invade Ghizni, which greatly intimidated Ibrahim, as he was not then in a condition to oppose him. But knowing that policy is sometimes a good substitute for strength, he wrote letters to the principal Omrahs of Malleck's army, which he dispatched by a messenger, who had received his instructions how to proceed. The purport of those letters was to importune the Omrahs, to whom they were directed, to hasten the King's march to Ghizni, lest their scheme should be prematurely discovered; and that they might depend upon his fulfilling his engagements to their satisfaction.

Policy of Ibrahim.

King of the Siljcki deceived.

The messenger accordingly took an opportunity one day, when Malleck was hunting, upon the road to Ghizni, to come running towards him; but upon discovering the King, he stole slowly away, which creating suspicion, he was pursued by some horsemen, and brought before the King. He was immediately searched, and the pacquet was found upon him; though he had previously suffered himself to be severely bastinadoed, without confessing any thing. The King having read these letters, the power of the supposed conspirators was such, that there was great danger in accusing them; bnt it raised such a diffidence in his mind, that he, from that time, was desirous of peace, and gave over all thoughts of his expedition.

Ibrahim's expedition to Hindostan.

When the mind of Ibrahim was quieted from any apprehensions from that quarter, he sent an army towards India, and conquered many places in that country, which before had not been visited by the Mussulman arms. In the year 472, he marched in person towards that country, and extended his conquests to the fort of Ajodin, called now Palanshukurgunge. This place being taken, he turned to another fort called Rupal, which was built

built upon the summit of a steep hill; a river enclosed it on three sides, and a small peninsula joined it to the other hills, which were entirely covered with an impervious wood, and much infested by venomous serpents. This, however, did not discourage the King from his attempt. He ordered some thousand hatchet-men to clear the wood, which they effected in spite of all opposition; and the rock being soft, the miners forced their way in a short time under the walls, which were brought down in ruins. The place was immediately taken, and the garrison made prisoners.

A.D. 1079. Higer. 472.

Takes Rupal.

He marched from thence to another town in the neighbourhood, the inhabitants of which came originally from Chorassan, and were banished thither, with their families, by Afransiab*, for frequent rebellions. Here they formed themselves into a small independent state, being encircled by impassable mountains; and had preserved their ancient customs and rites, without intermarrying with any other people. The King having, with infinite labour, cleared a road for his army over the mountains, advanced towards the town, which was well fortified. He was overtaken by the rainy season, and his army was greatly distressed; during three months he was obliged to remain idle before it. But when the rains began to abate, and the country to dry up, he summoned the town to surrender and acknowledge the faith.

Ibrahim's proposals being rejected, he commenced the siege, which continued some weeks, with great slaughter on both sides. The town at length was taken by assault, and the Mussulmen found much wealth in it, and one hundred thousand unfortunate persons, whom they carried bound to Ghizni. Some time after, the King accidentally

* A name common to a long race of Persian Kings.

saw

A.D. 1079. Higer. 472. ſaw one of thoſe unhappy men carrying a heavy ſtone, with great difficulty and labour, to a palace which was then building. This awakened his pity; he commanded him to throw it down, and gave him his liberty.

This ſtone happened to lie upon the public road, and proved troubleſome to paſſengers; but as the King's rigid adherence to his commands was univerſally known, none would attempt to remove it. A courtier one day, having ſtumbled with his horſe over this ſtone, took occaſion to mention it to the King; inſinuating, that he thought, if his Majeſty pleaſed, that it was adviſeable to have it removed. To which the King replied; "I have commanded it to be thrown there, and there it muſt remain; as a memorial of the misfortunes of war, and my own pity: For it is better for a King to be obſtinate, even in his inadvertencies, than to break his royal word." The ſtone was accordingly permitted to remain, where it is ſhewn as a curioſity to this day.

The want of materials muſt render our hiſtory of the reign of Ibrahim extremely ſhort. After his expedition to India, and the pacification with the Siljoki Tartars, he ſeems to have few foreign affairs to mind. His adminiſtration of domeſtic juſtice was ſudden, equitable and deciſive. The lower people were happy, and his chiefs loved and obeyed him. Profound peace furniſhes few materials for hiſtory; a well-regulated monarchy gives birth to no extraordinary events, except in expedition and foreign war.

Ibrahim had thirty-ſix ſons and forty daughters by a variety of women. The latter he gave in marriage to learned and religious men. In the year 492, he left this mortal ſtate, after having reigned in tranquillity and happineſs forty-two years. In his time flouriſhed Abul Farrhe, the famous

famous writer, who was a native of Seiſtan, according to ſome, but as others affirm, of Ghizni. He is eſteemed a maſter in poetry; and the famous Anſuri was one of his diſciples. A.D. 1098. Higer. 492.

When Ibrahim acceded to the throne of Ghizni, Togril Beg, the firſt of the dynaſty of the Siljokides, ſat upon that of Perſia and the Weſtern Tartary. Togril was ſucceeded by his nephew Alp-Arſlan, in the 465th of the Higera. Malleck Shaw, the ſon of Alp-Arſlan, poſſeſſed the empire, after the death of his father, and Barkiaroc, the ſon of Malleck Shaw, reigned in Perſia at the death of Ibrahim. Marriages between the family of Ghizni and that of the Siljoki contributed to that tranquillity which Ibrahim enjoyed during a very long reign; and the paſſiveneſs of the Indians permitted the empire to retain its former bounds on the ſide of Hindoſtan. State of Aſia at the death of Ibrahim.

MUSAOOD

MUSAOOD III.

A. D. 1015. Higer. 509. Musaood a good Prince.

MUSAOOD*, the ſon of Ibrahim, mounted the throne upon the demiſe of his father. He was endowed with a benevolent and generous diſpoſition: nor was he leſs famous for his juſtice and ſound policy. He reviſed the ancient laws and regulations of the ſtate, and, abrogating ſuch as were thought unreaſonable, ſubſtituted others in their place, founded upon better principles. He took the daughter of Sinjer King of the Siljoki, whoſe name was Mehid of Perſia, in marriage, which cemented the peace between them.

Tigha Tiggi's expedition.

Peace bleſſed the reign of Muſaood, and his hiſtory muſt, therefore, be ſuccinct. Under him Tigha Tiggi was honoured with the command of a great expedition, which he formed againſt Hindoſtan. Croſſing the Ganges he carried his conqueſts further than any Muſſulman, except the Emperor Mamood; and, having plundered many rich cities and temples of their wealth, returned in triumph to Lahore, which now became, in ſome meaſure, to be reckoned the capital of the empire; eſpecially as the Siljoki had ſtripped the Ghiznian family of moſt of their Perſian and Tartar provinces.

Muſaood dies.

After Muſaood had reigned ſixteen years, without domeſtic troubles or foreign wars, he entered

* Alla ul Dowla Muſaood, ben Ibrahim.

his

his eternal abode, in the latter end of the year five hundred and eight. We are told, that after his death, his son Shere placed his foot upon the imperial throne. He enjoyed it only one year, being assassinated by the hand of his own brother Arsilla, who assumed the diadem. A.D. 1115. Higer. 509.

Barkiaroc, the fourth of the dynasty of the Siljokides, sat on the throne of Persia at the accession of Musaood; and Mahommed, the fifth Sulton of the race of Seljuk, died the same year with the King of Ghizni. Sinjer, governor of Chorassan, succeeded his brother Mahommed as King of Persia, and we shall find in the sequel, that he interfered in the succession of the sons of Musaood, who were his nephews. The Indian provinces, conquered by his ancestors, remained in tranquillity to Musaood. State of Asia at the death of Musaood.

ARSILLA.

A R S I L L A.

A.D. 1115. Higer. 509. Arſilla confines his brothers.

WHEN Arſilla*, the ſon of Muſaood, by means of aſſaſſination, became King of Ghizni, he ſeized upon all his brothers, excepting one who eſcaped, and confined them. Byram, who was ſo fortunate as to get out of the King's hands, fled for protection to Sinjer, who then, on the part of his brother Mahommed, king of Perſia, ruled the province of Choraſſan. Sinjer, who was uncle to Arſilla, having demanded the releaſement of the other brothers, which was not complied with, made the cauſe of Byram a pretence for invading the kingdom of Ghizni; and he accordingly advanced the ſtandard of hoſtility towards that city.

Arſilla, hearing of the intended invaſion, wrote letters of complaint to Sinjer's elder brother, the Emperor Mahommed, that he might command him back; and that monarch pretended to be inclinable to make peace between them. But Sinjer was found to continue his march, which convinced Arſilla that he could have no dependance upon any thing but his ſword. But his mother, Mehid princeſs of Perſia, being offended with him for the murder of his brother Muſaood, and his inhuman treatment of her other children, with well-diſſembled affection, prevailed upon him to ſend

Arſilla deceived by his mother.

* Sultan ul Dowla, ARSILLA Shaw, ben Muſaood.

her

her to negotiate a peace, with a great ſum of money, ſufficient to reimburſe her brother Sinjer for the expence of his expedition. When ſhe arrived in the camp, ſhe, according to her deſign, excited Byram her ſon, and her brother Sinjer, to proſecute the war with all expedition. A.D. 1117. Higer. 509.

Sinjer immediately marched with thirty thouſand horſe, and fifty thouſand foot, from Buſt in Choraſſan, where he then lay, and, without oppoſition, advanced within one pharſang of Ghizni, where he beheld the army of Arſilla drawn out in order of battle to receive him. He therefore inſtantly ordered the line to be formed, dividing his horſe into ſquadrons, and placing battalions of ſpearmen in the intervals, with elephants in the rear, to be ready to advance upon occaſion. Encouraging then his troops, he advanced ſlowly toward the enemy, who ſtood firm to receive the charge. The ſhock was ſo violent upon both ſides, that order and command yielded to rage and confuſion. The gleam of arms that illuminated the field, was ſoon quenched in blood, and darkened by clouds of duſt, that took away all diſtinction. At length, by the uncommon bravery of Abul Fazil, governor of Seiſtan, the troops of Ghizni were put to flight, and Arſilla, unable to renew the combat, fled with the remains of his army towards Hindoſtan. Sinjer engages Arſilla.

Sinjer entered Ghizni in triumph, where he remained forty days, giving the kingdom to his nephew Byram, and then returning to his own country. When Arſilla had heard of the departure of Sinjer, he collected all his troops in the Ghiznian provinces of Hindoſtan, and returned to recover his capital. Byram, unable to oppoſe him, ſhut himſelf up in the fort of Bamia, till he could be ſuccoured by his uncle Sinjer. Sinjer again took the field, and drove Arſilla a ſecond time back to Hindoſtan.

A.D. 1117. Higer. 509. Hindoſtan. But he was ſo cloſely purſued, that his army was diſperſed, while a few of his Omrahs, who remained, laid hands upon him, and brought him to Byram, to procure their own pardon. Arſilla ſuffered a violent death in the 27th year of his age, after he had reigned three years. In this reign hiſtorians report, that, among other prodigies, there fell a ſtorm of fire upon the city of Ghizni, which conſumed a great part of its buildings. He was a weak and wicked prince, as unworthy of empire, as his father and grandfather were deſerving of a throne.

Arſilla taken and ſlain.

BYRAM.

B Y R A M.

BYRAM*, the son of Musaood the third, was blessed with a noble and generous disposition. He had an uncommon thirst after knowledge; he was a great promoter of literature, and a liberal patron of learned men. Many men of letters resorted to his court, particularly Shech Nizami, and Seid Hassen, both poets and philosophers of great fame. Many books were, in this reign, translated from various languages into the Persian tongue; among the most famous of which was an Indian book, called the Killila Dumna, a fabulous story, pregnant with sound morality, policy, and entertainment. A.D. 1118. Higer. 512. Byram, a good Prince.

This book was sent formerly before the dissolution of the Hindoo empire of India, by the King of that country, accompanied with a Chess table, to Noshirwan, sirnamed The Just, king of Persia. Buzurg Chimere his vizier, sirnamed The Wise, was so well versed in all the known languages, that in a few days he translated the Killila Dumna into Phelevi or antient Persic, to the astonishment of the ambassador, who imagined the Sanscrita language was entirely unknown in those parts. But he could form no conception of the chess-board, as that game was, at that time, unknown in Persia. He therefore had recourse to A digression.

* Moaz ul Dowla, Byram Shaw, ben Musaood.

the

A.D. 1150. Higer. 545. the ambaſſador, who was eſteemed the beſt player in Hindoſtan, to have this matter explained to him, who having accordingly diſcovered to him the principles, Buzurg ſat down with him to play. The firſt game he obliged the ambaſſador to draw; the ſecond he chaced his King ſolitary; and the third he gave him check-mate. The ambaſſador was ſo mad to be foiled at his own weapons, that he would play no more. Buzurg then invented the game of backgammon, returning a ſet of thoſe tables by the ambaſſador, who having related his adventure with Buzurg, and given an account of the genius and government of Noſhirwan, his maſter gave up all thoughts of an invaſion, which he had been meditating againſt that King. The preſent of the cheſs-board was intended as an experiment upon the genius of the miniſter, and to indicate that, in the great game of ſtate, attention and capacity were better friends than fortune. While the book, in its whole tenor, ſtrongly inculcated that wiſe maxim, that true wiſdom and policy is always an overmatch for ſtrength. The backgammon table, which was returned, ſignified, that attention and capacity alone cannot always inſure ſucceſs, but that we muſt play the game of life according to the caſts of fortune.

Byram ſettles the affairs of Hindoſtan.

But to return to our hiſtory. Byram, in the days of his proſperity, went twice into Hindoſtan, chaſtiſing his refractory ſubjects and collectors of the imperial revenue. The firſt time he went to reduce Balin, who had poſſeſſion of the government of Lahore, on the part of his brother the Emperor Arſilla, whom he defeated and took, the 27th of Ramzan, in the year 512; but having pardoned him, upon ſwearing allegiance, he was again reinſtated in his government, and the King returned to Ghizni. In the mean time, Balin built the fort of Nagore, in the country of Sewalic,

walic, whither he conveyed all his wealth, family, and effects; then raising an army, composed chiefly of Arabs, Persians, Afghans, and Chilligies, he committed great devastations upon the Indian independent princes, which success so puffed him up, that he aspired at length to the empire. Byram being apprized of the intentions of Balin, collected his army, and a second time marched towards Hindostan. Balin, with his ten sons, who had each the command of a province, advanced to meet the King, as far as Moultan, with a powerful army. A dreadful battle ensued; but the curse of ingratitude was poured, in a storm, upon the head of the perfidious rebel, who, in his flight, with his ten sons and attendants, fell headlong into a deep quagmire, where they were totally overwhelmed, and every one of them perished.

A.D. 1150. Higer. 545.

The King, after this compleat victory, settled the affairs of the Indian provinces, and, appointing Hussein to the chief command of the conquered part of India, returned himself to Ghizni. He soon after publicly executed Mahommed prince of Ghor, who was son-in-law to the rebel Balin. This, in its consequences, proved the ruin of the family of Ghizni. Seif ul dien, surnamed Souri, prince of Ghor*, brother to the deceased, raised a great army to revenge his death. He marched directly to Ghizni, which Byram, unable to oppose him, evacuated, and fled to a place called Kirma, upon the borders of India. This Kirma had been built by the Afghans to guard a pass in the mountains. The prince of Ghor, without further opposition, entered the capital, where he established himself, by the consent of the people,

Obtains a compleat victory over Balin.

Ghizni invaded by the Prince of Ghor.

* A province of the Ghiznian empire, the princes of which had been reduced into a dependence upon the family of Subuctagi, by the Emperor Mamood.

A. D. 1151. Higer. 546. sending Alla, his brother, to rule his native principality of Ghor. Notwithstanding all he could do to render himself popular at Ghizni, the people, from an attachment to the imperial family, began to dislike his government, and secretly wished the re-establishment of their former King. Some of the Omrahs, who were of the same principles, laying hold of this favourable disposition, informed Byram of their ripeness for an insurrection, if he could by any means favour it.

Byram marches against him. It was now winter, and most of the followers of the prince of Ghor had returned, upon leave, to their families, when Byram, unexpectedly, appeared before Ghizni, with a great army. Seif ul Dien being then in no condition to engage him with his own troops, and having little dependance upon those of Ghizni, was preparing to retreat to Ghor, when the Ghiznians intreated him to engage Byram, and that they would exert themselves to the utmost in his service. This was only a trick for an opportunity to put their design in execution. As the unfortunate prince was advancing to engage Byram, he was surrounded by the troops of Ghizni, and taken prisoner, while Byram in person put the forces of Ghor to flight.

Seif ul dien betrayed, disgraced, tortured, and put to death. The unhappy captive was inhumanly ordered to have his forehead made black, and then to be put astride a sorry bullock, with his face turned towards the tail. He, in that manner, was led round the whole city, insulted and hooted by the mob. He was then put to the torture, and his head sent to Sinjer, king of Persia, while his vizier, Seid Mujud, was impaled alive.

His brother Alla marches to revenge his death. When this news was carried to the ears of his brother Alla, he burnt with rage, and, resolving upon revenge, with all his united powers, invaded Ghizni. Byram hearing of his coming, prepared himself to receive him. He wrote him a letter, a letter, and endeavoured to intimidate him with the superiority of his troops, advising him not to plunge the whole family of Ghor into the same abyss of misfortune. Alla replied, "That his threats were as impotent as his arms: That it was no new thing for Kings to make war upon their neighbours; but that barbarity like his was unknown to the brave, and what he had never heard to have been exercised upon Princes. That he might be assured that God had forsaken Byram, and ordained Alla to be the instrument of that just vengeance which was denounced against him, for putting to death the representative of the long-independent and very ancient family of Ghor." A.D. 1152. Higer. 547.

All hopes of accommodation being past, Byram advanced, with a numerous army, to give Alla battle. The offer was gladly accepted by his adversary, and the bloody conflict commenced with great fury on both sides. At first the troops of Ghizni, by their superior numbers, bore down those of Ghor; till Alla, seeing his affairs almost desperate, called out to two gigantic brothers, whose name was Chirmil, the greater and the lesser, whom he saw in the front, like two rocks bearing against the torrent. He forced on his elephant towards Byram, these two heroes clearing all before him. Byram observing him, stood off; but his son Dowlat, accepting the challenge, advanced to oppose Alla. The elder of the heroick Chirmils intervening, ripped up the belly of Dowlat's elephant, and was himself killed by his fall. Alla, in the mean time, nailed the brave prince, with his spear, to the ground. The other Chirmil, attacked the elephant of Byram, and after many wounds, brought the enormous animal to the ground; but while he was rising from under the elephant's side, being much bruised by the fall, Byram escaped with his life, and instantly mounting a horse, The battle. Byram overthrown.

A.D. 1152. Higer. 547. a horſe, joined the flight of his army, which was now repulſed on all ſides. The troops of Ghor emulating the bravery of their leader, had made ſuch a violent attack as to be no longer reſiſtible.

Dies. Byram fled, with the ſcattered remains of his army, towards Hindoſtan; but he was overwhelmed with his misfortunes, and ſunk under the hand of death, in the year five hundred and forty-ſeven, after a reign of thirty-five years. He was, upon the whole, a good and virtuous prince; though his too precipitate ſeverity, in the caſe of the prince of Ghor, cannot be reconciled to humanity or ſound policy.

State of Aſia at the death of Byram. The long reign of Byram was peaceable but inglorious; the empire had been long upon the decline, and though he was a virtuous prince, he had not ſufficient abilities to retrieve its vigor. Sinjer, his uncle, by the mother, the ſixth Emperor of Perſia, of the Siljokan race, was upon the throne, in full poſſeſſion of the empire conquered by his anceſtors, when Byram became king of Ghizni.——Sinjer reigned over Perſia more than forty years. The Indian provinces ſubject to Ghizni, remained entire to Byram.

CHUSERO

CHUSERO I.

CHUSERO*, the son of the Emperor Byram, upon the death of his father, continued his march to Lahore, leaving the kingdom of Ghizni to his enemies, and was there saluted King, by the unanimous voice of his people. In the mean time, the conqueror entered Ghizni with little opposition, and that noble city was given up to flame, slaughter, rapine, and devastation. The massacre continued for the space of seven days, in which time pity seemed to have fled the earth, and the fiery spirits of demons to actuate the bodies of men. For which inhuman cruelty the barbarous Alla was justly denominated Allum Soze, or the incendiary of the world. But, insatiable of revenge, he carried a number of the most venerable priests, learned men, and citizens, in chains to Ghor, to adorn his triumph. There,—we shudder to relate it! he ordered their throats to be cut, tempering earth with their blood, with which he plaistered the walls of his city.

A. D. 1158. Higer. 547. Chusero.

Ghizni taken and destroyed.

Alla's unheard-of cruelty.

After the return of Alla to Ghor, Chusero, hoping to recover his lost kingdom of Ghizni, and depending upon the assistance of Sinjer, king of Persia, collected all his forces, and marched from Lahore. But when he had arrived upon the borders of Ghizni, he received intelligence that

Chusero attempts to recover Ghizni.

* Zehiri ul Dowla, Chusero Shaw, ben Byram Shaw Ghiznavi.

Sinjer

A.D. 1159. Higer. 555. Sinjer had been defeated and taken priſoner by the Turks of Ghiza, who were then marching down with a great army to Ghizni, to appropriate that kingdom to themſelves. This obliged him to retreat again to Lahore, being in no condition to oppoſe them. He governed the Indian provinces in peace, with the common juſtice of virtuous kings. The Turks of Ghiza, in the mean time, drove out the troops of Ghor, and kept poſſeſſion of Ghizni for two years. But they were expelled in their turn by the Ghorians, who did not long enjoy it for that time, being vanquiſhed by Aſſumud, general to Chuſero, the ſecond of that name, who, for a ſhort ſpace, recovered and held that kingdom.

Chuſero dies. Chuſero the firſt died at Lahore, in the year five hundred and fifty-five, after he had reigned ſeven years, with no great ſplendor; but he deſerved and attained the character of a good and peaceable prince.

CHUSERO

CHUSERO II.

WHEN Chusero the first departed from this house of grief, towards the mansions of joy and immortality, his son Chusero*, the second of that name, ascended the throne, which he adorned with benevolence and justice, extending his dominions to all the provinces formerly possessed by the Emperors Ibrahim and Byram. But Mahommed, brother to the prince of Ghor, invaded the kingdom of Ghizni, which he reduced, and not satisfied with that, marched an army into India, overrunning the provinces of Peshawir, Afghanistan, Moultan, and the Indus. He advanced at length to Lahore, and, in the year 576, invested the Emperor Chusero in his capital, but not being able to take the place, there was a kind of treaty concluded between them. Mahommed evacuated the country, carrying Chusero, the son of the Emperor, a child of four years of age, hostage for the performance of the treaty. A.D. 1159. Higer. 555. Chusero II. a good Prince.

But the terms not being kept properly by Chusero, Mahommed, in the year 580, returned to Lahore, and besieged it to no purpose. He however subjected the open country to fire and sword. He then built the fort of Salcot, where he left a strong garrison, and then returned to Ghizni. In his absence, the Emperor Chusero, in alliance with Lahore besieged.

* Chusero Malleck, ben Chusero Shaw.

the

A. D. 1184. Higer. 580. the Gickers, besieged the fort of Salcot, but their enterprize proving unsuccessful, they were obliged to desist.

Lahore taken by treachery. Some time after these transactions, Mahommed collected all his forces, and the third time resolved to reduce the city of Lahore, which he effected by treachery, in the following manner. While he was preparing for the expedition, he gave out, that it was intended against the Siljokies, writing, at the same time, to Chusero, that he was desirous of accommodating all their differences, by a treaty of peace. To convince him of the sincerity of his intentions, he now returned his son Chusero, with a splendid retinue; who had orders to make short marches, while the Emperor, his father, impatient to see him, advanced a part of the way to meet him. In the mean time, Mahommed, with twenty thousand horse, with incredible expedition, marched by another way, round the mountains, and cut off Chusero from Lahore, having surrounded his small camp in the night. The Emperor, having waked in the morning from his dream of negligence, saw no hope of escape left, which obliged him to throw himself upon the mercy of his adversary. He demanded possession of the capital for the King's release, accordingly the gates of that city were thrown open to receive him; and thus the empire passed from the house of Ghizni to that of Ghor, as we shall see more fully in the history of that race.

The Empire transferred to the house of Ghor.

State of Asia. The year in which the family of Ghizni was extinguished, proved also fatal to the elder branch of the royal family of the Siljokides in Persia. Disputes about the succession, and the weakness of the princes who reigned after Sinjer, seemed to conspire in the ruin of an empire, which fell as suddenly as it rose. The governors of the provinces, no uncommon thing in Asia, assumed independence,

dependence, with great facility, when their masters had not abilities of mind to counteract the power which the crown vested in its viceroys. Some governments, in the distractions of the empire, became hereditary, and many ambitious Omrahs rendered themselves independent, in the debilitated reign of the second Togril. Tacash viceroy of Charizm, a part of the ancient Transoxiana, not only assumed the ensigns of royalty in his government, but being invited into the western Persia, annexed that country to his new kingdom, by the defeat and death of Togril. A.D. 1184. Higer. 580.

MAHOMMED

MAHOMMED GHORI.

The origin of the house of Ghor.

MOR CHAN the hiſtorian tells us, that about the time when Feredoon, an ancient king of Perſia ſubdued Zohac Tazi, two brothers of the royal family, Souri and Sam, were taken into favour by the conqueror; but having by ſome means incurred his diſpleaſure, they fled with a party of their friends to Hawind, in the mountains between India and Perſia, where they took up their abode, poſſeſſing themſelves of a ſmall territory. Souri took the government of this diſtrict, appointing his brother to the command of his ſmall army, and gave his daughter in marriage to his ſon Suja.

Suja the firſt of that race.

Suja, after his father's deceaſe, enjoyed his place. But ſome private enemies having traduced him to his uncle, inſpired him with jealouſy and enmity to ſuch a degree, that he wanted to take his daughter away from him. When Suja found this, he was determined to ſeek his fortune elſewhere. He accordingly, in the night, with ten horſemen and a few camels, laden with his effects, ſet out, with his wife and children, to the mountains of Ghor, where he built a houſe, and called it Romijandiſh, or the careleſs habitation. Here he was gradually joined by many of his friends, who built a ſtrong fort, which he held out againſt the troops of Feredoon for ſome time, but at length he was obliged to ſubmit and pay tribute.

Thus

Thus the race of Zohac, one after another, ſucceeded to this government, which began to gain ſtrength by degrees, till the time of the prophet, when it was ruled by Shinſub, who, ſome ſay, was converted to the faith by the great Ali, the ſon-in-law of Mahommed, who confirmed him in his kingdom. The genealogy of the kings of Ghor, according to the moſt authentic hiſtorians, could be traced up, by the names, for three and twenty generations, and downwards nine generations, from Ali to Mamood, the ſon of Subuctagi, Emperor of Ghizni, who gave it to Ali the vanquiſhed prince's ſon, to hold it of the Empire. But Ali endeavouring to throw off the yoke of Mamood, he was depoſed, and the country given to Abas his nephew, in whoſe reign there were ſeven years drought in Ghor, ſo that the earth was burnt up, and thouſands of men and animals periſhed with heat and famine. Abas, deſirous of rendering himſelf independent, commenced a war againſt the Emperor Ibrahim, by whom he was defeated and taken priſoner; the kingdom being conferred upon his ſon Mahommed, who ſwore allegiance to the empire of Ghizni. He was ſucceeded by his ſon Huſſein, who was killed by an arrow in the eye, in attacking a certain fort, when he rebelled againſt Ghizni.

The genealogy of the houſe of Ghor.

Upon the death of Huſſein, his ſon Sham was obliged to fly to India, where he followed the buſineſs of a merchant; and having acquired much wealth, he returned up the Indus to his native country. But unfortunately he was wrecked, narrowly eſcaping with his life upon a plank, with his ſon Huſſein, after driving with the tide for three days. When they got foot on ſhore, they made towards a town that appeared in ſight, but, it being late before they arrived, they could find no lodgings, and were obliged to creep in under a balcony,

The adventures of Sham.

a balcony, where they might ſleep out of the rain. The watch going the rounds perceived them, and without further examination, concluding they were thieves, carried them to priſon. They were condemned to ſlavery for ſeven years, during which time the ſon died. When Sham obtained his liberty, he proceeded towards Ghizni, on the way to which he was met by a gang of robbers, that had for a long time infeſted the roads. When they ſaw him a man of great ſtrength and of a bold appearance, they inſiſted upon enrolling him in the gang, to which he was obliged to conſent; but unfortunately that very night, a party of the troops of the Emperor Ibrahim ſurrounded them, and carried them all in chains to the royal preſence, and the King immediately condemned them to death.

Condemned to death, and ſaved by accident.

When the executioner was binding up the eyes of Sham, he raiſed a grievous complaint, proteſting, and calling God to witneſs, that he was innocent, which ſoftened the ſteely heart of the executioner to pity. He deſired him to relate what he had to ſay in his own defence, which he did in ſuch a circumſtantial and probable manner, that the magiſtrate who attended, believing him innocent, petitioned the King to give him a hearing. This being accordingly granted, he acquitted himſelf with ſuch modeſty and eloquence, that the King commanded him to be releaſed, and admitted him into his particular friendſhip and favour. Ibrahim, ſome time after, created Sham an Omrah, and appointed him maſter of requeſts, in which ſtation he acquitted himſelf ſo honourably, that he roſe daily in rank and honours, till the Emperor Muſaood, the ſon of Ibrahim, put him in poſſeſſion of his hereditary kingdom. He then married a princeſs of the houſe of Ghizni, by whom

whom he had ſeven ſons, denominated the ſeven ſtars.

After the death of Sham, his ſons became divided into two factions; one headed by the governor of Tariſtan and Hiatilla, whoſe name was Muſaood, the eldeſt ſon: And the other by the fourth ſon, Mahommed, who took poſſeſſion of Ghor. The ſecond ſon, Cuttub, took poſſeſſion of the hills, and founded the city of Firoſe Ko, which he made his capital; and raiſing himſelf in a few years to great power, he meditated an attempt upon the empire of Ghizni, collecting ſoldiers of fortune from all parts. But Byram the Emperor, being privately acquainted of his intentions, treacherouſly invited him in friendſhip to Ghizni, where, contrary to all the laws of honour and hoſpitality, he ordered poiſon to be adminiſtered to him, which proved the fatal cauſe of the war between the houſes of Ghor and Ghizni. History of his ſons.

Seif ul dien the fifth ſon, who had accompanied his brother, eſcaped the ſnare, and fled to Firoſe Ko. He there placed himſelf at the head of his brother's army, and marched towards Ghizni to revenge his death, as we have ſeen in the hiſtory of that kingdom. He took Ghizni, and Byram fled to India. But Byram returning again in the winter, when the troops of Seif ul dien were moſtly gone to Firoſe Ko and Ghor, from whence they could not eaſily return, on account of the roads and deep ſnow, Seif ul dien, as before related, was treacherouſly delivered up to him, and, with his vizier, put to a moſt ignominious death. The conſequence of this impolitic cruelty was, that Sham, the ſixth brother, prepared to invade Byram, with an army from Firoſe Ko and Ghor; but dying in the interim, the command devolved upon the ſeventh brother, Alla the incendiary, Their attempts on the empire.

who

who took and deſtroyed Ghizni. He carried his ravages ſo far as to deſtroy every monument and tomb of the Ghiznian Kings, excepting thoſe of the Emperors Mahmood, Muſaood, and Ibrahim, throwing fire into their very graves, and defacing their inſcriptions upon all public edifices. When he returned to Ghor, he appointed his nephews Yeas ul dien and Mahommed Sham, to the government of a province of Ghor called Sinjia. But when they found the revenues of that province could not ſupport the figure which they endeavoured to make, by their unbounded generoſity and liberality to military men, whom they began to collect from all parts; they began to extend their limits. This having reached the ears of Alla, he ſent a force againſt them, and ſeizing them both, confined them in the fort of Goriſtan.

Alla. Alla then turned the hoſtile ſpear againſt the brother of the King of Perſia and governor of Choraſſan, Sinjer, to whom his father had paid tribute. He overrun the provinces of Balich and Herat; but coming to an engagement with Sinjer, he was defeated and taken priſoner. Notwithſtanding all which, Sinjer had compaſſion upon him, and again confirmed him in the kingdom of Ghor, where he died in the year five hundred and fifty-one. Alla was ſucceeded by his ſon Mahommed, who upon his acceſſion releaſed his two couſins from their confinement at Goriſtan, and beſtowed again the government of Sinjia upon them. In little more than a year, he commenced a war with the tribe of Turkumans called Ghiza, and in the day of battle was killed by one of his own men.

Yeas ul dien. He was ſucceeded by his eldeſt couſin, Yeas ul dien, who appointed his brother, Mahommed Ghori, his general. This illuſtrious hero, under the

the name of his brother, subdued Chorassan, and a great part of India; and Yeas annexed the titles of those countries to his own. His death happened, as shall afterwards appear, in the year 599 of the Higera. A.D. 1171. Higer. 567.

Mahommed Ghori was left by his brother, when he acceded to the throne of Ghor, to command in Tunganabad, in the province of Chorassan. He continued from thence to make incursions upon Ghizni, as we have observed in the history of that kingdom. In the year 567, Yeas ul dien marched in person against the Omrahs of Chusero, the last of the imperial house of Ghizni, and entirely reduced them. He gave the government of Ghizni to his brother Mahommed, who, according to the imperial orders, in the year 572, led an army towards Moultan, which he entirely subdued. He marched from thence to Adja. The prince of that place shut himself up in a strong fort. Mahommed began to besiege the place; but finding it would be a difficult task to reduce it, he sent a private message to the Raja's wife, promising to marry her if she would make away with her husband. Mahommed Ghori.

The base woman returned for answer, that she was rather too old herself to think of matrimony, but that she had a beautiful young daughter, whom, if he would promise to espouse, and leave her in free possession of the country and its wealth, she would in a few days remove the Raja. Mahommed basely accepted of the proposal, and the wicked woman accordingly, in a few days, found means to assassinate her husband, and to open the gates to the enemy. Mahommed confirmed his promise, by marrying the daughter, upon acknowledging the true faith; but he made no scruple to deviate from what respected the mother; for, instead of trusting her with the country, he sent her His policy.

off

A.D. 1179. Higer. 575. off to Ghizni, where ſhe ſoon died of grief and reſentment. Nor did the daughter reliſh her ſituation better; for, in the ſpace of two years, ſhe alſo fell a victim to grief.

Mahommed defeated in Guzerat. Mahommed having conferred the government of Moultan and Adja upon one Ali, returned to Ghizni; from whence, in the year 574, he again marched to Adja and Moultan, and from thoſe places continued his courſe through the ſandy deſert, to Guzerat. The prince Bim Deo advanced thither with a great army, to give him battle, in which the Muſſulmen were defeated, with great ſlaughter, and ſuffered many hardſhips in their retreat, till they arrived at Ghizni.

Makes peace with Chuſero II. In the year following, Mahommed marched his recruited army towards Peſhawir, which he in a ſhort time brought under ſubjection. He proceeded in the courſe of the next year, towards Lahore, where he inveſted Chuſero, the laſt of the Ghiznian race, who had been ſo weakened at that time, by wars with the Indian princes and the Afghans, that he could not oppoſe him in the field. But Mahommed, finding he could not reduce the place, intimated a deſire of treating with Chuſero, who, glad to get rid of him, made him ſome preſents, and gave his ſon as an hoſtage for the performance of the reſt of the agreement between them. Mahommed upon this returned to Ghizni, but he could not reſt long in peace. He, the very next year, drew his army towards Dewil, in the province near the mouth of the Indus, and ſubdued all the country to the ſea coaſt, returning loaded with rich ſpoil.

Beſieges Lahore. In the year 580, he returned again to Lahore, where Chuſero ſhut himſelf up as before, ſuſtaining a long ſiege, which at length Mahommed was obliged to raiſe. He, in this expedition, built the fort of Salcot, in which he left a gar-

riſon

rison to command the countries between the rivers Ravi and Chinab, under the government of Hussein Churmili, while he himself returned to Ghizni. This fort, as we have before related, was effectually besieged by Chusero, in the absence of Mahommed, which occasioned that prince's third expedition towards Lahore, which he took in the year 582, by the perfidious stratagem mentioned in the conclusion of the history of Ghizni. He sent Chusero and his family, prisoners to his brother at Firose Ko, who confined them in a fort in Ghirgistan, where they were some time afterwards put to death, on account of something the astrologers had predicted concerning them.

A.D. 1191. Higer. 587.

Extirpates the royal family of Ghizni.

When Mahommed had settled the provinces of Lahore, he left the government of that place in the hands of Ali governor of Moultan, and retired to Ghizni. In the year 587, he marched again towards Hindostan, and proceeding to Ajmere, took the capital of Tiberhind, where he left Malleck Zea, with above a thousand chosen horse, and some foot, to garrison the place. He himself was upon his way back, when he heard that Pittu Ra, the prince of Ajmere, with his brother Candi Ra, king of Delhi, in alliance with some other Indian princes, were marching towards Tiberhind, with two hundred thousand horse, and three thousand elephants. Mahommed determined to return to the relief of the garrison. He met the enemy at the village of Sirauri, upon the banks of the Sirsutti, fourteen miles from Tannassar, and eighty from Delhi, and gave them battle. Upon the first onset his right and left wings retired, being outflanked by the enemy, till, joining in the rear, his army was formed into a circle. Mahommed, who was in person in the center of the line when first formed, was told that his right and left wings were defeated, and advised

He marches to Hindostan.

A.D. 1192. Higer. 588. to provide for his own ſafety. Enraged at this counſel, he ſmote the imprudent adviſer, and ruſhed on towards the enemy, among whom he commenced, with a few followers, a great ſlaughter. The eyes of Candi Ra, king of Delhi, fell upon him. He drove the elephant, upon which he was mounted, directly againſt him. Mahommed riſing from his horſe, threw his lance with ſuch force at the elephant, that he drove out three of his back teeth. In the mean time the King of Delhi, from above, pierced the Sultan through the right arm, and had almoſt thrown him to the ground; when ſome of his chiefs advanced to his reſcue. This gave an opportunity to one of his faithful ſervants, to leap behind him as he was ſinking from his horſe, and ſupporting him in his arms, he carried him from the field, which, by this time, was deſerted almoſt by his whole army. The enemy purſued them near forty miles.

A ſingle combat between the King and the Raja of Delhi.

He is overthrown.

After this defeat, and when he had recovered of his wound at Lahore, he appointed governors to the different provinces he poſſeſſed in India, and returned in perſon to Ghor with his army. At Ghor he diſgraced all thoſe Omrahs who had deſerted him in battle. He obliged them to walk round the city, with their horſes mouth-bags, filled with barley, hanging about their necks; at the ſame time forcing them to eat, or have their heads ſtruck off; the former of which they chiefly choſe to do. We are told by Eben Aſire, contrary to all other authority, that when Mahommed was wounded, he fell from his horſe, and lay upon the field among the dead, till night. And that, in the dark, a party of his own horſe returned to ſearch for his body, and carried him off to his own camp.

Upon

Upon the retreat of Mahommed Ghori, the allied Rajas continued their march to Tiberhind, which they besieged for one year and one month, and at last were obliged to give favourable terms of capitulation. Mahommed remained a few months with his brother at Ghor, who still kept the imperial title, and then returning to Ghizni, spent the ensuing year in indolence and festivity. But ambition again fermenting in his mind, he recruited a noble army, consisting of one hundred thousand chosen horse, Turks, Persians, and Afghans, many of whom had their helmets ornamented with jewels, and their armour inlaid with silver and gold. With these he marched in martial splendor, from Ghizni towards India, without disclosing to his friends any part of his intentions.

A.D. 1192. Higer. 588. The combined Rajas take Tiberhind.

When his victorious spears had advanced as far as Peshawir, an old sage of Ghor, prostrating himself before him, said, "O King, we trust in thy conduct and wisdom; but as yet thy design has been a subject of much dispute and speculation among us." Mahommed replied, "Know, old man, that since the time of my defeat in Hindostan, notwithstanding external appearances, I have never slumbered in ease, or waked but in sorrow and anxiety. I have therefore determined, with this army, to recover my lost honour from those idolaters, or die in the noble attempt." The sage, kissing the ground, said, "Victory and triumph be thy attendants, and fortune be the guide of thy paths. But, O King, let the petition of thy slave find favour, and let those Omrahs you have so justly disgraced, be permitted to take this glorious opportunity of wiping away their dishonourable stains." The Prince listened to his request, and sent an order to Ghizni to release the disgraced Omrahs from their confinement, and that such of them as were desirous of recovering their

Mahommed marches into India.

A.D. 1192. Higer. 588. honour, might now attend his ſtirrup. They accordingly obeyed the order, and were each honoured with a chelat, according to their rank. The next day the royal ſtandard was put in motion, and the army advanced to Moultan, where Mahommed conferred titles and employments upon all who had been firm to his intereſt. He then proceeded to Lahore, from whence he diſpatched Humza, one of his principal Omrahs, ambaſſador to Ajmere, with a declaration of war, ſhould the Indians reject the true faith.

The Indians oppoſe him with a great army.

Pittu Rai, King of Ajmere, gave a diſreſpectful anſwer to the embaſſy, and immediately wrote for ſuccours to all the neighbouring Princes. Nor did his allies delay their coming, and therefore he ſoon advanced to meet Mahommed, with an army conſiſting, according to the loweſt and moſt moderate account, of three hundred thouſand horſe; beſides above three thouſand elephants, and a great body of infantry. The Hindoos again waited to receive Mahommed upon the former field of battle. The two armies incamped in ſight of each other, with the river Surſutti between them.

The haughty letter of the Rajas.

The Indian princes, of whom there were one hundred and fifty, in this enormous camp, having aſſembled, rubbed Tica upon their foreheads, and ſwore by the water of the Ganges, that they would conquer their enemies, or die martyrs to their faith. They then wrote a letter to Mahommed, in theſe haughty terms. "To the bravery of our troops we imagined you was no ſtranger; and to our great ſuperiority in number, which daily increaſes, your eyes will bear teſtimony of the truth. If you are wearied of your own exiſtence, yet have pity upon your troops, who may ſtill think it a happineſs to live. It were better then you ſhould repent in time, of the fooliſh reſolution

resolution you have taken, and we shall permit you to retreat in safety. But if you have determined to force your evil destiny, we have sworn by our Gods to advance upon you with our rank-breaking elephants, war-treading horses, and blood-thirsting soldiers, early in the morning, to crush the unfortunate army which your ambition has led to ruin." A.D. 1193. Higer. 589.

Mahommed returned them this politic answer. ——"That he had drawn his army into India, by the command of his brother, whose general he only was, and that honour and duty bound him to exert the utmost of his capacity in his service That therefore he could not retreat without his leave, but would be glad to obtain a truce, till he informed him of the situation of affairs, and received his answer." Mahommed's answer.

This letter produced the intended effect, for the enemy imagined that Mahommed was intimidated, and they spent the night in riot and revelry, while he was preparing for a surprise. He accordingly forded the river a little before the dawn of the morning, drew up his army on the sands, and had entered part of the Indian camp, before the alarm was spread. Notwithstanding the confusion that naturally reigned on this occasion among the Hindoos, their camp was of such an amazing extent, that the greater part had sufficient time to form the line which served to cover the rout, so that now they began to advance with great resolution and some order, in four lines. He surprises their camp.

Mahommed, upon seeing this, ordered his troops to halt, and his army, which had been divided into four parts, were commanded to renew the attack by turns, wheeling off to the rear after they had discharged their bows a certain number of times upon the enemy, giving ground gradually as they advanced with their elephants. In this manner The Indians overthrown.

A.D. 1193. Higer. 589. manner he retreated and fought, till the ſun was approaching the weſt, when thinking he had ſufficiently wearied the enemy, and deluded them with a ſecurity of victory, he put himſelf at the head of twelve thouſand of his beſt horſe, whoſe riders were covered with ſteel, and giving orders to his generals to ſecond him, he made a reſolute charge, and carried death and confuſion among the Hindoo ranks. The diſorder increaſed every where, till at length it became general. The Muſſulman troops, as if now only ſerious in fight, made ſuch a dreadful ſlaughter, that this prodigious army once ſhaken, like a great building, was loſt in its own ruins. The enemy recoiled, like a troubled torrent, from the bloody plain.

Candi King of Delhi, and many other princes, were ſlain in the field, while Pittu Rai King of Ajmere was taken in the purſuit, and afterwards put to death. The ſpoil of the camp, which was immenſely rich, fell into the hands of the conquerors, and the forts of Surſutti, Samana, Koram and Haſſi, ſurrendered after the victory. Mahommed in perſon went to Ajmere, and took poſſeſſion of it, after having barbarouſly put ſome thouſands of the unfortunate inhabitants to the ſword, reſerving the reſt for ſlavery. But, upon a promiſe of a punctual payment of a large tribute, he gave up the country to Gola the ſon of Pittu Rai. He then turned his ſtandards towards Delhi, but he was prevailed upon by the new king, with great preſents, to abandon that enterprize. He left his faithful ſlave and friend Cuttub in the town of Koram, with a conſiderable detachment, and marched himſelf, with the body of his army, towards the mountains of Sewalic, which lie to the north of India, deſtroying and plundering all the countries in his way to Ghizni. After the return of Mahommed, his general Cuttub, who

Mahommed ſettles the conquered countries.

who had been formerly a ſlave, raiſed an army, and took the fort of Merat, and the city of Delhi, from the family of Candi Rai. It was from this circumſtance that foreign nations ſay, that the empire of Delhi was founded by a ſlave. In the year 589, he alſo took the fort of Kole, and making Delhi the ſeat of his government, there eſtabliſhed himſelf in ſecurity, obliging all the diſtricts round to acknowledge the Muſſulman faith. A.D. 1194. Higer. 591.

Mahommed, in the mean time, marched from Ghizni towards Kinnoge, and engaged Rai Joy, who was prince of Kinnoge and Benaris, and who commanded a very numerous army of horſe, beſides four hundred elephants. This prince led his forces into the field between Chundwar and Atava, where he received a total defeat from the vanguard of the Ghiznian army, led by Cuttub, and all his baggage and elephants were taken. Mahommed then marched to the fort of Aſſi, where Rai Joy had laid up his treaſure, which in a few days he took, and found there, gold, ſilver, and precious ſtones, to a great amount. He marched from thence to Benaris, and broke down the idols in above one thouſand temples, which he purified and conſecrated to the true God. Here he alſo found immenſe plunder. He returned then to the fort of Kole, where he again confirmed Cuttub in the viceroyſhip of India, and from thence, laden with treaſure, he took the rout of Ghizni. Invades the eaſtern provinces. Mahommed takes Aſſi and Benaris.

In the mean time, one of the relations of Pittu Rai, late king of Ajmere, whoſe name was Himrage, invaded Gola the ſon of Pittu Rai, and drove him out of Ajmere. Gola immediately had recourſe for aſſiſtance to Cuttub. Cuttub accordingly marched, in the year 591, from Delhi againſt Himrage, who, having collected a great army, gave the Muſſulmen battle, in which he loſt the victory and his life. Cuttub, after this victory, Actions of Cuttub.

appointed

A. D. 1202. Higer. 599. appointed a governor of his own faith to ſuperintend the Raja, then led his army to Narwalla, the capital of the province of Guzerat, and defeating Bim Deo, took ample revenge for the overthrow given to his Lord. He plundered that rich country; but he was ſoon recalled, by orders from Ghizni, and commanded to proceed immediately to Delhi.

Mahommed again invades Hindoſtan. In the year following, Mahommed formed again a reſolution of returning to Hindoſtan, and proceeding to Biana. He took it and conferred the government upon Tughril; and leaving with him the body of his army, he commanded him to beſiege Gualier, and returned himſelf to ſettle ſome affairs at Ghizni. In the mean time, the ſtrong fort of Gualier was taken, after a long ſiege. Tughril, ambitious of extending his conqueſts further, led his army againſt the Rajaputs of the ſouth. But he received a terrible defeat, and was obliged to take the protection of his forts. In the year 593, Cuttub marched again from Delhi, and reduced Narwalla of Guzerat, with all its dependencies. He, after his return, took the forts of Callinger, Calpee and Budaoon.

Sultan Yeas ul dien dies. Mahommed was in the mean time engaged in an expedition to Toos and Sirchus towards Perſia. News was then brought to him of the death of his brother Yeas ul dien, who retained nothing of the empire but the name. Mahommed, upon this, acceded to the empire. He turned by the way of Badyeiſh, and ſubdued the country of Choraſſan, recovering it out of the hands of the Siljoki, and he divided it among the family of Sam, giving the government of Firoſe Ko and Ghor to Malleck Zea, who was ſon-in-law to his brother Yeas ul dien, the deceaſed Emperor. Buſt, Ferra and Iſphorar he gave to Mamood, his brother's ther's son; and the government of Herat and its districts to Nasir, his nephew by a sister. A.D. 1203. Higer. 600.

Mahommed, after these transactions, returned to Ghizni, where, according to the will of the deceased Emperor, he was crowned in form; and mounted the imperial throne. In the same year, he heard of the death of Zireck, prince of Murve, and in the beginning of the next, marched to the conquest of that country, advancing by the way of Charizm, and Tacash the King of that country, not able to oppose him in the field, shut himself up in the city. The King pitched his camp on the banks of the great canal, which the Chilligies had formerly dug to the westward of that city. He forthwith attacked the place, and in a few days lost many brave nobles in the pursuit of glory. In the mean time, news arrived, that Aibeck, the general of the King of Chitta, in Tartary, and Osman King of Samarcand, were advancing with great armies, to the relief of Charizm. Mahommed was so unwilling to abandon his hopes of taking the city, that he delayed till the allied armies advanced so near, that he was under a necessity of burning all his baggage, and to retreat with the utmost expedition towards Chorassan. But an army from the city pressed so close upon his heels, that he was obliged to give them battle. He was totally defeated, losing all his elephants and treasure.

Mahommed crowned at Ghizni.

Marches into Charizm and besieges the city.

In the mean time, the confederate Kings, who had taken a circuit, to cut off Mahommed's retreat, met him full in the face, as he was flying from the King of Charizm. Under a fatal necessity, he was obliged to rally his army, who now saw no safety in flight. Surrounded thus by the enemy, he commenced a desperate carnage. But valour was overpowered by numbers in the end, and of his late mighty army, there now remained

He is again totally overthrown.

scarce

A.D. 1203. Higer. 600. scarce a hundred men, who still defended their King, and in spite of innumerable foes, hewed him out a passage, and conducted him safe to the fort of Hindohood, which was at a small distance from the field. Mahommed was besieged here by the enemy, but upon paying a great ransom to Osman, King of Samarcand, and giving up the place, he was permitted to return in sorrow to his own dominions.

Birka's villainy. When the Emperor was defeated, one of his officers of state, named Birka, escaped from the field, and imagining the King was slain, with very great expedition made his way to Moultan, without mentioning the affair to any body. He waited immediately upon Hassen, governor of that province, and told him that he had a private message from the King. Hassen retired with him into his closet, where the villain, whispering in his ear, drew out a dagger, and stabbed him to the heart. He ran instantly to the court yard, where he proclaimed aloud, that he had killed the traitor, Hassen, in obedience to the King's command. Producing then a false order and commission, to take the government into his own hands, he was acknowledged by the army and the people.

The chief of the Gickers aspires to the throne. The chief of the tribe of mountaineers, called Gickers, at this time, hearing that the King was certainly slain, aspired to the empire, and raising a great army, advanced towards Lahore; kindling the war between the rivers Gelum and Sodra. When Mahommed, from the fort of Hindohood, had arrived at Ghizni, his own slave Ildecuz having seized upon the supreme authority in the city, presented himself to oppose his entrance, which obliged the King to continue his route to Moultan. There Birka also rebelled against him; but Mahommed, being by this time joined by many of his friends, gave him battle, and obtaining a complete

plete victory, took the traitor prisoner. He then, with all the troops of the borders of India, who now joined his standard, marched to Ghizni, and the citizens, presenting him with the head of the rebellious slave, obtained their pardon. Mahommed, at this time, concluded a treaty of peace with the King of Charizm; and then, in order to chastise the Gickers, drew his army towards India. Cuttub attacked them on the other side with his army from Delhi, and the Gickers being defeated and dispersed, the King parted, at Lahore, with Cuttub, who returned to his government of Delhi. A.D. 1205. Higer. 602.

During the residence of Mahommed at Lahore, the Gickers, who inhabited the country from that branch of the Indus which is called the Nilab, up to the fort of the mountains of Sewalic, began to exercise unheard-of cruelties upon the Mussulmen; so that the communication between the provinces of Peshawir and Moultan was entirely cut off. These Gickers were a race of wild barbarians, without either religion or morality. It was a custom among them, as soon as a female child was born, to carry her to the market place, and there proclaim aloud, holding the child in one hand, and a knife in the other, that any person who wanted a wife might now take her, otherwise she was immediately put to death. By this means, they had more men than women, which occasioned the custom of several husbands to one wife. When this wife was visited by one of her husbands, she set up a mark at the door, which being observed by any of the other, who might be coming on the same errand, he immediately withdrew, till the signal was taken away. This barbarous people continued to make incursions upon the Mahommedans, till, in the latter end of the Emperor's reign, their chieftain was converted to the Mussul- The Gickers a tribe of barbarians.

man

A. D. 1205. Higer. 602. man faith, by one of his captives. He, upon this change of principles, addressed the King, who advised him to endeavour to convert his people; and at the same time honoured him with a title and dress, and confirmed him in the command of the mountains. A great part of these mountaineers, being very indifferent about religion, followed the opinions of their chief, and acknowledged the true faith. At the same time, about four hundred thousand of the inhabitants of Teraiba, who inhabited the mountains between Ghizni and the Indus, were converted, some by force and others by inclination.

Mahommed proposes to invade Turkestan.

Mahommed having settled the affairs of India in peace, marched, in the year 602, from Lahore to Ghizni. He conferred the government of Bamia upon his relation Baka ul dien, with orders, that when he himself should move towards Turkestan, to take satisfaction for his former defeat, to march at an appointed time, with all the forces of those parts, and encamp on the banks of the Amu, where he would receive further orders, and at the same time to throw a bridge over the river.

A conspiracy.

The Emperor, upon the second of Shaban, having reached the banks of the Nilab, one of the five capital branches of the Indus, at a place called Rimeik, twenty Gickers, who had lost some of their relations in their wars against Mahommed, entered into a conspiracy against his life, and sought an opportunity to put their wicked purpose in execution. The weather being close and sultry, the King ordered the Canats, or the screens, which surround, in the form of a large square, the imperial tents, to be struck, to give free admission to the air. This gave them an opportunity of seeing the King's sleeping tent. They

cut

cut their way through the ſcreens in the night, and hid themſelves in a corner, while one of them advanced to the door; but being there ſtopt by one of the guards, who was going to ſeize him, he buried his dagger in his breaſt. The groans of the dying man being heard within, alarmed the reſt of the guards in the outer tent, who running out to ſee what was the matter, the other aſſaſſins took that opportunity of cutting their way through the King's tent behind. They found him aſleep, with two ſlaves fanning him, who ſtood petrified with terror, when they beheld the aſſaſſins advancing towards the Emperor. They at once plunged all their daggers in his body. He was afterwards found to have been pierced with no leſs than forty wounds.

A. D. 1205. Higer. 602.

Mahommed aſſaſſinated.

Thus tragically fell that great king and conqueror Mahommed Ghori in the year 602, after a reign of thirty-two years from the commencement of his government over Ghizni, and three from his acceſſion to the empire, the honours and titles of which he permitted his elder brother to retain during his life. One daughter only remained of his race. He was certainly one of the greateſt men that ever ſat upon the throne of India; and though he was, in ſome inſtances, cruel, he was not altogether an unvirtuous prince.

His character.

The Vizier, Chaja ul Muluck, took ſome of the aſſaſſins, and put them to a cruel death. He then called the chiefs together, and having obtained their promiſe of fidelity, in protecting the King's treaſure, which was loaded on four thouſand camels, he prevented the army and the ſlaves, who had propoſed to plunder it, from putting their ſcheme in execution. He carried the body in mournful pomp towards Ghizni. But when they reached Peſhawir, a great conteſt aroſe about the ſucceſſion. The Omrahs of Ghor inſiſting upon

Diſputes about the ſucceſſion.

Baha

A.D. 1205. Higer. 602. Baha-ul-dien, the King's coufin, governor of Bamia, and one of the feven fons of Huffein; and the Vizier, and the officers of the Turkifh mercenaries, on Mamood, fon of the former Emperor, the brother of Mahommed Ghori. The Vizier therefore wanted to go by the way of Kirma, where he knew that the governor Ildecuz was in the intereft of Mamood, hoping, by his affiftance, to fecure, at leaft, the treafure for his own party. The Omrahs of Ghor were equally defirous of proceeding by that road which lay neareft to Bamia, that they might be the fooner fupported by Baha-ul-dien. At length, being upon the eve of open hoftility, the point was given up to the Vizier.

When they arrived near Kirma, after having fuffered greatly by the mountaineers, Ildecuz came out to meet the Vizier and the King's hearfe; upon fight of which he tore off his armour, threw duft upon his head, and expreffed all the variety of forrow. He attended the funeral to Ghizni, where the Emperor was buried in a new tomb which he had built for his daughter. The forrow of Ildecuz was the more extraordinary, that, in the King's misfortunes, he had fhewn fuch difrefpect to him, as to be acceffary to the fhutting of the gates of his capital againft him. It will, however, hereafter appear, that Ildecuz's grief was political. The treafure Mahommed left behind him is almoft incredible: we fhall only mention, as an inftance of his wealth, that he had, in diamonds of various fizes alone, five hundred maunds*; for he had made nine expeditions into Hindoftan; returning every time, excepting twice, laden with wealth.

The body carried to Ghizni.

* The fmalleft maund is twenty-five pounds Avoirdupoife.

Though

Though Tacash, King of Charizm, had, by the death of Togril, the last of the Siljokides of Persia, rendered himself independent, and annexed the greatest part of the Persian empire to his government of Maver-ul-nere, the distractions which arose from the revolution furnished an opportunity to Mahommed Ghori to seize upon the extensive province of Chorassan, and to become so powerful in the north, as to block up the King of Charizm in his capital. The defeat, which ensued, not only weakened the power of Mahommed, but encreased that of Tacash so much, that he was enabled to extend his dominion over all Persia and the Western Tartary. His son Mahommed succeeded Tacash in his vast empire, and the family of Ghor were obliged to confine themselves to the ancient dominions of the house of Ghizni.

A.D. 1205. Higer. 602. State of Asia at the death of Mahommed.

CUTTUB.

C U T T U B.

A. D. 1205. Higer. 602. THE death of Mahommed Ghori may, in ſome degree, be ſaid to have put an end to the empire of Ghizni. The unambitious character of the ſurviving princes of the family of Ghor, gave an opportunity to two of the imperial ſlaves, to divide among them the empire, which Mahommed had been at ſo much pains to acquire. Ildecuz, or, as he is ſometimes called, Eldoze, kept poſſeſſion of Ghizni and the northern provinces, and Cuttub, the favourite friend and faithful ſervant of the late Emperor, was already viceroy of the empire, over the conqueſts in India. As it was from Cuttub the Mahommedan empire of the Patans, or Afgans, in India commenced, we ſhall begin with his hiſtory.

Cuttub's character, Cuttub * was of a brave and virtuous diſpoſition, open and liberal to his friends, and courteous and affable to ſtrangers. In the art of war and government he was inferior to none, nor was he a mean proficient in literature. In his childhood he was brought from Turkeſtan to Neſhapoor, and there ſold by a merchant, to Caſi the ſon of Abu, who, finding that Heaven had endued him with a great genius, ſent him to ſchool, where he made a wonderful progreſs in the Perſian and Arabic lan-

* His titles at full length were Cuttub-ul-dien, Abiek.

guages,

guages, and in all the polite arts and sciences. But his patron and master dying suddenly, he was sold as part of his estate, by his relations, and bought by a rich merchant, for a great sum of money, and presented for sale to the Emperor, Mahommed Ghori. That monarch purchased him, and called him by the familiar name of Abiek, from having his little finger broke. He behaved himself in such a becoming and assiduous manner, that he soon attracted the notice of his prince, and daily gained confidence and favour. One night Mahommed kept a magnificent festival at court, and ordered a liberal distribution of presents and money to be made among his servants. Abiek partook largely of his munificence, but had no sooner retired, than he divided his share among his companions. The King having heard of this circumstance, asked him the cause, and Abiek, kissing the earth, replied; "That all his wants were amply supplied by his Majesty's bounty. He had therefore no desire of burdening himself with superfluities, his favour being a certain independence." This answer so pleased the King, that he immediately gave him an office near his person, and, in a little time, was so satisfied with his diligence and capacity, that he appointed him master of the horse.

A.D. 1205. Higer. 602.

His rise, generosity, affability, capacity,

In one of the expeditions of Mahommed against the king of Charizm, in order to expel that prince from Chorassan, Abiek went out with a detachment to forage on the banks of the Murgaab. He was there surrounded by a numerous party of the enemy. But though he did the utmost justice to valour, he was, after the loss of most of his men, taken prisoner, and carried to the king of Charizm, who put him in chains. But that monarch being defeated, Abiek was left in this manner, sitting upon a camel in the field, and carried

and valour.

to

to his victorious master; who pitying his condition, received him with great kindness.

Made governor in Hindostan.

In the year 588, when Mahommed took revenge of his enemies, the Hindoos, for the defeat they had given him, he, upon his return, appointed Abiek, who was then dignified with the title of Cuttub-ul-dien*, to the chief command of the army left to protect his conquests. In discharge of this duty, Cuttub took possession of many districts around, and reduced the fort of Merat. He also drew his army towards Delhi, and invested it. But the garrison, finding that their own numbers triply exceeded the besiegers, marched out of the place, and drew up in order of battle, which was gladly accepted by Cuttub. When the slaughter became great on both sides, and the river Jumna was discoloured with blood, the Rajaputs were at length put to flight, taking protection within their walls. The garrison, after a desperate siege, were at last obliged to capitulate.

Defeats the Jits,

In the year 589, the Jits, who were subject to the prince of Narwalla, in Guzerat, advanced with an army to besiege Hassi. Cuttub marched with his forces to protect it, and obliging them to raise the siege, pursued them to their own frontiers. In the year following, he crossed the Jumna, and took the fort of Kole by assault. He found there a thousand fine horses, and much spoil, and being informed of Mahommed's expedition towards Kinnoge, he thought proper to proceed as far as Peshawir to meet him, presenting him with a hundred fine horses, and two great elephants, one of which carried a chain of gold and the other a chain of silver. He mustered there, before the King, fifty thousand horse, and was honoured with an

* The Pole-star of religion.

honorary

honorary dress, and with the command of the van of the royal army.

With the van he defeated the prince of Benaris, who, upon seeing his army retreat, pushed forward his elephant, in despair, against his enemy; but Cuttub, who excelled in archery, sunk an arrow in the ball of his eye, which brought him down from his elephant to the ground. It is said, that the number of slain was so great, that the body of the Raja for a long time could not be found by his friends, who were permitted to search for it. But, at last, he was discovered by his artificial teeth, which were fixed in by golden wedges and wires. The Emperor Mahommed, following with the body of the army, entered the city of Benaris, and took possession of the country, as far as the boundaries of Bengal, without opposition. He broke down all the idols, and loaded four thousand camels with the most valuable spoils. Cuttub presented the King with above three hundred elephants, taken from the Raja of Benaris. The riders had a signal given them to make the elephants fall upon their knees to the King at once, which they all did, except one white elephant. This animal was esteemed an inestimable curiosity, but upon this occasion, though extremely tractable at other times, had almost killed his rider, when he endeavoured to force him to pay his obedience. and the Raja of Benaris.

The King, when he was setting out for Ghizni, sent the white elephant back, in a present to Cuttub, and adopted him his son in his letter. Cuttub, ever afterwards, till his death, rode the white elephant; and when he died, the affectionate animal pined away with visible sorrow, and expired the third day after. This was the only white elephant of which we have ever heard in Hindostan; but it is said, that the King of Pegu keeps always two white elephants, and that, when one of them Cuttub adopted by the King.

 dies,

dies, he iſſues out an order over all his dominions, to ſearch the woods for another to ſupply his place. Cuttub, after the departure of the King, remained ſome days at Aſſi, where the Raja's treaſure was found. He then returned to Delhi, and there received advice that Himrage, the couſin of the diſcomfited prince of Ajmere, was marching down from the mountains of Abugur, and had driven Gola, the reigning prince, towards Rintimpore, and that Himrage's general was marching, with another army, towards Delhi, before which he ſoon arrived, and began to deſtroy the country. Cuttub marched out to chaſtiſe him, and ſeparating twenty thouſand horſe from the reſt of his army, he ſet out in front, and engaging the enemy, put them to flight. The enemy, ſome days after, rallying their defeated army, retreated towards Ajmere, and were purſued all the way by the conqueror. Himrage being joined by his general, in confidence of his ſuperior numbers, formed his army in order of battle. When they came to blows, he diſtinguiſhed himſelf by his bravery, as well as by his conduct; but, being ſlain, his army took the way of infamy before them. Thus Ajmere was reſtored to the Mahommedan government, and was afterwards ruled by its laws.

Cuttub ravages the territory of Narwalla.

In the year 590, Cuttub turned his arms towards Narwalla, of Guzerat, and Setwan, the general of Bimdeo, who was encamped under the walls, fled upon his approach. But being purſued, he drew up his army, and fought till he loſt his life, and then his army reſumed their flight. Bimdeo, upon intelligence of this defeat, fled from his dominions, and Cuttub ravaged the country at leiſure, and found much ſpoil. He marched from thence to the fort of Haſſi, which he repaired, then having viſited Koram, returned to Delhi.

Delhi. He in the mean time received advice, from the governor of the districts near Rintimpore, that the brother of Gola, prince of Ajmere, who lived in the hills, was marching down with an army to invade him. This obliged Cuttub to move immediately to his relief. The enemy, upon hearing this, fled; and Cuttub paid a visit to Gola, who entertained him magnificently, and, at his departure, presented him with some fine jewels, and two melons of gold. When he had settled the country, he again returned to Delhi, from whence he wrote to the King a particular account of his conquests, which so pleased Mahommed, that he ordered his attendance at Ghizni, for which place he set out, and was received with every demonstration of joy and respect.

Cuttub, some time after, obtained leave to return to his government, and, on his way, married the daughter of Tagi, governor of Persian Kirman*, making a magnificent rejoicing upon the occasion, when he returned to Delhi. He soon after marched his army to the siege of the fort of Biana, and, when he was on his way, he heard that the Emperor Mahommed, his master and patron, had taken the route of Hindostan. To shew his respect for the King, Cuttub returned back as far as Hassi to meet him. Both returned to Biana, besieged and took the place, which Mahommed submitted to the command of Tugril, one of his particular and trusty slaves. They then took the route of Gualier, where the prince of that country agreed to pay tribute, and bought peace with a great sum of ready money, and with jewels. The King, immediately after these transactions, returned to Ghizni, leaving Cuttub viceroy of all the conquered provinces of India.

Reduces Biana

and Gualier.

* The ancient Carmania.

About

Marches against the Rajaputs,

About this time, news arrived that many Indian independent princes had entered into an alliance with the king of Narwalla, and had formed a design to recover Ajmere from the Mahommedans. The troops of Cuttub being dispersed over the provinces, he was forced to march against the Indians, with what small part of the army lay in Delhi, to prevent their junction with the forces of Narwalla; but he was defeated, received six wounds, and was often dismounted; yet he fought like a man who had made death his companion. Forced at last, by his own friends, to abandon the field, he was carried in a litter to Ajmere.

and is defeated.

Besieged in Ajmere.

Tittura, chief of the Indians, rejoicing at this victory, joined the forces of Narwalla and Guzerat, and sat down before Ajmere, Intelligence of this unfortunate event coming to the Emperor Mahommed, he sent a great force from Ghizni, to the relief of Cuttub. Ajmere held out till the arrival of the Ghiznians, who obliged the enemy to raise the siege. Cuttub pursued them to Narwalla, in the year 593, taking, in his way, the forts of Tilli and Buzule. He there received advice that Walin and Daraparifs, in alliance with the king of Narwalla, were encamped near the fort of Abugur, to guard the passes into Guzerat. Cuttub, notwithstanding the difficulties of the road, and disadvantages of ground, resolved to attack them, which he did with such bravery and conduct, that, having trodden down their ranks, above fifty thousand of the enemy, with their blood, tempered the dust of the field. Twenty thousand were taken prisoners, and an immense spoil fell into his hands.

Marches to Guzerat.

When he had given his army some respite from slaughter and fatigue, he pursued his route into Guzerat, and ravaged that country without further opposition, taking the city of Narwalla, where an

Omrah

Omrah with a ſtrong garriſon was left. He then returned to Delhi, by the way of Ajmere, and ſent a great quantity of jewels and gold, and alſo many ſlaves, to Mahommed, at Ghizni, and divided the remainder among his truſty partners in the glories of the field. In the year 599, he muſtered his forces, and marched to the ſiege of Calinger, where he was met by Gola, the tributary prince of that country, whom he defeated; and diſmounting his cavalry, began to beſiege him in his fort. Gola, ſeeing himſelf hard preſſed, offered Cuttub the ſame tribute and preſents which his anceſtors had formerly paid to the Emperor Mamood. The propoſal was accepted, but the vizier, who wanted to hold out without coming to any terms, found means to make away with the Raja, while the preſents were preparing to be ſent. The flag of hoſtility was again hoiſted upon the fort, and the ſiege recommenced. The place, however, was in a ſhort time reduced, on account of the drying up of a ſpring upon that hill whereon the fort ſtood, and which ſupplied the garriſon with water. There is a tradition among the natives of the place, that the above fountain always dries up upon the diſcharging the artillery of the place. This ſtory may poſſibly, from a natural cauſe, have ſome foundation. But we are rather tempted to believe, that the preſent drying up of this ſpring was owing to the increaſe of inhabitants, and the thirſt occaſioned by hard duty; for, beſides the garriſon, Cuttub found there fifty thouſand male and female.

The plunder of this city was very great, in gold, jewels and precious effects. Cuttub then marched to the city of Mhoba, the capital of the principality of Calpee. He alſo took that place, together with Budaſo, between the rivers Jumna and Ganges. Mahommed Chilligi, who had been appointed

Takes Mhoba and Budaſo.

A.D. 1205. Higer. 602. appointed governor of Behar by the Emperor, but had, for ſome time back, been refractory to the imperial commands, came at this time to pay him a viſit, laying rich preſents at his feet, and Cuttub having entertained him magnificently, returned to Delhi.

Joins the Emperor againſt the Gickers. When Mahommed Ghori, after his defeat in Turkeſtan, returned to India, he was joined by Cuttub, by whoſe valour and fidelity he defeated the Gickers in ſeveral actions, and recovered his fallen glory. When matters were peaceably ſettled in this quarter, he returned to his government; and the Emperor, upon his way to Ghizni, was inhumanly aſſaſſinated by the Gickers. Mahommed's nephew, Mamood, aſſumed the imperial titles at Ghor, and upon his acceſſion, ſent all the enſigns of royalty, a throne, an umbrella, ſtandards, drums, and the title of King to Cuttub, deſirous of retaining him in his intereſt, as he was by no means able to oppoſe his power.

Raiſed to the Empire. Cuttub received thoſe dignities with a proper reſpect, at Lahore, where he aſcended the throne in the year 602, upon the 18th of Zicada; returning from thence in a few days to Delhi. In the mean time, Ildecuz, or Eldoze, marched an army from Ghizni, with an intention to take Lahore, which he effected by the treachery of the governor, whom he afterwards turned out. Cuttub marched to diſpute the point with Eldoze, as ſoon as he received intelligence at Delhi of this tranſaction. In the year 603 the flames of war began to aſcend between them, while bravery, on both ſides, became apparent. Eldoze, at length, was beat out of the city, and obliged to fly towards Kirman. Cuttub purſued him as far as Ghizni, in which city he was again crowned, taking that kingdom into his own hands.

Cuttub,

Cuttub, after this, unaccountably gave himself up to wine and pleasure, till the citizens of Ghizni, disgusted with his luxury and indolence, sent privately to Eldoze, acquainting him of the King's negligence, and intreating his return. Eldoze, upon this, recruiting an army with all secrecy and expedition, advanced towards Ghizni, and in a manner surprized Cuttub, who had no intelligence of his design till the day before his arrival. It was now too late to put himself in a proper state of defence, and he was obliged to abandon the kingdom, and retire to Lahore. He then became sensible of his own weakness, repented of his evil habits, and exercised himself in the practice of justice, temperance and morality. He regulated his kingdoms according to the best laws of policy and wisdom till his death, in the year 607, which happened by a fall from his horse in a match at ball, which adverse parties endeavoured to carry off on the point of their spears.

A.D. 1210. Higer, 607. Cuttub turns indolent and luxurious.

He dies.

His reign, properly speaking, was only four years, though he enjoyed all the state and dignities of a king, for upwards of twenty, if we reckon from his taking of Delhi, when he may be said to have become king of India; though he assumed only the title of commander in chief for his patron Mahommed. He was certainly an accomplished warrior, and had nearly equalled the greatest heroes in fame, had not his loss of the kingdom of Ghizni tarnished his glory. He was famous for his great generosity all over the east, for which he got the sirname of Bestower of Lacks. When a man is praised for generosity in India, they say to this day, " He is as generous as Cuttub-ul-dien.

His character.

Mahommed,

A.D. 1210. Higer. 607. State of Asia. Mahommed, the ſon of Tacaſh, reigned over Charizm and all Perſia, during the ſhort reign of Cuttub. He invaded the ſmall provinces in poſſeſſion of the Patan empire, to the north of the Indus; and, taking Ghizni, reduced all Zabuliſtan beneath his command.

ELDOZE.

MAHOMMED GHORI, during his reign, having no children of his own excepting one daughter, had taken a particular pleasure in educating Turkish slaves, whom he afterwards adopted as his children. Four of those slaves, besides Cuttub, became great princes, of whom the present Eldoze was one. The King having observed him to be a youth of genius, advanced him gradually, till at last he bestowed upon him the government of Kirma and Shinoran, which lay between Ghizni and India. His situation gave him an opportunity of frequently entertaining his prince, upon his expeditions to and from that country, which he always did with great magnificence and festivity, making presents to all the King's attendants. Eldoze's rise.

Mahommed, in his last expedition, favoured Eldoze so much, that he bestowed upon him the black standard of the kingdom of Ghizni, by this intimating his will, that he should succeed to that throne. But, upon the death of that monarch, the Turkish Omrahs were desirous that Mamood, the son of the former Emperor, should come from Ghor and reign at Ghizni. Mamood being a man of an indolent disposition declined it; and said, that he was content with the throne of his an- Ascends the throne of Ghizni.

ceſtors. He, however, aſſumed the imperial title, proclaimed Eldoze king of Ghizni, and was content to maintain the appearance of that power which he would not, or rather durſt not enforce.

King of Charizm takes Ghizni.

The firſt thing Eldoze did after his acceſſion, was to croſs the Indus, and invade Punjab and Lahore, as we have ſeen in the former reign. He was defeated by Cuttub, and in conſequence loſt his own kingdom; which, however, he ſoon after recovered. He afterwards, in conjunction with the Emperor Mamood of Ghor, ſent an army to Herat, which they conquered, as alſo a great part of Seiſtan, but making peace with the prince of that country, they returned. On the way, making war upon the great Mahommed king of Charizm, they were both defeated, and the conqueror purſuing his fortune, took Ghizni, while Eldoze retired to Kirma, his former government, on the borders of India. Eldoze, finding the northern troops too hard for him, recruited an army, and marched ſome time after the death of Cuttub, with a view to conquer India. But, after reducing ſome of the northern provinces, he was defeated near Delhi, by the Emperor Altumſh, and being taken, died in confinement. The time of his reign was nine years.

Eldoze defeated and taken, dies.

Tughril a brave and virtuous Omrah.

As we have already given the hiſtory of two of Mahommed Ghori's adopted ſlaves who arrived at the imperial dignity, it may not be improper here to ſay ſomething of Tughril, who raiſed himſelf from the ſame low ſituation. Tughril was a chief of ſome repute in the ſervice of Mahommed; brave, and of a virtuous diſpoſition. They relate, that when Mahommed took the fort of Biana, he gave the command of it to Tughril, and proceeded himſelf to Gualier, as we have ſeen before. But after he left Hindoſtan, Tughril continued to infeſt the country about

Gualier;

Gualier; the King having told him at his departure, that if he conquered the place, he would confirm him in the government of it. When he found that this manner of war had no effect, as they always found some opportunity of supplying the place, he ordered small forts to be built all round, which he garrisoned, and by this means the fort was effectually blockaded. Yet it held out for near a whole year, when, being distressed for provisions, they sent an embassy privately to Cuttub to come and take possession of the place, for they had conceived an implacable resentment against Tughril. Cuttub accordingly sent his troops to seize upon Gualier; upon which, war had almost ensued between him and Tughril. Death however interfering, put an end to the dispute; for, at this juncture, Tughril suddenly expired. The actions of the other two princes, formerly slaves to Mahommed, will be seen in the history of Sind and Punjab, to which they more properly belong.

ARAM.

A R A M.

A. D. 1210. Higer. 607. Aram a weak prince.

AFTER the death of Cuttub, his ſon Aram * mounted the throne of Delhi; but was no ways equal to the government of ſo great an empire. Naſir, one of the adopted ſlaves of Mahommed Ghori, marched with an army towards Sind, which he conquered, as alſo Moultan, Otch, Shinoran and other places. Another ſlave, Mahommed of Chilligi, poſſeſſed himſelf of the kingdom of Bengal, and aſſerted his own independence. At the ſame time, ſeveral dependent princes blew up the flames of rebellion in many parts of the empire.

Defeated and depoſed.

Upon theſe misfortunes, Ali Iſmaiel, Daood Delhi, and all the Omrahs, became diſcontented, ſending a perſon to call Altumſh, who was the ſon-in-law and adopted ſon of Cuttub, and then governor of Budaoon†, to aſcend the throne. Altumſh accordingly marched with his army to Delhi, and by the aſſiſtance of the faction within, eaſily reduced it. Aram, afraid of truſting himſelf in his capital, had previouſly withdrawn into the country, recruited a fine army, and advanced to give Altumſh battle. A warm engagement enſued in ſight of the city. Aram loſt the victory and his empire, which he had enjoyed ſcarce one year.

* Sultan Aram Shaw.

† The country beyond the Ganges, N. E. from Delhi, now poſſeſſed by the Rohillas.

ALTUMSH.

A L T U M S H.

WE are told that Altumsh * was descended of a noble family in the Tartarian Chitta, and that his father's name was Elim, a great and famous general. But in his youth, being the favourite of his father, he was envied by the rest of his brothers. They therefore determined to get rid of him, and as they were out one day hunting, they stript him, and sold him to a company of travelling merchants for a slave. The merchants carried him to Bochara, and sold him to one of the relations of Jehan, prince of that country, from whom he received a liberal education. Upon the death of his master he was again exposed to sale, and bought by a merchant, who sold him to another, who carried him to Ghizni. The Emperor Mahommed heard at Ghizni of Altumsh's beauty and talents, but could not agree with the merchant about his price. He was therefore carried back to Bochara, as none durst buy him, on account of the King's displeasure, till Cuttub, obtaining his leave, made that purchase at Delhi, whither he had invited the merchant, for fifty thousand pieces of silver. Cuttub, at the same time,

The family of Altumsh.

* Shumse ul dien Altumsh.

A. D. 1210. Higer. 607. time, bought another ſlave, whom he called Taga, and appointed him afterwards governor of Tibberhind, where he was ſlain in the battle between Cuttub and Eldoze. Altumſh, in the mean time, was made maſter of the chace, and afterwards roſe to ſuch favour that he became the adopted ſon of his patron, Cuttub, and was advanced to the government of Gualier and Birren, and from thence to the viceroyſhip of Budaoon. He accompanied Cuttub in his war againſt the Gickers, and greatly diſtinguiſhed himſelf in bravery and zeal for the ſervice. He killed in one action, with the troops of Budaoon, upwards of ten thouſand of the enemy. This behaviour ſo pleaſed Cuttub, that he declared him free, and made him many honorary preſents.

Accedes to the throne. Thus by degrees, Altumſh roſe, till he was created captain general of the empire; and married the daughter of Cuttub, and upon his death, as we have before related, he advanced againſt the capital, and, expelling Aram from the throne in the year 607, declared himſelf Emperor by the title of Shumſe ul dien Altumſh. Upon his acceſſion he was acknowledged by many chiefs and princes; but ſome of his generals taking diſguſt, went off with the greater part of his Turkiſh horſe, which were the flower of his army. They joined themſelves with other malecontents, and advanced with a great force towards Delhi. They were met before the city by Altumſh, and defeated, their chief general Firoch being killed, and the reſt ſo cloſely purſued, that in a ſhort time they were all either killed or taken, which for that time eſtabliſhed Altumſh in peace. But ſoon after, the governor of the fort of Gollore rebelled, and refuſed to pay the revenues of that country. This obliged the King to march and reduce him to obedience. Eldoze King of Ghizni,

at

at this time, sent him the ensigns of royalty, pretending to confirm Altumsh in the empire of Hindostan. But soon after, when Eldoze himself was defeated by the troops of Charizm, and retired to Kirma and Shenoran, he turned his views towards the conquest of Hindostan. Eldoze seized upon the country of Punjaab and the city of Tannasar in the year 612, and endeavoured, by his emissaries in the court of Delhi, to raise a faction in his own favour. Altumsh, in the mean time, drew together his forces, and advancing towards him, they fought on the confines of Tirowri, about one hundred and fifty miles from Delhi. Eldoze was defeated, as before related, and, with many of his Omrahs, taken and imprisoned in Budaoon, where he died a natural death, according to some; but, according to others, was poisoned.

A. D. 1217. Higer. 614.

Defeats and takes Eldoze.

In the year 614, Altumsh engaged Nasir, who was also son-in-law to Cuttub, upon the banks of the Chinaab, where Altumsh proved victorious. The governor of Chilligi, in the mountains, the year following, being defeated by Nasir, fled for protection to Altumsh, who, taking part in his quarrel, marched against Nasir, and a second time overthrew him, recovering the countries lost by the Viceroy of Chilligi, upon which he himself returned to Delhi. In the year 618, the famous but unfortunate Jellal ul dien King of Charizm being defeated in the north, by the great conqueror Zingis Chan, retreated towards Lahore, where Altumsh opposed him with all his forces. This obliged the brave though unfortunate Jellal to retreat towards the Indus, where he was opposed by Nasir, who defeated him, and pursued him, by the way of Kutch and Muckeran, the maritime provinces of Persia.

Zingis Chan.

A. D. 1225. Higer. 622. Altumsh reduces Bengal, and Behar.

In the year 622, Altumsh led his army towards Behar and Bengal, where he obliged Yeas ul dien of Chilligi, then prince of Bengal, whose history we shall see in its proper place*, to pay him tribute and allegiance. He struck the currency in his own name, and appointing his own son Nasir to the government of Bengal, he left Yeas ul dien in the government of Behar, and then returned to Delhi. But soon after, war broke out between Nasir prince of Bengal, and Yeas ul dien of Behar. The latter was defeated and slain; Nasir taking possession of his principality and treasure, out of which he sent ample presents to his friends at Delhi.

Altumsh marches towards the Indus.

In the mean time, Altumsh led out his forces against Cabaja, who possessed the provinces on the Indus, and unable to oppose him in the field, left a strong garrison in Outch, and returned himself to Backar. The Emperor detached Nizam Jinaidi with half the army in pursuit of Cabaja, while, with the other half, he himself laid siege to Outch, which he took in two months and twenty days. When the news of the fall of Outch reached Cabaja, he sent his son Alla to intreat the Emperor for peace. The terms were not settled when news was brought, that Nasir, already mentioned, had been obliged by Nizam to attempt to cross the river, and that he was unhappily drowned. The whole country submitted to the imperial power. Altumsh then drew his forces towards the fort of Rintimpore, which he besieged and took.

* The historian alludes to another work which he wrote concerning the transactions of the principalities of Hindostan.

In

In the year 624, he marched towards the fort of Mendu, which he reduced with all the country of Sewalic. At this time, the noble Ruhani, the most learned and most famous poet and philosopher of that age, fled from Bochara, that city being taken by the great Zingis, and took protection at Delhi, where he wrote many excellent pieces. The Emperor, at the same time, had an embassy from the Arabian Princes, with the royal robes of the Caliphat, which he assumed with joy, making a great festival, and distributing rich presents. In the same year, he received intelligence of the death of Nasir, his eldest son, prince of Bengal, which threw him into mourning and sorrow. He soon after conferred the tit e upon his younger son, whom he carried with him to that province in the year 627, to invest him with the government, which had run into confusion after the death of the former prince. Having entirely settled this country in peace, he left Eaz ul Muluck to superintend the kingdom, and returned with his son to Delhi.

A. D. 1231. Higer. 629. Reduces Sewalic.

Altumsh formed a design, in the year 629, to reduce the fort of Gualier, which had, during the reign of his predecessor Aram, fallen into the hands of the Hindoos. He accordingly besieged it for a whole year, when the garrison being reduced to great streights, the governor made his escape in the night, and the troops capitulated; but above three hundred of them, for treacherous behaviour, were punished.

Reduces Gualier.

After the reduction of this place, he marched his army towards Malava, and reducing the fort of Belsay, took the city of Ugeïn, where he destroyed the magnificent and rich temple of Makal*,

* MA signifies Great, in the Indian language; and KAL Tim., or sometimes Death.

A. D. 1231. Higer. 629. formed upon the ſame plan with that of Sumnat, which had been building three hundred years, and was ſurrounded by a wall one hundred cubits in height. The image of Bickermagit, who had been formerly prince of this country, and ſo renowned that the people of Hindoſtan date their time from his death, as alſo that of Makal, both of ſtone, with many other figures of braſs, he ordered to be carried to Delhi, and broken at the door of the great moſque.

Dies. After his return from this expedition, he drew his army again towards Moultan, to ſettle the affairs of that province; but this enterprize proved unſucceſsful on account of his health. He fell ſick on his march, which obliged him to return to Delhi, where he died on the 20th of Shaban, in the year 633. His vizier, towards the latter end of his reign, was Aſſami, who had been formerly vizier of the Calipha of Bagdat for thirty years. He was renowned for wiſdom and learning, but had left that court on account of ſome diſguſt, and travelled to Delhi, where he was deemed a great acquiſition, and honoured with the vizarit. The moſt famous for letters in this reign, was Mahommed Ufi, who wrote the Jame ul Hickaiat, a valuable collection of hiſtories, and other books. The reign of Altumſh was twenty-ſix years. He was an enterprizing, able, and good prince.

State of Aſia at the death of Altumſh. In the 13th year of the reign of Altumſh, Zingis Chan, the great conqueror of Aſia, marched againſt Mahommed, King of Charizm and all Perſia. The ſtate of Aſia, juſt preceding the revolution brought about by the arms of Zingis, was as follows: China was divided into two empires, that called the Song Kingdom in the ſouth, and Kitay in the north. The greateſt part of Tartary was ſubject to Zingis, after the defeat and death of Aunac, the Grand Chan; the Weſ-

tern

tern Tartary and all Persia were comprehended in the empire of Charizm, under Mahommed; the three Arabias, the Arabian Irac, Mesopotamia, and a small territory on the side of Persia, owned the authority of the Calipha, Nasser, of the noble house of Abassi: The successors of the famous Jellal ul dien, corruptly called Saladin, possessed Syria and Egypt; and a younger branch of the Siljokides of Persia reigned in the lesser Asia, under the title of Sultans of Iconium. All Hindostan, except the Decan, was subject to the Afgan or Patan empire, under Altumsh. From the thirteenth to the twenty-sixth year of Altumsh, which was the last of his reign, the face of affairs in Asia became totally changed. Zingis conquered that immense continent, from the sea of China to Syria, and from the Indus to the Arctic circle. That great prince being bent upon the complete conquest of China, India escaped an invasion, which, in all human probability, would have forced it to share the same fate with the rest of Asia.

A.D. 1231. Higer. 629.

FEROSE I.

A. D. 1235. Higer. 633. Ferose,

THE prince Ferose * succeeded his father Altumsh in the throne of Delhi. In the year 625, his father appointed him governor of Budaoon, and, after the reduction of Gualier, conferred upon him the viceroyship of Lahore. He chanced, at the Emperor's death, to be at Delhi on a visit, and immediately ascended the throne. The Omrahs made their offerings, and swore allegiance; while the poets of the age vied with one another in his praise, for which they received liberal donations.

a weak and dissolute Prince.

But, when he acquired the imperial dignity, he spread the flowery carpets of luxury, and withdrew his hand from the toils of state. He expended his father's treasure upon dancing-women, comedians, and musicians, and left the affairs of government to the management of his mother. This woman had been a Turkish slave, and now became a monster of cruelty, murdering all the women of Altumsh's Haram, to gratify her inhuman hatred to them, as also the youngest of that Emperor's sons. The minds of the people began to be filled with disgust, and Mahommed, the

* Ruckun ul dien, Ferose Shaw.

younger

A.D. 1235. Higer. 633.

younger brother of the King, and governor of Oud, intercepted the revenues from Bengal, and began to assert independence. At the same time, Mahommed, Suba of Budaoon, Chani, governor of Lahore, Cabire, viceroy of Moultan, and Kugi, governor of Hassi, entering into a confederacy, exalted their standards of hostility against the Emperor. Ferose collected a vast army, and marched to Kilogurry, where he was deserted by his vizier Junedi, with part of his army. The vizier went towards Kole, where he joined some of the insurgents. They from thence proceeded to Lahore, where they were joined by the nobles of these provinces. The Emperor, in the mean time, continued his march towards them, and when he reached Munsurpoor, seven of his principal chiefs deserted from him, and retired with their troops to Delhi. There they advanced Sultana Rizia, the eldest daughter of Altumsh, to the throne, and imprisoned the Emperor's mother.

When this news reached the Emperor, he hastened back with his army towards Delhi, and having reached Kilogurry, Rizia, on the 18th of Ribbi ul Awil, in the year 634, advanced against him. He was delivered up into her hands, and died in confinement some time after; so that he reigned only six months and twenty-eight days.

SULTANA

SULTANA RIZIA.

A.D. 1236. Higer. 634. An excellent Princeſs.

SULTANA RIZIA * was adorned with every qualification neceſſary in the ableſt kings; and the ſtricteſt ſcrutineers of her actions could find in her no fault but that ſhe was a woman. In the time of her father, ſhe entered deeply into the affairs of government, which diſpoſition he encouraged, finding ſhe had a remarkable talent in politicks. In that year in which he took the fort of Gualier, he appointed her regent in his abſence. When he was aſked by the Omrahs, why he appointed his daughter to ſuch an office, in preference to ſo many of his ſons, he replied, "that he ſaw his ſons gave themſelves up to wine, women, gaming, and the worſhip of the wind†; that therefore he thought the government too weighty for their ſhoulders to bear; and that Rizia, though a woman, had a man's head and heart, and was better than twenty ſuch ſons."

The rebels diſperſe.

Rizia, upon her acceſſion, changing her apparel, aſſumed the imperial robes, and every day gave public audience from the throne, reviſing and confirming the laws of her father, which had

* Malleke Doran, Sultana Rizia.

† Flattery.

been

been abrogated in the last reign, and distributing justice with an equal hand. In the mean time, the vizier Junedi, and the confederate Omrahs, who had met at Lahore, advanced with their armies to Delhi, and encamping without the city, commenced hostilities. They, at the same time, sent circular letters to all the Omrahs of the empire, to draw them from their allegiance. This news reaching the Suba of Oud, he collected his forces, and hastened to the relief of the Empress; but when he had crossed the Ganges, he was engaged by the confederates, defeated, and taken prisoner, in which condition he soon died. The Empress found means, in her own policy, to sow dissension among the confederates; till, finding themselves in a dangerous situation, they retreated each to his own country, while some of them, being pursued by the Empress, were taken and put to death, the vizier escaping to the hills of Sirmore, where he died. A.D. 1239. Higer. 637.

The prosperity of the Sultana daily gaining ground, she gave the vizarit to Chaja Ghiznavi, who had been deputy to the former vizier, with the title of Nizam, and the chief command of her forces to Abiek, with the title of Kilic Chan. Kabirc, having subjected himself to her authority, was confirmed in the government of Lahore, while the countries of Bengal, and the northern provinces, were also confirmed to their respective viceroys, on their promise of future obedience. In the mean time, Kilic Chan, general of the Sultana's armies, died, and Hassen, being appointed to succeed him, was sent with a force to raise the siege of Rintimpore, which was then invested by the independent Indian princes. But, at the approach of the imperial forces, they raised the siege, and retreated. After Hassen's departure from Rintimpore, Tiggi was advanced to the dignity

Rizia settles the Empire.

Promotions at court.

A.D. 1239. Higer. 637. dignity of lord of the privacy, and master of requests. Jammal gaining great favour with the Empress, was also appointed Master of the Horse, from which station he was presently advanced to that of Captain General of the Empire.

The governor of Lahore rebels, The nobles were greatly disgusted at this promotion, as the favourite was originally an Abassinian slave. The first who began openly to express his discontent, was the viceroy of Lahore, in the year 637, who threw off his allegiance, and began to recruit his army. The Empress, collecting also her forces, marched out against him, and the viceroy, being disappointed by some of his confederates, was obliged to make every concession to obtain pardon. This he effected with so much art, that the Empress, upon her departure, either believing him to be her friend, or desirous of binding him over to her interest by gratitude, continued him in his viceroyship, and added to it that of Moultan, which had been governed by Kirakus.

and the Suba of Tiberhind. In the same year, Altunia, the imperial governor of Tiberhind, exalted the hostile standard against the Empress, on account of her imprudent partiality to the Abassinian. The Empress, upon this intelligence, marched with her army towards Tiberhind, but, about half way, all the Turkish chiefs in her army mutinied with their forces. A tumultuous conflict ensued, in which her Abassinian general was killed, and she herself seized and sent to the fort of Tiberhind, to Altunia. The army then returned to Delhi, where the Turkish Omrahs set up her brother Byram, the son of the Emperor Altumsh.

Rizia is deposed, In the mean time, Altunia, governor of Tiberhind, having married the Empress, in a short time, by her influence, raised a great army of Gickers, Jits, and other nations, near the banks of

of the Indus, with many Omrahs of diſtinction, A.D. 1239. Higer. 637.
and marched with her towards Delhi. Byram, the new Emperor, upon this, ſent Balin, ſon-in-law to Altumſh, with his forces to oppoſe her. The two armies meeting near Delhi, an obſtinate engagement enſued, in which the unfortunate Empreſs being defeated fled to Tiberhind.

She ſome time after collected her ſcattered forces, and was ſoon in a condition to make another bold effort for the empire. She advanced with a numerous army towards Delhi, but her forces being compoſed of the troops of India, were no ways a match for the mercenaries of Tartary, which chiefly compoſed the Emperor's army. Balin, who was again ſent to oppoſe her, gave her another defeat at Keitel, the 4th of the firſt Ribbi, in the ſame year. She and her huſband being taken in the purſuit, were inhumanly put to immediate death; while others relate, with leſs probability, that they were both carried bound to Byram, who ordered them to be aſſaſſinated in priſon. Thus died the Empreſs Rizia, deſerving a better fate, after a reign of three years ſix months and ſix days.

and put to death.

BYRAM

BYRAM II.

A. D. 1239. Higer. 637. Byram mounts the throne.

WHEN the Empreſs Rizia was priſoner in the fort of Tiberhind, Byram*, the ſon of the late Emperor Altumſh, upon Monday the 27th of Ramſan, in the year 637, by conſent of the Omrahs, aſcended the throne of Delhi, and confirmed all the laws and cuſtoms then in force. Tiggi, in conjunction with the vizier, by degrees took the whole government of the empire upon himſelf, taking the ſiſter of the Emperor to wife, and mounting an elephant upon guard, at his gate, which was an honour peculiar to royalty. This circumſtance raiſed diſguſt and jealouſy in the Emperor's mind. He therefore ordered two Turkiſh ſlaves to put on the appearance of drunkenneſs, and endeavour to aſſaſſinate Tiggi and the vizier. Accordingly, upon a certain day, theſe two Turks, when the King gave public audience, preſſed among the crowd, and began to be very troubleſome. Tiggi, who ſtood firſt in the rank of Omrahs, went to turn them out. They drew their daggers, and plunged them into his breaſt, then, running to the vizier, they gave him two wounds; but he eſcaped through the crowd. The

* Moaz ul dien, Byram Shaw.

ſlaves

ſlaves were immediately ſeized, and thrown into chains, but in a few days after they were pardoned.

A. D. 1239. Higer. 637.

The vizier kept his bed for ſome days, on account of his wounds, but, as ſoon as he recovered, he appeared again at court, and officiated in his employ. Sunkir Rumi, who was then maſter of the requeſts, formed a ſcheme to ſuperſede him. He, for this purpoſe, placed himſelf at the head of a powerful faction at court, and collecting the Omrahs together, and, among the reſt the vizier, at the houſe of the chief juſtice of the empire, he began to concert with them a plan to bring about a revolution. The chief juſtice was ſecretly averſe to the meaſure, and fearing that what was nominally meant againſt the vizier, ſhould actually turn upon his maſter, he ſent to the Emperor, and informed him of the whole affair. The meſſenger brought back with him a faithful ſervant of the King, in the habit of a fool, to overhear the converſation with the vizier. The vizier, though he actually entered into the meaſures of the meeting, excuſed himſelf from attendance at that time.

His ſcheme to ſuperſede the vizier.

The ſtory of the chief juſtice being confirmed by the perſon whom the Emperor ſent to overhear the Omrahs, a body of cavalry were immediately diſpatched to ſeize them; but they having had previous intelligence, diſperſed themſelves before the horſe arrived. The next day, Sunkir Rumi, who was one of the principal conſpirators, was ſent to be governor of Budaoon, while Caſi Jellal was turned out of his office. In a few months after, Rumi and Muza were aſſaſſinated at Budaoon by the Emperor's emiſſaries, while Caſi Jellal was trod under foot by elephants. Theſe proceedings raiſed fear and apprehenſion in the boſom of every body, which being improved by the

Conſpirators puniſhed.

A.D. 1241. Higer. 639. the faction, there was a general mutiny among the troops. In the mean time news arrived, that the Moguls of the great Zingis had invested Lahore upon the 16th of the first Jemmad, in the year 639; that Malleck, the viceroy of that place, finding his troops mutinous, had been obliged to fly in the night, and was actually on his way to Delhi; and that Lahore was plundered by the enemy, and the miserable inhabitants carried away prisoners.

The King, upon this urgent occasion, called a general council of state, in which it was determined to send the vizier, and Hassen Ghori, chief secretary of the empire, with other Omrahs, to oppose the Moguls at Lahore, with an army. When the imperial army advanced as far as the river Bea, where the town of Sultanpoor now stands, the vizier, who was privately an enemy to the Emperor, began to depreciate his government to the nobles, and to sow the seeds of sedition in their minds. But that he might completely effect his purpose, he wrote a private letter to the Emperor, accusing them of disaffection, and begging he would either take the field himself, or send other Omrahs and more forces, for that those now with the army could not be depended upon, and that therefore nothing could be done against the enemy.

Treachery of the vizier.

Attaches the Omrahs to his interest.

The Emperor, though he had been forewarned of the treachery of his vizier in the late conspiracy, yet the artful man had so well extricated himself, and gained such confidence, that Byram, who was not blessed with much discernment, gave entire credit to this accusation, and sent him an order, importing, that they deserved death; at the same time recommending to him to keep them quiet till he should find the means of bringing them to condign punishment. This was what the crafty

crafty vizier wanted. He immediately produced the King's order, which kindled the Omrahs at once into rage, while he misled them with respect to the accuser. He even pretended to be apprehensive for himself, and began to consult with them about the means of general security; and they all promised to support him. A.D. 1242. Higer. 640.

This news having reached the Emperor, he began to open his eyes when too late, and in great perturbation hastened to the house of Islaam, a venerable and learned Omrah, requesting him to set out for the camp, and endeavour, by proper representations, to bring over the disaffected chiefs to their duty. Islaam accordingly set out in private, but not being able to effect any thing, returned to Delhi. The vizier, in the mean time, advanced with the army to the capital, which he besieged for three months and an half. Rebellion spreading at last among the citizens, the place was taken on the eighth of Zicada, in the year 639. Byram was thrown into prison, where, in a few days, he came to a very tragical end, after a reign of two years one month and fifteen days. The Emperor sends to quiet the Omrahs. The Emperor slain.

The Moguls, in the mean time, plundered the provinces on the banks of the five branches of the Indus, and returned to Ghizni.

MUSAOOD

MUSAOOD IV.

A.D. 1242. Higer. 640. Musaood mounts the throne.

WHEN Byram had drank the cup of fate, Balin the elder raised a faction, and forcing his way into the palace, mounted the throne, and ordered himself to be proclaimed throughout the city. But the greater part of the princes and nobility, dissatisfied with his advancement, immediately took out Musaood * the son of Ferose, the late Emperor, from his confinement in the white castle, and deposing the usurper, placed him upon the throne the same day in which Balin had seized it. Hassin was made vakeel of the empire†; Nizam, vizier; and the late governor of Lahore, lord of requests.

The vizier is assassinated.

The vizier, who was a politic and ambitious man, still maintained an absolute power in the empire; but being of a haughty and oppressive disposition, he bore it with too high a hand among the nobles. They consequently began to combine against him, and in the month of the first Ribbi, in the year 640, found means to assassi-

* Alla-ul-dien, Musaood Shaw.

† This office of vakeel sultanit, or vakeel mutuluck, was the first in the empire; his business was to issue all orders from the closet to the vizier or other officers of state, who were to take measures for executing them.

nate

nate him one day when he was hunting. The vizarit was conferred upon the chief justice of the empire, and the younger Balin was made lord of the requests. Even Balin the elder was appointed viceroy of Nagore, Sind, and Ajmere. The Subaship of Budaoon was given at the same time to Tiggi; and other provinces fell to various chiefs, according to their rank and interest at court; and, in general, peace and content seemed to diffuse themselves over the kingdom. A.D. 1244. Higer. 642.

The Emperor releases his uncles.

The Emperor, about this time, released his two uncles Mamood and Jellal, who had been imprisoned by the Emperor Byram. He conferred upon the former the government of Barage, and to the latter he gave that of Kinnoge. Tiggi was appointed governor of Bengal. In the year 642, an army of Mogul Tartars made an incursion into Bengal, by the way of Chitta and Tibet. Musaood sent towards Bengal, Timur, to the aid of Tiggi, governor of that province, with a great army. The Moguls received a total defeat; but jealousy arising between Timur and Tiggi, they proceeded to open hostilities; and the Emperor ordered Tiggi to resign the government to Timur, and to return to Delhi. In the following year, intelligence arrived that another army of Moguls had crossed the Indus, and invested Outch. The King immediately ordered forces to be mustered, and putting himself at their head, directed the imperial standard towards the Tartars. When he had reached the banks of the river Bea, they raised the siege, and began to retreat; and Musaood, hearing that they had totally evacuated the country, returned to Delhi.

The Emperor deposed.

Musaood soon after gave himself up to wine and women, and exercised various modes of cruelty, injustice and oppression, despising all counsel, and placing the way of ruin before him. The

princes

A. D. 1244. Higer. 642. princes and Omrahs at length bound up their loins to hoſtility, having firſt privately ſent for Mamood, the King's uncle, from Barage. Mamood advanced with all the forces he could raiſe towards the capital. The Emperor was thrown into priſon, by the Omrahs, where he remained for life. He reigned four years one month and one day; a weak and fooliſh prince, a ſlave to his pleaſures, and without firmneſs of mind to entertain any one commendable virtue.

State of Aſia. Oktay, the ſon of Zingis, ſat upon the imperial throne of Tartary, during the ſhort reigns of Feroſe, Rizia, Byram, and Muſaood. Little alteration happened in the conqueſts of Zingis, and his poſterity were employed in extending the Tartar empire in the two extremities of Aſia. The dominions left by Altumſh remained intire when his ſon Muſaood was depoſed.

MAMOOD

MAMOOD II.

WE have already obſerved, that, when the eldeſt ſon of the Emperor Altumſh died in Bengal, he conferred the title and government of that principality upon his younger ſon Mamood*. But this was a nominal honour, Mamood being at that time too young for ſuch a charge. Upon his father's death he was confined by the cruel Empreſs, and remained in priſon till he was releaſed by the Emperor Muſaood, who gave him the government of Barage. During the time of his government, he waged ſucceſsful wars with the neighbouring independent princes, and rendered his province happy and flouriſhing. The fame of his juſtice and policy became to be noiſed abroad, which made the Omrahs turn their eyes towards him in the late revolution. He was then placed upon the throne of his father, which, even laying aſide his birth, his bravery, wiſdom and learning, his other good qualities very much deſerved to poſſeſs. During the time of his impriſonment, he wrote for his livelihood, deſpiſing the Emperor's allowance. He often ſaid, in the days of his misfortune, that he who could not

A. D. 1245. Higer. 643. Mamood

wiſe, learned, and politic.

* Naſir ul dien Mamood.

work

A.D. 1246. Higera 644. work for his bread did not deserve it. When he ascended the throne, he was the patron of learning, the protector of the people, and the friend of the poor. The poets of that age vied with one another for the prize at his coronation, which was gained by Minage, for his poem upon that occasion. This writer is also particularly famous for his valuable history called the Tibcaat Nazari.

The vizarit conferred upon Balin.

The office of vizier was now conferred upon Balin the younger, who formerly defeated the Sultana; and all the executive power was put into his hands. Shere, the Emperor's nephew, was appointed to the government of Lahore, Moultan, Batenize, and Tibberhind, where he was ordered to keep a great standing army, to watch the motions of the Moguls, who now had possessed themselves of the provinces beyond the Indus.

The Emperor's charge to Balin.

It is said, that when Mamood appointed young Balin vizier, he told him, he trusted his own glory to his loyalty and conduct; therefore, to do nothing for which he could not answer to God, or that would stain his name with injustice towards his people, or ingratitude towards his king. The vizier faithfully promised his best, and exerting himself with such unwearied diligence in his office, regulated so well the business of the state, that nothing escaped his eye, or passed his particular inspection.

The Gickers chastised.

In the month of Regib, the King took the field, and turned his arms towards Moultan. He encamped for some time upon the banks of the Sodra; and making his vizier captain general, he sent him towards the mountains of Jehud, and the territories near the Indus. Those countries were reduced, and the Emperor avenged himself upon the Gickers for their continual incursions, and for guiding the Moguls through their country

into

into Hindostan. These offences were too great to be pardoned, and therefore he carried some thousands of every age and sex into captivity. A. D. 1247. Higer. 645.

Some ancient Omrahs, who had estates conferred on them in the provinces near the Indus, had, for some time past, refused to supply their quotas to the army, for the maintenance of which they held these estates. By the advice of the vizier, they were arrested, and carried prisoners to Delhi. The King, however, gave their estates to their sons or relations, upon the old military tenure. The country of Punjaab and Moultan were by these means effectually settled, and the King's authority firmly established. The behaviour of Mamood, upon this occasion, puts us in mind of a story of a singular kind. Some authors inform us, that when Secunder * was on his way to India, some of his old generals, unwilling to proceed farther, began to draw their feet out of the circle of his obedience. The hero upon this, was thrown into great perplexity, not knowing how to proceed with them. In this dilemma, he sent a messenger to Greece to advise with his old master Aristotalise†, who, by reason of his age and infirmities, had not accompanied him. When the sage read the letter, he carried the messenger into the garden, where he gave orders to the gardener to root up all the old plants, and set young shoots in their places. Without saying more, or writing any answer, he told the messenger to return in haste to his master. When the messenger arrived, he fell upon his face before the King, and told him he could obtain no reply. Secunder was somewhat surprized, and enquired into the particulars of the interview. Hearing the above re- Refractory Omrahs punished.

* Alexander the Great.

† Aristotle, the Philosopher.

lation,

A.D. 1249. Higer. 647. lation, he ſmiled, and told the meſſenger he had brought him an excellent anſwer. He accordingly put ſome of the old mutinous officers to death, and caſhiered others; ſupplying their places with young men, who became more obedient to command; and thus re-eſtabliſhed his authority in the army.

The Emperor reduces Tilſinda.

In the month of Shaban 645, the Emperor Mamood returned with his troops through the country which lies between the two rivers Ganges and Jumna, and, after an obſtinate ſiege, the fort of Tilſinda yielded to his arms. He then continued his march towards Kurrah, Balin commanding the van guard. He was met at Kurrah by the Indian princes Dilleki and Millecki, whom he defeated, plundering their country, and taking many of both their families priſoners. Theſe two Rajas had ſeized upon all the country to the ſouth of the Jumna, deſtroying the King's garriſons from Malava to Kurrah, and held their chief reſidence at Callinger. After theſe exploits the Emperor returned to Delhi.

The vizier chaſtiſes the inhabitants of Rintimpore.

In the following year, he ſent the vizier with an army towards Rintimpore, and the mountains of Merwar, to chaſtiſe the rebellious inhabitants of theſe countries, which he effectually did, and returned to Delhi. The vizier's brother Abiek Cuſhli was promoted to the dignity of lord of the petitions, and Zingani to be chief ſecretary to the empire. In the ſame year, the Emperor's brother Jellal was called from his government of Kinnoge to Delhi. But, fearing that the King had ſome intentions againſt his life, he fled to the hills of Sitnoor, with all his adherents. The Emperor purſued him, but finding, after eight months labour, that he could not lay hands upon him, he returned to Delhi. Mamood, in the year 647, married the daughter of his vizier, Balin, and upon

upon the occasion made great rejoicings. He drew, in the year following, his army towards Moultan, and, upon the banks of the Bea, he was joined by his nephew Shere, governor of the northern provinces, with twenty thousand chosen horse. The King continued his march to Moultan, where he remained for some days. Having placed the elder Balin in the government of Nagore and Outch, and settled some other matters, he returned to his capital.

A.D. 1251. Higer. 649.

The elder Balin, in the year 649, threw off his allegiance, and stirred up a rebellion in those provinces. This obliged Mamood to put the imperial standard in motion towards Nagore. He put the rebel to flight; but such was the strange policy of the times, that he promised him his pardon, upon his submission; and afterwards actually continued him in his government. The Emperor, after returning from this expedition, remained only a few days at Delhi, before he proceeded to the siege of Narvar. He was met at Narvar by the Indian prince Sahir Deo, who had just built that fortress on a steep rock, with five thousand horse, and two hundred thousand foot. This immense host were defeated with great slaughter, and the place, being invested, was reduced, after a few months siege. The Emperor from thence continued his march to Chinderi and Malava, and having settled those countries, and appointed a suba to govern them, returned to Delhi. The vizier gained, in this expedition, great reputation for his conduct and personal valour.

Elder Balin rebels.

In the mean time, the Emperor's nephew Shere, viceroy of Lahore and Moultan, who was at that time reckoned a prodigy of wisdom, valour, and every royal virtue, had raised and disciplined a body of horse, with which he drove the Moguls out of the kingdom of Ghizni, and annexed it once

Shere recovers Ghizni from the Moguls.

A.D. 1252. Higer. 650. once more to the empire. He ſtruck the currency in the name of Mamood, and proclaimed him through all the provinces. The King, for theſe ſervices, added the government of Outch to his viceroyſhip, which, contrary to expectation, was quietly delivered up by the elder Balin, who returned to Delhi, and received the Jagier of Budaoon.

The vizier diſgraced.

Mamood, in the year 650, marched by the way of Lahore, into Moultan, and was joined by the governor of Budaoon, by the way of Sevan and Cuſhlu, with fine armies. In the beginning of the following year, Zingani, chief ſecretary of the empire, who had roſe to that dignity through the intereſt of the vizier, began to envy the fame and influence of that able miniſter. He took every opportunity to traduce his benefactor to the King in private. The Monarch's affections for the vizier began to cool viſibly, and he was even prevailed upon at laſt to diſcharge that great man from his office, when he only conferred upon him, in lieu of it, the ſmall government of Haſſi, for his ſubſiſtance, where his enemy ſought an opportunity to take his life.

Zingani in great favour with the King.

Zingani now became abſolute in the King's favour, and began his authority by turning out every perſon from their offices and governments, who had been appointed by the former vizier. He removed all Balin's friends and relations from the royal preſence, conſtituting Mahommed, who reſided at Delhi, vizier of the empire, and Cutchlew, lord of requeſts. When he returned to Delhi with the King, he every where diſturbed the public peace, and overſet the fundamental laws of the country. The Emperor again muſtered his army, and began his march towards the river Bea, for Shere had unfortunately, at this time, been defeated by the rebels of the province of Sind,

Sind, and loſt ſeveral forts in Moultan. This furniſhed the favourite with an opportunity of diſgracing him with the King, who turned him out of his viceroyſhip, which he conferred upon Arſilla, and then returned to his capital. In the mean time, the governor of Keital and Koram was aſſaſſinated by the zemindars, which prevailed on the Sultan to march his army to revenge his death, from which expedition he very ſoon returned again to Delhi. A.D. 1253. Higer. 651.

His inſolence. The government of the chief ſecretary became by this time ſo invidious to the whole empire, that almoſt all the governors of provinces entered into an aſſociation, and ſent an embaſſy to Balin, the former vizier, informing him, that the government of the country was quite ſubverted, and that the oppreſſion and arrogance of Zingani was beyond expreſſion; that they were therefore deſirous he ſhould proceed to Delhi, and take the empire, as formerly, under his wiſe conduct and direction. Balin conſented, and, according to appointment, all the Omrahs met, with their forces, in one day, at Koram.

A revolt. Mamood and his chief ſecretary Zingani, upon receiving this intelligence, marched with the imperial forces to diſperſe the inſurgents; but when the royal army advanced as far as Haſſi, Balin, and the reſt of the Omrahs, ſent an addreſs to the King, to the following purpoſe: "That they were his loyal ſubjects, and were ſatisfied to kiſs the foot of his throne, ſo be he would baniſh Zingani from his preſence." The Emperor was under the neceſſity of either conſenting to this requeſt, or to loſe his empire. He therefore diſmiſſed the obnoxious favourite from his preſence, and ſent him to Budaoon. The Omrahs preſented their offerings, and were honoured with royal dreſſes. Chani was appointed to command at Lahore, and Shere

was

A. D. 1257. Higer. 655. was confirmed in his former governments, and other diſtricts adjacent. Mamood returned peaceably to Delhi, and expreſſed great joy at ſeeing his old vizier, while the flower of deſire bloſſomed in the hearts of the ſubjects.

Inſurrections quelled. In the year 653, the Emperor conferred the government of Oud upon Cuttulich, of which, however, he wanted to deprive him in a few months for that of Barage, which was neither ſo lucrative nor ſo honourable. Cuttulich, upon this account, ſwerved from his allegiance, and, having brought over ſome other Omrahs to his party, raiſed a great army, which obliged Mamood to ſend the vizier againſt him. A general was diſpatched at the ſame time againſt Zingani, who had begun a diverſion about Budaoon. He was however ſoon defeated, taken priſoner, and put to death. Cuttulich was alſo routed by the vizier, and fled to Sitnoor. The vizier deſtroyed the place, but not being able to lay hold of the rebel, he returned to Delhi.

A conſpiracy in the imperial army, Diepal, the Indian prince of Sitnoor, in the year 655, entered into an alliance with the rebel Cuttulich, and raiſing a great army, advanced to meet the ſuba of Sind, who was in the ſame confederacy. All three joining their forces near Koram, became very formidable to the empire. The King again ordered his vizier, with a great army, to take the field. When the two armies approached one another, a mutiny was ſtirred up in the vizier's camp, by ſome Omrahs, who wrote private letters to the enemy, projecting the means of their

diſcovered and baffled by the vizier. taking the city, in which they had alſo ſet a faction on foot to favour them. The vizier having received good intelligence of this treaſonable correſpondence, acquainted the King of the particulars, who ordered them all to be confined. In the mean time, the enemy, according to the ſcheme projected,

projected, marched with a body of chosen cavalry two hundred miles, in two days, advancing to the gates of Delhi, where the traitors had promised to meet them that day with their forces; but finding themselves disappointed, and the imperial troops marching out against them, they entirely dispersed, the governor of Sind retreating to his government, but Cuttulich was never heard of afterwards. A.D. 1258. Higer. 657.

Towards the latter end of this year, a Mogul army crossed the Indus, which obliged Mamood to point his hostile spears towards that quarter; but the Moguls fled upon his approach; so that, without further trouble, he returned to his capital, giving the country of Punjaab to his nephew Shere, and sending Chani to the government of Bengal. In the year 656, Mamood marched his army towards Kurrah and Manickpoor, to chastise Arsilla and Calliche, who had not joined their forces in obedience to his orders, when he marched the year before to Punjaab. These subas, however, found means at court to mollify the King's resentment, and Arsilla found even interest to obtain the government of Bengal, which had been so lately disposed of to Chani, while the other obtained some districts by the foot of the mountains. The Moguls obliged to retreat.

Cutchlew, the vizier's brother, was, in the year 657, appointed to the government of Kole, Jellasore, Gualier, and Biana. Nothing else remarkable happened this season, but the death of the rebellious governor of Sind. The vizier, by the King's commands, led, next year, an army towards Sewalic and Rintimpore, where the Indians had begun to raise great disturbances, having collected a very numerous body of horse and foot, at the head of which they plundered and burnt the country. Upon the vizier's approach, they retired into strong posts and passes among the mountains,

A.D. 1258. Higer. 657. tains, where, however, he routed them, and continued to ravage their country four months with fire and ſword, ſetting a price upon their heads.

Some rebellious Rajas overthrown by the vizier. The princes of thoſe Rajaputs, rendered at length deſperate, collected all their forces, and ruſhed down from the mountains to be revenged of the Mahommedans. The vizier ſaw the ſtorm deſcending, and had time to draw up his army in order of battle to receive them. The attack of the enemy was violent and terrible, being actuated by rage, revenge, and deſpair. It was with much difficulty that the vizier could keep the imperial troops in the field, but the enemy overheating themſelves towards midday, they became hourly more languid and faint. The imperial general inſpiring his troops with freſh courage, for, till then, they had acted upon the defenſive, began to charge in his turn, and, before evening, purſued the enemy, with great ſlaughter, back to the hills. The vizier's loſs was very conſiderable in this action, and many brave Omrahs drank of the cup of martyrdom. Of the enemy above ten thouſand were ſlain, and ninety of their chiefs made priſoners, beſides a great number of common ſoldiers. The vizier having, by this action, relieved the fort of Rintimpore, which had been beſieged by ſome other tribes, he returned victorious to Delhi. The captive chiefs were cruelly ordered to be put to death, and their unfortunate ſoldiers condemned to perpetual ſlavery.

Embaſſy from Hallacu king of Perſia. In the month of the firſt Ribbi of this year, an ambaſſador arrived at Delhi, on the part of Hallacu, the grandſon of Zingis, and king of Perſia. The vizier went out to meet the ambaſſador with fifty thouſand foreign horſe, in the imperial ſervice, two hundred thouſand infantry in arms, two thouſand chain-elephants of war, and three thouſand carriages of fireworks. He drew up in order of of battle, formed in columns of twenty deep, with the artillery and cavalry properly disposed. Having then exhibited some feats of horsemanship, in mock battles, and fully displayed his pomp to the ambassador, he conducted him into the city and royal palace. There the court was very splendid, every thing being set out in the most gorgeous and magnificent manner. All the Omrahs, officers of state, judges, priests, and great men of the city were present, besides five princes of Persian Ayrac, Chorassan, and Maver-ul-nere, with their retinues, who had taken protection at Delhi, from the arms of Zingis, who, a little before that time, had overrun most part of Asia. Many Indian princes, subject to the empire, were there, and stood next the throne. A.D. 1265. Higer. 664.

This ceremony being concluded with great pomp, nothing particular occurred at Delhi, till the year 663, when the Emperor fell sick, and, having lingered some months on the bed of affliction, died on the 11th of the first Jemmad, in the year 664, much lamented by his people. The Emperor dies.

Mamood was very singular in his private character, for, contrary to the custom of all princes, he kept no concubines. He had but one wife, whom he obliged to do every homely part of housewifry; and when she complained one day, that she had burnt her fingers in baking his bread, desiring he might allow her a maid to assist her, he rejected her request, with saying, that he was only a trustee for the state, and that he was determined not to burden it with needless expences. He therefore exhorted her to persevere in her duty with patience, and God would reward her in the end. His singular character.

As the Emperor of India never eats in publick, his table was rather that of a hermit, than suitable to a great King. He also continued the whim-

A.D. 1265. Higer. 664. fical notion of living by his pen. One day, as an Omrah was infpecting a Coran of the Emperor's writing before him, he pointed out a word, which he faid was wrong. The King, looking at it, fmiled, and drew a circle round it. But when the critic was gone, he began to eraze the circle, and reftore the word. This being obferved by one of his old attendants, he begged to know his Majefty's reafon for fo doing; to which he replied, "That he knew the word was originally right, but he thought it better to eraze from a paper, than touch the heart of a poor man, by bringing him to fhame." Thefe might, indeed, be virtues in private life, but were certainly none in a fovereign; for, notwithftanding the praifes conferred upon him by hiftorians, we muft look upon him rather as the reprefentation than the real fubftance of a great monarch.

State of Afia. Kajuc, and, after him, Mengo Chan, fat on the throne of Tartary, during the reign of Mamood. The conqueft of the fouthern China goes on, and Hallacu, the grandfon of Zingis, extends his victories in the weft of Afia, and, having taken Bagdad, puts an end to the Caliphat, by the extirpation of the race of Abbas, who enjoyed it 523 years.

B A L I N.

MAMOOD leaving no ſons behind him, his vizier Balin*, who was of the ſame family, mounted, by the univerſal deſire of the nobles, the throne of Delhi. Balin was originally a Turk of Chitta, of the tribe of Alberi, a relation of the Emperor Altumſh. In his youth, he was carried priſoner by the Moguls, who conquered that country, and ſold to a merchant, who conveyed him to Bagdat. His father was a chief of great power, and commanded ten thouſand horſe in that unfortunate war in which our young hero was taken. He was bought at Bagdat in the year 630, by Jemmal of Buſſorah, who was then famous for his piety and learning. His patron having learned that he was a relation of the Emperor Altumſh, proceeded with him immediately to Delhi, and preſented him to that monarch, who rewarded him ſo handſomely, that he returned independent to Bagdat.

A. D. 1265.
Higer. 664.
Balin, his family.

Altumſh employed him firſt in the office of chief manager of falconry, in which he was very expert. He roſe from that ſtation, both by the influence of his brother, who happened to be then a noble, and in great favour at the court of Delhi, and by his own merit. He aſcended gradually, from one preferment to another, till he became an Omrah of the empire, and a man in

His gradual riſe in the ſtate.

* Yeas ul dien Balin.

great

A.D. 1265. Higer. 664. great eſteem. In the reign of Feroſe, when he commanded in Punjaab, hearing his enemies at court had enraged the King againſt him, he refuſed to obey his orders to return, and kept for ſome time poſſeſſion of that country. But having advanced to Delhi, with the confederate Omrahs who came to depoſe the Empreſs Rizia, he was taken priſoner in their flight, and remained there ſome time in confinement. He however made his eſcape, and joined the party of the Emperor Byram againſt the Empreſs, whom he twice defeated, as we have ſeen in that reign. This gained him great reputation; and he had the government of Haſſi and Raberi conferred upon him; in which office he diſtinguiſhed himſelf in ſeveral actions againſt the rebels of Mewat.

Succeeds to the empire. In the reign of Muſaood, he was advanced to the dignity of lord of requeſts, in which he gained great reputation; and in that of Mamood, he was raiſed to the vizarit, which high office he managed in ſuch a manner as to leave the King but the mere title of royalty. He therefore, upon the death of his ſovereign, mounted the throne, not only without oppoſition, but even by the general voice of the nobility and people.

Rids himſelf of his rivals. In the reign of Altumſh, forty of his Turkiſh ſlaves, who were in great favour, entered into a ſolemn aſſociation to ſupport one another, and, upon the King's death, to divide the empire among themſelves. But jealouſies and diſſenſions having aroſe afterwards among them, prevented this project from being executed. The Emperor Balin was of their number; and, as ſeveral of them had raiſed themſelves to great power in the kingdom, the firſt thing he did after his acceſſion, was to rid himſelf of all who remained of that aſſociation, either by ſword or poiſon; among whom

was

was a nephew of his own, Shere, a man of great bravery and reputation. A.D. 1265. Higer. 664.

His fears, after these assassinations, were entirely dispelled, and he became so famous for his justice and wise government, that his alliance was courted by all the Kings of Persia and Tartary. He took particular care that none but men of merit and family should be admitted to any office in his government; and for this purpose he endeavoured to make himself acquainted with the particular talents and connections of every person in his court. As he was very assiduous in rewarding merit, he was no less so in punishing vice; for whoever misbehaved in their station, were certain of being immediately disgraced. Courted by the Kings of Tartary and Persia.

He expelled all flatterers, usurers, pimps, and players, from his court; and being one day told, that an Omrah, an old servant of the crown, who had acquired a vast fortune by usury and monopoly in the Bazar, or market, would present him with some lacks of Rupees, if he would honour him with one word from the throne; he rejected the proposal with great disdain, and said, "What must his subjects think of a King who should condescend to hold discourse with a wretch so infamous?" An enemy to vice.

Balin was so famous for his generosity, that all the princes of the East, who had been overthrown by the arms of Zingis, sought protection at his court. There came upwards of twenty of those unfortunate sovereigns from Turkestan, Maver-ul-nere, Chorassan, Persian Iraac, Azurbaejan, Persia Proper, Room*, and Syria. They had a princely allowance, and palaces for their residence allotted them; and they were, upon public oc- His generosity,

* The lesser Asia, so called from being long a part of the Roman empire.

A.D. 1265. Higer. 664. casions, ranked before his throne, according to their dignity; all standing to the right and left, except two princes of the race of the Caliphas, who were permitted to sit on either side of the Musnud. The palaces in which the royal fugitives resided in Delhi, took their names from their respective possessors. In the retinue of those princes, were the most famous men for learning, war, arts and sciences, that Asia at that time produced. The court of India was therefore, in the days of Balin, reckoned the most polite and magnificent in the world. All the philosophers, poets, and divines, formed a society every night, at the house of the prince Shehîd, the heir apparent to the empire; and the noble Chusero the poet presided at those meetings. Another society of musicians, dancers, mimicks, players, buffoons, and story-tellers was constantly convened at the house of the Emperor's second son Kera, or Bagera, who was given to pleasure and levity. The Omrahs followed the example of their superiors, so that various societies and clubs were formed in every quarter of the city. The Emperor himself, having a great passion for splendor and magnificence in his palaces, equipages and liveries, he was imitated by the court. A new city seemed to lift up its head, and arts to arise from the bosoms of luxury and expence.

and magnificence. Such was the pomp and grandeur of the royal presence, that none could approach the throne without terror. The ceremonies of introduction were conducted with so much reverence and solemnity, and every thing disposed so as to strike awe and astonishment into the beholders. Nor was Balin less magnificent in his cavalcades. His state elephants were caparisoned in purple and gold. His horse-guards, consisting of a thousand noble Tartars in splendid armour, were mounted upon the

the fineſt Perſian ſteeds, with bridles of ſilver, and ſaddles of rich embroidery. Five hundred choſen men in rich livery, with their drawn ſwords upon their ſhoulders, ran proclaiming his approach, and clearing the way before him. All the Omrahs followed according to their rank, with their various equipages and attendants. The Monarch, in ſhort, ſeldom went out with leſs than one hundred thouſand men; which he uſed to ſay, was not to gratify any vanity in himſelf, but to exalt him in the eyes of the people.

A.D. 1265. Higer. 664.

His juſtice.

The feſtivals of Noroſe and Ide, as alſo the anniverſary of his own birth, were held with wonderful pomp and ſplendor. But amidſt all this glare of royalty, he never forgot that he was the guardian of the laws, and protector of his meaneſt ſubjects. It was before Balin's time a cuſtom in Hindoſtan, in caſes of murder, to ſatisfy the relations by a certain fine, if they conſented to accept of it. He aboliſhed this cuſtom, which has been ſince revived, and ordered the Subah of Budaoon, Malleck, to be put to death, upon the complaint of a poor woman for killing her ſon.

When Balin was only an Omrah, he gave into the then courtly vices of wine, women, and play. But, upon his acceſſion, he became a great enemy to all thoſe luxuries; prohibiting wine upon the ſevereſt penalties to be drank in his dominions; laying great reſtrictions upon women of pleaſure, and baniſhing all gameſters from his court. So zealous was Balin to ſupport his authority, that, for the diſobedience of one man, he would order a force to the remoteſt parts of the empire to bring him to puniſhment. In caſes of inſurrection or rebellion againſt his government, he was not content, as had formerly been the cuſtom, to chaſtiſe the leaders, but he extended the capital puniſhment of high treaſon to the meaneſt of their

His ſeverity to rebels.

A. D. 1266. Higer. 665. vaſſals and adherents. This ſeverity rendered it neceſſary for the Subas to have the King's mandate for every expedition or hoſtilities they were about to commence.

Rejects the advice of his council to reduce Malava.

That his army might be kept in conſtant exerciſe, he led them out twice every week to hunt, for forty or fifty miles round the city, and eſtabliſhed laws for the preſervation of the game. In the year 664, he was adviſed by his council, to undertake an expedition to reduce the kingdoms of Guzerat and Malava, which had been annexed to the empire by Cuttub, but were afterwards permitted to ſhake off the yoke. To this advice the Emperor would by no means conſent, ſaying, That the Mogul Tartars were become ſo powerful in the north, having conquered all the Muſſulmen princes, that he thought it would be much wiſer to ſecure what he poſſeſſed againſt thoſe invaders, than to weaken himſelf, and leave his country unguarded, by foreign wars.

The Mewats extirpated.

Mahommed Tatar, the ſon of Arſilla, who had begun to aſſert independence in Bengal, was, this year, however, reduced, and obliged to ſend his uſual tribute to Delhi. A great rejoicing was made upon this occaſion, at which the King was preſent, and gave public audience. Balin ordered, in the courſe of the ſame year, an army to extirpate a certain tribe of banditti called Mewats, who had poſſeſſed themſelves of an extenſive wilderneſs about eighty miles ſouth eaſt of the city towards the hills; from whence they uſed, in former reigns, to make incurſions, to the number of fifty thouſand, even to the gates of Delhi. It is ſaid, that, in this expedition, above one hundred thouſand of theſe wretches were put to the ſword; and the army being ſupplied with hatchets and other implements, cleared away the woods for above the circumference of one hundred miles.

The

The cleared ſpace afterwards proved excellent lands, and was well inhabited, as the people were protected by a line of forts along the foot of the mountains. A.D. 1266. Higer. 665.

The Emperor quells ſeveral inſurrections.

In the 665 year of the Higera, Balin ſent an army down between the Ganges and Jumna, to ſuppreſs ſome inſurrections in thoſe parts, with orders to puniſh the offenders without mercy. The Emperor ſoon after marched in perſon towards Kattal, Pattiali and Bhogepoor, whoſe inhabitants had begun to ſtop all intercourſe with Bengal, by the way of Jionpoor and Benaris. He put ſome thouſands of them to death, eſtabliſhing juſtice and public ſecurity in thoſe parts. He ordered forts to be built, which he garriſoned with Pattans, to cruſh any future diſturbance, and then returned towards Delhi. Soon after his arrival, he received intelligence of an inſurrection in Budaoon and Kuttur, whither he haſtened with five thouſand choſen horſe, and ordered a general maſſacre among the unfortunate inſurgents, and ſome thouſands of every age and ſex fell by the ſword. If ſuch cruelties can be any where excuſed, it muſt be in a government like that of Hindoſtan, where rebellions were in thoſe days ſo common, that, without the moſt vigorous meaſures, the peace and royal authority could not be at all eſtabliſhed.

Reduces Jehud.

Balin, after theſe tranſactions, marched his army towards the mountains of Jehud, where he employed them for the ſpace of two years, in taking forts, and reducing the wild inhabitants to obedience. This country was famous for breeding horſes, many thouſands of which were carried by Balin to Delhi. Wherever the King marched, there was an order for the Subas, Zemindars, Fogedars, and magiſtrates of the provinces, to meet him on their own frontiers, with their offerings,

A.D. 1268. Higer. 667. ferings, which was afterwards diſtributed among the poor. Balin, ſome time after, made a journey to Lahore, which city, having greatly ſuffered from the Moguls, he ordered to be put in a proper ſtate of defence and repair; and, after having erected ſome public buildings, he returned to Delhi.

Regulates the army. About this time, Balin was told by one of his Omrahs, that a great number of veterans, who had ſerved in the preceding reigns, were now become invalids, and incapable of attending their duty. The Emperor, upon this, ordered a liſt of their names to be taken, and ſettling half-pay upon them for life, diſcharged them from further ſervice. The old men, however, were diſſatisfied with this proviſion, and ſome of the principals of them were deputed by the reſt, to go to Malleck, chief magiſtrate of Delhi, with preſents, to repreſent their caſe to the King. This venerable magiſtrate, being in great favour with Balin, rejected their preſents, but told them, he would uſe his endeavour to get them continued upon full pay. He accordingly went next day to court, and while he ſtood in the preſence, put on the appearance of ſorrow, which being obſerved by the King, he enquired about the cauſe of his grief. The old man replied, "I was juſt thinking, that if, in the preſence of God, all the old men were rejected, what would become of me." The King was ſtruck with the reproof, and after ſome penſive ſilence, ordered the veterans to be continued in their uſual pay.

Shere dies. In the fourth year of the reign of Balin, Shere, the nephew of the late Emperor, who had, from the time of Mamood, governed the provinces upon the banks of the five branches of the Indus, and other diſtricts, died: Some ſay, by poiſon from the King; but this is not now believed, though

though reported by some malicious people in those days. He was esteemed a man of great genius, and an intrepid warrior; having defended his country from the incursions of the Moguls, who now became the terror of the East. Balin, upon the demise of Shere, gave Sunnam and Samana to the noble Timur, and the other countries were divided among other Omrahs of his court. The Moguls, encouraged by the death of Shere, began again their depredations in those provinces. The mutual jealousies and dissensions among the Subas, prevented them from doing any thing effectual for the public good.

A.D. 1268. Higer. 667.

The Emperor, therefore, was obliged to appoint his eldest son Mahommed, at that time bearing the title of the noble Malleck, afterwards famous by the name of Shehid, viceroy of all those frontier provinces. Mahommed was immediately dispatched to his government with a fine army, and some of the wisest and best generals in the empire. The Prince himself was blest with a bright and comprehensive genius, taking great delight in learning and the company of learned men. He, with his own hand, made a choice collection of the beauties of poetry, selected from the most famous in that art. The work consisted of twenty thousand couplets, and was esteemed the criterion of taste. Among the learned men in the Prince's court, the noble Chusero and Hassen bore the first rank in genius and in his esteem. These, with many more of his philosophical society, accompanied him on this expedition to Lahore. Mahommed was visited at Lahore by Osman Marindi, who was esteemed the greatest man of that age. But no presents or entreaty could prevail upon him to remain out of his own country; so that after a short stay he returned. We are told, that as he was one day

The prince Mahommed appointed governor of the frontiers.

A.D. 1268. Higer. 667. day reading one of his poems in Arabic before the Prince, all the poets who were present were transported into a fit of dancing. But the piece affected the Prince, to all appearance, in a quite contrary manner; for the tears began to flow fast down his cheeks. This might indeed be occasioned by excess of pleasure, though it was, at that time, attributed to that noble emulation which grieves for that excellence which it cannot attain.

He invites the famous poet Sadi to his court. The fame of the enlightened Sadi of Schiraz, the celebrated poet, being great at that time, Mahommed invited him twice to his court; but that renowned sage excused himself on account of his years, and, with much difficulty, was brought to accept of some presents. Sadi, in return, sent to Mahommed a copy of his works, and did honour to the abilities of the noble Chusero, the Prince's favourite, and president of his learned society. The Prince, every year, made a journey to see his father at Delhi, to whom he always behaved with the greatest filial affection and duty. Balin gave his younger son Kera, entitled Nasir ul dien, a Jagier of Sammana and Sunnam, whither the prince set out to reside. His father, at his departure, advised him to recruit and discipline a good army, to watch the motions of the Moguls; and that if he ever should hear of his giving himself up to wine and his former debaucheries, he would certainly withdraw him from that Subaship, and never put confidence in him again. The Prince took the advice of his father to heart, and entirely reforming his manners, gave great proofs of his natural abilities, though his mind had taken a wrong bias in his youth. A place of rendezvouz was appointed, in case of an invasion from the north, on the river Bea, near Lahore,

Lahore, where the two Princes were to join the Imperial army from Delhi. A.D. 1279. Higer. 678.

Every thing seemed now in perfect peace and security throughout the empire, when Tughril, who was intrusted with the government of Bengal, began to appear in arms. In the year 678, this bold and enterprizing man led an army against the Indian princes towards Jagenagur, whom he defeated, carrying off some hundreds of elephants and much wealth, out of which he made no acknowledgment to the King. Balin happened at that time to be very sick, insomuch that the news of his death was spread abroad. This intelligence having reached the ears of Tughril, he assumed the red umbrella with all the royal dignities, and declared himself King of Bengal. Balin hearing of this, wrote him an order to return immediately to his allegiance, which having produced no effect, he commanded Tiggi, governor of Oud, to raise his forces, and declaring him Suba of Bengal, sent Timur, Malleck, Jemmal, and other generals, to his assistance, with an army from Delhi, to reduce the traitor to obedience.

Tughril rebels in Bengal.

When Tiggi was joined by this force, he crossed the Sirju, now the Gagra or Deo, and proceeded towards Bengal, whence Tughril advanced with his forces to meet him. Tughril employed his money so well among the troops of Tiggi, that he drew many of the Turkish chiefs over to his party, and then engaging the imperial army, he gave them a total defeat. The King hearing this news, bit his own flesh with indignation. He ordered Tiggi to be hanged at the gate of Oud; and dispatched Turmutti, a Turkish general, with another army, against the rebel. Nor was the fate of Turmutti more fortunate than that of his predecessor. He was totally routed, and lost all his baggage and the public treasure.

Defeats the imperial army.

Balin,

A.D. 1279. Higer. 678. Balin prepares to march against him in person.

Balin, having intelligence of this second disgrace to his arms, was in great affliction, and prepared to take the field in person. He gave orders to build a large fleet of boats, with all expedition, to carry his baggage down the river. He, in the mean time, under pretence of going upon a hunting party, went to Sunnam and Samana, the Subaship of his younger son, whom he brought with his army with him to Delhi, leaving one Malleck in the government. Having collected the imperial army, he appointed the chief magistrate of the city, regent during his own absence.

He enters Bengal.

The Emperor crossing the Ganges, without waiting for the dry season, proceeded to Bengal by forced marches. But having met with great delay, on account of the roads and numerous rivers, Tughril heard of his approach, and had time to collect his army, and with all his elephants, treasure and effects, took the route of Jagenagur*, with intention to remain there till the King should return to Delhi. The Sultan having arrived in Bengal, remained there only a few days. He appointed Hissam governor of the province, and proceeded himself, with his army, towards Jagenagur. At Sunnarguam, the zemindar of that place joined him with his troops, and promised to guard the river against Tughril, if he should endeavour to escape that way.

Pursues the rebels into Orissa.

Balin continued his march with great expedition, but he could gain no intelligence of the enemy. He therefore ordered Malleck, with seven thousand chosen horse, to advance twenty miles, in front of the army, and, by all means, to endeavour to gain intelligence of the rebels; but, in

* A town in Orissa, near Cattack.

spite

ſpite of all enquiry, no ſatisfactory accounts could for ſeveral days be obtained. One day, however, Mahommed Shir, governor of Kole, being out from the advanced guard with forty horſe, reconnoitring the country, beheld ſome bullocks with pack-ſaddles, and having ſeized the drivers, began to enquire about the enemy. They obſtinately pretended ignorance; but the head of one of them being ſtruck off, the reſt fell upon their faces, and confeſſed that they had juſt left the enemy's camp, which was about four miles in front, that they had halted for that day, and intended to advance to Jagenagur.

A. D. 1270. Higer. 678.

Mahommed ſent the drivers to Malleck, who commanded the vanguard, that he might examine them, and proceeded himſelf, as directed, to reconnoitre the enemy's camp. He ſaw, from a riſing ground, the whole encampment, extended over a great plain, with the elephants and cavalry picqueted, and every thing in reſt and ſecurity. Having fixed his eye upon the rebels' tents, which were pitched in the center of the army, he determined to execute one of the boldeſt enterprizes perhaps ever attempted. He advanced on full ſpeed, with his forty attendants, whom he fired with the glory of the undertaking, towards the camp, which he was permitted to enter, being taken for one of their own parties. He continued his courſe to the uſurper's tents, and then ordered his men to draw; and ruſhing into the great tent of audience, which was crowded with men of diſtinction, put all they met to the ſword, crying, "Victory to Sultan Balin!"

A gallant exploit of Mahommed Shir.

Tughril, who imagined he was ſurprized by the imperial army, ſtarted from his throne in confuſion, and cut his way through the tent behind. He mounted a horſe without a ſaddle, and the cry having now ſpread through the camp, he was

Tughril flies,

A.D. 1279. Higer. 678. was confirmed in his fears, and fled towards the river, with an intention to crofs it, that he might make his efcape to Jagenagur. In the mean time, Malleck, the brother of the gallant Mahommed, having feen the rebel as he fled, purfued him to the river, and fhot him with an arrow as he was and is killed. croffing. Tughril immediately fell from his horfe, and Malleck, plunging into the ftream, dragged him out by the hair, and cut off his head. At that very inftant, feeing fome of the enemy coming that way, he hid the head in the fand, and fending the body down the ftream, begun to bathe himfelf in the river. The party queftioned him about their King, and then went off without fufpicion.

His army fly. Mahommed's party, in the mean time, having difpatched every body they found in the royal tents, difperfed themfelves in fuch a manner among the enemy, who were now in the greateft confufion, that moft of them efcaped in the crowd. Tughril being no where to be found, and the panic having run through the whole army, the flight became general, and none thought about any thing but perfonal fafety. Thofe who remained alive of the forty heroes, loitered in the rear, till the enemy were quite gone off the field. They then returned to the deferted camp, where they chanced to meet Malleck. He related the King's death to his brother, who inftantly fent the head to Balin. He at the fame time difpatched an exprefs to the vanguard, which came up that night, and took poffeffion of the camp.

The Sultan arrived the next day with the imperial army. He called to him the two gallant brothers, and commanded them to relate the particulars of this aftonifhing exploit. He heard it with furprize; but inftead of praifing them, as they expected, he told them, that the rafhnefs of their behaviour was inconfiftent with their duty and

and prudence, and much more to the ſame purpoſe. But he, in a few days, took them into favour, and conferred great titles and honours upon them. A. D. 1279. Higer. 678.

Balin, finding the enemy had entirely diſperſed, returned to Bengal, and put every one of the rebel's family, and principal adherents, to death. He did not even ſpare his innocent women and children; and he carried his cruelty ſo far, as to maſſacre a hundred Fakiers, and their chief Collinder, for having been in great favour with the rebel, who had given him a preſent of three maunds of gold to ſupport the ſociety. Balin appointed his ſon Kera, King of Bengal, beſtowing upon him all the enſigns of royalty, and the ſpoils of Tughril, except the elephants and treaſure, while he himſelf returned with his army towards Delhi. Balin was abſent upon this expedition three years. Upon his arrival, he conferred dignities upon Malleck, who had ruled Delhi with great wiſdom. He then viſited the learned men at their own houſes, made them princely preſents, and, at their inſtigation, publiſhed an act of grace to all inſolvent debtors who were in confinement, ſtriking off, at the ſame time, all old balances of revenues due to the crown. Notwithſtanding this appearance of humanity, either the policy or natural cruelty of his diſpoſition rendered him unmerciful to all rebels. He ordered ſpits to be erected in the market-place, for the execution of all the priſoners taken in the late expedition; and it was with the utmoſt difficulty, that the Caſies, Muftíes, and learned men, in a body petitioning their pardon, could obtain it. This venerable body at laſt ſoftened Balin into mercy, and he drew the pen of forgiveneſs over their crimes. Mahommed rewarded. Balin's cruelty.

A.D. 1282. Higer. 681. His eldest son returns to Delhi.

His eldest son, having heard of his father's arrival, proceeded to Delhi to visit him, and was received with the greatest affection and joy. He had not remained at the capital three months, during which his father and he were inseparable, when news was brought that the Moguls had invaded Moultan. Mahommed hastened his departure to oppose them; but, before he had taken leave, his father called him into a private apartment, and addressed him in the following manner:

His father's advice to Mahommed;

He told him, "That he himself had spent a long life in the administration and government of kingdoms; that, by study and experience, he had acquired some knowledge, which might be of service to Mahommed after his death, which, in the course of nature, now hastened apace. That therefore he desired he would lend him the ear of attention, and treasure up his maxims in his mind.

"When you shall ascend the throne, look upon yourself as the deputy of God. Have a just sense of the importance of your charge. Permit not any meanness of behaviour in yourself, to sully the lustre of your exalted station, nor let avaricious and low-minded men share your esteem, or bear any part in your administration.

"Let your passions be governed by reason, and beware of giving way to your rage. Anger is dangerous in all men; but in Kings it is the weapon of death.

"Let the public treasure be expended in the service of the state, with that prudent œconomy, yet benevolent liberality, which reason will dictate to a mind always intent on doing good.

"Let the worship of God be inculcated by your example, and never permit vice and infidelity, unpunished, to hold up their face to the day.

"Be

"Be ever attentive to the businefs of the ftate, that you may avoid the impofition of defigning minifters. Make it your ftudy to fee them execute your commands, without the leaft deviation or neglect, for it is by them you muft govern your people. A.D. 1282. Higer. 681.

"Let your judges and magiftrates be men of capacity, religion, and virtue, that the light of juftice may illuminate your realms. Let no light behaviour, in public or private, detract from that important majefty which exalts the idea of a King; and let every thing around you be fo regulated, as to infpire that reverence and awe which will render your perfon facred, and contribute to enforce your commands.

"Spare no pains to find men of genius, learning, and courage. You muft cherifh them by your benificence, that they may prove the foul of your council, and the fword of your power.

"Throw not down a great man to the ground for a fmall crime, nor entirely overlook his offence. Raife not a low man too haftily to a high ftation, left he forget himfelf, and be an eyefore to men of fuperior merit.

"Never attempt any thing, unlefs it is through neceffity, but what you are fure to accomplifh; and having once determined upon a meafure, let your perfeverance be never fhaken by doubt, nor your eye ever deviate from the object. For it is better for a King to be obftinate than pufillanimous, as in the firft cafe he may chance to be right, in the latter he is always fure to be wrong. Nothing more certainly indicates the weaknefs of a prince, than a fluctuating mind."

Balin, having ended his inftructions, embraced his fon tenderly, and parted with him in tears. The Prince immediately marched againft the enemy, and having defeated and flain the noble Mahommed, who marches againft the Moguls.

A.D. 1283. Higer. 682. Mahommed, chief of the Moguls, he recovered all the territories of which they had possessed themselves in the empire. The throne of Persia was at this time filled by Argunu, the son of Eback and grandson of Hallaku, who had conquered that empire about the year 656. Timur of the family of Zingis, who was then a prince of mighty renown in the empire, and of the race of the conqueror of Asia, governed all the eastern provinces of Persia, from Chorassan to the Indus, and invaded Hindostan with twenty thousand chosen horse, to revenge the death of his friend Mahommed, who had been killed the former year. Having ravaged all the country about Debalpoor and Lahore, he turned towards Moultan. The Prince Mahommed, who was then in Moultan, hearing of his designs, hastened to the banks of the river of Lahore, which runs through part of Moultan, and prepared to oppose him. When Timur advanced to the river, he saw the army of Hindostan on the opposite bank. But the prince, desirous of engaging so great a chief upon equal terms, permitted Timur to pass the river unmolested.

They are defeated by Mahommed, Both armies then drew up in order of battle, and engaged with great fury, for the space of three hours, in which both commanders eminently distinguished their valour and conduct. The Moguls were at last put to flight, and the nobles of India pursued them with imprudent disorder. Mahommed, fatigued by the pursuit, halted by a large pond of water, with five hundred attendants, to drink. He there fell prostrate upon the ground, to return God thanks for his victory.

who is surprized and slain. In the mean time one of the Mogul chiefs, who had hid himself, with two thousand horse, in a neighbouring wood, rushed out upon Mahommed,

hommed, and began a dreadful slaughter. The Prince had just time to mount his horse, and, collecting his small party, and encouraging them by his example, fell upon his enemies. He was at last overpowered by numbers, after having thrice obliged them to give ground, and he unfortunately received a fatal arrow in his breast, by which he fell to the ground, and in a few minutes expired. A body of the troops of India appearing at that instant, the Moguls took to flight. Very few of the unfortunate Mahommed's party escaped from this conflict. Among the fortunate few, was the noble Chusero the poet, who relates this event at large, in his book called Chizer Chani.

A. D. 1286. Higer. 685.

Grief of the army for his death.

When the army returned from the pursuit of Timur, and beheld their prince in his blood, the shouts of victory were changed to the wailings of woe. No dry eye was to be seen from the meanest soldier to the Omrah of high command. The fatal news reached the old King, who was now in his eightieth year. The fountains of his tears were exhausted, and life became obnoxious to his sight. However, bearing himself up against the stream of misfortune, he sent Kei Chusero his grandson, and the son of the deceased, to supply the place of his father. Kei Chusero, upon his arrival at Moultan, took the command of the army, and pouring the balm of benevolence and kindness upon the wounds of his afflicted people, began to adjust his government, and provide for the defence of the frontiers.

Balin sends for his son Kera to succeed him, and dies.

When the King found grief and infirmities began to conquer his vital strength, he sent for his son Kera, from Bengal, and appointed him his successor, at the same time insisting, that he should continue with him at Delhi till his death, and ap-

A.D. 1286. Higer. 685. point a deputy for his government of Bengal. To this Kera consented; but finding his father's illness was not likely to come soon to a crisis, he set out for Bengal without acquainting him of his departure. This undutiful behaviour in his son, threw the old man into the deepest affliction, so that death began now to press hard upon him. He in the mean time sent for his grandson Kei Chusero, from Moultan: the prince hastened to his presence, and a council of all the Omrahs being called, the succession was changed in his favour, all of them promising to enforce Balin's last will, in favour of this young prince. Balin in a few days expired, in the year 685, after a reign of twenty-two years. Immediately, upon the death of the Emperor, Malleck, chief magistrate of Delhi, having assembled the Omrahs, and being always in enmity with the father of Chusero, harangued them upon the present posture of affairs. He assured them that Chusero was a young man of a very violent and untractable disposition, and therefore, in his opinion, unfit to reign; besides, that the power of the prince Kera was so great in the empire, that a civil war was to be feared if the succession should not be continued in his family. That therefore, as the father was absent, it would be most prudent for the Omrahs to elect his son Kei Kobad, who was a prince of a mild disposition, and then present in Delhi. So great was the influence of the minister, that he procured the throne for Kei Kobad; and Chusero, glad to escape with life, returned to his former government of Lahore.

In the glorious reign of Balin, flourished at Delhi, besides the great men we have already mentioned, the renowned and learned Musaood Shukurgunge,

Shukurgunge, the enlightened Zeckeria, the flower of genius Arif, Budder a great philosopher, the high-learned Buchtiar Kaki, the unblemished Mola, and many more, eminent in all branches of science and literature. A. D. 1286. Higer. 685.

KEI KOBAD.

A.D. 1286. Higer. 685. Kei Kobad.

WHEN Balin was numbered with the dead, Kei Kobad * his grandſon, in his eighteenth year, aſcended the throne, and aſſumed all the imperial titles. He was a prince remarkably handſome in his perſon, and of an affable and mild diſpoſition. He had a talent for literature, and his knowledge that way was pretty extenſive. His mother was a beautiful princeſs, daughter to the Emperor Altumſh; and if purity of blood royal is of any real worth, Kei Kobad had that to boaſt, for a ſeries of generations.

Luxury prevails at Delhi.

As he had been bred up with great ſtrictneſs under the wings of his father, when he became maſter of his own actions he began to give a looſe to pleaſure without reſtraint. He delighted in love, and in the ſoft ſociety of ſilver-bodied damſels with muſky treſſes, ſpent great part of his time. When it was publickly known that the King was a man of pleaſure, it became immediately faſhionable at court; and in ſhort, in a few days, luxury and vice ſo prevailed, that every ſhade was filled with ladies of pleaſure, and every ſtreet rung with muſick and mirth. Even the magiſtrates were ſeen drunk in public, and riot was heard in every houſe.

* Moaz-ul-dien, Kei Kobad.

The

The King fitted up a palace at Kilogurry, upon the banks of the river Jumna, and retired thither to enjoy his pleaſures undiſturbed; admitting no company but ſingers, players, muſicians and buffoons. Nizam ul dien, who was nephew and ſon-in-law to the chief magiſtrate of Delhi, to whom Kei Kobad owed his elevation, was raiſed to the dignity of chief ſecretary of the empire, and got the reins of government in his hands; and Ellaka, who was the greateſt man for learning in that age, was appointed his deputy. Nizam, ſeeing that the King was quite ſwallowed up in his pleaſures, began to form ſchemes to clear his own way to the empire. The firſt object of his attention was Chuſero, who was now gone to Ghizni, to endeavour to bring that noble and royal Tartar, the ſon of the prince Mahommed, the King's couſin-german, Timur, over to his party, in order to recover the throne of Delhi; to which he claimed a title from his father's right of primogeniture, as well as from the will of the late Emperor. But in this ſcheme Chuſero did not ſucceed, and he was obliged to return from Ghizni in great diſguſt.

A. D. 1286. Higer. 685. Kei Kobad gives himſelf up to pleaſure.

In the mean time, Nizam endeavoured to make him as obnoxious as poſſible to the King, who was at length prevailed upon to entice Chuſero to Delhi. Nizam hired aſſaſſins to murder the unfortunate prince on the way, which they accompliſhed at the village of Hicke. The villanies of Nizam did not ſtop here. He forged a correſpondence between Chaja the vizier, and Chuſero, and thus effected that miniſter's diſgrace and baniſhment. He alſo privately aſſaſſinated all the old ſervants of Balin, inſomuch that a general conſternation was ſpread through the city, though none as yet ſuſpected Nizam as the cauſe. The more he ſucceeded in his villanies, he became leſs ſecret

Chuſero murdered.

A.D. 1288. Higer. 687. ſecret in the execution; and though he began to be deteſted by all ranks, his power and influence was ſo great with the King, that he was the terror of every man.

While things were in this ſituation, advices arrived of another invaſion of Moguls into the diſtricts of Lahore. Barbeck and Jehan were ſent with an army againſt them. The Moguls were defeated near Lahore, and a number of priſoners brought to Delhi. The next ſtep the traitor took, was to inſpire the King with jealouſy of his Mogul troops, who, as ſoldiers of fortune, had enliſted in great numbers in his ſervice. He pretended that, in caſe of a Mogul invaſion, they would certainly join their countrymen againſt him, inſinuating, at the ſame time, that he believed there was already ſome treachery intended.

The Moguls defeated.

Kei Kobad maſſacres the Moguls in his ſervice.

The weak prince liſtened to thoſe villanous intimations, and, calling their chiefs one day together, he ordered them to be ſet upon by his guards and maſſacred; confiſcating, at the ſame time, all their goods and wealth. He ſeized upon all the Omrahs who had any connections with the Moguls, and ſent them priſoners to diſtant garriſons in the remoteſt parts of the empire. So blind was Kei Kobad to his own ruin, and ſo infatuated by this deceitful miniſter, that when any of his father's friends, or well-wiſhers to himſelf and the ſtate, made any complaints againſt the traitor, he immediately called for Nizam himſelf, and, ſmiling, told him, that ſuch a perſon had been doing him ſuch and ſuch ill offices, with an intention to alienate his affections from him. The perſon who preferred the complaint became, by this means, a ſacrifice, while fear prevented others from falling martys to virtue and honeſty.

When

When Nizam thus carried all before him in the preſence, his wife was no leſs buſy in the Haram. She had all the ladies at her devotion; and, by way of particular reſpect, was called the King's mother. The old chief magiſtrate of Delhi, Malleck, who had now reached his ninetieth year, perceived the deſign of the treacherous miniſter, and called him to his houſe, and, by various arguments, endeavoured to ſuppreſs his ambitious ſchemes, and to lay the deformity of ſuch behaviour fully open to his view. The miniſter allowed the juſtice of his reaſoning, and affirmed that he had no further intentions than to ſecure himſelf in the King's favour. That having, unfortunately, diſobliged ſo many people, it was dangerous for him to permit his authority to decline.

A. D. 1288. Higer. 687. The miniſter carries all before him.

In the mean time, prince Kera, the Emperor's father, who had contented himſelf with the kingdom of Bengal, having heard how matters went on at the court of Delhi, penetrated into the deſigns of the miniſter, and wrote a long letter to his ſon, forewarning him of his danger, and adviſing him how to proceed. But his advice, like that of others, was of no weight with that vicious, luxurious, and infatuated prince. When Kera found that his inſtructions were ſlighted, and that things would ſoon be brought to a diſagreeable iſſue, he collected a great army, and directed his ſtandards towards Delhi, about two years after the death of Balin. Kei Kobad, hearing that his father had advanced as far as Behar, drew out his forces, and marched down to meet him, encamping his army upon the banks of the Gagera. Kera lay upon the Sirve, and both armies remained ſome days in hourly expectation of an action. The old man, finding his army much inferior to that of his ſon, began to deſpair of reducing

Kera's advice to his ſon is ſlighted.

Marches towards Delhi.

A.D. 1288. Higer. 687. reducing him by force, and accordingly began to treat of peace.

A conference proposed between the father and son. The young prince, upon this, became more haughty, and by the advice of his favourite prepared for battle. In the mean time, a letter came from his father, written in the most tender and affectionate terms, begging he might be blessed with one sight of him before matters were carried to extremities. This letter awakened nature, which had slumbered so long in Kei Kobad's breast, and he gave orders to prepare his retinue, that he might visit his father. The favourite attempted all in his power to prevent this interview, but finding the prince, for once, obstinate, he prevailed upon him to insist, as Emperor of Delhi, upon the first visit, hoping, by this means, to break off the conference. His design, however, did not succeed; for Kera, seeing what a headstrong boy he had to deal with, consented to come to the imperial camp, and ordered the astrologers to determine upon a lucky hour, and crossing the river, proceeded towards his son's camp.

Kei Kobad's insolence. The young Monarch, having prepared every thing for his father's reception in the most pompous and ceremonious manner, mounted his throne, and arrogantly gave orders, that his father, upon his approach, should three times kiss the ground. The old man accordingly, when he arrived at the first door, was ordered to dismount, and after he had come in sight of the throne, he was commanded to pay his obeisance in three different places as he advanced. The Emperor's macebearer crying out, according to custom, The noble Kera to the King of the world sends health.

Mollified upon seeing his father. The old man was so much shocked at this indignity, that he burst out into a flood of tears; which being observed by the son, he could no longer

longer ſupport his unnatural inſolence, but, leaping from the throne, fell on his face at his father's feet, imploring his forgiveneſs for his offence. The good old man melted into compaſſion, and, raiſing him in his arms, embraced him, and hung weeping upon his neck. The ſcene in ſhort was ſo affecting on both ſides, that the whole court began to wipe the tears from their eyes. Theſe tranſports being over, the young King helped his father to mount the throne, and paying him his reſpects, took his place at his right hand, ordering a charger full of golden ſuns to be waved three times over his father's head, and afterwards to be given among the people. All the Omrahs alſo preſented to him their preſents. A.D. 1288. Higer. 687.

Public buſineſs being then talked over, every thing was ſettled in peace and friendſhip, and Kera returned to his own camp. A friendly intercourſe commenced immediately between the two armies, for the ſpace of twenty days, in which time the father and ſon alternately viſited one another, and the time was ſpent in feſtivity and mirth. The principal terms ſettled between the two Kings were, that they ſhould reſpectively retain their former dominions; and then Kei Kobad prepared to return to Delhi, and his father to Bengal. Before they had taken leave, Kera called his ſon, the favourite miniſter, and his deputy, into a private apartment, and gave them a long lecture of advice on the art of government. He then embraced Kei Kobad, and whiſpered in his ear, to rid himſelf of Nizam as ſoon as poſſible. They both parted in tears, and returned to their reſpective capitals. Kera was much affected upon this occaſion, and told his friends, at his return to his own camp, "That he had that day parted with his ſon and the empire," ſtill apprehenſive of the A peace ſettled between them.

A.D. 1288. Higer. 687. the miniſter, and the wayward diſpoſition of the young man.

Kei Kobad beginning to reform, When Kei Kobad arrived at Delhi, the advice of his father for a few days ſeemed to take root in his mind. But his reformation was not the intereſt of the miniſter. He therefore ſoon brought back his prince to the paths of pleaſure. He, for this purpoſe, collected together all the moſt beautiful women, moſt graceful dancers, and ſweeteſt ſingers, from all parts of the empire; and theſe allurements to vice were occaſionally introduced to his view.

is again brought back to pleaſure; One day, as he was riding out, he was accoſted by a beautiful lady, mounted upon a fine Arabian horſe, with a crown of jewels upon her head, a thin white robe with golden flowers flowing looſely over her ſnowy ſhoulders, and a ſparkling girdle of gems around her ſlender waiſt. This fair one advancing before the royal umbrella, with a thouſand charms and ſmiles began to ſing a love ſong. Then, ſtopping ſhort, ſhe begged pardon for her intruſion, and would not, without much intreaty, proceed. The King was ſtruck with the beauty of this enchantreſs, and immediately diſmounting, ordered his camp to be pitched, and employed the evening in the pleaſures of love. This damſel was no leſs remarkable for her wit than for her beauty. The King, while ſhe was dancing, having broke out in rapturous verſes upon thoſe charms which ſhe diſplayed, ſhe anſwered every time extempore, in the ſame meaſure, with ſuch propriety and elegance as aſtoniſhed and ſilenced the greateſt wits of the court.

falls ſick. In ſhort, the King continued in this courſe of pleaſure, till wine, and intemperance in his other paſſions, had ruined his health. He fell ſick, and then began to recollect the advices of his father, and to conſider Nizam as the cauſe of all his diſtreſs.

distress. He immediately began to form schemes in his mind to rid himself of that wicked minister. He for this purpose ordered him to the government of Moultan; but Nizam, perceiving his drift, contrived many delays, that he might get a favourable opportunity to accomplish his villanous intentions. His designs, however, in the mean time reverted upon his own head. The Omrahs dispatched him by poison, some say without the King's knowledge, while others affirm that it was by his authority.

A.D. 1289. Higer. 688.

Nizam poisoned.

Malleck Ferose, the son of Malleck chief of the Afgan tribes called Chilligi, who was deputy governor of Sammana, came, by the King's orders, to court, and was honoured with the title of Shaista Chan, and made lord of requests, as also suba of Birren. Chigen was promoted to a high office at court, and Surcha was made chief secretary of the empire. These three divided the whole power of the government amongst them, while the King by this time became afflicted with a palsy, by which he lost the use of one side, and had his mouth distorted.

Promotion at court.

Kei Kobad becomes paralytic.

Every Omrah of popularity or power, began now to intrigue for the empire, which obliged the friends of the royal family to take Keiomourse, a child of three years, son to the reigning Emperor, out of the Haram, and set him upon the throne. The army, upon this, split into two factions, who encamped on opposite sides of the city. The Tartars * espoused the cause of the young King, and the Chilligies, a powerful tribe of Afghans, joined Ferose, who usurped the throne. Upon the first disturbance, those Tartars who had set up the young prince, jealous of the power of the Chilligies, assembled them-

His son raised to the empire.

* They were mercenaries in the imperial army.

selves,

A.D. 1289. Higer. 688. ſelves, and proſcribed all the principal Chilligian officers.

Feroſe rebels. Feroſe, being the firſt in the bloody liſt, immediately rebelled. Chigen had been deputed by the Tartar party, to invite Feroſe to a conference with the ſick King, and a plot was formed for his aſſaſſination. Feroſe diſcovering his deſigns, drew upon the traitor, who came to invite him, and killed him at the door of his tent. The ſons of Feroſe, who were renowned for their valour, immediately put themſelves at the head of five hundred choſen horſe, and making an aſſault upon the camp of the Tartars, cut their way to the royal tents, which were pitched in the center of the army, and ſeizing the infant King, carried him, and the ſon of Malleck ul Omrah, off, in ſpite of all oppoſition, to their father. They killed Surcha, who purſued them, with many other men of diſtinction. When this exploit began to be noiſed abroad in the city, the mob flew immediately to arms. They marched out in thouſands, and encamping at the Budaoon gate, prepared to go againſt Feroſe, and reſcue the infant King, for they greatly dreaded the power of the Chilligies, who were a fierce and ſavage race. Malleck ul Omrah, the old miniſter, ſo often mentioned, conſidering that this ſtep would occaſion the aſſaſſination of the young King, and of his own ſon, who was in their hands, exerted his great influence and authority among the people, and at length prevailed with them to diſperſe.

Kei Kobad aſſaſſinated. Feroſe, in the mean time, ſent an aſſaſſin to cut off the Emperor Kei Kobad, who lay ſick at Kilogurry. The villain found this unfortunate prince dying upon his bed, deſerted by all his attendants. He beat out the poor remains of life with a cudgel; then rolling him up in his bedclothes, threw him over the window into the river. This aſſaſſin

was

was a Tartar of ſome family, whoſe father had been unjuſtly put to death by Kei Kobad, and he now had a complete revenge. A. D. 1289. Higer. 688.

When this horrid deed was perpetrated, Feroſe aſcended the throne, and aſſumed the title of Jellal ul dien, having put an end to the dynaſty of Ghor, and commenced that of Chilligi. Chidju, nephew to the Emperor Balin, and who was now eſteemed the juſt heir of the empire, was immediately appointed governor of Kurrah, and ſent off to his government. Feroſe marched into the palace, and was proclaimed with great ſolemnity in the city; and to complete his cruel policy, he made away with the young prince, that he might reign with the greater ſecurity. Feroſe aſcends the throne.

This great revolution happened in the year ſix hundred and eighty-ſeven, the reign of Kei Kobad being ſomething more than three years; a time long and diſaſtrous, if we look upon the villanies of Nizam, and the conſequent overthrow of the family of Balin.

During the reign of Balin, and his grandſon Kei Kobad, Cubla, the grandſon of Zingis, ſat on the Tartar throne, and completed the conqueſt of China. Hallacu, and after him his ſon Abâca, ſurnamed Ilkan, reigned over the empire of Perſia and Syria, in ſubordination to Cubla. Zagatay the ſon of Zingis, and his poſterity, were in poſſeſſion of Maver-ul-nere, or Tranſoxiana, and the provinces to the north-weſt of the Indus, which had formerly compoſed the empire of Ghizni. State of Aſia.

FEROSE

F E R O S E II.

A.D. 1289. Higer. 688. Different opinions concerning the origin of the tribe of Chilligi.

NIZAM AHMUD ſays, in his hiſtory, that the tribe of Chilligi, of whom Feroſe * was deſcended, derived their origin from Calidge Chan. Calidge, continues that writer, having quarrelled with his wife, who was an imperious and vindictive woman, and fearing ſhe would draw the reſentment of her brother Zingis upon him, deſerted his army as he was paſſing the mountains of Ghor and Ghirgiſtan, in his return from the conqueſt of Perſia. Three thouſand of his friends followed Calidge, and took poſſeſſion of thoſe mountains, where they were afterwards joined by many of their countrymen, and even by ſome of the family of Zingis. Other hiſtorians, with equal improbability, affirm, that we ought to look for the origin of the Chilligies, as far back as Eaphs the ſon of Noo†, who, ſay they, had eleven ſons, one of whom was called Chilligi. But we have reaſon to think that neither of the accounts is authentic, the one being too modern, and the other too antient, to merit our faith. We hear of this tribe of Chilligi in the reigns of Subuctagi, and Mamood of Ghizni, which entirely deſtroys the former ſuppoſition; and we have great doubts concerning the exiſtence of Chilligi the ſon of

* Jellal-ul-dien Feroſe, Chilligi.

† Japhet, the ſon of Noah.

Eaphs,

Eaphs, being persuaded that this idle story took its rise from the natural vanity of nations, in tracing themselves back to remote antiquity. This tribe, however, as we have already observed, inhabited the mountains of Ghor and Ghirgistan, in the confines of Persia, and were a brave and hardy, though barbarous race. They made a business of war, and always served as mercenaries any power that chose to employ them. The father of that Ferose, who mounted the throne of Delhi, was Malleck. He was one of those soldiers of fortune, who subsist by the sword; and raised himself to some rank, in the army of the Emperor Balin. His son Ferose, being a man of genius, was appointed to the government of Sammana. He was called from thence, as before related, and usurped the empire. A.D. 1289. Higer. 689.

He reserved, for some months, the young prince Keiomours, as a cloak to his usurpation; and having established himself upon the throne, he ordered him to be put to death. He was seventy years of age when he mounted the Musnud. He, by way of plainness, changed the royal umbrella from red to white; laid entirely aside his cruelty, after the death of the young prince; and became remarkable for his humanity and benevolence. He had no great confidence in the loyalty of the people of Delhi, and therefore resided always at Kilogurry, which he strengthened with works, and adorned with fine gardens, and beautiful walks by the side of the river. The Omrahs, following the Emperor's example, built palaces around, so that Kilogurry became known by the name of the new city. Egherish, the Emperor's brother, was appointed receiver-general of all petitions to the throne; and the Emperor's eldest son was dignified with the title of first of the nobles: the second son, with the title of Arkali; and the third with

The infant Emperor murdered.

A. D. 1290. Higer. 689. with that of Kuder Chan. They had all governments conferred upon them, and maintained separate houſeholds. Chaja Chatire was appointed vizier, and the old chief magiſtrate of the city, Malleck, was continued in his office.

Feroſe courts popularity. The citizens of Delhi, perceiving the wiſdom, lenity, and juſtice of the King, were gradually weaned from their attachment to the old family, and became friends and ſupporters of the new government. Feroſe himſelf was at much pains to cultivate popularity, and, for that purpoſe, he gave great encouragement to the learned of that age, who, in return, offered the incenſe of flattery at the altar of his fame. In the ſecond year of Feroſe, Chidju, nephew to Balin, and Nabob of Kurrah, in alliance with Halim, Nabob of Oud, aſſumed the enſigns of royalty, and ſtruck the currency of the country in his own name, which he changed to that of Moghiz ul dien. He brought over to his party all the Rajas and Jagierdars of thoſe parts, and, raiſing a great army, advanced towards Delhi.

Advices of this inſurrection arriving in the capital, Feroſe collected his forces, and marched out to meet the rebels. He ſent the Chilligian cavalry, who excelled at the bow, a few miles in his front, under the command of Arkilli his own ſon. A rebellion quaſhed. Arkilli, encountering the enemy about twenty-five miles from the city, after an obſtinate engagement, defeated them. He took ſeveral Omrahs priſoners in the purſuit, whom he mounted upon camels, with branches hung round their necks; and in that plight ſent them to his father. When Feroſe ſaw them in this diſtreſs, he immediately ordered them to be unbound, to have a change of linen given them, and an elegant entertainment to be provided. He called them before him, and repeated a verſe to this purpoſe, " That evil for

evil

evil was eaſily returned, but he only was great who could return good for evil." He then ordered them to retire, in full aſſurance of his forgiveneſs. Chidju, ſome days after, was taken by the zemindars, and ſent priſoner to the King. Inſtead of condemning him to death, as was expected, Feroſe gave him a free pardon, and ſent him to Moultan, where he had a handſome appointment for life, as priſoner at large. This lenity of the King gave great umbrage to the Omrahs of Chilligi, who addreſſed him upon the occaſion, and adviſed him to purſue the policy of Balin, who never pardoned a traitor. They deſired, that, at leaſt, a needle ſhould be paſſed through the eyes of Chidju, to be an example to others. If that was not done, they averred, that treaſon would ſoon raiſe its head in every quarter of the empire; and, ſhould the Tartars once gain the ſuperiority, they would not leave the name of Chilligi in Hindoſtan. The King anſwered, That what they ſaid was certainly according to the true policy of government; but, my friends, ſays he, I am now an old man, and I wiſh to go down to the grave without ſhedding blood. A. D. 1290. Higer. 689. Clemency of the Emperor

This behaviour of the Emperor, it muſt be acknowledged, had ſoon the effect which the Chilligian chiefs foreſaw. Clemency is a virtue which deſcends from God, but the degenerate children of India did not deſerve it. There was no ſecurity to be found in any place. The ſtreets, the highways, were infeſted by banditti. Houſebreaking, robbery, murder, and every other ſpecies of villainy, became a buſineſs all over the empire. Inſurrections were heard of in every province, numerous gangs of robbers ſtopt all commerce and intercourſe, and the Nabobs refuſed or neglected to ſend any account of their revenues or adminiſtration. occaſions diſturbances.

A.D. 1290. Higer. 689. The Omrahs confpire againft him.

The Omrahs of Chilligi were greatly alarmed at thefe proceedings, and began to lengthen the tongue of reproach againft their Sovereign. They even began to confult about depofing him, and to raife their kinfman Kugi, who was a man of influence, courage, and refolution, to the throne. For this purpofe they met one day, at an entertainment in his houfe; but having intoxicated themfelves with wine, they began openly to talk of affaffinating the Emperor, quarrelling about which of them fhould have the honour of that undertaking. While they were in this fituation, one of the company privately withdrew, and, running to Ferofe, repeated very circumftantially every particular of what he had heard. The Emperor immediately ordered a guard to furround the houfe, who, having feized the Omrahs, brought them all before him. He upbraided them with their treafon, he drew his fword, and throwing it down upon the ground, challenged the boldeft of them to wield it againft him. But they fell upon their faces, and remained filent and confounded. One of them, however, whofe name was Malleck Nuferit, was gifted with more impudence than the reft, and told the King, that "the words of drunkennefs were but wind: Where can we ever find fo good and gracious a King, if you fhould be no more? Or where can the King get fo faithful fervants, were he to condemn us for a little unguarded folly?" The unguarded Prince was pleafed with this, and, fmiling, called for wine, and gave him another cup with his own hand. He then upbraided the reft for their conduct, advifed them to behave better for the future, and difmiffed them all with his pardon.

Are difcovered and pardoned.

Remarkable ftory of a Dirvefh.

The execution of a Dirvefh is one of the moft remarkable events in this reign. The name of the Dirvefh was Seid Molah, and the whole affair has

has been thus delivered down in history. Malleck, the Cutwal or chief magistrate of Delhi, dying about this time, all the great men, who, by his interest, held estates, and places at court, were deprived of them, and reduced to want. Among other dependants of the venerable Cutwal, that became destitute by his death, were twelve thousand readers of the Coran*, and some thousands of his Sipais and servants. All these turned their face towards Seid Molah for their maintenance. Molah was a venerable sage, in a mendicant dress, who travelled from Girjan, in Persia, towards the east, where he visited various countries, and men famous for piety and knowledge. He then turned his face towards Hindostan, to visit Sech Ferid of Shuckergunge, a famous poet and philosopher of that age, with whom he resided, some time, in great friendship. But, in the reign of Balin, having an inclination to see Delhi, he took leave of his friend, who advised him to cultivate no intimacy with the great men of the court, otherwise it would prove fatal to him in the end. A.D. 1290. Higer. 689.

Molah arriving at Delhi, set up a great academy, and house of entertainment for travellers, fakiers, and the poor of all denominations, turning none away from his door. Though he was very religious, and brought up in the Mahommedan faith, yet he followed some particular tenets of his own, so that he never attended public worship. He kept no women nor slaves for himself, and lived upon rice only; yet his expences in charity were so great, that, as he never accepted of any presents, men were astonished whence his finances were supplied, and actually believed that he possessed the art of transmuting other metals into gold. Upon His arrival at Delhi;

* Each of these was obliged to read the Coran over once a day.

A.D. 1290. Higer. 689. the death of Balin he launched out more and more in beſtowing great ſums in charity, and expended a princely revenue in his entertainments, which were now frequented by all the great men of the city; for he made nothing of throwing three or four thouſand pieces of gold into the boſom of a noble family in diſtreſs. In ſhort, he diſplayed more magnificence in his feaſts than any of the princes of the empire. His charity was ſo unbounded, that he expended daily, upon the poor, about thirty thouſand pounds of flower, fifteen thouſand of meat, two thouſand of ſugar, beſides rice, oil, butter, and other neceſſaries in proportion. The mob, at length, crouded his gates in ſuch numbers, that it was almoſt impoſſible to paſs that way. In the mean time, the ſons of the Emperor and all the princes of the court reſorted to him with their retinues, and ſpent whole days and nights in innocent feſtivity and philoſophical converſation. After the death of the chief magiſtrate of Delhi, the Dirveſh ſtretched forth his hand to his numerous dependants, and ſupported them in plenty and eaſe.

His magnificence and charity.

In the mean time, Jellal, a man of an intriguing turbulent diſpoſition, wrought himſelf into the favour and confidence of Seid Molah, and being endued with art and plauſibility of tongue, began to inſpire the philoſopher with ambitious views. He told him, that the people looked upon him as ſent from God to deliver the kingdom from the tyranny and oppreſſion of the Chilligies, and to bleſs Hindoſtan with a wiſe and juſt government.

Aſpires to the throne.

The philoſopher, in ſhort, ſuffered his imagination to be deluded by the ſplendid ideas of royalty, and privately began to beſtow titles and offices upon his diſciples, and to take other meaſures to execute his deſigns. He engaged Cutwal and Palwan, two of his particular friends, to join in the

the King's retinue on Friday, as he went to the public mosque, and to aſſaſſinate him; while he himſelf prepared about ten thouſand of his adherents to ſupport his uſurpation. But one of his followers, underſtanding that ſome others of leſs merit than himſelf were appointed to be his ſuperiors, became diſguſted, went privately to the King, and diſcloſed to him every particular of the conſpiracy. A.D. 1290. Higer. 689. Conſpires againſt the King.

The King ordered Seid Molah and Jellal to be immediately ſeized and brought before him for examination. But they perſiſted in their innocence, and no other witneſs appeared againſt them, which rendering the accuſation doubtful, Feroſe ordered a great fire to be prepared in the field of Bahapoor, that they might be put to the ordeal trial. He himſelf marched out of the city to ſee the ceremony performed, and ordered a ring to be made round the pile. The fire being kindled, Feroſe commanded Seid Molah and the two aſſaſſins to be brought, that they might walk through the flames to prove their innocence. Having ſaid their prayers they were juſt going to plunge into the fire, when the Emperor ſtopped them ſhort, and, turning to his miniſters, ſaid, "That the nature of fire was to conſume, paying no reſpect to the righteous more than to the wicked. Beſides, ſaid he, it is contrary to the Mahommedan law to practiſe this heatheniſh ſuperſtition." He is ſeized.

He therefore ordered Jellal to Budaoon, and Seid Molah to be thrown into chains in a vault under the palace, and the two men who were to perpetrate the aſſaſſination to be put to death. He, at the ſame time, baniſhed a number of thoſe who were ſuſpected of the conſpiracy. When they were carrying Seid Molah through the court to his priſon, the King pointed him out to ſome Collinders who ſtood near him, and ſaid, "Behold Ordered to perpetual impriſonment.

A. D. 1291. Higer. 690. "Behold the man who was projecting such an evil against us! I therefore leave him to be judged by you, according to his deserts." At the word, a Collinder, whose name was Beri, started forth, and running towards the prisoner began to cut him with a razor. The unfortunate Molah told him to be more expeditious in sending him to God. He then addressed himself to the King, who was looking over the balcony, and said, I am rejoiced that you have thought of putting a period to my life; yet to distress the pious and the innocent is an evil, and be assured that my curse will lie heavy upon you and your unfortunate posterity. The King, hearing these words, became pensive and perplexed. His son the prince Arkilli, who hated Seid Molah for the great intimacy between him and his elder brother, seeing the Emperor's irresolution, beckoned to an elephant rider, who stood in the court mounted, to advance, which accordingly he did, and commanded his elephant to tread Seid Molah to death.

Put to a cruel death.

Birni, in his history of Ferose, informs us that he himself was at that time in Delhi, and that immediately upon the death of Seid Molah, a black whirlwind arose, which, for the space of half an hour, changed day into night, drove the people in the streets against one another, so that they could scarce grope their way to their own habitations. The same author relates, that no rain fell in these provinces during that year, and the consequence was a most terrible famine, by which thousands daily died in the streets and highways; while whole families drowned themselves in the river. But these were the throes of nature, and not the rage of the elements, for Seid Molah. This event happened in the year 690, and the loss of the Dirvesh was much regretted; for many believed him entirely innocent of the charge.

A prodigy.

The

The prosperity of the King began visibly to decline, for every day new factions and disputes arose, which greatly disturbed his administration. Private misfortunes pressed hard upon him at the same time; among the number of which was the madness of his eldest son, heir apparent of the empire. No medicines could cure that prince, and the distemper, hourly gaining ground, soon terminated in his death.

A.D. 1291. Higer. 690. The good fortune of the King declines.

The King, after the decease of his son, marched his army towards Rintimpore to quell an insurrection in those parts. He left his son Arkilli to manage affairs in his absence. The enemy having retired into the fort of Rintimpore, and the King having reconnoitred the place, despaired of reducing it. He marched towards a small fort called Jain, which he took; then breaking down the temples of Malava, plundered them of some wealth, and again returned to Rintimpore. He summoned the fort a second time to surrender, but finding the rebels paid no attention to his threats, he gave orders to undermine the walls. He however changed his resolution, and decamped, saying, That he found the place could not be taken without the loss of many lives, and therefore he would lay aside his designs against it. Amed Chip, who was one of the pillars of the empire, replied, That Kings, in the time of war, should make no account of those things, when compelled to it by justice and the necessity of supporting their authority, which was now plainly the case. The King, in wrath, asked him, How he came to think that these were not his sentiments; "but I have often, said he, told you, that now being on the brink of the grave, I am unwilling to entail the curse of widows and orphans upon the reign of a few days." He therefore continued his march to Delhi.

He marches to Rintimpore.

In

A. D. 1291. Higer. 691. The Moguls invade Hindostan.

In the year 691, one of the kinſmen of Hallacu, grandſon of the great Zingis, and King of Perſia, in ſubordination to his couſin, the Emperor of Tartary, invaded Hindoſtan with ten tomans * of Moguls. Feroſe, having received advices of the approach of the enemy, collected his army, and moved forward to oppoſe them. When he reached the frontiers of Biram, he ſaw the Moguls in front beyond a ſmall river. Both armies encamped for the ſpace of five days upon either ſide of this ſtream, during which time their advanced poſts ſkirmiſhed frequently, and many were killed.

The armies at laſt, by mutual conſent, pitched upon an extenſive plain where they might have room to contend for the victory. Accordingly, on the ſixth morning, they drew up in order of battle, and cloſed up the dreadful interval of war.

Overthrown by Feroſe.

The Moguls, after an obſtinate conteſt, were overthrown, many of their chiefs killed, and about a thouſand men taken priſoners. Among the latter were two Omrahs and ſeveral officers of rank. The Emperor, notwithſtanding this victory, was afraid to purſue it, and offered them peace, upon condition of their evacuating his dominions. They accordingly gladly accepted thoſe terms, and preſents were exchanged between them. When the Moguls were retreating, Allaghu, grandſon to the great Zingis joined Feroſe with three thouſand men. They all became Muſſulmen, and their chief was honoured with one of Feroſe's daughters in marriage.

Arkilli made governor of Lahore.

The King, about this time, appointed his ſon Arkilli viceroy of Lahore, Moultan, and Sind, with whom he left a ſtrong force, and returned himſelf to his capital. To Allaghu, and the reſt of the Moguls who had now become true belie-

* A Toman conſiſted of 10,000 men.

vers,

vers, was allotted a certain district near the city, where they built for themselves houses, and raised a considerable town, known by the name of Mogulpurra. A. D. 1292. Higer. 692.

In the year 692, the Emperor was under the necessity of marching his army again to quell an insurrection about Mindu, which fort he took, and put the enemy to flight. In the mean time, Alla-ul-dien, the King's nephew, and governor of Kurrah, requested to be permitted to march against the Hindoos of Belsa, who infested his province. Having obtained leave, he marched the same year to Belsa, which he took, and, having pillaged the country, returned with much spoil, part of which was sent as a present to the Emperor; among other things there was a large brazen idol, which was thrown down, by the Budaoon-gate. Ferose was greatly pleased with the success and behaviour of his nephew upon this expedition, for which he rewarded him with princely presents, and annexed the subadary of Oud to his former government of Kurrah. The expeditions of Alla,

Alla, upon this preferment, acquainted the King, that there were some princes of great wealth towards Chinderi, whom, if the King should give him permission, he would reduce to his obedience, and send their spoils to the royal treasury. The King, through covetousness, consented to this proposal, to which Alla was moved by the violent temper of his wife Malleke Jehan, the King's daughter, who threatened his life. To avoid therefore her resentment and that of her father, he looked round for some remote country which might afford him an asylum. Accordingly, in the year 693, he took leave of the King at Delhi, and, proceeding towards Kurrah, took many chiefs of distinction into his service. He marched with eight thousand chosen horse, by the nearest road, against Ramdeo, into the Decan.

A.D. 1293. Higer. 693. Ramdeo, prince of the Decan, who poſſeſſed the wealth of a long line of Kings.

Alla, arriving upon the frontiers of the Decan, preſſed forward againſt the capital of Ramdeo's dominions, which, not being fortified, he was in hopes of ſurprizing. Though this attempt ſeemed too bold to be attended with ſucceſs, yet he perſiſted in his reſolution, and by ſurprizing marches reached Elichpoor, where he made a ſhort halt to refreſh his ſmall army. He marched from thence with equal expedition towards Deogire, the capital. Intelligence of Alla's progreſs coming to the prince, who, with his ſon, had been abſent upon ſome ſervice in a diſtant part of his dominions, he returned with great expedition to intercept the enemy with a numerous army. He accordingly threw himſelf between Alla and the city, engaged him with conſummate bravery, but in the end he was defeated with great loſs.

Overthrows Ramdeo.

Another account of this expedition.

This expedition is otherwiſe recorded by the author of the Tibcat Naſiri. Alla, ſays that writer, left Kurrah on pretence of hunting, and having paſſed through the territories of many petty Rajas, avoided all hoſtilities, giving out that he had left the Emperor in diſguſt, and was going to offer his ſervices to the Raja of the Tellingana, who was the moſt powerful King in the Decan. Accordingly, after two months march, he arrived without any remarkable oppoſition at Elichpoor, from whence, at once changing his courſe, he decamped in the night, and in two days ſurprized the city of Deogire, the capital of Ramdeo. The Raja himſelf was in the city, but his wife and his eldeſt ſon had gone to worſhip at a certain temple without the walls.

Alla takes Deogire.

Ramdeo, upon the approach of Alla, was in the greateſt conſternation. He however collected three or four thouſand citizens and domeſticks, engaged

Alla

Alla at one of the gates of the city, but, being defeated, retired into the citadel. This fort having no ditch, and not being ſtored with proviſions, he had no hopes of defending it long. Alla immediately inveſted the place. In the mean time he gave out, that he was only the vanguard of the Emperor's army, who were in full march to the place. This ſtruck univerſal terror into all the Rajas round, who, inſtead of joining for the general ſafety, began to ſecure themſelves. Alla having pillaged the city and ſeized upon the merchants, brahmins, and principal inhabitants, tortured them for their wealth; while he at the ſame time carried on the ſiege of the citadel. A.D. 1293. Higer. 693. His cruelty.

Ramdeo ſeeing he muſt ſoon be obliged to yield, and imagining that the Emperor intended to make a general conqueſt of the Decan, endeavoured to procure a peace before any other forces arrived. He therefore wrote after this manner to Alla. "Your invaſion of this country was certainly impolitic and raſh, but fortunately for you, having found the city unguarded, you have been permitted to range at large. It is however poſſible that the Rajas of the Decan, who command innumerable armies, may yet ſurround you, and not permit one of your people to eſcape from our dominions alive. Suppoſing even that you ſhould be able to retreat from hence undiſturbed, are not the princes of Malava, Candez and Gundwarra in your way, who have each armies of forty or fifty thouſand men? Do you hope they will permit you to eſcape unmoleſted, after this perfidious attack on their brethren, in religion and Gods? It is therefore adviſeable for you to retire in time, by accepting a ſmall reward, and what ſpoil you have already got, to indemnify you for your expence and labour." Ramdeo propoſes terms of peace,

Alla was very glad to accept of thoſe propoſals, and having received fifty maunds of gold, a large quantity which Alla accepts.

A.D. 1293. Higer. 693. quantity of pearls and jewels, fifty elephants, and ſome thouſand horſes, which were taken in the Rajas ſtables, he releaſed his priſoners, and promiſed to abandon the place in the morning of the fifteenth day from his firſt entrance. But when Alla was preparing to retreat, Ramdeo's eldeſt ſon, who had fled with his mother, on the firſt appearance of the imperial troops, to collect forces, advanced with a numerous army, within a few miles of the city. Ramdeo ſent a meſſage to his ſon, informing him, that peace was concluded, and whatever was done, was done. He therefore ordered him not to open again the door of diſturbance, for that he perceived the Tartars were a warlike race, whoſe peace was better than their war. The young Prince, however, underſtanding that his army was thrice the number of the enemy, and hourly expecting to be joined by other princes, with numerous forces, liſtened not to the commands of his father, but wrote to Alla in theſe terms: "If you have any love for life, and deſire ſafety, ruſh out of this horrible whirlpool, into which you have plunged yourſelf. Whatever you have plundered and received, you muſt return, and take your way homeward, rejoicing in your happy eſcape." Alla, upon reading this inſolent letter, kindled the fire of rage, and blackening the face of the meſſenger, hooted him out of the city. He left Malleck Nuſerit to inveſt the citadel with a thouſand horſe, and immediately marched with the reſt of his army to attack the Raja's ſon, and drew up in the front of his camp.

Ramdeo's ſon advances with an army.

His inſolent letter to Alla.

The Indian did not decline the offered battle. He drew forth his numerous ſquadrons, and the battle commenced with ſuch violence, that the ſtout heart of Alla began to quake for the victory. His troops began to fall back on all ſides. In the mean time Malleck Nuſerit, having learned by his

Is overthrown.

ſcouts

ſcouts the ſituation of affairs, left the citadel without orders, and galloping up to the field of battle, with his thouſand horſe, changed the fortune of the day. The duſt having prevented the enemy from diſcovering the force of Nuſerit, ſome perſon cried out, that the Tartar army, of whom they had been told, was arrived. This ſpread inſtantly a panic through the Indian ranks, and they at once turned their face to flight. Alla did not think proper to purſue them far, but immediately returned into the city, and inveſted the citadel.

A.D. 1293. Higer. 693.

A ſcene of cruelty and horror now commenced. The Tartars, enraged at the perfidy of the Hindoos, for their breach of the treaty, began to ſpread fire and ſword through the city; from which no diſcipline could reſtrain them. Several of the Rajas kindred, who had been taken priſoners, were in chains, thrown down in ſight of the enemy. Ramdeo, in the mean time, ſent expreſs upon expreſs, to haſten the ſuccours which he expected from the Kings of Kilbirga, Tellingana, Malava, and Candez: but was informed that there remained no proviſions in the place, for that a great number of bags, in which they had reckoned upon rice, had been found, upon examination, to be ſalt.

Cruelty of the Tartars.

Ramdeo was greatly perplexed; he commanded that this ſhould be concealed from the troops, and began a ſecond time to propoſe a treaty with Alla. " It muſt be known to you, ſaid the Prince, O! my lord, that your well-wiſher, Ramdeo, had no hand in the late quarrel. If my ſon, in the way of folly and the pride of youth, exalted the ſpear of valour and hoſtility, let not your reſentment be kindled againſt me for his raſhneſs." Ramdeo told the meſſenger privately, that there were no proviſions in the place, and that if the enemy ſhould perſiſt a few days, they muſt be informed of their diſtreſs, which would inevitably bring on the ruin of the

The Raja in great diſtreſs.

Propoſes terms.

A.D. 1294. Higer. 694. the whole. For, ſaid the Prince, ſuppoſing we ſhould be able to hold out the place againſt the aſſaults of the enemy, yet famine cannot be withſtood; and there is now ſcarce ſix days proviſion left. Uſe then art, and take any means to perſuade the army of Iſlam*, to evacuate the country.

A peace concluded.

But Alla, from the behaviour of Ramdeo, perceived the true cauſe of his propoſals, and therefore ſtarted every day ſome new difficulty to retard the treaty, till the garriſon was in the utmoſt diſtreſs. But at length it was concluded, according to our author, upon the following almoſt incredible terms; that Alla ſhould receive, upon conſideration of evacuating the country, ſix hundred maunds of pure gold, according to the weights of the Decan†, ſeven maunds of pearl, two maunds of diamonds, rubies, emeralds, and ſapphires, one thouſand maunds of ſilver, four thouſand pieces of ſilk, and a long liſt of other precious commodities that ſurpaſs all belief. This ranſom was not only required, but alſo the ceſſion of Elichpoor, and its dependencies, where Alla might leave a ſmall garriſon, which ſhould remain there unmoleſted, to collect the revenues.

Alla retreats with an immenſe treaſure.

Alla having ſettled affairs to his ſatisfaction, releaſed all his priſoners, and marched in triumph out of the city with his plunder, and proceeded on his way homeward, on the twenty-fifth day after his taking the city. He conducted his retreat with ſuch ſurprizing addreſs, that he opened his way through extenſive and powerful kingdoms; through Malava, Conduana, Candez, and others, though he was ſurrounded by numerous armies, who, admiring his order and reſolution, made but faint and irreſolute attacks, which ſerved only to adorn his

* That is, the Mahommedans.

† The maund of the Decan is 25lb. avoirdupoiſe.

triumph.

triumph. We may here juſtly remark, that, in the long volumes of hiſtory, there is ſcarcely any thing to be compared to this exploit, whether we regard the reſolution in forming the plan, the boldneſs of the execution of it, or the fortune which attended the attempt. We cannot help to lament, that a man, formed for ſuch great exploits, ſhould not be actuated by better motives than rapine, violence, and the thirſt of gain.

A. D. 1295. Higer. 695.

When Alla marched to Deogire, all communication with Kurrah being ſtopt, no news was heard of him for ſome months. The perſon, whom he left his deputy, to make the King eaſy, wrote, that he had accounts of his being buſy in the conqueſt of Chinderi, and amuſed him every day with falſe intelligence. But as the King, for the ſpace of ſix months, had received no letters from under his own hand, he began to ſuſpect treaſon; and in the year 695, under a pretence of hunting, ordered out his retinue, and proceeded towards Gualier, where he encamped, and built a Choultry, inſcribing a verſe to this purpoſe, over the door.—"I who preſs with my foot the celeſtial pavement, what fame can I acquire by a heap of ſtones and mortar? No! I have joined theſe broken ſtones together, that perhaps, under their ſhade, the weary traveller, or broken-hearted, may find repoſe."

The King ſuſpects Alla of treaſonable deſigns.

In the mean time Feroſe received private intelligence, that Alla had conquered Deogire, and had acquired there ſuch wealth, as had never been poſſeſſed by an Emperor of Delhi, and that he was now upon his march towards Kurrah. The King was greatly pleaſed with this intelligence, and reckoned upon the ſpoil, as if already in his own treaſury. But men of more wiſdom thought otherwiſe, and juſtly concluded, that it was not to fill the royal coffers that Alla, without the King's authority,

Alla returns towards Kurrah.

A.D. 1295. Higer. 695. thority, had undertaken ſuch a daring expedition. They however waited to ſee the event, without informing the King of their ſuſpicions.

Feroſe conſults his council concerning Alla. The King having one day aſſembled his council, and told them, that Alla was now on his march to Kurrah with immenſe plunder, requeſted their advice, whether it was moſt prudent to remain where he was, and command Alla to his preſence, to march towards him, or to return to Delhi. Ahmed Chip, who was renowned for his wiſdom and penetration, expreſſed his ſuſpicions to the King, in a rational and plauſible manner. He adviſed Feroſe, at the ſame time, to advance with his army towards Chinderi, and to encamp in the way between Alla and Kurrah. This, ſaid he, will diſcover Alla's intentions, before he has time to augment his army. Ahmed added further, "That, upon the appearance of the imperial army, it was highly probable, that the troops of Alla, being laden with ſpoil, and within their own country, would not care to hazard the loſs of it by an action; but would rather endeavour to ſecure their wealth among the mountains. That, by this means, Alla would be deſerted by the greateſt part of his ſmall army, which would oblige him to think of nothing but peace, and to lay all his wealth at the foot of the throne. That the King, in that caſe might take all the gold, jewels, and elephants, permitting him to retain the remainder for himſelf, and either leave him his government, or carry him to Delhi, according to the royal pleaſure."

They differ in opinion. Kudgi, chief magiſtrate of Delhi, though he was ſenſible of the prudence of this advice, yet turning his eyes upon the Emperor, he perceived he did not at all approve of it; and therefore began to this effect: "The news of Alla's return, the amount of his plunder, and the truth of his conqueſt, has not yet been confirmed but by flying reports,

reports, which we all know are often vague and extravagant. Supposing even that this account is true, is it not natural to imagine, that when he shall hear of the approach of the imperial army, that the fear of false accusation, or evil designs against him, will prevail on him to retreat among the mountains? From whence, as the rainy season is at hand, it will be impossible to dislodge him. Let us not therefore cast off our shoes, before we reach the river, but wait till Alla shall arrive at Kurrah. If then it shall appear, that he cherishes his treasonable views, one assault of the imperial army will crush his ambition." A.D. 1295. Higer. 695.

Ahmed, having heard this perfidious advice, was kindled into generous resentment, and replied; "The time passes.—As soon as Alla shall have escaped us, will he not proceed by the way of Oud to Bengal, where his treasure will soon enable him to raise such an army as neither you nor I will be able to oppose? O shame! that men should know better, yet not have the honesty to give salutary advice." Ferose was displeased with those words, and spoke thus to the Omrahs who stood near him. "Ahmed does always ill offices to Alla. He endeavours to raise my suspicion and resentment against my nephew; but such private rancour shall have no weight with the King; I am so well assured of the loyalty of Alla, whom I have nursed in my bosom, that I should sooner believe treason in my son than in him." Ahmed, upon this, shut the door of argument, and, rising with some emotion, walked out, striking one hand upon the other, and repeating a verse to this purpose: "When the sun of prosperity is eclipsed, no advice can enlighten the mind." The King, bestowing great commendations on Kudgi, marched back with his army to Delhi.

A.D. 1295. Higer. 695. Alla's insidious message to the King.

Not many days after the King's arrival at the capital, the address of Alla was brought to him, setting forth, that "he was the King's slave, and that all his wealth was consecrated to him; that being wearied with tedious march, he begged for some repose at Kurrah. That he intended to kiss the footstool of the throne, but that, knowing he had some enemies at court, who might have, in his absence, defamed him, and deprived him of his majesty's favour, he, and the chiefs who accompanied him in the expedition, in which he was sensible he had exceeded his orders, were apprehensive that some punishment might be inflicted upon them. That he therefore requested to have a letter of grace, to assure him and his followers of perfect safety, under the royal protection." The King having received this address, expressed great joy, and entirely laid aside all suspicions of Alla. He ordered a letter full of kindness, and the most solemn assurances of protection, to be wrote to him, and dispatched by the hands of two messengers of distinction.

Alla prepares to retreat to Bengal.

In the mean time Alla was preparing to retreat to Bengal. He was now joined by all the Zemindars of the neighbouring districts, who inlisted themselves under his fortunate banners. The messengers perceived plainly his intentions, but they were detained, and watched so strictly, that they could send no advices to the King. Almass, who was also son-in-law and nephew to Ferose, in the mean time received advices from his brother Alla, "That it was now become public at Kurrah, that the King intended certainly to take his life, for proceeding to Deogire contrary to his orders: That he repented the occasion, and had taken his majesty's displeasure, which to him was worse than death, so much to heart, that he was afraid excess of sorrow would put an end to his melancholy life:

He

He therefore requested, that his brother should inform him before the King put his design in execution, that he might either take poison, or look out for a place of security." A.D. 1295. Higer. 695.

His insidious letters to the court.

Letters to the same purpose were, day after day, wrote to his brother, Almass, who, being in the plot, was constantly at court, and shewed them to the King, seemingly distracted, lest his brother should lay violent hands upon himself, or fly his country. He used a thousand delusive arts to inveigle the King to Kurrah, who no less feared the loss of the treasure than his nephew's life. The old man, at last, took the golden bait, and embarked, with a thousand horse and a small retinue, on the Ganges, ordering Ahmed Chip to follow with the army by land.

Ferose sets out for Kurrah.

Alla, hearing of the departure of Ferose from Delhi, crossed the Ganges with his army, and encamped near Mannickpoor, upon the opposite bank. When, upon the seventeenth of Ramzan, the imperial umbrella appeared in sight, Alla drew out his army, on pretence of doing honour to the Emperor, and sent his brother Almass, who had come on before to concert measures to introduce Ferose into camp. This artful traitor represented to Ferose, that if he should take the thousand horse with him, Alla might be alarmed; for that some bad people had confirmed him so strongly in his fears, that all he could say to him was not sufficient entirely to expel his suspicions.

Persuaded to leave his retinue behind him.

The weak old King, suspecting nothing of this horrid treachery from a man whom he had cherished from his infancy in his bosom, gave into this proposal. He ordered a few of his select friends into his own boat, and commanded the fleet to remain some distance behind. When they came near the camp, Almass again opened the mouth of delusion, and told the King, that his brother, seeing so many men in compleat armour, might possibly be startled;

 that

A. D. 1295. Higer. 695. that therefore, as he had taken ſuch ridiculous notions into his head, which nobody could remove, it were better to avoid the leaſt appearances to favour them. The King might have ſeen that this was overdoing the matter, but perhaps he thought it now too late to reveal his ſuſpicions, being near the ſkirts of the camp, and that an open confidence might be his beſt ſecurity. He therefore ordered all his attendants to unbuckle their armour, and lay their weapons aſide. Charram, chief ſecretary of the Empire, oppoſed this ſtep with great vehemence, for he plainly ſaw into the bottom of their perfidy. But the traitor had ſuch a ſoft and plauſible tongue, that at laſt he yielded, though with great reluctance.

They had now reached the landing place, and Alla appeared upon the bank with his attendants, whom he ordered to halt. He himſelf advancing alone met the Emperor juſt after he had landed upon the beach, and fell down proſtrate at his feet. The old man in a familiar manner tapped him on the cheek, and raiſing him up, embraced him, ſaying, "I who have brought you up from your infancy, and cheriſhed you with a fatherly affection, holding you dearer in my ſight, if poſſible, than my own offspring, and who have not yet waſhed the odors of your infant ſmiles from my garments, how could you imagine I ſhould entertain a thought to your prejudice." Then taking him by the hand, he was leading him back into the royal barge, when the hard-hearted villain made a ſignal to his aſſaſſins who ſtood behind. Mamood, Barbarouſly aſſaſſinated. the ſon of Salim, ruſhing immediately forward, wounded the King with his ſword in the ſhoulder. The unfortunate Monarch ran forward to gain the barge, crying, "Ah! villain Alla, what doſt thou?" but before he had reached the boat, another of the aſſaſſins, whoſe name was Achtiar Hoor, coming up, ſeized the old man, and throwing him on the ground,

ground, barbarously cut off his head, just as the sun sunk in the west as if to avoid the horrid sight*. A.D. 1295. Higer. 695.

All his attendants were then murdered. They fixed the venerable head of their lord upon the point of a spear, and carried it through the camp and city, as a bloody spectacle to the gazing rabble. But the rabble were shocked at the sight, and were heard to cry: "Behold the reward of him who fixeth his mind upon this perfidious world: who nourisheth his relations with the blood of his liver, in the arms of kindness, and to their gratitude confideth his strength." Reflections upon his death.

Alla immediately exalted the white umbrella over his own head; but the vengeance of heaven soon after fell heavy on all who were concerned in the assassination of Ferose. They relate, that when Alla visited a reverend sage, named Shech Karrick, who is buried at Kurrah, and whose tomb is held sacred to this day, he rose from his pillow, and repeated an extempore verse, to the following purpose: "He cometh, but his head shall fall in the boat, and his body shall be thrown into the Ganges;" which, they say, was explained a few hours after, by the death of the unfortunate King, whose head was thrown into the boat upon that occasion. Mamood, the son of Salim, one of the assassins, about a year after, died of a horrid leprosy, which dissolved the flesh, piece by piece, from his bones. Achtiar Hoor, the other assassin, fared no better, for he became mad, crying out incessantly, that Ferose was cutting off his head. Thus the wretch suffered a thousand deaths, in imagination, before he expired. Almass, the brother of Alla, and others who planned this horrid tragedy, in hopes of great advancement, fell into such a scene of misfortunes, that, in the space of four years, there was no remembrance of them, but their villanies, upon the face of the earth. The miserable end of the assassins.

* He reigned seven years and some months.

ALLA

A L L A I.

A.D. 1295. Higer. 695. Ruckun-ul-dien raised by his mother to the throne.

INTELLIGENCE of the murder of the King having reached Ahmed Chip, who was advancing with the army, he retreated to Delhi. Malleke Jehan, the wife of Ferose, and Queen regent, imprudently, and without consulting the chiefs, raised to the diadem Ruckun, her youngest son; Arkilli, the elder son, being then at Moultan. She accompanied him from Kilogurry to Delhi, and placed him on the throne in the green palace, though as yet but a boy, and altogether unacquainted with the affairs of state. She also divided the provinces among her own party. Arkilli, who was the true heir to the empire, and possessed all the qualities of a king, was greatly afflicted at this news, but thought proper, for the present, to remain at Moultan.

Alla prepares to march to Delhi.

Alla, upon receiving intelligence of those transactions at Delhi, laid aside his intended expedition to Bengal, and prepared to march to the capital, though it was then the rainy season. He raised a great army in his government, and conferred titles and rewards upon his friends. Almass was honoured with the title of Elich Chan, Nuserit of Jallisiri with that of Nusirit Chan, Malleck Hiziber was distinguished with the name of Ziffer Chan, and Sinjer, Alla's wife's brother, received the title of Acta. They all received estates upon their advancement to those honours. Alla, by the advice of Nuserit, distributed presents among the army, and wherever he encamped he amused himself with throwing gold from a sling among the people.

This

This liberality, in a ſhort time, brought a world of ſoldiers under his banners. The Queen-mother was thrown into great perplexity, by the advices ſhe daily received concerning Alla. She diſpatched an expreſs to Moultan, for her ſon Arkilli; but that prince returned for anſwer, That now the time was loſt, for that, before he could arrive, the imperial troops would join the enemy; that therefore his coming would be of no real ſervice: That the ſtream might have been diverted at its ſource, but when it became a river, no dams could oppoſe it. A.D. 1295. Higer. 695.

Alla made no delay on his march. He croſſed the Jumna, and encamped without the north-eaſt gate of Delhi. Ruckun, fluttering like a ſolitary fowl, collected all his forces, and marching out of the city, paraded it before the enemy. But when he ſaw them preparing for battle, he retreated into the city. He was that night deſerted by a great number of Omrahs, who went over with their forces to Alla. Ruckun ſaw now no ſafety but in flight. Taking therefore his mother, the Haram and treaſure with him, he ſet out for Moultan, accompanied by Rijib, Olavi, Ahmed, and Jellal. The citizens, after the departure of the young King, crouded forth to pay their reſpects to Alla. He immediately ordered the current money to be ſtruck in his own name, and making a triumphant entry into Delhi, in the latter end of the year 695, aſcended the throne, and kept his court at the red palace. He exhibited ſhows, and made grand feſtivals, encouraging every ſpecies of riot and debauchery; which ſo pleaſed the unthinking rabble, that they ſoon loſt all memory of their former King, and the horrid villany of the reigning Emperor. He who ought to have been hooted with deteſtation, became the object of admiration, to thoſe who could not ſee the darkneſs of his deeds, through the ſplendor of his magnificence. Sits down before Delhi, which ſubmits.

Whilſt

A.D. 1295. Higer. 695. Promotions.

Whilst he gained, by these means, popularity among the vulgar, he secured the great with titles, and bought the covetous with gold. The office of vizier was bestowed upon Chaja Chatire, a man renowned for his virtue in those degenerate times. Arif was made chief justice of the court of equity, and Omdat was raised to the office of principal secretary of the Divan, being a man of great learning and genius, and a favourite of the King. Nuserit was appointed chief magistrate of Delhi, Kudgi was raised to the dignity of chief justice in the courts of law, and Ziffer to that of chief secretary of the empire; with many others, to high offices, which are too tedious to mention. Alla, having advanced six months pay to his whole army, began to concert means to extirpate the descendents of Ferose. He dispatched Elich, his brother, and Ziffer, with forty thousand horse, towards Moultan, who, upon their arrival, invested that city. After a siege of two months, the citizens and troops betrayed the cause of the prince Arkilli, and gave up the place to the enemy. The two unfortunate brothers, being driven to great distress, surrendered themselves at last to Elich, upon promise of personal safety.

The family of Ferose extirpated.

The object of this expedition being thus completed, Elich wrote to his brother an account of his victory, which was read in all the public pulpits after divine worship, and great rejoicings were ordered to be made upon the occasion. Elich proceeded in triumph with his army and state prisoners to Delhi. He was met on his way by Nuserit, chief magistrate of the city, who had been sent by the Emperor to put out the eyes of the prisoners. This cruel order was executed upon the two princes, upon Alaghu, the grandson of the great Zingis, upon Ahmed Chip, and others of less note, and all their effects confiscated. The two unfor-

tunate

tunate princes were then confined in the fort of Hassi, where, soon after, they were both assassinated; and the Queen-mother, with all the ladies of the former Emperor's seraglio, and his other children, confined at Delhi. A.D. 1296. Higer. 696.

In the second year of this reign, Chaja Chatire, not falling entirely in with Alla's policy, was dismissed from the office of vizier, which was conferred upon Nuserit, chief magistrate of Delhi. This minister redemanded all the sums which the King, upon his accession, had bestowed upon the nobility and people, which occasioned great disgust and disturbance. A new vizier.

During these transactions, advices came to Delhi, that Dova, king of Maver-ul-nere, had sent an army of one hundred thousand Moguls, with a design to conquer Moultan, Punjab, and the provinces near the mouth of the Indus: That they were advancing with great expedition, carrying all before them with fire and sword. Alla immediately ordered his brother Elich, with a great force, to expel them. The two armies having met in the districts of Lahore, a bloody conflict ensued, in which the Moguls were defeated, with the loss of twelve thousand men, and many of their principal officers, besides a number of prisoners of all ranks, who were put to the sword some days after, without sparing the poor women and children who had been taken in the Mogul camp. These two victories raised the fame of the Emperor's arms to a high pitch of reputation, established his authority at home, and overawed his foreign enemies. Alla, about this time, by the advice of his brother Elich, seized upon many Omrahs, who, in the late revolution, taking advantage of the distresses of the prince Arkilli, and the Queen-mother, had extorted great sums of money for their services. He ordered the extortioners to be blinded, and their Invasion of the Moguls. Are overthrown.

estates

A. D. 1297. Higer. 697. estates to be confiscated, which brought great wealth into the treasury.

Alla sends an army to reduce Guzerat.

In the beginning of the year 697, Elich, the King's brother, and Nuserit the vizier, were sent with a great army to reduce Guzerat. They accordingly laid waste that country with death and rapine, took the capital city Narwalla, which was deserted by its prince, who fled and took protection under Ramdeo, king of Deogire, in the Decan. By the aid of that prince he soon after returned and took possession of Buckelana, one of the districts of Guzerat, bordering upon Ramdeo's dominions. But his wives, children, elephants, baggage and treasure fell into the hands of the enemy when he fled. The vizier, with a part of the army, proceeded then to Cambaat, which being a rich country, and full of merchants, yielded a prodigious treasure to those sons of cruelty and rapine. When they had sufficiently glutted their avarice, and quenched their thirst for blood, they appointed subas to the provinces, and leaving part of the army for their defence, returned with their plunder towards Delhi.

A mutiny in the army.

The two generals having, on the march, made a demand of the fifth of the spoil from the troops, besides what they had already extorted from them, a mutiny arose in the camp. Mahommed, general of the mercenary Moguls, with many other chiefs, at the head of their several divisions, attacked Malleck Eiz, the brother of the vizier, and having slain him and a number of his people, continued their march. Elich, the Emperor's brother, fled in the disguise of a footman, to the tent of the vizier. The mutineers rushing in, killed the King's nephew, and the son of Elich, whom he had left upon the couch asleep, supposing him to be Elich. The vizier immediately ordered the drums of war to be beat and the trumpets to be sounded. All

who

who had not been concerned in the mutiny imagined that the enemy was coming upon them, and quickly formed the line. The mutineers divided and dispersed themselves all over the camp, and escaping in the confusion, fled, by different routes, to a place of rendezvous. They were, however, closely pursued the next day, and forced to retreat with some loss, to the districts of the Indian prince of Rintimpore, where they took protection. Elich and the vizier continued then their march to Delhi. A. D. 1298. Higer. 698.

Alla, upon seeing Cumladè, the captive wife of the prince of Guzerat, who, for her beauty, wit and accomplishments, was the flower of India, took her in marriage. But this did not satisfy his abominable lusts. Chaja Cafoor, a slave who had been taken on that expedition, engaged his unnatural passion, which he publickly indulged, to the disgrace and debasement of human nature. The vizier, by the Emperor's order, basely massacred all the families of those Moguls, or others, who had been concerned in the late mutiny. He pitied not the weeping mothers, nor the smiling infants who clung to their breasts. This was a new species of tyranny at Delhi, and occasioned some private murmuring, but those slaves possessed not the virtue or bravery to shake off the tyrant. The King's abominable lust.

About this time, Jildoo, a Mogul chief, and his brother, came down with a considerable force, and took the fort of Seostan. Ziffer marched against him, and having invested the place, he took it. Jildoo, and about two thousand Moguls, were taken prisoners, and sent in chains to Delhi. But Ziffer had distinguished himself so much as a brave commander in this expedition, that his fame awaked the jealousy of Alla. He therefore designed to deprive him of his government, but was prevented from this measure, by a great invasion of Moguls, under Cuttulich, the son of Dova, king of Maver- Invasion of the Moguls.

ul-nere.

A.D. 1298. Higer. 698. ul-nere. The army of the invaders consisted of two hundred thousand horse, and they promised to themselves the entire conquest of Hindostan. Cuttulich, accordingly, took possession of all the countries beyond the Indus on his march, and protected them from all violence. He then crossed the river, and proceeded to Delhi, without opposition, Ziffer retreating with his army before him.

They besiege Delhi. The whole country, in terror of the Moguls, crowded into the city. The crowd became so great, that the streets were rendered impassable, and all business and communication were interrupted. This however was but the beginning of their misfortunes. In the space of a few days, the consumption being great, and no supplies procured, a dreadful famine began to rage, and distraction to stare in every countenance. Alla, upon this pressing occasion, called a council of his Omrahs, and, having regulated his plan of action, prepared for battle, notwithstanding they all endeavoured to dissuade him from it. He left the care of the city to the noble Alla, marched out at the Budaoon gate, with three hundred thousand horse, and two thousand seven hundred elephants, besides foot without number. He drew up in order of battle on the plains beyond the suburbs; where the enemy were already formed to receive him. From the time that first the spears of Islam * were exalted in Hindostan, two such mighty armies had not joined in fight.

The Moguls overthrown. Alla gave the command of his right wing to Ziffer, the greatest general of that age, where all the troops of Punjaab, Moultan, and Sind, were posted. The left was intrusted to his brother Elich, and to Akit his brother-in-law. The King posted himself in the center, with twelve thousand inde-

* The Mahommedans.

pendent

pendent volunteers, who were mostly gentlemen of A.D. 1298. Higer. 698.
ruined families, and soldiers of fortune. With the choice of his elephants, he formed a tremendous line in his front, and he supported his rear with another chosen body of cavalry, under the vizier. Ziffer began the action with great impetuosity on the right, and breaking, with his elephants, the enemy's line, commenced a dreadful slaughter, and bore them like a torrent before him. Inclining then to the left, he pressed upon their flank, and put their whole army to flight, before the action was well begun in the center. Alla, seeing the victory complete, ordered his brother Elich, who commanded on the left, to advance and pursue the enemy. But the perfidious man, jealous of the glory of Ziffer, stopt at a small distance, while Ziffer continued the slaughter for upwards of thirty miles. One of the Mogul chiefs, who commanded the left, seeing Ziffer was not supported, rallied with ten thousand horse, and sending advice to his general Cuttulich, he also returned with ten thousand more, and attacked Ziffer in the rear. The brave general saw into his error, but it was now too late to retreat. He drew up his troops, which were not half the enemy's number, divided into two squadrons, and again renewed the conflict, exhibiting wonders by his own valour. At last his horse's leg being cut off by a sabre, he fell to the ground. He however rose again, seized a bow and quiver, and being a dexterous archer, sent death on the wings of his arrows. The most part of his men were, by this time, either killed or fled; and Cuttulich, admiring his bravery, called out to him to submit, and his valour should be rewarded with such honours as he deserved. Ziffer replied sternly, "I know no greater honour than to die in discharging my duty." Then he began to deal his arrows around. The Mogul prince, upon this, ordered a party of horse

A.D. 1298. Higer. 698. to ſurround him, and endeavour to take him alive; but Ziffer refuſed to ſubmit, and was at laſt cut in pieces, with a few truſty ſervants who ſtood by him to the laſt.

They retreat. This advantage however did not diſpel the fears of the Moguls. They continued their retreat, and evacuated India with all expedition. The bravery of Ziffer became famous among the Moguls. When their horſes ſtarted, or were unruly, they uſed wantonly to aſk them, Whether they ſaw the ghoſt of Ziffer? Alla, it is ſaid, eſteemed the death of this great general, as a ſecond victory, and could not help expreſſing his ſatisfaction upon the occaſion; and thus diſplayed his own baſe ingratitude, for that brave life which had been thrown away in his unworthy ſervice. Great rejoicings were made at Delhi, to celebrate the victory; and the principal officers were rewarded with titles and governments, according to their behaviour and intereſt at court. Some who had behaved ill were diſgraced, particularly one Omrah, who was led upon an aſs all round the city.

Extraordinary ſchemes of the King. In the third year of the reign of Alla, when proſperity ſhone upon his arms, he began to form ſome extraordinary projects. One of theſe was the formation of a new ſyſtem of religion, that, like Mahommed, he might be held in veneration by poſterity. He often conſulted upon this ſcheme his brother Elich, Nuſerit his vizier, and Akit, over a bottle; from which we may ſuppoſe he had no deſign to prohibit the uſe of wine. His other deſign was equally romantic. He propoſed to leave a viceroy in India, and, like the great Secunder*, to undertake the conqueſt of the world. In conſequence of this project, he aſſumed the title of Secunder Sani†, which was ſtruck upon the currency

* Alexander the Great. † Alexander the Second.

of

of the empire. Notwithstanding these lofty ideas, Alla was so illiterate, that he even did not possess the common knowledge of reading and writing; yet he was so obstinate in his ridiculous opinions, that men of learning, who disdained to prostitute their judgment, avoided the court, or stood silent in his presence. There were not however wanting slaves, who, though they knew better, extolled his every word to the skies, and seemed to feed upon his crude imaginations. A. D. 1298. Higer. 698.

Alla-ul-Muluck, the chief magistrate of the city, who was an old man, and so fat that he was not able to attend the court above once a month, being one day sent for by the King, to give his advice about the execution of his religious project, he determined, however fatal the consequences might be, to oppose every measure against the doctrine of the Mahommedan faith, and to dedicate the few years he had to live, by the course of nature, to martyrdom. With this firm resolution he waited upon the King, whom he found drinking wine with a great number of his principal Omrahs. The King beginning to confer with Alla upon the occasion, the old man told him, he had something to say to him in private, and would be glad he should order the wine and the company away. The King smiled, and desired all the company to retire except four. The advice of the chief magistrate of Delhi.

The old magistrate then fell upon his face, and having kissed the ground at his feet, rose up and thus spoke; "O King! Religion is the law of God, by his spirit inspired in his prophets, nor depends it upon the opinions of mortals. We are taught by his word to believe, that the spirit of prophecy ended with Mahommed, the last and greatest messenger of God. Since this therefore is known to great and small, to all nations and degrees of people, should your intentions against their faith be once known, it is impossible to conceive what hatred should Against his scheme of a new religion.

A.D. 1298. Higer. 698. ſhould riſe againſt you, and what blood and diſturbance muſt enſue. It is therefore adviſeable, that you ſhould eraze with the chiſſel of reaſon, thoſe conceptions, from the ſurface of your bleſſed mind, as the accompliſhment of your intention exceeds all mortal power. Did not Zingis, the moſt powerful of monarchs, and his ſucceſſors, labour for ages to ſubvert our faith, that they might eſtabliſh their own? What rivers of blood were ſpilt in the conteſt, till at length the ſpirit of truth prevailed, and they became proſelytes to that religion which they had laboured ſo long to deſtroy!" The Emperor having liſtened with attention, replied, "What you have ſaid is juſt, and founded on friendſhip and reaſon. I will for ever lay aſide all thoughts of this ſcheme, which has ſo long engaged my attention. But what do you think of my project of univerſal conqueſt?"

Againſt his project of univerſal conqueſt. The venerable magiſtrate replied, "Some Kings, in former ages, formed the ſame great reſolution which your Majeſty does at preſent, and your power, perſonal bravery, and wealth, gives you at leaſt equal hopes of ſucceſs. But the times are not ſo favourable, and the government of India ſeems not to ſtand upon ſo firm a baſis, as to ſupport itſelf in your abſence. Perfidy and ingratitude daily appear. Brothers become traitors to one another, and children againſt their parents conſpire. How much is this degenerate age unlike to the virtuous times of Secunder? Men were then endued with honourable principles, and the cunning and treachery of the preſent times were then held in utter abomination. Your Majeſty has no counſellors like Ariſtotalice*, who kept, by his wiſdom and policy, not only his own country in peace and ſecurity, but brought other nations, by voluntary conſent, under his maſ-

* Ariſtotle.

ter's

ter's protection. If your Majesty can put equal confidence in your Omrahs, and can depend so much upon the love of your people, as Secunder, you may then carry your scheme into execution; if not, we cannot well reconcile it to reason." A.D. 1299. Higer. 699.

The King, after musing a while, said, "What you have told me bears the face of sincerity and truth. But what availeth all this power in armies, in wealth, and in kingdoms, if I content myself with what I already possess; nor employ it in acquiring conquest and glory?" Alla-ul-Mulück replied, "That there were two undertakings in which his treasure might be expended to good purpose. The first was, the conquest of the southern kingdoms of Hindostan; and the second, the reduction of all the western provinces, which had been invaded by the Moguls, and lay beyond the Indus. This, said the chief magistrate, would secure the peace of Hindostan, and procure to the King immortal honour, in bestowing happiness upon his people; a thing greater in itself, than if he should consume the world in the flames of war; but even to succeed in this project, it is requisite that the King should abstain from excess of wine, and from luxurious pleasures." The Emperor, contrary to the old man's expectations, took all this advice in good part, and, praising him for his fidelity, presented him with a royal honorary dress, ten thousand rupees, two horses caparisoned, and two villages in freehold. The other Omrahs, who, though they themselves wanted the virtue or resolution to speak their minds, were extremely pleased with the Cutwal, and sent him also presents to a great amount. Conquest of the unsubdued provinces proposed.

The King, in the year 699, according to the advice of Alla-ul-Muluck, called his brother Elich from Semana, the vizier from Kurrah, and others The imperial army invading Rintimpore.

 from

A.D. 1299. Higer. 699. from their reſpective ſubadaries, and ſent them, with a great army, againſt the Indian prince of Rintimpore. They ſoon took the fort of Jain, and afterwards inveſted the capital. Nuſerit the vizier, advancing near the wall, was cruſhed to death by a ſtone from an engine. And the Raja, at the ſame time, ſallying with forty thouſand men, drove Elich back to Jain with great loſs.

A conſpiracy. Elich wrote to Delhi the particulars of this defeat. Alla flew into a violent rage, and immediately took the field. Upon his march he halted for a day at a place called Jilput, and went out a hunting. Having wandered far from his camp, in the chace, he remained with his attendants all night in the foreſt. In the morning, before ſunriſe, he placed himſelf upon a riſing ground, where he ſat down with two or three attendants, and commanded the reſt to hunt in his view. Akit obſerving this, recollected that it was now in his power to cut off the King, in the ſame manner as the King himſelf had cut off his predeceſſor. He thought, that being nephew and brother-in-law to the Emperor, he might claim by that, and the influence he had by being chief ſecretary of the empire, the ſame title which Alla himſelf had to the throne*. Akit imparted his reſolution to a few choſen horſemen, who accompanied him on this party. They immediately rode up to the King, ſaluted him with a flight of arrows, two of which entered his body, ſo that he lay for dead on the ground. Akit, upon this, drew his ſword, and ran to cut off his head; when he was told by one of the King's attendants, that he was quite dead; that therefore to cut off his head would be an unneceſſary piece of cruelty.

* Alla was himſelf nephew and ſon-in-law to Feroſe, whom he had murdered.

Akit

Akit being thus prevailed upon to desist from his intentions, set out for the camp with all expedition, mounted the throne; and proclaimed the King's death. The army was thrown into great confusion; but where loyal affection and patriotism are things unknown, mankind are satisfied to bow their necks to any new master. The great men assembled to pay their court, and present their presents upon the occasion; the customary service was read from the Coran; the Chutba was proclaimed aloud; and the singers ordered to extol his praise. Akit then rose from the throne, and proceeded towards the Haram; but Dinar, the chief eunuch, with his guard; stopped him at the door, swearing, that till he shewed him Alla's head, or put him to death, he should not enter. Alla, in the mean time, recovered his senses, and, having his wounds bound up, imagined that Akit's treason and treachery was a preconcerted conspiracy of the Omrahs. He signified his intentions to fly to his brother Elich at Jain, with about sixty servants, who still attended him. Malleck Hamid, deputy porter of the presence, advised the King against this resolution. He told him, that he ought immediately to go to his own camp, and there shew himself to his army; for that the usurper had not yet time to establish himself; and that, upon seeing the Emperor's umbrella, he doubted not but the whole army would immediately return to their duty. He observed, at the same time, that the least delay might render his affairs irrecoverable.

A.D. 1299. Higer. 699. Akit mounts the throne.

Alla saw the propriety of this resolute advice; and mounting his horse, with great difficulty, spread the white umbrella, which lay on the field, over his head, and with his small retinue, proceeded towards the army. When he appeared in sight, being joined by some foraging parties on the way, he

He is defeated and slain.

A. D. 1299. Higer. 699. he was now guarded by about five hundred men. He ascended an eminence, in full view of the camp, where he was at once seen by the whole army. They crouded in thousands towards him; and the court of the usurper was immediately broke up, and in a few minutes he found himself alone. In this situation he mounted his horse, and, distracted with fear, fled towards Binour. Alla now marched down from the eminence towards the royal pavilion, and mounting the throne, gave public audience; sending, at the same time, a party of horse after the usurper. They soon came up with him, and brought back his head. The King ordered the usurper's brother Cuttulich, and the chief conspirators, to be put to death.

Alla besieges Rintimpore.

When Alla recovered of his wounds, he continued his march to Rintimpore, where he was joined by his brother Elich, and began to besiege the place. But the Hindoos so well defended themselves, that numbers of the imperial army daily fell. Alla however continued his attacks with redoubled obstinacy, while detachments of his army ravaged the adjacent territories of Malava and Daar. But the siege being protracted for some months without much effect, Omar and Mungu, who were both nephews to the Emperor, and held the governments of Budaoon and Oud, rebelled, and raised a great army. Alla wrote letters to the several Omrahs of those provinces whom he thought loyal, as also to the neighbouring subas and zemindars, and they levied forces, engaged, defeated, and took the rebels, and sent them both prisoners to the royal camp. The Emperor ordered their eyes to be put out, and then to torture them to death, as a barbarous example to others.

A rebellion quashed.

Notwithstanding

Notwithſtanding this ſeverity, one of the moſt extraordinary conſpiracies recorded in hiſtory was undertaken by one Mola, the ſon of a ſlave of the old chief magiſtrate of the city, who died in the former reign. This ambitious youth, ſeeing Alla buſied in the ſiege of Rintimpore, began to form the ſcheme of a revolution in the empire. He was perhaps moved to this ſcheme by the murmuring of the citizens againſt the chief magiſtrate's deputy, Tirmazi, who, in his maſter's abſence in camp, oppreſſed the people, having the government entirely in his hands. The firſt thing however that Mola publickly did, was, in the heat of the day, when every body was gone to reſt, to collect a mob of citizens, by a forged order from the King. With theſe he haſtened to the houſe of Tirmazi, and ſent in to tell him that a meſſenger had arrived with an order from the King. Tirmazi, out of reſpect to the imperial order, haſtened to the door, when the young impoſtor, ſhowing him the paper in one hand, cut him down with the other. He then read aloud the forged mandate for that purpoſe.

A. D. 1299. Higer. 699. An extraordinary conſpiracy.

The mob now encreaſing, Mola ſent parties to ſecure the city gates, and diſpatched a perſon to Alla Eaz, who was chief magiſtrate of the new city, to come and ſee the King's order. This magiſtrate however, having heard of the diſturbance, paid no regard to the meſſage, but ſhut his own gates. Mola, in the mean time, with his mob, entered the red palace, and releaſed all the ſtate priſoners, taking out all the arms, treaſure, and valuable effects, which he divided among his followers. He then, by force, placed Allavi, one of the priſoners, who was deſcended from the Emperor Altumſh, upon the throne, and imperiouſly commanded all the principal men of the city to pay him allegiance. The Emperor, having advice of theſe

A ſedition at Delhi.

A.D. 1300. Higer. 700. theſe ſtrange tranſactions, was ſtruck motionleſs with aſtoniſhment, but ſtirred not a ſtep from the ſiege. He however wrote to Hamid, his foſter-brother, who, raiſing a party in the city, ſeized the Budaoon gate the ſeventh day after the uſurpation, and took the field, where he was joined by a great multitude from the new city and the country around. With theſe he again, by ſurprize, entered the city at the Ghizni gate, but he was met at the ſecond gate, called Beder, by Mola and his aſſociates, and a ſharp conflict enſued. Hamid being diſmounted, run up to Mola, who was leading on his party with great bravery, and pulling him from his horſe, threw him down in the ſtreet, and ſlew him. He himſelf, in the mean time, received ſeveral wounds; quaſhed. but the faction of Mola, diſpirited by his death, gave ground, and diſperſed themſelves all over the city. Hamid then proceeded to the red palace, dragged from thence the unfortunate Allavi and ſent his head round the city upon the point of a ſpear, which put an end to this ſtrange conſpiracy.

Elich Chan ſent to puniſh the rebels. Elich, the Emperor's brother, was in the mean time ſent by Alla to Delhi, to puniſh all who were ſuppoſed to have had any hand in this rebellion. The ſons of the chief magiſtrate, and the old Cutwal himſelf, were put to death merely on ſuſpicion, as the rebel had been one of their dependents. But the moſt probable cauſe was their great wealth, which was confiſcated to the King.

Rintimpore taken. Rintimpore had now been cloſely beſieged for a whole year, and Alla, after trying all other means, fell upon the following expedient to take the place. He collected together a great multitude of people, and provided each of them with a bag, which they filled with earth, and having begun at ſome diſtance from the rock, with immenſe labour, formed an aſcent to the top of the walls, by which the troops entered the place, and put the Indian prince Amir Deo,

Deo, his family, and the garrison, to the sword. This fort is esteemed the strongest in Hindostan. Mahommed, the Mogul general, who had taken refuge in Rintimpore, after the mutiny at Jallore, having lost most of his men in the defence of the fort, was himself lying ill of his wounds when Alla entered the place. Alla, finding the unfortunate Mahommed in this condition, asked him, in an insulting manner, "What gratitude would he express for his lord, should he command his wounds to be immediately cured." The Mogul fiercely replied, "I would put him to death for a tyrant, and endeavour to make the son of Amir Deo, to whom my gratitude is due, King." The Emperor, enraged at this reply, threw him beneath the feet of an elephant. But considering afterwards that he was a brave man, and one of whose gallant behaviour he himself had been often witness, he ordered his body to be put in a coffin, and interred with decent solemnity. Alla then commanded that the Raja's vizier, who had deserted over to him with a strong party during the siege, should, with all his followers, be massacred. Saying, upon the occasion, that "Those who have betrayed their natural lord, can never be true to another!" Having bestowed the government of Rintimpore, with all the riches taken in it, upon his brother Elich, he returned with his army to Delhi. But Elich, about six months after, fell sick, and died on his way to the capital.

A. D. 1300. Higer. 700.

Alla being, in the course of this year, apprehensive of conspiracies and insurrections, called together the Omrahs who were most renowned for their wisdom, and commanded them to give their opinion without reserve, how he should conduct matters, so as to prevent disturbances and rebellions in the empire. He, at the same time, desired them to explain what they thought were the principal

The King convenes a council of the Omrahs.

A.D. 1300. Higer. 700. principal cauſes of the diſorders. The Omrahs, after conſulting among themſelves, replied, that there were many cauſes concurring in a ſtate from which convulſions, diſagreeable in their conſequences, proceeded. That, as thoſe misfortunes could not be obviated at once, they would only mention, for that time, a few of thoſe evils, from which danger to the empire muſt have aroſe.

The cauſes of diſturbances in the empire.

"At the head of this liſt," ſaid the Omrahs, "we muſt place the King's inattention to advance the good, or to redreſs the wrongs of the people. The public uſe of wine is the ſource of many diſorders; for when men form themſelves into ſocieties for the purpoſe of drinking, their minds are diſcloſed to one another, while the ſtrength of the liquor, fermenting in their blood, precipitates them into the moſt deſperate undertakings. The connections formed by the great men of the court, are pregnant with danger to the ſtate. Their numerous marriages, and the places in their gift, draw the ſtrength of the government into the hands of a few, who are always able, by aſſociating themſelves together, to create revolutions in the empire. The fourth, and not the leaſt cauſe of diſturbance is, the unequal diviſion of property; for the wealth of a rich empire is circulated in a few hands, and therefore the governors of provinces are rather independent princes, than ſubjects of the ſtate."

Alla begins to redreſs grievances.

Alla approved ſo much of the remarks of his Omrahs, that he immediately began to carry into execution the plan which they laid before him. He firſt applied himſelf to a ſtrict inquiry into the adminiſtration of juſtice; to redreſs grievances, and to examine narrowly into the private as well as public characters of all men of rank in the empire. He laid himſelf out to procure intelligence of the moſt ſecret diſcourſes of families of note in the

city,

city, as well as of every transaction of moment in the most distant provinces. He executed justice with such rigour and severity, that robbery and theft, formerly so common, were not heard of in the land. The traveller slept secure upon the public highway, and the merchant carried his commodities in safety from the sea of Bengal to the mountains of Cabul, and from Tellingana to Cashmire. A.D. 1300. Higer. 700.

He published an edict against the use of wine and strong liquors upon pain of death. He himself set the example to his subjects, and emptied his cellars in the street. In this he was followed by all ranks of people, so that, for some days, the common sewers flowed with wine.

He issued out orders that no marriage, among the nobility, should be ratified without a special licence from him: that no private meetings or conversation should be held among the Omrahs, which proved a severe check on the pleasures of society. This latter order was carried into such rigorous execution, that no man durst entertain his friends without a written permission from the vizier.

He then lengthened the hand of violence upon the rich. He seized upon the wealth, and confiscated the estates of Mussulmen and Hindoos without distinction, and by this means he accumulated an immense treasure. Men, in short, were almost reduced to a level over all the empire.

All emoluments were cut off from the different offices, which were filled with men whose indigence and dependence rendered them implicitly obedient to the dictates of government.

He ordered a tax of half the real annual produce of the lands to be raised over all the empire, and to be regularly transmitted to the exchequer. He appointed officers to superintend the collectors, who were to take care that the zemindars should take

An equal land tax established.

A.D. 1303. Higer. 703. take no more from the poor farmers, than in proportion to the estimate which they had given in of their estates; and in case of disobedience or neglect, the superintendants were obliged to refund the overplus, and to pay a fine for the oppression. The farmers, at the same time, were confined to a certain proportion of land, and to an appointed number of servants and oxen to cultivate the same. No grazier was permitted to have above a certain number of cows, sheep and goats, and a tax was paid out of them to the government. So strictly did the Emperor look after the behaviour of the collectors and other officers of the revenue, that many of them, who formerly kept great retinues, were obliged to dismiss them, and to have all the menial offices of their families performed by their wives and children. Neither were they permitted to resign their employs, till they found others as capable as themselves to execute the duties of their office.

These regulations were good, but they were arbitrary and severe. He broke through all laws and customs, which, according to the Mahommedan law, were left to the decision of the courts justice. Other Monarchs left all but state affairs to the common course of justice. Alla descended to all the inferior departments of government. It was with him a common saying, "That religion had no connection with civil goverment, but was only the business, or rather amusement of private life; and that the will of a wise prince was better than the variable opinions of bodies of men."

The King applies himself to letters. As the King was known to be illiterate, it became a maxim with the learned men at court, to talk upon no subjects which they knew must be beyond the King's knowledge. He was however so sensible of the disadvantages which he laboured under by his ignorance of letters, that he applied himself

himself privately to study, and, notwithstanding the difficulty of acquiring the knowledge of the Persian manner of writing, which generally requires ten or twelve years study, he soon read all addresses, and made himself acquainted with the best authors in the language. After he had proceeded so far as to be able to hold part in learned discourses, he encouraged literary subjects, and showed particular favour to all the eminent men of that age, particularly to Casi Molana, Corami, and Cuzi Biana. He appointed the last of those learned men to explain the law to him; which he did according to the true spirit, in every point upon which he was consulted. He did not however do it without fear and trembling, where it differed from the King's violent maxims of government.

A. D. 1303. Higer. 703.

Reduces Chitor.

Alla, much about this time, sent an army, by the way of Bengal, to reduce the fort of Arinkil, which was in the possession of the Raja of Tellingana. He himself moved the royal standard towards Chitor, which had never before been reduced by the troops of the Mahommedans. After a siege of six months he took the place, in the year 703, conferred the government of it upon his eldest son Chizer, and called it the city of Chizer. He at the same time bestowed upon Chizer regal dignities and authority.

The Moguls invade Hindostan.

Intelligence of this expedition arriving at Maver-ul-nere, Jirghi, who distinguished himself formerly against Ziffer, thinking that Alla would be a long time absent, seized that opportunity for invading Hindostan. Alla, hearing of this dangerous inroad, abandoned all his schemes against the Decan, and made what haste he could with his army to Delhi. Jirghi, with twelve tomans of Mogul horse, approached, in a few days, the city, and encamped upon the banks of the Jumna. The horse of the imperial army being absent on the

Advance towards Delhi,

expedition

A.D. 1303. Higer. 703. expedition to Arinkil, the King was in no condition to face, upon equal terms, so powerful and warlike an enemy in the field. He therefore contented himself with entrenching his army in the plain beyond the suburbs, till he could draw the forces of the distant subas together. But the Moguls, having the command of the adjacent country, prevented the succours from joining the King, and proceeded so far as to plunder the suburbs, in the King's presence, without his being able to prevent them. In this situation stood affairs for two months; and then Alla, say some authors, had recourse to supernatural aid. He applied to a saint of those days, whose name was Nizam Aulia. The saint, in one night, without any visible cause, struck the Mogul army with a panic, which occasioned their precipitate retreat to their own country. But we have no reason to ascribe the flight of the Moguls to so weak and superstitious a cause; as private orders, intelligence, or the improbability of success, brought about their sudden departure more than the power of the saint. The King, during this alarming period, was heard to confess, that his ideas of universal conquest were idle and ridiculous, for that there were many heads in the world as hard as his own.

but retreat.

Alla levies a great army.

Alla, being relieved from the perils of this invasion, built a palace upon the spot where he had entrenched himself, and ordered the citadel of Delhi to be pulled down and built anew. He then began to recruit his army, with an intention to retaliate upon the Moguls their repeated inroads. He encreased his forces to such a prodigious number, that, upon calculating the expence, he found his revenues, and what treasures he had himself, could not support them above six years. He resolved therefore to reduce the pay, but it occurred to him that this could not be done with propriety, without

without lowering, proportionably, the price of horses, arms and provisions. This he did by an edict, which he strictly enforced all over the empire, settling the price of every article at about half the common rate, which, in fact, was just doubling his treasures and revenues. A.D. 1303. Higer. 703.

To establish this reduction of the price, with respect to grain, he ordered great magazines to be built upon the rivers Jumna and Ganges, and other places convenient for water carriage, under the direction of Malleck Cabuli. This collector received half of the land tax in grain; and the royal agents supplied the markets at a stated price. To prevent any monopoly in this article, every farmer was allowed to retain only a certain quantity, according to the number of his family, and send the overplus, as soon as it was threshed out, to market, for which he was obliged to take the standing price. The importation of grain was encouraged; but to export it, or any other article of provision, was a capital crime. The King himself had a daily report laid before him, of the quantity sold and remaining in the several royal granaries, and spies were appointed in the different markets, to inform him of abuses, which he punished with the utmost rigour. The prices of grain regulated;

Alla appointed also a public office, and inspectors, who fixed the price of the various kinds of cloth, according to its quality, obliging the merchants to open their shops at certain hours every day, and sell their goods at the stipulated price. He at the same time opened a loan, by which they were enabled to procure ready money to import cloth from the neighbouring countries, where the poverty of the people rendered their manufactures cheaper. But what is somewhat unaccountable, the exportation of the finer kind of manufacture was prohibited, yet not permitted to be worn at home, and of cloth.

A. D. 1304. Higer. 704. home, except by ſpecial authority from the King, which favour was only conferred upon men of rank.

Of horſes. As horſes had roſe to an immenſe price, by an aſſociation of the dealers, who only bought up a certain number from the Perſian and northern merchants to inhance the price; the King publiſhed an edict, by which they were obliged to regiſter the prices paid for them, and to ſell them at a certain profit within ſuch a time, if that price was offered them, otherwiſe the King took them upon his own account. The price of the horſe was at the ſame time according to his quality, and care was taken, by that means, that the merchants and dealers in thoſe animals ſhould not have an opportunity, by ſecret connivance, to raiſe the price. Many frauds being found in this article ſome time after, a great number of horſe-dealers were whipt out of the city, and others put to death. Oxen, ſheep, goats, camels, and aſſes, were alſo taken into conſideration; and in ſhort every uſeful animal, and all commodities, were ſold at a ſtated price in the markets.

Settles the pay of the army. The King having thus regulated the prices of things, his next care was to new-model his army. He ſettled the pay of every horſeman, for himſelf and horſe, from 234 rupees a year, down to 80, according to the goodneſs of the horſe; and, upon a muſter, he found his cavalry to conſiſt of four hundred and ſeventy-five thouſand.

The Moguls overthrown. In the mean time Ali, one of the grandſons of Zingis Chan, and Chaja, with forty thouſand horſe, made an irruption into Hindoſtan, but the Emperor ſending Tughlick, with a force againſt them, they were defeated, with the loſs of ſeven thouſand. Ali, and Chaja, with nine thouſand of their troops, were taken priſoners. They were ſent in chains to the King, who ordered the chiefs to be thrown

thrown under the feet of an elephant, and the soldiers to be inhumanly massacred. He appointed Tughlick, for this service, viceroy of Punjab. A.D. 1305. Higer. 705.

Malava reduced.

Alip Chan was, about this time, appointed captain-general of Guzerat, and sent thither with a great force. Moultani, an Omrah of great fame, was at the same time ordered with a numerous army to the conquest of Malava. He was opposed by Kokah, the prince of Malava, with forty thousand Rajaput horse and one hundred thousand foot. An engagement ensued, in which Moultani proved victorious, and took the cities of Ugein, Mindu Daranagurri, and Chanduri. He, after these successes, dispatched a Fatte Namma * to the Emperor, who, upon receiving it, ordered a rejoicing of seven days throughout the city of Delhi. The Indian prince of the fort of Jallore, terrified by the conquests of Moultani, gave up that place upon terms of capitulation.

The Prince of Chitor makes his escape,

The prince of Chitor, who had been prisoner since the Emperor took that place, found in the mean time means to make his escape, in a very extraordinary manner. Alla, having heard extravagant things in praise of the beauty and accomplishments of one of the Raja's daughters, told him, that if he would send her, he should, upon her account, be released. The Raja, who was very ill treated in his confinement, consented, and sent for his daughter, with a manifest design to prostitute her to the King. The prince's family, hearing this dishonourable proposal, concerted means of poisoning the Raja, to save their own reputation. But the daughter, being a girl of invention, proposed a stratagem to release her father,

* A writing of victory. Pompous accounts of his actions, according to their custom.

A.D. 1305. Higer. 705. ther; and at the ſame time to preſerve her own honour. She accordingly wrote to her father to give out, that ſhe was coming with all her attendants, and would be at Delhi upon a certain day, acquainting him with the part ſhe intended to act. Her contrivance was this; She ſelected a number of enterprizing fellows, who, in complete armour, concealed themſelves in doolies or cloſe chairs, in which the women are always carried; ſhe provided for them a choſen retinue of horſe and foot, as cuſtomary to guard ladies of rank. She herſelf, by this time, had, by her father's means, received the imperial paſſport, and the whole cavalcade proceeded to Delhi, and were admitted without interruption. It was now night, and, by the King's permiſſion, they were permitted to ſee the Raja. The chairs being carried into the priſon, and the attendants having taken their ſtations without; the armed men ſtarted out of the chairs, and putting all to the ſword within the courts, carried the Raja out, and, having horſes prepared for him, he mounted, and, with his attendants, ruſhed out of the city before any oppoſition could be made, and fled to his own country.

by the contrivance of his daughter.

The Moguls overthrown.

In the year 705, Kabeik, an Omrah of Dova, prince of Maver-ul-nere, with deſign to revenge the death of Ali and Chaja, invaded Hindoſtan with a great army, and, ravaging Moultan, proceeded to Sewalic. Tughlick, in the mean time, collecting his forces, cut off the retreat of the Moguls, before any troops arrived from Delhi, and defeated them with great ſlaughter. Thoſe who eſcaped the ſword, finding it impoſſible to force their way home, retired into the deſert, where thirſt and the hot winds which blow at that ſeaſon, put an end to their miſerable lives; ſo that out of fifty-ſeven thouſand horſe, beſides their attendants, who

who were ſtill more numerous, only three thouſand, who were taken priſoners, ſurvived this horrid ſcene. The unhappy captives were only reſerved for greater miſery. They were ſent to Delhi with their unfortunate chief, Kabeik, where they were all trodden to death by elephants, except ſome women and children, who were ſold in the market for ſlaves.

A.D. 1305. Higer. 705.

These repeated misfortunes did not however diſcourage the Moguls. Aekbalmund, a chief of great reputation, ſoon after invaded Hindoſtan with a powerful army. But Tughlick defeated him alſo, with great ſlaughter; and ſent ſome thouſand priſoners to Delhi, who were diſpatched by the cuſtomary inhumanity of Alla. Fear, from this time forward, took poſſeſſion of the Moguls, and they gave over all thoughts of Hindoſtan for many years. They were even hard preſſed to defend themſelves: for Tughlick made incurſions into their country every year, plundering the provinces of Cabul, Ghizni, Candahar, and Garrimſere, or laying them under heavy contributions.

The Moguls again overthrown.

In the mean time Alla was employed in ſettling the internal policy and government of his empire; and with ſuch fortunate perſeverance in whatever he undertook, that the ſuperſtition of the times aſcribed his ſucceſs to ſupernatural power, amazed at the good effects that flowed from the ſtrictneſs of his government. Ram Deo, King of Deogire in the Decan, having neglected to ſend the revenues of that diſtrict, which he aſſigned over to the Emperor by treaty, Cafoor, the favourite of Alla, with many Omrahs of renown, and a great army, was ordered to conquer the Decan. Cafoor was one of the Emperor's catamites, and originally a ſlave, taken by force from a merchant of Guzerat,

The King buſy in ſettling the police of the empire.

A.D. 1306. Higer. 706 as we have already mentioned. The Emperor's affection for Cafoor exceeded all the bounds of decency and prudence upon the present occasion. He gave him the title of Malleck Naib Cafoor*, commanding the Omrahs who attended him, to pay their respects to him every day, as to a sovereign. This created among them great disgust, but they durst not murmur. Chaja was appointed his lieutenant; a man much esteemed in those days for his good principles. In the beginning of the year 706, they marched from Delhi, with an army of an hundred thousand horse, and were joined in their way, by Moultani, governor of Malava, and Alip, suba of Guzerat, with their forces.

Comladè's addrefs to the Sultan. One of the Emperor's wives, the fair Comladè, formerly mentioned, hearing of this expedition, addressed herself to the King, and told him, that before she was taken prisoner, she had two beautiful daughters to her former husband. That one of them, she heard, had since died; but that the other, whose name was Dewildè, was still alive. She therefore begged that the Emperor should give orders to his generals to endeavour to get her into their possession, and send her to Delhi. The King consented, and gave orders accordingly.

Cafoor enters the Decan. Cafoor, having passed through Malava, encamped upon the borders of the Decan. He sent the imperial order to the Prince Kirren, to deliver up his daughter Dewildè, which was now urged as a pretext for commencing hostilities in case of a refusal. The Raja could by no means be brought to agree to this demand. Cafoor therefore marched from his camp at Nidderbar, while Alip, with his forces from Guzerat, was taking the

* That is, a viceroy; with all the ensigns of royalty.

route

route of the mountains of Buckelana, to enter the Decan by another paſs. He was oppoſed by Kirren, who defeated all his attempts for two months, in which time ſeveral undeciſive actions were fought. A.D. 1306. Higer. 706.

Singeldeo, the prince of Deogire, who had been contracted to the young Dewildè, without conſent of his father, ſent his brother Bimedeo with preſents to Kirren, perſuading him, that as Dewildè was the occaſion of the war, if he ſhould deliver her over to him, the troops of the Mahommedans, in deſpair of obtaining their ends, would return to their own country. Kirren, who depended much upon the young prince's aid, conſented to this propoſal, and gave his daughter, then in her thirteenth year, in marriage to Singeldeo. Singeldeo demands Dewildè in marriage.

Alip, hearing this news, was greatly terrified leſt the King ſhould impute this circumſtance to his ſlowneſs, and was reſolved, at all events, to ſeize her before her departure, as he was certain his own life depended upon his ſucceſs. He acquainted all the Omrahs with his intentions, who readily ſeconded the attempt. He then entered the mountains with his army, and engaging the Raja, gave him a total defeat; upon which, Kirren fled to Deogire, leaving all his elephants, tents and equipage upon the field. Alip purſued him through the hills for ſome days, but, at length, entirely loſt his track, and all intelligence concerning him and his daughter. But, in the end, accident threw this pearl in his way. Halting to refreſh his army two days among the mountains, ſome of his troops without leave, to the number of three hundred, went from the camp to ſee a famous mountain in the neighbourhood of Deogire, from Alip Chan deſigns to intercept her.

 which

A.D. 1306. Higer. 706.

which city he was not then far diſtant. In their excurſion they ſaw a great troop of horſe, whom they apprehended to belong to Singeldeo, and to be in purſuit of them. As there was no ſafety in flight, they were determined to ſtand on their defence, and accordingly drew up to receive the enemy. This troop proved to be the retinue of Bimedeo, who was carrying the young bride to his brother. The two parties, in ſhort, engaged, and the Hindoos were put to flight, while an unfortunate arrow having pierced the horſe of Dewildè, the unhappy fair one was abandoned in the field. The conquerors ſeeing her, gathered round her horſe, and commenced a bloody ſcuffle about the prize. This might have proved fatal to the beautiful Dewildè, had not one of her female ſlaves told aloud her name and quality, conjuring them to carry her to their commander with that reſpect which was due to her rank and ſex. Upon hearing this they knew the peril of treating her with any indignity; and, while an expreſs was diſpatched with the news to Alip, they conducted her with great care and reſpect to the camp.

Seizes her by an accident.

Alip, having obtained this prize, was exceedingly rejoiced, knowing how acceptable it would be to his prince, over whom the lady's mother had great influence. He therefore proſecuted his conqueſts no further, but returned to Guzerat, and from thence carried Dewildè to Delhi, and preſented her to her mother. In a few days her beauty inflamed the heart of the Emperor's ſon Chizer, to whom ſhe was given in marriage. The hiſtory of the loves of this illuſtrious pair is wrote, in an elegant poem, by the noble Chuſero.

He conducts her to Delhi.

Let

Let us now return to Cafoor, whom we left entering the Decan. He first subdued the country of the Mahrattors, which he divided among his Omrahs, then proceeded to the siege of Deogire, since known by the name of Dowlat-abad. Ramdeo being in no condition to oppose this great army, prudently left his son Singeldeo in the fort, and advanced himself, with great presents, to the conqueror, to procure peace, which was accordingly settled between them. Cafoor, upon this, wrote a writing of victory to the King, and some time after brought Ramdeo, with rich presents and seventeen elephants, to pay his allegiance to him at Delhi, where he himself was received with the most extravagant marks of favour and distinction. Ramdeo had royal dignities conferred upon him, with the title of Rai Raian*, and had not only the government of his own dominions restored to him, but others were also added; for all which he did homage, and paid tribute to the Sultan. The King moreover gave him the district of Nosari, near Guzerat, by way of Jagier, and a lack of rupees to bear his expences home. Thus he dismissed Ramdeo with princely generosity; having, in some measure, looked upon the wealth, of which he had formerly robbed him, as the foundation of all his own greatness. And he perhaps thought that some grateful return was due to the Raja upon this account.

A.D. 1306. Higer. 706. Cafoor's transactions in the Decan.

During the absence of Cafoor in his expedition to the Decan, the King employed himself in taking a strong fort to the southward of Delhi, called Sewana, which had often been attempted in vain. When the prince of this place found

The King besieges and takes Sewana.

* Prince of Princes.

A. D. 1307. Higer. 707. he could hold out no longer, he sent his own image, which had been cast in pure gold, to Alla, with a chain round its neck, in token of obedience. This present was accompanied with a hundred elephants, and other precious effects, in hopes of procuring peace. Alla received the presents, but returned him for answer, that unless he came and made his submission in person, he could hope little from his dumb representative. The Raja, finding the Emperor inexorable, threw himself upon his mercy, and delivered up the place. He plundered and again restored it. But he alienated a great part of the Raja's country to his favourite Omrahs, and bound him over to pay homage for the rest. He then proceeded to Jallire, which he took, and returned to Delhi.

Cafoor marches towards Arinkil.

The Emperor, much about this time, was informed that the expedition, by the way of Bengal, to Arinkil, in the country of Tellingana, had not succeeded, and that his army on that side had been obliged to retreat in great distress. In the year 709, he dispatched Cafoor with a great force to invade that country, by the way of Deogire; with orders, that if Lidderdeo, Prince of Arinkil, should consent to give him a handsome present, and promise an annual tribute, to return without prosecuting the war any further. When Cafoor and Chaja had reached Deogire, Ramdeo came out to meet them with offerings, and carrying them home, entertained them with great hospitality, ordering his market to the camp, with strict orders to sell every thing according to the Emperor's established price in his own dominions.

Enters Tellingana.

Cafoor having marched from Deogire, appeared at Indore, upon the frontiers of Tellingana, and issued orders to lay waste the country with fire and sword;

ſword; which ſtruck the unhappy people, who had never injured their wanton enemies, with great terror and conſternation. In the mean time, the neighbouring princes haſtened with all their forces to ſupport Lidderdeo, in this alarming juncture. But as the imperial army proceeded with great expedition, he was forced, before the arrival of his allies, to ſhut himſelf up in the fort of Arinkil, which was a place of great ſtrength. The allied Rajas, upon this, alſo took poſſeſſion of divers ſtrong holds round the country.

A.D. 1310. Higer. 710.

Cafoor immediately inveſted the place, and began his attacks, which were carried on and repelled with great ſlaughter on both ſides. Notwithſtanding the interruptions that Cafoor received from the auxiliary princes without the place, Arinkil, after ſome months ſiege, was taken by aſſault, and the garriſon maſſacred without mercy, for the citadel to which Lidderdeo had retired, was not ſufficient to contain the whole. Lidderdeo, driven to this extremity, bought his peace with three hundred elephants, ſeven thouſand horſes, and money and jewels to a very great amount; agreeing, at the ſame time, to pay an annual tribute. Cafoor, after this advantageous peace, returned with his army to Delhi. He diſpatched before him the news of his victories, which was read from the pulpit, and a public rejoicing ordered. Upon his approach to the city, the King himſelf came out and met him at the Budaoon gate, and there the conqueror laid all the ſpoils at his feet.

Beſieges and takes Arinkil.

In the year 710, the King ſent Cafoor and Chaja, with a great army, to reduce Dhoor, Summund and Maber in the Decan, where he had heard there were temples very rich in gold and jewels. When they had proceeded to Deogire, they found that Ramdeo

Cafoor's expedition to the Decan.

A.D. 1311. Higer. 711. Ramdeo the old King was dead, and that the young prince Singeldeo, was not so well affected to them as they thought. They therefore left some Omrahs in a strong post upon the banks of the Ganges, and continued their march. When they had passed the Raja's territories, they began their inhuman cruelties, and, after three months march from Delhi, arrived in the countries which they were commanded to subdue. They engaged Bellal Deo, sovereign of the Carnatic, and defeating him, took him prisoner, and then ravaged his whole country. They found in the temples a prodigious spoil in idols of gold, adorned with the most precious stones; and other rich effects, consecrated to their worship. Here the conqueror built a small mosque, and ordered divine service to be read according to the Mahommedan faith, and the Chutba to be pronounced in the Emperor's name. This mosque remains intire in our days, for the Caffers*, esteeming it a house consecrated to God, would not destroy it†.

The Raja of the Carnatic overthrown.

An immense treasure discovered.

Cafoor, having wearied his own inhumanity and avarice, in destroying and robbing an unfortunate people, resolved to return to Delhi with the spoil. The night before his intended march, a quarrel arose among some Brahmins, who had taken protection in his camp, from the plundering parties that scoured the country. Some body who understood their language, found the quarrel was about

* The Mahommedans give the name of Caffers or Infidels to all nations who do not profess their own faith.

† This observation of our author sets the two religions in very opposite lights, and is perfectly consistent with the principle of universal charity of the Hindoos, who think that the same God is the object of all religions, however much they may differ in ceremonies and tenets.

the

the divifion of fome hidden treafure, which was immediately communicated to the fuperintendant of the market, who feized them, and carried them to Cafoor to be examined. They were at firft very obftinate, but their lives being threatened, and each being queftioned apart, they were afraid one would inform againft the other, by which means they difcovered all they knew. Seven different places were pointed out near the camp, where immenfe treafures were concealed. Thefe being dug up and placed upon elephants, Cafoor turned the points of his fpears to Delhi, where he arrived, without any remarkable occurrence, in the year 711. He prefented the Emperor with 312 elephants, 20,000 horfes, 96,000 maunds of gold, feveral chefts of jewels and pearls, and other precious things*. Alla upon feeing this treafure, which exceeded that of Baadawird or Purvez, thofe wealthy and magnificent Kings of Perfia, was greatly rejoiced, and opened the doors of his bounty to all. He gave to each of the principal Omrahs ten maunds, and to the inferior five. The learned men of his court received one maund, and thus in proportion he diftributed wealth to all his fervants, according to their rank and quality. The remainder was melted down, coined and lodged in the treafury. It is faid, that during this expedition to the Carnatic, the foldiers threw the

A.D. 1311.
Higer. 711.

* This treafure may appear to exceed all belief in the eyes of Europeans: But if we confider the Hindoos as a mercantile people, and not difturbed perhaps by wars for thoufands of years; and add to this, that it is the invariable cuftom of that race, to live with the abftinence of hermits in the midft of wealth, our wonder will ceafe, and the credit of our author remain intire. The gold alone amounts to about one hundred millions of our money.

filver

A.D. 1311 Higer. 711. silver they found away, as too cumbersome, where gold was found in such plenty. No person wore bracelets, chains, or rings of any other metal than gold, while all the plate in the houses of the great, and in the temples, was of beaten gold; neither was silver money at all current in that country, should we believe the reports of those adventurers.

Alla's inhumanity to the Mogul mercenaries. Soon after this accession of wealth, the tyrannical Alla exhibited a scene in the capital too dreadful to be varnished over by his great abilities. The Mogul converts in his army having incurred his displeasure, he ordered them to be all discharged. Some of them engaged themselves in the service of the Omrahs, but the greater number remained at Delhi in great distress, in hopes that the Sultan would relent by seeing their wretched poverty. He however remained obdurate, and some daring fellows among them, forced by their misfortunes, entered into a conspiracy to murder the King. This plot being discovered, Alla, instead of punishing the conspirators, extended his inhuman rigour to the whole body. He ordered them all to be instantly put to the sword; so that fifteen thousand of those unhappy wretches lay dead in the streets of Delhi in one day. All their wives and children were enslaved. The King was so inexorable and vindictive, that no one durst attempt to conceal, however nearly connected they might be, any of the unfortunate Moguls, so that not one of them escaped.

His pride and magnificence. The King, elevated by his good fortune, gave himself over to pride. He listened to no advice, as he sometimes condescended to do in the beginning of his reign, but every thing was executed by his irrevocable word. Yet the empire never flourished

riſhed ſo much as in this reign. Order and juſtice travelled to the moſt diſtant provinces, and magnificence raiſed her head in the land. Palaces, moſques, univerſities, baths, ſpires, forts, and all kinds of public and private buildings ſeemed to riſe, as by the power of enchantment, neither did there in any age appear ſuch a concourſe of learned men from all parts. Forty-five ſkilled in the ſciences were profeſſors in the univerſities. In poetry, Chuſero and Delavi held the firſt rank. In philoſophy and phyſic, Molana of Damaſcus. In divinity, Shatibi. In aſtrology, Nizam Awlia acquired much fame. Others diſtinguiſhed themſelves in muſic, morality, languages, and in all the fine arts then known in the world.

A.D. 1311. Higer. 711.

His impolitic proceedings.

But when the King ſeemed to have carried every thing to the heighth of perfection, and to the extent of his wiſhes, he, all at once adopted every meaſure that evidently tended to ſubvert the great fabrick which he had raiſed. He reſigned the reins of government entirely into the hands of Caſoor, whom he blindly ſupported in his moſt impolitic and tyrannical actions. This gave great diſguſt to the Omrahs, and ſpread univerſal diſcontent over the face of the people. He neglected the education of his own children, who were let out of the ſeraglio when very young, and intruſted with independent power. Chizer was made viceroy of Chitor when as yet a boy, without any perſon of wiſdom to adviſe him, or to ſuperintend his conduct, while Shadi, Mubarick and Shab-ul-dien, his other ſons, had appointments of the ſame important nature.

The

A. D. 1312. Higer. 712. Cafoor proposes an expedition to the Decan.

The prince of Tellingana, about this time, sent some presents and twenty elephants to the King, with a letter informing him that the tribute which he had agreed to pay in his treaty with Cafoor, was ready to be paid. Cafoor, uppon this, desired leave of the King, to make another expedition into the Decan, promising that he would not only collect the revenues which had fallen due, but bring the Raja of Deogire and others, who had withheld their allegiance and tribute, under due subjection. He was principally moved to this by his jealousy of Chizer, the declared heir to the empire, whose government lay most convenient for that expedition; and, whom he feared the King intended to send.

He enters the Decan and reduces it.

Alla consented to Cafoor's proposal, and he accordingly proceeded the fourth time to the Decan with a great army. He seized the Raja of Deogire, and inhumanly put him to death; then ravaging the countries of Mahrat, Connir, Dabul, Giwil, Raijore and Mudkil, took up his residence at Deogire. He raised the tribute from the princes of Tellingana and the Carnatic, and, in the year 712, dispatched the whole to the Emperor.

The King falls sick.

Alla by this time, by his intemperance in the seraglio, ruined his constitution, and was taken extremely ill. His wife Mallecke Jehan, and her son Chizer, neglected him entirely, and spent their time in riot and revelry, which added new strength to the King's disorder. He therefore ordered Cafoor from the Decan, and Alip from Guzerat. He told them in private of the unpolitic, undutiful and cruel behaviour of his wife and

Cafoor aspires to the throne.

and ſon. Cafoor, who had before aſpired, in his mind, to the empire, now began ſeriouſly to form ſchemes for the extirpation of the royal line. He, for this purpoſe, inſinuated to the King, that Chizer, the Queen, and Alip, had conſpired againſt his life. What gave colour to this wicked accuſation was, that at this time the Sultana ſolicited Alla to get one of Alip's daughters for her ſon Shadi. The traitor did not fail to improve this circumſtance to his own advantage. The King at length ſuffered ſuſpicion to ſteal into his breaſt, and ordered Chizer to Amrohe, and there to continue till he himſelf ſhould recover. Though Chizer was mad with the follies of youth, this command of his father made a deep impreſſion on his mind, and at his departure he made a private vow, that if God ſhould ſpare the life of his father, he would return all the way on foot. When he accordingly heard that his father's health began to return, he performed his vow, and waited upon him at Delhi. The traitor Cafoor turned this filial piety entirely againſt Chizer. He inſinuated that his behaviour, by ſuch a ſudden change, could be imputed to nothing but hypocriſy, and urged his diſobedience, by coming without his father's leave, pretending, at the ſame time, that he was intriguing with the Omrahs about kindling a rebellion in the empire. Alla could not give entire credit to theſe inſinuations. He ſent for Chizer into his preſence, embraced him to try his affection, and, ſeeing him weep, ſeemed convinced of his ſincerity, and ordered him into the Seraglio, to ſee his mother and ſiſters. But unhappily for this Prince, the flights of his youth made him deviate

A.D. 1312. Higer. 712.

Plots againſt Chizer.

A.D. 1316. Higer. 716. viate again into his former wild amufements. He neglected for feveral days to vifit his father; during which time his fubtle enemy bribed over to his own intereft the Emperor's private fervants, and called upon them to witnefs his afperfions againft Chizer. He at length, by a thoufand wiles and ftratagems, accomplifhed his purpofe, and prevailed upon the King to imprifon his two fons Chizer and Shadi, in the fort of Gualier, and their mother in the old citadel. He at the fame time procured an order to feize Alip, who was unjuftly put to death, and his brother Nizam, fuba of Jallore, was affaffinated by Cummal, who affumed his place.

who is imprifoned.

Difturbances in the empire.

Thus far the traitor's fchemes advanced in the direct road of fuccefs. But now the fire, which had long been fmothered, began to flame, kindling firft at Guzerat into a general infurrection. The King, to fupprefs this rebellion, fent Cummal thither with a great army; but the forces commanded by the friends of Alip defeated him with great flaughter, and put him to a cruel death. In the mean time the governor of Chitor threw the imperial officers over the wall, and affumed independence; while Hirpal Deo, the fon-in-law of Ramdeo, ftirred up the Decan to arms, and took a number of the imperial garrifons.

The Sultan dies.

Alla, upon receiving this intelligence, could do nothing but bite his own flefh, in refentment. His grief and rage ferved to ftrengthen his diforder, which would yield to no power of medicine. On the evening of the fixth of Shawal, in the year 716, he gave up that life, which, like a comet, had fpread terror and defolation through

through an aſtoniſhed world; but not without ſuſpicion of being poiſoned by the villain whom he had raiſed from the duſt to power. He reigned twenty years and ſome months. A.D. 1316. Higer. 716.

If we look upon the government and policy of Alla-ul-dien, a great King ariſes to our view. If we behold his hands, which are red, an inexorable tyrant appears. Had he come by better means to the throne, his abilities deſerved it well; but he began in cruelty, and waded through blood to the end. Ambition was the favourite paſſion of his ſoul, and from it ſprung forth like branches, injuſtice, violence, and rapine. Had fortune placed him at firſt on high, his glory would not perhaps be tarniſhed with meanneſs and deceit; but in whatever way that flame was to paſs through the world, his tract, like that of a ſtorm, muſt have been marked with ruin. He had ſome right, as a warrior, to the title of the Second Alexander; but theſe two Princes reſembled one another in nothing but in ſucceſs and bravery. The firſt was poliſhed and generous, the latter was dark and rude. They were both magnificent, and each of them might conquer the world, and could command it. The ſervants of his houſehold amounted to ſeventeen thouſand, and his pomp, wealth and power, were never equalled by any Prince who ſat before him on the throne of Hindoſtan. His character.

Ahmed, Argun, Ganjatû, Baidû, Kazân and Aljaptu, all of the poſterity of Zingis, reigned ſucceſſively in Perſia, during the reigns of Feroſe and Alla in India. Cubla was on the imperial throne of Tartary and China, till the ſixth year of Feroſe; Timur, Hayſan and Ajuli Palipata ſucceſſively State of Aſia, during the reigns of Feroſe and Alla.

A.D. 1316. Higer. 716. successively held the sceptre of the Moguls, in the reign of Alla. The family of Zagatay still held their government on the confines of Tartary, Persia, and India. All Hindostan was comprehended in the Patan empire, at the death of Alla.

OMAR.

O M A R.

IN the hiſtory of Sidder Jehan of Guzerat, we are informed that, the day after the death of Alla, Cafoor aſſembled the Omrahs, and produced a ſpurious teſtament of the deceaſed King, in which he had appointed Omar, Alla's youngeſt ſon, his ſucceſſor, and Cafoor himſelf regent, during the prince's minority, ſetting aſide the right of primogeniture in the perſon of Chizer, and the other princes. Omar, then, in the ſeventh year of his age, was placed on the throne, and Cafoor began his adminiſtration. The firſt ſtep which the traitor took, was to ſend a perſon to Gaulier, to put out the eyes of the princes Chizer and Shadi. His orders were inhumanly executed; and the Sultana, their mother, was put into cloſer confinement, and all her wealth ſeized. Mubarick, the third ſon of Alla, was alſo taken into cuſtody, with an intention to have his eyes put out, like his unhappy brothers. There is ridicule in what we are to relate. Cafoor, though an eunuch, married the mother of Omar, the late Emperor's third wife. But the mother of Mubarick, Alla's ſecond wife, having heard that the regent intended to put out the eyes of her ſon, acquainted Nizam of her intelligence, and he gave her ſome hopes that the threatened misfortune ſhould be prevented.

Omar placed upon the throne by Cafoor.

Cafoor, in the mean time, to cloak his wicked deſigns, placed the young King every day upon the

Sends to put out the eyes of Mubarick,

A.D. 1316. Hig. 716. the throne, and ordered the nobles to pay their reſpects, as uſual, to the Emperor. He ſent one night ſome aſſaſſins to cut off the prince Mubarick; but when they entered his apartment, he conjured them to remember his father, whoſe ſervants they were; then untying a ſtring of rich jewels from his neck, which perhaps had more influence than his intreaties, he gave it them. They immediately abandoned their purpoſe; but quarrelling about the diviſion of the jewels, when they had got out, it was propoſed to carry them to the chief of the foot-guards, and acquaint him of what the Prince had ſaid, and of their inſtructions from Cafoor.

Aſſaſſinated. The commander of the foot-guards, who owed every thing to the favour of the deceaſed King, was ſhocked at the villany of Cafoor, and finding his people of the ſame ſentiments, he immediately formed a conſpiracy againſt the tyrant, and accordingly he and his lieutenant entered the regent's apartment, a few hours after, and aſſaſſinated him, with ſome of the principal eunuchs, who where attached to his intereſt. This happened thirty-five days after the Emperor Alla's death, and thus the world was rid of a monſter too horrid to exiſt among mankind.

Mubarick aſcends the throne. When, with the return of day, the tranſactions of the night became public, they gave general ſatisfaction. The prince Mubarick was releaſed from his confinement, and had the reins of government placed in his hands. He however did not immediately aſſume the throne, but acted for the ſpace of two months, as regent or vizier for his brother, till he had brought over the nobles to his intereſt. He then claimed his birthright to the diadem, depoſed his brother, and acceded to the imperial dignity. But, according

cording to the barbarous cuſtom and policy of those days, he deprived Omar of his eyes, and confined him for life in the fort of Gualier, after he had borne the title of King for three months and ſome days. A. D. 1317. Hig. 717.

MUBARICK I.

Mubarick's cruelty and ingratitude,

UPON the feventh of Mohirrim, in the year feven hundred and feventeen of the Higera, Mubarick * mounted the throne. The commander of the foot-guards, who had faved his life, and raifed him to the imperial dignity, as alfo his lieutentant, were ungratefully and inhumanly put to death by his orders, under no better pretence than that they prefumed too much upon the fervices they had done him. It is probable he was inftigated to this bafe action by his fears, as, in fome meafure, appears by his immediately difperfing all the old foldiers, who were under their command, into different parts of the country. Mubarick began to difpenfe his favours among the nobles, but he difgufted them all by raifing fome of his flaves to that dignity.

Promotions at court,

Dinar Shenapil was dignified with the title of Ziffer. Moula, the Emperor's uncle, received the name of Shere, and Malana Zea, that of Sidder Jehan. In the mean time Kerabeg was made one of the counfellors of ftate; and Haffen one of his flaves, the fon of a feller of rags at Guzerat, received the title of Chufero, and through the King's unnatural affection for him, became the greateft man in the empire. He was appointed to the command of the armies of Cafoor and Chaja, thofe joint conquerors of the Decan, and at the fame time to the honour of the office of Vizier, without any one good quality to recommend him to thofe high employs.

* Cuttub-ul-dien, Mubârick Shaw Chilligi.

The

The emperor, whether to affect popularity, or in remembrance of his late situation, ordered all the prisons to be opened, by which means seventeen thousand were blessed with the light of day, and all the exiles were by proclamation recalled. He then commanded to give to the army a present of six months pay, and conferred upon them many other private benefits. He at the same time issued orders to give free access to all petitioners. He eased the petitioners of some of their taxes; but by too much relaxing the reins of government, disorder and tumult arose, which threw down to the ground the great fabrick raised by his father Alla. He gave himself up entirely to wine, revelry, and lust. These vices became fashionable at court, from whence the whole body of the people were soon infected.

A.D. 1317. Hig. 717. The Emperor affects popularity.

Mubarick, in the first year of his reign, sent an army, under the command of the famous Moultani, into the province of Guzerat, which had revolted. Moultani was an Omrah of great abilities. He soon defeated the insurgents, cut off their chiefs, and settled the country in peace. The King conferred the government of Guzerat upon Ziffer, whose daughter he had taken in marriage. Ziffer soon after marched his army to Narwalla, the capital of Guzerat, where some disturbances had happened, reduced the rebels, confiscated their estates, and sent their moveable wealth to the King.

Guzerat reduced;

Mubarick, in the second year of his reign, raised a great army, and marched towards the Decan, to chastise Hirpaldeo, the son-in-law of Ramdeo, who, by the assistance of the other princes of the Decan, had recovered his country. Mubarick at his departure appointed Shahin, the son of a slave, to whom he gave the title of Offa Beg, governor of Delhi, during his absence. When he arrived near Deogire, Hirpaldeo and the

and the Decan.

A. D. 1318. Hig. 718.

the other princes, who were then besieging the place, fled. But some Omrahs being ordered to pursue Hirpaldeo, he was brought back prisoner, flead alive, and beheaded. His head was fixed above the gate of his own capital. The Emperor ordered his garrisons to be re-established as far as the sea, and built a mosque in Deogire, which still remains. He then appointed one of his father's slaves, to command in the Decan. He, in imitation of Alla, gave his catamite Chusero the ensigns of royalty, sending him towards Malabar, with part of his army, then returned himself to Delhi.

A conspiracy.

Assid, son to the Emperor's grand-uncle, seeing the King daily drunk, and negligent of all the duties of a king or commander, began to entertain thoughts of the empire, and formed a conspiracy against his life. This plot however was discovered by one of the conspirators, and Assid was condemned to death. Whether Mubarick had found proofs that his brothers were concerned in this conspiracy, we cannot learn, but at that time he sent an assassin to Gualier, and these two unfortunate blind princes were inhumanly murdered, and the fair Dewildè brought to the royal Haram.

The Emperor abandons himself to every species of vice.

Mubarick, finding himself in quiet possession of all the kingdoms of India, abandoned those popular manners which he at first affected, and grew perverse, proud, vindictive, and tyrannical, despising all counsel, ill-treating all his friends, and executing every thing, however bloodly or unjust, by his obstinate, blind, arbitrary will. Ziffer, the imperial governor of Guzerat, among others, fell a victim to his tyranny, and also Offa Beg, upon whom he had heaped such favours, without any plausible pretence against either. He was infamous, in short, in every vice that can taint the human mind, and descended so far from the

the royal character, as to dress himself often like a common prostitute, and go with the public women to dance at the houses of the nobility. At other times, he would lead a gang of those abominable prostitutes, stark naked, along the terraces of the royal palaces, and oblige them to make water upon the nobles as they entered the court. These and such other vices and indecencies, too shocking to mention, were the constant amusements of this monster in the form of a man. A. D. 1318. Hig. 718.

After the death of Ziffer, Hissam, uncle to the famous slave Chusero, who was also one of the Emperor's catamites, in the absence of the detestable slave, obtained the regency of Guzerat, where he had not been established long, till, in confederacy with a few nobles, he rebelled; but the other omrahs of Guzerat rising in arms, defeated him, and sent him prisoner to Delhi, where he was not only pardoned, but permitted to resume his place in the King's favour; Odgi being sent to Guzerat, in his stead. About this time news arrived, that Eclikki, governor of the Decan, had rebelled. The Emperor sent a great army to suppress that insurrection, who found means to seize the rebel and his principal adherents, and to send them to Delhi, where Eclikki had his ears cut off, and the others were put to the torture. The gallant Moultani was advanced to the viceroyship of the Decan. Several insurrections quashed.

Chusero, who had gone to Malabar, stayed there about one year. He plundered the country of about one hundred and twenty elephants, a perfect diamond of 168 Ruttys, with other jewels and gold to a great amount. His ambition was increased by his wealth, and he began to aspire to the throne. Not being able to join to his interest any of the great officers of his army, he formed the means of their destruction. For this Chusero aspires to the throne.

A. D. 1319. Hig. 719. this purpoſe he called one Tilbiga from the government of the iſland of Koohe, Timur and Malleck Affghan, who were on different ſervices, and gave out that he had orders to return to Delhi. Theſe nobles, having intelligence of his intentions, diſobeyed his commands, and wrote a remonſtrance to the Emperor, accuſing Chuſero of a conſpiracy againſt the ſtate. Mubarick, on this, ordered them to ſeize him, and ſend him priſoner to Delhi, which accordingly they found means to execute. But when he came before the King, he pleaded his own innocence ſo artfully, and blamed his accuſers with ſuch plauſibility of truth, that the Emperor, believing the whole proceeded from the diſguſt of their being commanded by his favourite, he recalled them; and notwithſtanding they gave undoubted proofs of their aſſertions, he was determined to liſten to nothing againſt this vile catamite.—He diſhonoured them, confiſcated all their eſtates, turning them out to poverty and the world. The other Omrahs, ſeeing that the enemies of Chuſero, right or wrong, were devoted to deſtruction, the men of the beſt principles among them made excuſes, and obtained leave to retire to diſtant parts of the empire; while the abandoned to all honour joined themſelves to the catamite, who was now the object of univerſal dread, as well as the ſource of all benefits and promotion. This ſlave, in the mean time, cheriſhed his own ambitious views, and began again to form meaſures for his own advancement.

Chuſero continues his deſigns. To accompliſh his purpoſe, he told the King, "That as his own fidelity and ſervices had been by his Majeſty ſo generouſly rewarded, and as he might ſtill have occaſion for them in the conduct of his military affairs, while the Omrahs, from the pride of family, were ſeditious and diſobedi-

ent

ent to his commands, he begged that he might be permitted to call ſome of his relations from Guzerat, in whom he could more certainly confide." Mubarick agreed to this requeſt; and Chuſero ſent a great ſum of money, by ſome of his agents, to Guzerat, who collected about twenty thouſand of the dregs of the people, and brought them to Delhi. Every place of profit and truſt were conferred upon thoſe vermin, which bound them faſt to Chuſero's intereſt; and alſo upon all the villains about the city, who were remarkable for their boldneſs and addreſs. A.D. 1320. Hig. 720.

The Emperor, in the mean time, going to hunt towards Jirſava, a plot was formed to aſſaſſinate him. But this was laid aſide, on account of ſome difference in opinion among the conſpirators: and therefore they reſolved to perform their tragedy in the palace. Mubarick returned to Delhi, and, according to cuſtom, gave himſelf up to his debaucheries. Chuſero was warm in his project, and took the opportunity of a favourable hour to beg leave of Mubarick to entertain his friends in the outer court of the palace. The Emperor not only conſented, but iſſued orders to give them free acceſs at all times; by which means the courts of the palace became crouded with thoſe vermin. In the mean time, the Caſi Zea, who was famous for his ſkill in aſtrology, though upon this occaſion, we imagine, he conſulted his own judgment and not the ſtars, ran into the preſence, and kiſſed the ground. "O King," ſaid he, "Chuſero is concerting means for your aſſaſſination. If this ſhould prove falſe, his honeſty will be the better eſtabliſhed; if otherwiſe, caution is neceſſary, becauſe life is a moſt ineſtimable jewel." Mubarick ſmiled at the old man, who had been one of his preceptors, and told him, he would make enquiry into that affair: while inſtantly Chuſero entered in a female

Conſpires againſt the Emperor's life.

male

A.D. 1321. Hig. 721.

male dreſs, with all the affectations of a girl. The Emperor, upon ſeeing the infamous catamite, repeated a verſe to this effect: "If my beloved were guilty of ten thouſand crimes, one ſmile from him and I forget them all." He then embraced Chuſero, and actually did forget all that the Caſi had ſaid.

The old Caſi murdered.

That night, as the Caſi was ſupicious of treaſon, he could not go to reſt, but walked out about midnight, to ſee whether the guards were watchful. In their rounds, he met Mundul, uncle to Chuſero, who engaged him in converſation. In the mean time, one Jaherba came behind him, and, with one ſtroke of a ſword, ſtretched him upon the ground, leaving him only ſtrength to cry out, "Treaſon! Treaſon! Murder and treaſon are on foot!" while two ſervants, who attended him, run off, ſcreaming aloud, that the Caſi was aſſaſſinated. The guards ſtarted up in confuſion, but they were inſtantly attacked by the conſpirators, and maſſacred, before they could prepare for their own defence.

The Emperor aſſaſſinated.

The Emperor, alarmed by the noiſe, aſked Chuſero, who lay in his apartment, the cauſe of it. The villain aroſe to enquire, and going out on the terrace, ſtood for ſome time, and returning told the king, that ſome of the horſes belonging to the guard had broke looſe from their picquets, and were fighting, while the people were endeavouring to lay hold of them. This ſatisfied Mubarick for the preſent; but, ſoon after, the conſpirators having aſcended the ſtairs, and got upon the terraces which led to the royal ſleeping apartment, they were ſtopped by Ibraham and Iſhaac, with all the porters of the private chambers, whom they immediately put to the ſword. The Emperor, hearing the claſh of arms and groans of dying men ſo near him, roſe up in great terror and confuſion, running towards the Haram,

ram, by a private paſſage. Chuſero, fearing he might eſcape, ruſhed cloſe after him, and ſeizing him by the hair in the gallery, ſtruggled with him for ſome time. Mubarick being the ſtronger man, threw Chuſero on the ground; but as he had twiſted his hand in his hair, he could by no means diſengage himſelf, till ſome of the other conſpirators came, and, with a ſtroke of a ſabre, cut off his head and threw it down into the court, proclaiming the deed aloud to thoſe below.

A.D. 1321. Hig. 721.

The conſpirators in the court below began to be hard preſſed by the guards and the ſervants, who had crouded from all quarters, but upon hearing of the Emperor's fate, they all haſtened out of the palace. The conſpirators then ſhut the gates, and maſſacred all who had not the good fortune to eſcape; particularly the younger children of the Emperor Alla, Feredoon, Ali, and Omar. Then breaking into the Haram, committed all manner of violence upon the poor women. Thus the vengeance of God overtook and exterminated the race of Alla, for his ingratitude to his uncle Feroſe, and the ſtreams of innocent blood which flowed from his hands. Heaven alſo puniſhed Mubarick, whoſe name and reign are too infamous to have a place in the records of literature; did not our duty, as a hiſtorian, oblige us to this diſagreeable taſk. But notwithſtanding we have, in ſome places, been obliged to throw the veil of oblivion over circumſtances too horrid to relate.

A general maſſacre in the palace.

This maſſacre happened on the fifth of the firſt Ribbi, in the year 721. In the morning, Chuſero, ſurrounded by his creatures, mounted the throne, and, ridiculouſly, aſſumed the title of the ſupporter of religion.* He then ordered all the ſlaves and ſervants of Mubarick, who he thought

Chuſero mounts the throne.

* Naſir-ul-dien.

A. D. 1321. Hig. 721. thought had the leaſt ſpark of honeſty, to be put to death, and their wives and children to be ſold for ſlaves. His brother was dignified with the title of Chan Chanan, or chief of the Omrahs, and married to one of the daughters of the Emperor Alla, while he took Dewildè, the widow of Mubarick, to himſelf. He diſpoſed of all the other ladies of the ſeraglio among his beggarly friends. The army now remained to be bribed, who loved nothing better than a revolution; for they had always, upon ſuch an occaſion, a donation of ſix months pay immediately divided from the treaſury. This trifle bought thoſe diſſolute ſlaves, who were loſt to all ſenſe of gratitude or honour.

Honours conferred upon the conſpirators

The ſon of Kimar, the chief of a gang of thieves, received the title of Shaiſta, and was made chief ſecretary of the empire, while Ain ul Malleck was appointed captain general of the imperial armies. Jonah had the title of Chuſero, and the appointment of maſter of the horſe, with many other diſtinguiſhing favours, with an intention to gain over the allegiance of his father, Ghazi, governor of Lahore and Debalpoor, of whom the uſurper was in great fear. Notwithſtanding his promotion, Jonah was touched to the ſoul to ſee the empire ridden by a gang of villains.

Ghazi revolts.

His father alſo, who was reckoned a man of great bravery and honour in thoſe days, was diſcontented at the infamous proceedings at court, and rouſed himſelf to revenge. He acquainted his ſon of his purpoſe, and Jonah took the firſt opportunity to fly from Delhi, and join his father. The uſurpur was in great perplexity upon the flight of Jonah, and began already to give his hopes to the wind. Ghazi immediately prepared for hoſtilities, and, by circular letters, invited all the Omrahs to join his ſtandard. A great many of the ſubas of the provinces put their troops immediately

mediately in motion; but Mogulti, the governor of Moultan, jealous of precedence, refused to join; upon which occasion, Byram, a chief of some note in those parts, was prevailed upon to assassinate him. Eclikki, governor of Samana, notwithstanding the usurper had been the occasion of his losing his ears, transmitted the circular letter of Ghazi to court, informing him of the rebellion, and, taking the field against the confederates, received a signal defeat, and, in his flight to Delhi, was fallen upon by the zemindars, and cut to pieces. The usurper sent his brother, and Sufi, with all on whom he could depend, against the confederates

A.D. 1321. Hig. 721.

Defeats the usurper's army.

Ghazi, now joined by Byram with the army from Moultan, and other subas, advanced to meet the usurper's army, which he did upon the banks of the Sirusti. But as the troops of Ghazi were experienced in frequent wars with the Moguls, and those of Chusero enervated by indolence and debaucheries, and besides lost to all sense of military honour, they were broke at the first onset, and all the public treasure, elephants and baggage, were taken. This booty was divided in the field among the conquerors. They then continued their march in triumph towards Delhi. The usurper, in great embarrassment, marched out of the city, and took possession of a strong post near the great pond of Alahi, with the citadel in his rear, and many gardens with high walls in his front. He then opened the treasury, and gave three years pay to his troops, leaving nothing but the jewels, of some of which he also disposed. The confederates advancing in sight, an action was expected next morning. But that night, Moultani drew off his forces from the usurper, and took the rout of Mindu. This struck great terror into Chusero's army. They however drew up in order of battle; and Tilbiga and Sha-

ista

A. D. 1321. Hig. 721.

ista opposing the confederates with great bravery, as they advanced through the lanes, were at length overpowered and slain. But their situation gave such advantages to the usurper's army, that they maintained their post till the evening; when the infamous Chusero fled, with a few of his friends, towards Jilput. In the way he was deserted by all his attendants, and obliged to conceal himself in a tomb, from whence he was dragged the next day, and ordered to be put to death, together with his brother, who was taken in a neighbouring garden.

Chusero overthrown, taken, and slain.

The day after this action, being the first of Shaban, all the Omrahs and magistrates of the city came to pay their respects to the victor, and made him a present of the keys of the capital. He mounted his horse, and entered Delhi in triumph. When he came in sight of the palace of a thousand pillars, he began to weep, crying with a loud voice! "O ye subjects of this great empire, I am no more than one of you, who unsheathed my sword to deliver you from oppression, and rid the world of a monster. My endeavours, by the blessing of God, have been crowned with success. If therefore any of the royal line remain, let them be brought, that justice may take place, and that we, his servants, may prostrate ourselves before his throne. But if none of the race of kings have escaped the bloody hands of tyranny and usurpation, let the most worthy of the illustrious order be elected among you, and I shall swear to abide by your choice."

Ghazi's moderation

He mounts the throne.

The people cried out with one voice, that none of the princes were now alive; that as he had shielded them from the vengeance of the Moguls, and delivered them from the rage of a tyrant, none was so worthy to reign. Then seizing him, in a manner by violence, they placed him upon the throne, and hailed him king of the world.

But

But he aſſumed the more modeſt title of Yeas-ul-dien Tuglick, or the reformer of religion. The reign of Chuſero was five months. Nothing in hiſtory can exhibit ſuch an example of the diſſolute and infamous manners of any age or nation, as we are preſented with in the accounts of this wicked and ſhameful uſurpation, though it was ſcarcely more diſhonourable to mankind than the reign of the abandoned Mubarick, who had ſome right to the empire. A.D. 1321. Hig. 721.

During the ſhort uſurpations of the two Cafoors, and the reign of Mubarick, there were very few alterations in the ſtate of Aſia. Ajuli Palipata ſat on the Mogul throne of Tartary and China; and Abuſaid, of the race of Zingis, on that of Perſia. State of Aſia.

TUGLICK I.

A. D. 1321. Hig. 721. His pedigree uncertain.

WE have no true accounts of the pedigree of Tuglick *. It is generally believed that his father, whofe name was Tuglick, had been, in his youth, brought up as an imperial flave, by Balin. His mother was one of the tribe of the Jits. But indeed the pedigrees of the Kings of the Patan empire make fuch a wretched figure in hiftory, that we could wifh to omit them, were it not to fhow how far the depravity and corruption of a people can plunge them into the fink of flavery, and fubject them to the vileft of men.

A wife prince.

When Tuglick mounted the throne, he began to regulate the affairs of government, which had fallen into the utmoft diforder, by the moft falutary and adviseable methods, which gained him general efteem. He repaired the palaces and fortifications, founded others, and encouraged induftry and commerce. Men of genius and learning were called to court; inftitutes of laws and government were eftablifhed and founded upon the Coran, and the ancient ufages of the empire.

Promotions t court.

Jonah, the Emperor's eldeft fon, was declared heir apparent, with the title of Ali, and all the royal enfigns conferred upon him. His other four fons were entitled Byram, Ziffer, Mamood, and Nuferit. Byram Iba, who had had fo effectually affifted him with the army from Moultan, was

* Sultan Yeas-ul-dien Tuglic Shaw.

adopted

adopted his brother, by the title of the noble Chusero, and appointed viceroy of the provinces upon the Indus. Affid, his nephew, was appointed lord of the presence; and Malleck Baha, his other nephew, chief secretary of the empire. Shadi, the Emperor's brother and son-in law, was made vizier. Burhan had the government of Deogire conferred upon him; and Tartar, the government of another district in that country called Ziffer-abad. A. D. 1322. Hig. 722.

The Emperor, in the mean time, stationed troops upon the frontiers towards Cabul, and built forts to defend the country from the incursions of the Moguls, which he did so effectually as not to be troubled by these invaders during his reign. In the second year from his accession, Jonah, the Emperor's eldest son, with some of the old Omrahs, and the troops of Chinderi Budaoon, and Malava, was dispatched towards Tillingana, to chastise Lidderdeo, the Indian prince of Arinkil, who had, during the late disturbances, wrested his neck from the yoke, and refused to send his tribute, while the Raja of Deogire had also swerved from his allegiance. Jonah having advanced into those countries, began a barbarous war with fire and sword. Lidderdeo opposed him with some vigour, but was in the end obliged to retreat into the city of Arinkil, which Jonah immediately invested. Troops stationed on the frontiers.

The siege was carried on with great loss on both sides, till the walls were battered down, and a practicable breach made. The Mahommedan army, in the mean time, on account of the hot winds and bad water, were seized with a malignant distemper, that swept hundreds to their graves every day. Many became desirous to return home, and spread false reports through the camp, which threw universal consternation among Arinkil besieged.

A. D. 1322. Hig. 723. the army. As there had been no advices for above a month from Delhi, Zuda Dimiſki the poet, and ſome others who were companions of Jonah, raiſed a report, by way of jeſt, that the Emperor was dead, and that a great revolution had happened in Delhi. Not content with this, they went to the tents of Timur, Afghan, Cafoor Mordar, and Tiggi, who were the principal Omrahs in the camp, and told them, ſuch and ſuch was the ſtate of affairs at Delhi, and that Prince Jonah, knowing them, as old Omrahs, to have an equal right with himſelf to the empire, had reſolved to diſpatch them.

Siege raiſed. The Omrahs, giving implicit belief to this falſe information, fled that night, with all their dependants from the camp. Jonah, thus deſerted, was under the neceſſity of retreating, in great diſorder, towards Deogire, whither he was purſued by the beſieged, with great ſlaughter. In the mean time advices arrived from Delhi, that all was well, and Jonah halted at Deogire, to collect his ſcattered army. The four Omrahs who fled, having diſagreed among themſelves, had each taken a ſeparate rout, by which means they were fallen upon by the Indians, plundered of their elephants, camels and baggage, and otherwiſe greatly haraſſed in their march. Timur and Tiggi were both ſlain, while Afghan and Cafoor were ſeized by their own troops, and brought priſoners to Deogire. An enquiry was made into their conduct, the authors of the diſturbance ſeized, and all of them ſent priſoners to Delhi. The Emperor ordered the propagators of the falſe intelligence to be buried alive, with this ſevere ſarcaſm: "That they had buried him alive in jeſt, but that he would bury them alive in good earneſt."

Prince

Prince Jonah was obliged to retreat from Deogire, and brought only back three thouſand horſe, of all his great army, to Delhi. He in two months, however, made great preparations, and, with a more numerous army than the former, took the rout of Arinkil. He took in his way the city of Bedir, on the frontiers of Tillingana, and other places, where he left garriſons. He then advanced to the capital, renewed the ſiege, and, in a ſhort time, reduced it. Some thouſands of the unfortunate Hindoos were maſſacred, and Lidderdeo, with his family, taken priſoners. Jonah ſent the priſoners, their treaſure, elephants, and effects, to Delhi, under charge of Kuddir and Chaja. Upon their arrival, great rejoicings were made in the new citadel, which the Emperor had built, by the name of Tughlickabad. The Prince, having appointed truſty Omrahs to govern the country of Tillingana proceeded in perſon towards Jagenagur *. In that place he took forty elephants from the Raja, and ſent them to his father. Returning then to Arinkil, he ſtaid there a few days, and continued his march to Delhi.

A, D, 1323, Hig. 723, Arinkil again beſieged.

In the beginning of the year 724, complaints arrived from Bengal of the great oppreſſions committed by the governors of that kingdom. Tughlick appointed his ſon Jonah to the government of Delhi, and, with a great army, marched towards Bengal. When he had reached Nahib, Nazir, the grandſon of the Emperor Balin, who had remained in that government ſince the death of his father, arrived, in a reſpectful manner, from Bengal, with many valuable preſents. He was confirmed in his government of the whole kingdom of Bengal, and honoured with royal

The Emperor marches towards Bengal,

 dignities;

* Now Cattack in Oriſſa.

A.D. 1325, Hig. 725, dignities; and the Emperor prepared for his return. When he was paſſing near the hills of Turhat, the Indian prince of thoſe parts appearing in arms, he purſued him into the woods. Finding his army could no longer continue the purſuit, he alighted, and calling for a hatchet, cut down one of the trees with his own hand. The troops, upon ſeeing this, ſet to work with ſuch ſpirit, that the foreſt ſeemed to vaniſh before them, till they arrived at a fort ſurrounded with ſeven ditches full of water, and a high wall. The King immediately inveſted it, began the ſiege, filled up the ditches, and broke down the wall in three weeks. He took the Raja, his family and wealth, and conferred the government of Turhat upon the noble Ahmed, and returned with his army towards Delhi.

Killed by accident, When the Emperor had reached Afghanpoor, he was met by Prince Jonah, with all the nobles of Delhi, to congratulate him upon his ſafe return. But his death was now approaching. His ſon had in that place raiſed a wooden houſe, in three days time, for his father's reception. The entertainment being over, the King was preparing to mount, and every body haſtened out to be ready to accompany him. The roof of the building fell inſtantly in, and killed the Emperor, and five of his attendants, as he was riſing to follow the Omrahs.

His death aſcribed to various cauſes, Some authors attribute this accident to the newneſs of the buildng, and the motion of the elephants that were preparing without. Others give it to deſign, with which they charge Jonah, as the raiſing this unneceſſary building ſeems indeed to indicate. But others aſcribe it to lightning; ſo that the matter ſtill remains in doubt. The death of Tughlick happened in the month of the firſt Ribbi of the year 725, after a reign of four years

and

and some months. The poet, the noble Chusero, who lived down to the end of this Emperor's reign, has favoured posterity with his history at large, by which it appears that he was a great and virtuous prince.

MAHOM-

MAHOMMED III.

A. D. 1325. Hig. 725. Jonah, by the name of Mahommed, mounts the throne.

AFTER the King's funeral obſequies were performed, his eldeſt ſon, Jonah, aſcended the throne by the name of Mahommed, and proceeded from Tughlick Abad to Delhi. The ſtreets of that city were ſtrowed with flowers, the houſes adorned, the drums beating, and every demonſtration of joy exhibited. The new Emperor ordered ſome elephants, loaded with gold and ſilver, before and behind him, which was ſcattered among the populace. Tatar, whom the Emperor Tughlick had adopted, and appointed to the government of Zifferabad, was now honoured with the title of Byram, and preſented with a hundred elephants, a crore of golden rupees, two thouſand horſe, and the government of Bengal. To Sinjer of Buduchſhan, Mahommed gave ſeventy lacks in ſilver. To Malleck, eighty lacks; and to Molana, his preceptor, forty lacks, all in one day. The learned Molana Cumi had an annual penſion of one lack, and Malleck of Ghizni, the poet, another to the ſame amount.

His generoſity.

His generoſity, in ſhort, was, like his wealth, without bounds; which no man could well account for, there being no great ſum in the treaſury upon his acceſſion. It is therefore probable, that he had concealed the riches of the prince of Arinkil, from Tughlick, and that his liberality was ſupplied from the wealth of the Decan, which

which circumſtance ſtrengthens our ſuſpicion that he was acceſſary to his father's death. Some writers, notwithſtanding this ſuſpicion, make long panegyricks upon his virtues and accompliſhments. He, it muſt be acknowledged, aimed at univerſal knowledge, was converſant in all the literature of the times, and a patron of learned men, giving them profuſely penſions for a magnificent ſubſiſtence. Mahommed was, at the ſame time, very ſtrict with regard to public and private worſhip. He ordered prayers to be read in the moſques five times every day. He diſcouraged all intemperate pleaſures, and ſet the example by his own ri id life. But it is to be ſuſpected, that he acted the mean character of a hypocrite, for he was vindictive and inhuman, delighting in the blood of his ſubjects, and condemning them, without diſtinction of right or wrong, to cruel and ignominious deaths.

A. D. 1325. Hig. 725.

His learning, religion, and cruelty.

In the beginning of the reign of Mahommed, before the empire was properly ſettled, iri, chief of the tribe of Zagatay, a Mogul general of great fame, invaded Hindoſtan, in the year 727, with an innumerable army, with a view to make an entire conqueſt of it. Having ſubdued Limghan, Moultan, and the northern provinces, he advanced towards Delhi with incredible expedition, and inveſted it. Mahommed, ſeeing he could not cope with the enemy in the field, and that the city muſt ſoon fall, began to ſue for peace; he ſent an immenſe preſent in gold and jewels, to ſoften the Mogul chief, who at laſt conſented, upon receiving almoſt the price of the empire, to return to his own country, taking Guzerat and Sind in his way, which he plundered of a world of wealth.

The Moguls invade Hindoſtan.

Mahommed turned his thoughts to war, and the regulation of his army. He ſubdued, by different generals, many diſtant countries, ſuch as Door,

The Emperor's conqueſts.

A.D. 1326 Hig. 727. Door, Summudir, Maber, Compila, Arinkil, ſome of which provinces had revolted, and others had never been ſubjected by the arms of the Iſlamites. He ſoon after reduced the Carnatic to the extremities of the Decan, and from ſea to ſea, obliging all the Rajas to pay him tribute, by which means he again filled the treaſury with money.

The cauſe of diſturbances in the empire.

But, during the convulſions which ſoon after ſhook the empire, all theſe foreign conqueſts were wreſted from the yoke. The cauſes of the diſturbances were chiefly theſe; the heavy impoſts, which were, in this reign, tripled in ſome provinces; the paſſing copper money for ſilver, by public decree; the raiſing 370,000 horſe for the conqueſt of Choraſſan and Maver-ul-nere; the ſending 100,000 horſe towards the mountains between India and China; the cruel maſſacre of many Mahommedans, as well as Hindoos, in different parts of India; and many other leſſer reaſons, which, for the ſake of brevity, we ſhall forbear to mention.

Heavy impoſts.

The impoſts upon the neceſſaries of life, which were levied with the utmoſt rigour, were too great for the power of induſtry, and conſequently the country was involved in diſtraction and confuſion. The farmers were forced to fly to the woods, and to maintain themſelves by rapine. The lands being left uncultivated, famine began to deſolate whole provinces, and the ſufferings of the people obliterated from their minds every idea of government, and ſubjection to authority.

Copper money.

The copper money, for want of proper regulations, was productive of no leſs evils than that which we have already ſpecified. The King, unfortunately for his people, adopted his ideas upon currency, from a Chineſe cuſtom of uſing paper upon the Emperor's credit with the royal ſeal appended, for ready money. Mahommed, inſtead

of

of paper, ſtruck a copper coin, which, being issued at an imaginary value, he made current by a decree throughout Hindoſtan. The mint was under very bad regulations. Bankers acquired immenſe fortunes by coinage, whilſt the merchants made their payments in copper to the poor manufacturers, at the ſame time that they themſelves received for their exports, ſilver and gold. There was much villany alſo practiſed in the mint; for a premium to thoſe who had the management of it, the merchants had their coin ſtruck conſiderably below the legal value; and theſe abuſes were overlooked by the government. But the great ſource of the misfortunes conſequent upon this debaſement of the coin, was the known inſtability of government. Public credit could not long ſubſiſt in a ſtate ſo liable to revolutions as Hindoſtan; for how could the people in the remote provinces receive for money, the baſe repreſentative of a treaſury that ſo often changed its maſter?

A. D. 1329. Hig. 730.

Villainies in the mint.

From theſe evils general murmurs and confuſions aroſe throughout the empire. The Emperor, to eaſe the minds of the people, was obliged to call in the copper currency. But there had been ſuch abuſes in the mint, that, after the treaſury was emptied, there ſtill remained a heavy demand. This he was forced to ſtrike off, and thouſands were ruined. The Emperor himſelf was ſo far from winning by this indigeſted ſcheme, that he loſt all he had in his treaſury; and the bankers accumulated immenſe fortunes; on the ruin of their ſovereign and the people. Mahommed, by the advice of Amir Norole, a Mogul chief, who, with thouſands of his tribe, had entered into the ſervice, raiſed a great army. The Mogul buoyed up the Emperor's mind with the facility of reducing both Perſia and Tartary; but before theſe mighty projects could be put in execution,

Mahommed obliged to call in the copper money.

A.D. 1337. Hig. 738. cution, he fell in arrears to his forces. They, finding they could not ſubſiſt without pay, diſperſed themſelves over the empire, and carried pillage, ruin, and death, to every quarter. Theſe misfortunes comprehended the domeſtic tranſactions of many years. The public treaſury being ſquandered by impolitic ſchemes and follies of various kinds, the King entered into a project to repair his finances, equally abſurd with that by which they were principally ruined.

Projects the conqueſt of China. Having heard of the great wealth of China, Mahommed formed a reſolution to ſubdue that kingdom; but, to accompliſh his deſign, it was firſt neceſſary to conquer the country of Himmatchil, which lies between the borders of China and India. He accordingly, in the year 738, ordered one hundred thouſand horſe, under the command of his ſiſter's ſon Chuſero, to ſubdue the mountainous country of Himmatchil, and fix garriſons as far as the frontiers of China. When this ſhould be done, he propoſed to advance in perſon, with his whole force, to invade that empire. The Omrahs and counſellors of ſtate went ſo far, as plainly to tell him that the troops of India never yet could, and never would advance a ſtep within the limits of that mighty empire, and that the whole was a viſionary project. The Emperor inſiſted upon making the experiment, and accordingly this army was put in motion, and, having entered the mountains, began to build ſmall forts on the road, to ſecure a communication; proceeding in this manner to the boundaries of China, where a numerous army appeared to oppoſe them. As their numbers were by this time greatly diminiſhed, and much inferior to that of the enemy, the troops of Hindoſtan were ſtruck with univerſal diſmay, upon conſidering their diſtance from home, the rugged ways they had paſſed, and the rainy ſeaſon which

was

was now approaching; besides the scarcity of provisions, which now began to be severely felt. In this consternation, they bent their march towards the foot of a mountain, where the savage inhabitants of the hills poured down upon them, and plundered their baggage, while the Chinese army lay in their front. A.D. 1337. Hig. 738.

In this distressful situation they remained for seven days, suffering the extremities of famine without knowing how to proceed. At length such a heavy rain fell, that the cavalry were up to their bellies in water, which obliged the Chinese to remove their camp to a greater distance. Chusero then determined to endeavour to make his retreat, but the low country was quite covered with water, and the mountains with impervious woods. Their misfortunes now came to a crisis. Having lost the road, they found themselves in such an unfortunate situation, that they could find no way out but that by which they entered, which was now possessed by the enemy. This whole army in short, in the space of fifteen days, fell a prey to famine, and a victim to false ambition; scarce a man coming back to relate the particulars, except those who were left behind in the garrisons. A few of them escaped indeed the rage of the enemy, but could not escape the more fatal tyranny of their Emperor, who ordered them to be put to death, upon their return to Delhi. His army destroyed.

Baha, the Emperor's nephew, an Omrah of great reputation, known more generally by his original name Kirshasib, who possessed a government in the Decan called Saghir, began to turn his thoughts upon the empire, and gained over many of the nobles of the Decan to his party. By their influence, and the great riches which he had accumulated, his power became very formidable. He then attacked some Omrahs who continued Rebellion in the Decan.

A. D. 1338. Hig. 739. tinued firm in their allegiance, obliging them to take refuge in the fort of Mindu. Mahommed having intelligence of the revolt, commanded Jehan, with many other Omrahs and the whole power of Guzerat, to chastise the rebel. When the imperial army arrived before Deogire, they found Kirshasib drawn up in order of battle to receive them: but, after a gallant contest, he was defeated. He fled towards his government; but not daring to remain there, he carried off his family and wealth to Campala in the Carnatic, and took protection in the dominions of the Raja of that place, with whom he had maintained a friendly intercouse.

Kirshasib taken and flead alive.

Mahommed, in the mean time, took the field, and arrived soon after at Deogire. He sent from thence Jehan with a great force against the prince of Campala, by whom the imperialists were twice defeated: but, fresh reinforcements arriving from Deogire, Jehan engaged the Raja a third time, and carried the victory. He took the prince prisoner, but Kirshasib fled to the court of Bellaldeo, who, fearing to draw the same misfortunes upon himself, seized upon him, and sent him bound to the general, and acknowledged his subjection to the empire. Jehan immediately dispatched the prisoner to court, where the Emperor ordered him to be flead, and shewn a horrid spectacle, all around the city; while the executioner proclaimed aloud, "Thus shall all traitors to their King perish."

The Emperor makes Deogire his capital.

The Emperor was so much pleased with the situation and strength of Deogire, that, considering it more centrical than Delhi, he determined to make it his capital. But, upon proposing this affair in his council, the majority were of opinion, that Ugein was a more proper place for that purpose. The King, however, had previously formed his resolution. He therefore gave orders that the

the city of Delhi, which was then the envy of the world, ſhould be rendered deſolate, and that men, women, and children, with all their effects and cattle, ſhould make a grand migration to Deogire. To add magnificence to the migration, he commanded trees to be tore up by the roots, and planted in regular rows along the road, to yield the emigrants a ſhade, and that all who had not money to defray their charges, ſhould be maintained at the public expence. He ordered that for the future Deogire ſhould be called Dowlatabad, or the fortunate city; raiſed noble buildings, and dug a deep ditch round the walls, which he repaired and beautified. Upon the top of the hill upon which the citadel ſtood, he formed large reſervoirs for water, and made a beautiful garden. This change however greatly affected the empire, and diſtracted the minds of the people. But the emperor's orders were ſtrictly complied with, and the ancient capital left deſolate. A. D. 1338. Hig. 739. Deſtroys Delhi.

Mahommed having effected this buſineſs, marched his army againſt the fort of Gundana, near Jinner. Nack-naig, who was chief of the Colies, oppoſed him with great bravery, but was forced to take refuge within his walls. As the place was built upon the ſummit of a ſteep mountain, inacceſſible but by one narrow paſs cut in the rock, the Emperor had no hopes of reducing it but by famine. He accordingly ordered it to be blockaded, and, at the ſame time, made ſome ineffectual attacks, in which he was repulſed with great loſs. The garriſon becoming ſtraitened for proviſions, and having no hopes of Mahommed's retreat, delivered up the place at the expiration of eight months; and he ſoon after returned to Dowlatabad.

He had not been long in his capital, when he heard that his father's firm friend Ibah, the viceroy of Moultan, had rebelled, and was then reducing The vicero of Moultan revolts.

A. D. 1340. Hig. 741. ducing the country about the Indus with a great army. The cause of the revolt was this: Mahommed having sent an order to all his Omrahs to send their families to Dowlatabad, the messenger who was dispatched to Moultan, presuming too much upon the King's authority, upon observing some delay, proceeded to impertinent threats. He one day told Ibah's son-in-law, that he believed his father was meditating treason against the King. High words upon this arose between them, which soon ended in blows; and the messenger had his head struck off, by one of Ibah's servants. Ibah knowing the vengeful disposition of Mahommed, was sensible that this disrespect to his authority would never be forgiven, and resolved to seek refuge in arms.

He is overthrown and slain. The Emperor, upon these advices, put his spears in motion, and hastened towards Moultan; and Ibah, with a numerous army, prepared to dispute the field. Both armies at last met, and, eager for victory, engaged with great resolution; but after a great slaughter on both sides, misfortune darkened the standards of Ibah, and his troops turning their backs upon glory, abandoned the field. Mahommed immediately gave orders for a general massacre of the inhabitants of Moultan; but the learned Shech Rukun interceded for them, and prevented the effects of this horrible mandate. Ibah was taken in the pursuit, and his head brought to the King, who returned towards Delhi.

Mahommed resides at Delhi two years. At sight of their native country and city, all those who had been forced to Dowlatabad began to desert the imperial army, and to disperse themselves in the woods. The Emperor, to prevent the consequences of this desertion, took up his residence in the city; whither he invited them, and remained there for the space of two years. But then he again revolved in his mind the scheme of of making Dowlatabad his capital. He removed his family, obliging the nobles to do the ſame, and carried off the whole city a ſecond time, to the Decan; leaving that noble metropolis a habitation for owls, and the wild beaſts of the deſert. A.D. 1341. Hig. 742.

Oppreſſions, and unheard-of cruelty of the Emperor.

About this time the taxes were ſo heavily impoſed, and exacted with ſuch rigour and cruelty, by the officers of the revenue, that the whole extent of that fertile country, between the two rivers Ganges and Jumna, were particularly oppreſſed. The farmers, weary of their lives, in one day, ſet fire to their own houſes, and retired to the woods, with their families and cattle. The tyrant, having received intelligence of this circumſtance, ordered a body of troops to maſſacre theſe unhappy people if they reſiſted, and if they ſhould be taken, to put out their eyes. Many populous provinces were, by this inhuman decree, laid waſte, and remained ſo for ſeveral years. The colony of Dowlatabad was alſo in great diſtraction; the people, without houſes, without employment, were reduced to the utmoſt diſtreſs. The tyrannies of the cruel Mahommed exceeded, in ſhort, any thing we have met with in hiſtory, of which the following is a horrid inſtance. When he remained at Delhi, he led his army out to hunt, as is cuſtomary with princes. When they arrived in the territory of Birren, he plainly told them, that he came not to hunt beaſts but men; and, without any obvious reaſon, began a general maſſacre of the wretched inhabitants. He had even the barbarity to bring home ſome thouſands of their heads, and to hang them over the city walls. He, upon another occaſion, made an excurſion of the ſame nature towards Kinnoge, and maſſacred all the inhabitants of that city, and the adjacent country for many miles, ſpreading terror and deſolation wherever he turned his eyes.

But

A. D. 1341. Hig. 743. A rebellion in Bengal.

But to return to the chain of hiſtory: during this time, Fuchir, after the death of Byram, rebelled in Bengal, having ſlain Kuddir, and poſſeſſed himſelf of the three provinces of Bengal.* The Emperor, at the ſame time, received advices, that Seid Haſſen had rebelled in Maber. He ordered Ibrahim the ſon of Haſſen, and all his family, to priſon; then marched in the year 742, from the ſacking of Kinnoge, towards Maber. When he had reached Dowlatabad, he laid a heavy tax upon that city and the neighbouring provinces, which awakened the people into rebellion; but his numerous army ſoon reduced all the unhappy inſurgents to their former ſlavery. From that place he ſent back a part of his army, and Chaja Jehan, to Delhi, while he himſelf marched with another force towards Maber, by the way of Tillingana.

Mahommed buries, with great ſolemnity, one of his teeth.

When Mahommed arrived before Arinkil, there happened to be a plague in that city, by which he loſt a great part of his army. He himſelf had a violent ſtruggle for his own life, and was obliged to leave one of his Omrahs, Ahmed, to command the army, and return towards Dowlatabad. On the way he was ſeized with a violent toothach, and loſt one of his teeth, which he ordered to be buried with much ceremony at Beir, and a magnificent tomb to be reared over it, which ſtill remains a monument of human vanity and folly. Having arrived at Patan, he found himſelf better, and halted, to take medicines for ſome days. In this place, he gave to Sultani the title of Nuſerit Chan, and the government of Bidder on the Indus, with its dependencies, which yielded annually a revenue of one crore of rupees. He, at the ſame time, conferred the government of Dowlatabad and of the country of the Maharattors upon [illegible]ttilich his preceptor.

He

* Bengal, at this time, was divided into three governments.

He proceeded from Patan in his palankie to Delhi, having heard of ſome diſturbance among the Patan ſoldiers, ſtationed in that capital. He, at this period, gave leave to ſuch of the inhabitants of Dowlatabad as were willing to return to Delhi, to follow him. Many thouſands returned, but they had almoſt periſhed on the way by a famine, which then deſolated the countries of Malava and Chinderi. When they came to Delhi, they found that the famine raged with redoubled violence in that city, inſomuch that very few could procure the neceſſaries of life. Mahommed, for once, ſeemed affected with human miſeries. He even for ſome time entirely changed his diſpoſition, and took great pains to encourage huſbandry, commerce, and all kinds of induſtry. He opened the treaſury, and divided large ſums to the inhabitants for theſe purpoſes. But as the people were really in great diſtreſs, they expended the money in the neceſſaries of life, and many of them were ſeverely puniſhed upon that account.

A. D. 1342. Hig. 743. He returns to Delhi.

The miſery of the inhabitants.

Shahoo, a chief of the Mountain Afgans, about this time, commenced hoſtilities to the northward, poured down like a torrent upon Moultan, which he laid waſte, and killed Begad, the imperial viceroy, in battle, and put his army to flight. Mahommed, having prepared an army at Delhi, moved towards Moultan, but Shahoo, upon the King's approach, wrote him a ſubmiſſive letter, and fled to the mountains of Afganiſtan. The Emperor, perceiving that it was idle to purſue him, returned to Delhi. The famine continued ſtill to rage in the city ſo dreadfully, that men eat one another. He ordered, in this diſtreſs, another diſtribution of money towards the ſinking of wells, and the cultivation of lands, but the people, weakened by hunger, and diſtracted by private diſtreſſes in their families, made very little progreſs, while the drought continued, and

Rebellion of the Afgans.

A. D. 1342. Hig. 743. rendered their labour vain. At the ſame time, the tribes of Mindahir, and others who inhabited the country about Samana, unable to diſcharge their rents, fled into the woods. The Emperor marched forthwith againſt them with his army, and maſſacred ſome thouſands of theſe poor ſlaves.

The Gickers invade Punjâb. In the year 743, the chief of the Gickers invaded Punjâb, and killed Tatar the viceroy of Lahore in action. Jehan, upon this, was ſent againſt him. Mahommed, in the mean time, began to entertain a ridiculous notion, that all the misfortunes of his reign proceeded from his not being confirmed in the empire by the Calipha of Mecca. He therefore diſpatched preſents and ambaſſadors to Arabia, and ſtruck the Calipha's name, in the place of his own, on all the current coin, and prohibited all public worſhip in the moſques, till the Calipha's confirmation ſhould arrive. In the year 744, one of the race of the prophet, named Sirſirri, returned with the ambaſſador, and brought the Calipha's confirmation, and a royal dreſs. He was met without the city by the King in perſon, who advanced to receive him on foot, putting the patent of the Caliphat upon his head, and opening it with great ſolemnity. Returning into the city, he ordered a grand feſtival to be celebrated, and public ſervice to be read in all the moſques, ſtriking out every King's name from the Chutba, who had not been confirmed from Mecca. Among the number of thoſe degraded monarchs, was the Emperor's own father. He even carried this whim ſo far as to write the Calipha's name upon his houſes, robes, and furniture. Theſe, and ſome other ridiculous actions of the life of Mahommed, may reaſonably make us ſuſpect the ſoundneſs of his head. The Arabian ambaſſador, after being royally entertained, was diſmiſſed with a letter to his maſter,

An embaſſy ſent to Mecca.

master, full of respect, and with presents of immense value, and accompanied by Kabire, chief of the life-guards. A. D. 1343. Hig. 744.

This year Kisnanaig, the son of Lidderdeo, who lived near Arinkil, went privately to Bellaldeo, the prince of the Carnatic, and told him, "That he had heard the Mahommedans, who were now very numerous in the Decan, had formed a design of extirpating all the Hindoos; that it was therefore adviseable to prevent them in time." What truth there might be in this report we know not, but Bellaldeo acted as if he was convinced of such a scheme. He called a council of his nobles, in which it was resolved, that Bellaldeo should first secure his own country, by fixing his capital in a pass among the mountains, to exclude the followers of Mahommed from all those kingdoms. Kisnanaig in the mean time promised, when matters should be ripe, to raise all the Hindoos of Arinkil and Tillingana to his assistance.

Schemes for a revolt, formed in the Decan.

Bellaldeo accordingly built a strong city upon the frontiers of his dominions, and called it Bigen, from the name of his son, to which the word Nagur, or city, is now added. He then began to raise an army, and sent part of it under the command of Kisnanaig, who reduced Arinkil, and drove Ahmed, the imperial viceroy, to Dowlatabad. Bellaldeo, and Kisnanaig, having joined their forces with the princes of Maber and Doorsummund, who were formerly tributaries to the government of the Carnatic, they seized upon those countries, and drove the Mahommedans before them on all sides. In short, within a few months, Mahommed had no possessions in the Decan, except Dowlatabad.

The Decan lost to the empire.

The tyrannical Mahommed, upon receiving intelligence of those misfortunes, grew vengeful, splenetic, and cruel, wreaking his rage upon his

Emperor's tyranny, and distractions in the empire.

A.D. 1345. Hig. 746. unhappy ſubjects, without crime, provocation, or diſtinction. This conduct occaſioned rebellion robbery, and confuſion, in all parts of the empire. The famine became daily more and more dreadful, inſomuch that the Emperor, not able to procure proviſions even for his houſehold, was obliged to abandon the city, and to open the gates, and permit the ſtarved inhabitants, whom he had before confined, to provide for themſelves. Thouſands crouded towards Bengal, which, as we have before obſerved, had revolted from the empire. Mahommed encamped his army near Cumpula, on the banks of the Ganges, and drew ſupplies from the countries of Oud and Kurrah. He ordered his people to build houſes, which at length became a city under the name of Surgdewarie.

Inſurrections quaſhed

In the year 745, Nizam Bain, a zemindar, poſſeſſed of ſome lands in the province of Oud, and a fellow of an infamous character, collected a mob of the diſcontented farmers, and aſſumed the royal umbrella, under the name of Alla. But before Mahommed marched againſt him, the ſuba of Oud raiſed his forces, and, defeating him, ſent his head to court. Nuzerit, in the ſame year, who had taken the whole province of Bidder, at one crore of rupees, payable to the treaſury, finding himſelf unable to make good that contract, rebelled; but Cutulich, being ordered againſt him from Dowlatabad, expelled him from that government. During this period, Ali, who was ſent from Dowlatabad to collect the rents of Kilbirga, finding that country deſtitute of troops, aſſembled his friends, raiſed an army with the collections, and, in the year 746, erected his rebellious ſtandards, and took poſſeſſion of Kilbirga and Bidder. Mahommed, on this occaſion, ſent a reinforcement to Cutulich to ſuppreſs him. Cutulich arriving on the confines of Bidder, Ali

came

came out and gave him battle; but being defeated, he ſhut himſelf up in the city. He was however ſoon obliged to capitulate, and was ſent priſoner to the King, who baniſhed him and his brother to Ghizni. A.D. 1345. Hig. 746.

The ſuba of Oud, having paid great attention to the King, and entirely gained his favour, was appointed to the viceroyſhip of Dowlatabad and Arinkil, in the room of Cutulich. But he himſelf looked upon this appointment as an impolitic ſtep in the King, conſidering the ſervices Cutulich had done to his affairs in the Decan, and the power he then enjoyed; and therefore thought it a ſnare laid to draw him quietly from his own ſubaſhip, and then to deprive him of both. In the mean time, a number of the clerks of the revenues, being convicted of abuſes in their office, were ordered to be put to death. Some of thoſe who ſurvived found means to eſcape to the ſuba, and endeavoured to confirm him in his former opinion of the King's intentions. He accordingly diſobeyed the King's order, and erected the ſtandard of rebellion, ſending a detachment of horſe under the command of his brother, who, before Mahommed received any intelligence of his deſigns, carried off all the elephants, camels, and horſes, that were grazing or foraging near the royal camp. The Emperor, in great perplexity, called the troops of the adjacent diſtricts to his aſſiſtance; while Jehan joined him, with an army from Delhi. He moved his ſtandards againſt the revolted ſuba, who, with his brothers, had now croſſed the Ganges, and were advancing towards him, in great hopes that the imperial army, tired and diſguſted with their ſovereign's tyrannical behaviour, would join them. Suba of Oud meditates a rebellion.

Mahommed, enraged at their preſumption, mounted his horſe, and engaging them, after a ſhort conflict, put them to flight. The ſuba was taken Mahommed overthrows and pardons him.

A. D. 1346. Hig. 747.

taken prisoner, and his brother Shoralla drowned in the Ganges, as he was swimming across, having been wounded in the action, while another brother was slain in the field. The Emperor was so prejudiced in favour of the suba, that he pardoned him, and restored him to his former dignities, saying, that he was certain that Muluck was a loyal subject, though he had been instigated to this rebellion by the malice and falsehood of others. Mahommed marched from thence to Barage, to pay his devotions at the tomb of Musaood, one of the family of the great Mamood, Emperor of Ghizni, who had been killed there by the Hindoos in the year 557. He distributed great sums among the Fakiers, who resided at Barage, and then returned to Delhi. Another ambassador arrived at that time from the Calipha, and was received with the same distinguishing marks of respect as the former, and dismissed with rich presents. Not long after, a prince of the noble house of Abassi arrived at Delhi, and was met by Mahommed, at the village of Palum, and he presented him with two lacks of rupees, a large territory, a palace, and fine gardens. By way of respect to the Caliphat, he placed him upon his right hand, and even sometimes ridiculously condescended to sit down upon the carpet before him, and pay him obeisance.

Cuttulich recalled from the Decan.

Some of the courtiers calumniated Cuttulich, governor of Dowlatabad, accusing him of oppressions and other abuses in his government, though a man of justice and integrity. The King recalled Cuttulich to Delhi, ordering his brother Molana, to whom he gave the title of Alim, to take charge of what remained to the empire of the Decan, till he should send some person from court. When the King's order arrived, Cuttulich was digging a great pond or reservoir, which he begged his brother to complete, and prepared to return to Delhi,

Delhi, with all the revenues of the Decan, which he had previously secured in a fort called Daragire, upon a mountain close to the city. Mahommed, after the arrival of Cuttulich, appointed four governors for the Decan, having divided it into four provinces, and determined to reduce it, as before, to his obedience. To accomplish his purpose, he ordered a numerous army, under the command of Ahmed, late governor of Arinkil, an Omrah of great reputation, to march to Dowlatabad, and entered into articles with him, that he and the other chiefs should pay into the treasury seven crores of rupees * annually for their governments. To make up this sum, and to gratify their own avarice, they plundered and oppressed that unfortunate country. At the same time, Mahommed conferred the government of Malava upon Aziz, a mean fellow, formerly a vintner, and told him, that the Amirs of Sidda † were dangerous persons in that country, therefore to endeavour to extirpate them.

A. D. 1346. Hig. 747.

Encourages husbandry.

Mahommed then marched back to his old cantonments at Surgdewara, and began to encourage cultivation, upon a new plan which he himself had invented. He appointed an inspector, for the regulation of all that related to husbandry, by the name of Amir Kohi, who divided the country into districts of 60 miles square, under a deputy, who was to be answerable for its cultivation and improvement. About one hundred deputies received their appointments at once, and seventy lacks of rupees were issued out of the treasury, to enable them to carry on this work.

A cruel massacre at Bedar.

Aziz, when he arrived at Bedar, invited the Mogul chiefs to an entertainment, and assassinated

* Near ten millions of our money.

† Mogul captains, who entered into his service with Amir Norose.

A.D. 1347. Hig. 748. ed eighty of them, with their attendants. He wrote to the Emperor an account of this horrible maſſacre, who ſent him back a preſent of a dreſs and a fine horſe, for his loyal ſervices. Such were the morals of thoſe wretched days! The tyrannical Mahommed had now taken it into his head, that he would be better ſerved by people of low birth, than by the nobility. He accordingly promoted Litchena a ſinger, Pira a gardener, Munga his ſon, Baboo a weaver, Muckbil a ſlave, and other low fellows, to the degree of Omrahs, and gave them the command of provinces and high offices at court. He, in this, forgot the advice of the poet, who writes, that "He who exalts the head of a beggar, and hopes great things from his gratitude, inverts the nature of things, and nouriſhes a ſerpent in his boſom." This reſolution of the Emperor was occaſioned by a noble refuſal of the Omrahs to put his cruel orders in execution.

Diſturbances in Guzerat. In the mean time, the ſlave Muckbil, with the title of Chan Jehani, governor of Guzerat, with the treaſure, and the Emperor's horſes, ſet out for Delhi. The mercenary Moguls of thoſe parts, hearing of his intentions, waylaid him with a body of horſe, and having robbed him, retired to Narwalla, the capital of Guzerat. Mahommed hearing of this robbery, in a great rage prepared for Guzerat, leaving Feroſe, his nephew, governor at Delhi, and, in the year 748, marched to Sultanpoor, about 30 miles without the city, where he waited for ſome reinforcements. An addreſs came from Aziz the vintner, begging leave to go againſt the Mogul chiefs being nearer, and having a ſufficient force, as he imagined, for that purpoſe. The Emperor conſented to his requeſt, at the ſame time expreſſing much doubt of his ſucceſs, knowing him to be a daſtardly and unexperienced officer. Aziz

advanced

advanced towards the rebels; but, in the beginning of the action, he was struck powerless with terror, and fell headlong from his horse. He was taken, and suffered a cruel death; his army being defeated with some loss. A.D. 1347. Hig. 748.

Birni's reply to the Emperor.

Mahommed, being informed of this disaster, marched from Sultanpoor. It was on this march that he is said to have asked Birni the poet, what crimes a King ought to punish with severity? The poet replied, that seven sorts of criminals deserved severe punishment; these were, apostates from their religion, shedders of innocent blood, double adulterers, rebellious persons, officers disobeying lawful orders, thieves, and perverters of the laws. When he had reached the hills of Abu, upon the confines of Guzerat, he sent one of his principal Omrahs against the rebels, who met them in the districts of Bai, and gave them a total defeat. The Emperor, having halted at Barage, sent Muckbil after them, who, coming up with them as they were crossing the Nirbuda, put the greatest part to the sword. The few who escaped, taking protection with Madeo, prince of Buckelana, were all plundered of their wealth.

The Emperor's cruelty in Cambait and Guzerat.

The Emperor, upon this occasion, massacred many of the Mogul chiefs, and plundered Cambait and Guzerat of every thing valuable, putting all who opposed him to the sword. He then sent to Dowlatabad, to seize upon all the Siddas of those parts, to bring them to punishment. Muckbil, according to the orders, summoned Siddas from Raijor, and many other places. The Siddas, conformable to those orders, prepared for Dowlatabad, and when they were all collected, Muckbil dispatched them, under a guard of fifteen hundred horse, to the royal presence. When the Siddas, or Mogul chiefs, were arrived upon the frontiers of Guzerat, fearing that Mahommed

A.D. 1347, Hig. 748. hommed had a design upon their lives, they entered into a conspiracy for their own security. They, with one accord, fell upon their guard, slew Ahmed their chief, with many of his people, while the rest, under the command of one Ali, fled to Dowlatabad. The Siddas pursued them, and, before any advices could arrive to put the place in a posture of defence, they took it by assault, being favoured by the troops within, who became seditious. Muckbil, with whose behaviour they were satisfied, was spared. but all the rest of the Emperor's officers were put to death, and the treasure divided among the conspirators. The Siddas of Guzerat, and other parts, who were skulking about in the woods and mountains, hearing of the success of their brethren, joined them. Isaiel, one of the nobles of their faction, was proclaimed King, by the name of Nasir. Mahommed, hearing of this revolution at Dowlatabad, left Barage, and hastened towards that city. The usurper, having drawn out his army, waited to give battle to the King. The two armies accordingly met, and the Moguls, though greatly inferior in number, roused by their danger and wrongs, assaulted the imperial troops with such violence, that the right and left wings were beat back, and the whole army upon the point of flight. But many of the chieftains who fought in the van being killed, four thousand of the Siddas fled; and night coming on, left the victory undecided, so that both armies lay on the field of battle.

The impolitic conduct of the Siddas. A council of war being, in the mean time, called by the Siddas, who had suffered greatly in the engagement, it was determined that Ismaiel should retire into Dowlatabad, with a good garrison, and that the remainder should shift for themselves, till Mahommed should leave the Decan;

Decan; when they resolved to assemble again at Dowlatabad. This wretched conduct was accordingly pursued. The Emperor ordered Ahmed, who was then at Elichpoor, to pursue the fugitives, while he himself laid siege to the city. A.D. 1347. Hig. 748.

In the mean time, advices arrived, that one Tiggi, heading the Siddas of Guzerat, was joined by many of the zemindars, by which means he had taken Narwalla, the capital, and put Muziffer, the deputy governor of Guzerat, to death; imprisoned Moaz the viceroy, and was now marching to lay waste Cambait, having in his rout blockaded Barage. Mahommed, upon this, left an Omrah to carry on the siege of Dowlatabad, and, with the greater part of his army, marched with great expedition to Guzerat. He was plundered in his way of many elephants, and a great part of his baggage, by the Indians: he lost also a great many men in defending himself. Having, however, arrived at Barage, Tiggi retreated to Cambait, and was pursued by Buckera, whom the Emperor had detached after him. Tiggi, having engaged the pursuers at Cambait, turned the chace upon them, killed Buckera and many other Omrahs, while the rest retreated to the Emperor. The rebel ordered all the prisoners taken in the action, as well as those whom he had formerly in confinement, to be put to death; among the latter was Moaz, viceroy of Guzerat. An insurrection in Guzerat.

Mahommed, hearing of this cruelty, breathed revenge. He hastened to Cambait, and Tiggi, unable to oppose him, retreated; but was closely pursued thither by Mahommed. The rebel continued his flight to Narwalla, and, in the mean time, the Emperor, on account of a prodigious rain, was obliged to halt at Assawil a wole month. Advices were brought him at Assawil, that Tiggi, Mahommed pursues.

having

A.D. 1347. Hig. 748. having recruited his army at Narwalla, was returning to give him battle. He immediately ſtruck his tents and met the rebel at Kurri. Tiggi, having injudiciouſly ordered his men to intoxicate themſelves with ſtrong liquors, they attacked the imperialiſts with the fury of madmen; but the elephants in front ſoon repreſſed this borrowed valour, and repulſed and threw into confuſion the rebels. An eaſy conqueſt was obtained: five hundred priſoners were taken and put to death; and an equal number fell in the field. The Emperor immediately diſpatched the ſon of Buckera in purſuit of the runaways, by the way of Tatta, near the mouth of the Indus, whither Tiggi had fled; while the King went in perſon to Narwalla, and employed himſelf in ſettling Guzerat.

and overthrows the rebels.

A rebellion in the Decan.

News, in the mean time, arrived from the Decan, that the Mogul officers had aſſembled again under Haſſen Caco, had defeated Ahmed, who had fallen in the action, and had driven all the imperial troops towards Malava: That Iſmaiel had reſigned his regal dignity, which Haſſen Caco had aſſumed under the title of Alla. Mahommed was exceſſively chagrined, upon receiving this intelligence, and began to conſider his own tyranny as the cauſe of all thoſe diſorders. He therefore reſolved to govern with more mildneſs and humanity for the future. He called his nephew Feroſe, and other nobles, with their troops, in order to diſpatch them againſt Caco.

The Emperor reſolves to march in perſon againſt the rebels.

Before thoſe Omrahs arrived, the King was informed that the uſurper's army was prodigiouſly increaſed. He therefore determined firſt, to ſettle Guzerat and Carnal *, and then to march

* Now Joinagur.

in

in perſon to the Decan ; but this buſineſs was not ſo ſoon accompliſhed, as he at firſt imagined ; for he ſpent a whole year in regulating Guzerat, and in recruiting his army. The next year was alſo ſpent in beſieging the fort of Carnal, reducing Cutch, and the adjacent territories. Some authors, affirm, that Mahommed took the fort of Carnal ; but others of better authority, ſay, that he deſiſted from that attempt, upon receiving ſome preſents from the Raja. The poet Birni informs us, that Mahommed, one day, about this time, told him, that the diſeaſes of the empire were of ſuch a malignant nature, that he had no ſooner cured them in one place, than they broke out to another. He would therefore be glad to know what remedy now remained, to put a ſtop to this contagion. A. D. 1349 Hig. 750.

The poet replied, that when diſaffection and diſguſt had once taken root in the minds of the people, they were not to be exterminated, without tearing up the vitals of the ſtate : that the Emperor ought to be, by this time, convinced how little was to be hoped from puniſhment. That it was therefore his opinion, in this caſe, that the King ought to inveſt his ſon with the government, and retire ; which would obliterate all former injuries, and diſpoſe the people to peace and tranquillity. Mahommed, ſays Birni, anſwered in an angry tone, "That he had no ſon whom he could truſt, and that he was determined to ſcourge his ſubjects for their inſolence, whatever might be the event." He is adviſed to reſign the crown to his ſon.

The Emperor, ſoon after this converſation with Birni, fell ſick at Kondal. He had previouſly ſent Jehad and Ahmed to Delhi, on account of the death of the viceroy, and called moſt of the principal men of the empire to the royal camp. Having recovered a little from his diſorder Falls ſick.

A. D. 1351. Hig. 752. diſorder, he muſtered his army, and ſent to collect boats along the Indus, which he ordered towards Tatta. Marching then from Kondal, he arrived on the banks of the Indus, which he croſſed in ſpite of Tiggi; and was, on the other ſide, joined by five thouſand Mogul horſe. From thence he took the rout of Tatta, to chaſtiſe the Sumrahs, for giving the rebel protection. Arriving within ſixty miles of that city, he halted to paſs the firſt days of the Mohirrim; and when that faſt was over, having eat fiſh to exceſs, he was ſeized with a fever. He would not however be prevailed upon to ſtop, but, getting into a barge, he proceeded to within thirty miles of Tatta, and upon the banks of the Indus, on the twenty-firſt of Mohirrim, in the year 752, this tyrant was conquered by death, and ſhut up in the dark dungeon of the grave. He reigned twenty-ſeven years; during which time, he ſeems to have laboured with no contemptible abilities, to be deteſted by God, and feared and abhorred by all men.

Dies.

His execrable character.

State of Aſia.

Seventeen years before the death of Mahommed, the Mogul empire of Perſia fell into pieces, at the death of Abuſaid. A number of petty dynaſties aroſe out of the ruins; ſome of the imperial family of Zingis, and others of governors who had rendered themſelves independent in their provinces, between Tartary, Perſia and India, ſubject to the houſe of Zagatay, fell into anarchy and confuſion, about the time of Mahommed's death. Shotepala, Yeſun-Temur, Hoſila, Tu-Temur and Tohan-Temur, ſucceſſively mounted the Mogul throne of Tartary and China, during the reigns Tughlick and Mahommed in India. The Patan empire declined greatly under the impolitic government of

Mahom-

Mahommed. The [illegible] and eastern provinces were lost; and the territories of the Kings of Delhi were reduced to the same limits which bounded them [illegible] the successful reign of Alla. A.D. 1351. Hig. 752.

[illegible]

FEROSE

FEROSE III.

A. D. 1351. Hig. 752. Ferose.

WHEN the death of Mahommed happened his cousin Ferose * was in the imperial camp. He was nephew to the Emperor Tughlick; and Mahommed, having conceived great friendship for him, designed to make him his successor, and, for that purpose, recommended him upon his death-bed to the Omrahs. Upon Mahommed's demise the army fell into the utmost confusion. Ferose having gained over the majority of the Omrahs to his party, prevailed, with presents, upon the Mogul mercenaries to move to some distance from the camp to prevent disturbances, till he should reduce the rest of the army to obedience. Amir Norose, a Mogul chief, who commanded a great body of the imperial troops, deserted that night, and, having joined Altu, the general of the Mogul mercenaries, told him, that now was the time to plunder the late Emperor's treasure, and to retreat to their native country. Altu was easily prevailed upon to adopt this lucrative scheme. They therefore returned next morning to the camp, which was still in very great confusion, and, after a very sharp skirmish, loaded some camels with treasure. Ferose, to secure himself from further depredations, led the army to Sewan, and took every possible means to defend himself

† Moazim Mohizzib Ferose Shaw, ben Sallar Regib.

against the avarice of the mercenaries. The Omrahs, the day after this movement, waited upon Ferose, and intreated him to mount the throne. After many pretended excuses, he favoured the Omrahs with his consent, and was accordingly proclaimed Emperor.

A.D. 1351. Hig. 752. mounts the throne.

He, the very first day of his reign, gave orders to ransom many prisoners, who, during the late confusion, had fallen into the hands of the people of Tatta: and, upon the third day, he marched against the Mogul mercenaries, took many of their chiefs prisoners, and forced the rest to fly towards their own country. He, soon after, directed his march to the fort of Bicker, and gladdened the face of the court with princely presents, and gave very liberally to the zemindars of Bicker and Sewistan. He from thence sent Ahmed and Ali Ghori against the rebel Tiggi, with a part of his army, and marched himself towards Outch, where he did many acts of benevolence and charity.

Defeats the Mogul mercenaries.

At Outch the Emperor received advices from Delhi, that Jehan, who was a relation of the late Emperor, now about ninety years of age, had placed upon the throne a boy whom he had adopted, by the name of Mahommed, and had massacred a number of the citizens who had refused to pay him allegiance. Ferose sent Shanapir, to expostulate with the old man, who, he thought, was now in the dotage of years, with promises of forgiveness and favour, if he would relinquish his ridiculous scheme. The Emperor himself, in the mean time, remained with the army, to regulate the territory of Outch. He was soon after joined by Muckbil the vizier of the empire, who received an honorary dress, and a confirmation of his former dignity.

Affairs at Delhi.

Ferose having reached Hassi, on his way to Delhi, met an ambassador from Jehan, acquainting

Jehan sends an embassy to the Sultan.

A. D. 1351, Hig. 752. ing him, that now the empire was in the hands of Mahommed's family, and therefore, that it would be no more than juſtice in him, to acknowledge the title of the young King, and act as regent during the minority. Feroſe immediately convened the Omrahs before the ambaſſador, and aſked them, whether they knew any of the male iſſue of Mahommed. They all declared, that unleſs Molana Cumal, an Omrah then preſent, knew, they were perfectly ſtrangers to any ſurviving iſſue of Mahommed. Molana made anſwer, that though one ſhould remain of the iſſue of the former Emperor, it was now adviſeable to ſtand by what was already done. We have reaſon to believe, from this circumſtance, that the youth who was ſet up at Delhi, was actually a ſon of Mahommed, though it was, at that time, prudent in the Omrahs not to acknowledge him.

who deſires to accommodate matters amicably. The Emperor, after the council, ſent Zada the ambaſſador back to acquaint Jehan of what had paſſed, and to adviſe him to accommodate matters in an amicable way. When Zada arrived in the city, a number of the principal men in the place haſtened to the camp of Feroſe, and made their ſubmiſſion. Much about the ſame time, advices were received from Guzerat, that the rebel Tiggi was defeated by Ahmed: and, that very day, a ſon was born to the Emperor, whom he named Fatti. Theſe fortunate circumſtances concurred to ſtrenghen the intereſt of Feroſe.

Jehan ſubmits. Jehan, perceiving that he could not ſupport the young King, made overtures towards an accommodation to Feroſe. He ſent ſome reſpectable Omrahs to intercede with the Emperor for his pardon, and to ſolicit leave to pay his reſpects in perſon. Feroſe conſented, and accordingly the old man, with his head bare, and his

turban

turban hung round his neck, came, accompanied by ſome of the principal men of his party, to make his ſubmiſſion. The King according to his promiſe, gave him his life, but ordered the chief magiſtrate of Haſſi to take him under his care, which was a kind of impriſonment. Chattab, one of Jehan's aſſociates, was baniſhed to Karkinda, and Guſtami expelled the court. A. D. 1352. Hig. 753.

Upon the ſecond day of Regib, in the year 752, Feroſe marched into Delhi, and mounted the imperial throne. He immediately began to adminiſter impartial juſtice to his people, who flocked from all quarters, with their petitions. He, in the mean time, conferred offices and titles upon his Omrahs. Upon the fifth of Siffer, in the following year, he, in order to hunt, removed his court towards the hills of Sirmore, and reduced ſeveral zemindars to obedience. He, in the mean time, had a ſon born to him at Delhi, whom he named Mahommed, and ordered great rejoicings to be made upon the occaſion; diſtributing his favours with a liberal hand. Feroſe arrives at Delhi.

In the year 754, the Emperor hunted at Collanore. He ordered, upon his return, a palace to be built upon the banks of the Surſuti; and towards the end of the year, appointed one Jehan to the viceroyſhip of Delhi. He himſelf, in the mean time, marched towards Bengal, to ſubdue Elias, who had aſſumed the imperial title, and poſſeſſed himſelf of all Bengal and Behar, even to Benaris. When he had arrived in the neighbourhood of Gorupoor, the zemindars of that place, having brought proper preſents, were admitted to his preſence. Feroſe having penetrated as far as Pundua, one of the reſidences of the princes of Bengal, Elias retreated to a ſtrong poſt, whither the Emperor purſued him. An action enſued, but Elias ſecured himſelf in his poſt, which obliged the Emperor to ſurround Rebellion in Bengal.

 him,

A.D. 1353. Hig. 754. him, the place being almost inacceſſible. Things having continued in this ſituation for twenty days, Feroſe, intending to change his ground, and to encamp on the banks of the Ganges, went out to reconnoitre. The enemy, imagining that he meditated a retreat, advanced out of their poſt, and drew up in order of battle. But, when they ſaw that the Emperor was preparing to attack them, they again retreated within their works, but with ſuch precipitation and confuſion, that 44 elephants, and many ſtandards, fell into the Emperor's hands. The rainy ſeaſon coming on with great violence, a kind of peace was patched up between them, and Emperor returned diſappointed to Delhi.

Feroſe employs himſelf in public works.

In the year 755, Feroſe built the city of Feroſeabad, adjoining to that of Delhi; and in the following year marched to Debalpoor, where he made a canal 100 miles in length, from the Suttuluz to the Jidger. In the year 757, between the hills of Mendouli and Sirmore, he cut a channel from the Jumna, which he divided into ſeven ſtreams; one of which he brought to Haſſi, and from thence to Beraiſen, where he built a ſtrong caſtle, calling it by his own name. He drew, ſoon after, a canal from the Cagar, paſſing by the walls of Sirſutti, and joined it to the rivulet of Kera, upon which he built a city, named after him, Feroſeabad. This city he watered with another canal from the Jumna. Theſe public works were of prodigious advantage to the adjacent countries, by ſupplying them with water for their lands, and with a commodious water-carriage from place to place.

Bengal and the Decan become independent.

An embaſſy about this time arrived, with preſents and new conditions of peace from Bengal, which Feroſe accepted, and ſoon after ratified the treaty. Bengal became, in a great meaſure, independent of the empire, paying only a ſmall acknow-

acknowledgement annually, by way of present. He exacted no other terms of the Decan; so that these two great members were now lopt off from the government of Delhi. In the year 759, the king of Bengal sent a number of elephants and other rich presents, to Delhi, which was amply repaid in Arabian and Persian horses, jewels, and other rich curiosities. But when the imperial embassy arrived at Behar, they received news of the death of Shumse king of Bengal, and that his son Ascunder had acceded to the throne. They thought proper not to proceed further, and returned to Delhi. The Emperor being, in the same year, encamped at Semana, received advices that the Moguls had made an incursion as far as Debalpoor. He forthwith ordered a general, with a great army, against them; but the Moguls, before his arrival, had laden themseves with spoil, and retreated towards their own country. A. D. 1357. Hig. 759.

Notwithstanding the treaty of 757, Ferose, in the year 760, resolved upon another expedition into Bengal. Having arrived at Zifferabad, he cantoned there his army, during the rains. When he lay at this place, Bustami, who had been banished, returned embassador from the Calipha of Egypt †, with a chelat; for which he was graciously received, and dignified with the title of Azim. An embassy having been, in the mean time, dispatched to Ascunder, the new king of Bengal, returned with another on his part, and with rich presents. The King not being satisfied with these concessions, marched, after the rains were over, towards that country, and, on The Emperor invades Bengal.

† After the taking of Bagdat by Halacu, king of Persia, the grandson of Zingis, one of the family of Abassi assumed the title of Calipha in Egypt.

his

A. D. 1358. Hig. 760. his way, conferred the enſigns of royalty upon the prince Fatti his ſon. He gave him maſters for his inſtruction, to whom the royal youth gave great attention. Feroſe having arrived at Pundwah, Aſcunder, after the example of his father, retreated to Ackdalla, and ſhut himſelf up in that place. Being however cloſely inveſted, and reduced to great ſtraits, he ſent 48 elephants, and other preſents, to the Emperor, with overtures of peace. In a few days the terms were agreed upon, and Feroſe marched to Jionpoor, where he cantoned his army for another ſeaſon, and then moved down behind the mountains, towards Jagenagur.

Feroſe ravages Jagenagur. Feroſe having croſſed the river Mendri, arrived at the capital of the Indian prince of Jagenagur, which was alſo called Benaris. The Raja, upon the Emperor's approach, fled towards Tillingana. Having plundered the country, Feroſe returned, and, upon his way, was met by the prince of Beerban, who preſented him with 37 elephants, and other valuable preſents, upon conſideration of not ravaging his country. The Emperor having received the preſents, changed his rout, and, as he paſſed through the woods of Pudmawitti, which abounded with elephants, he caught 33 of them, and killed a few in the chace. He then continued his march, and arrived at Delhi, in the year 762.

Schemes for improving the lands of Sirhind. Feroſe, who had much at heart the improvement of his country, was informed, that near Hirdar, in the province of Sirhind, there was a mountain from which there iſſued a great ſtream of water, which fell into the Suttuluz; and that beyond that place there was a ſmall rivulet called Selima, divided only by a riſing ground from the large ſtream which we have juſt mentioned. The Emperor conſidered, that, by making a cut through this eminence, the great ſtream might be carried into the rivulet, and ſo form a river

to

to water the countries of Sirhind and Munsurpoor, from whence it might be carried to Sunnam, and so render great tracts of land fertile. He therefore marched immediately that way, and ordered fifty thousand labourers to be collected together to cut the passage. When the workmen were in this place employed in digging to great depth, they found some immense skeletons of elephants in one place, and, in another, those of a gigantic human form, the arm-bones of which measured one yard. Some of the bones were in their natural state, and others petrified. A. D. 1360. Hig. 762.

The Emperor, having finished this great work, built a fort at Sirhind, which he called Ferosepoor. He, from that place, marched towards the mountains of Nagracut, where he was overtaken by a storm of hail and snow. He however reduced the Raja of those parts, after sustaining some loss on his side, and confirmed him again in his dominions; changing the name of Nagracut, to that of the city of Mahommed, in honour of the former Emperor. Ferose was told here, that the Goddess, whom the Hindoos worshipped in the temple of Nagracut *, was the image of Noshaba, the wife of the great Secunder, which that conqueror had left with them. The name of the idol is now changed to that of Jewallamucki. In the temple there was also, at that time, a fine library of the books of the Ferose reduces Nagracut.

* Some authors relate, that the image now worshipped at Nagracut, is not that of Noshaba, which, say they, Ferose sent to Mecca, where it was buried before the door of the great Mosque. It is not improbable, but Alexander, who penetrated to the Indies, might have left an image of the Grecian Goddesses upon the frontiers of his conquests. The Brahmins might have, with less absurdity, converted this foreign Goddess into one of their own growth, than those holy persons at Rome, who have changed the statue of Jupiter Tonans into one of St. Peter; disgracing, with a parcel of keys, that hand which formerly held the thunder.

Brahmins

A. D. 1372. Hig. 774. Bramins, consisting of one thousand and three hundred volumes. Ferose ordered one of those books, which treated of philosophy, astrology, and divination, to be translated into the Persian language, and called it the arguments of Ferose.

Invests Tatta. The Emperor, after the conquest of Nagracut, moved down the Indus towards Tatta, where Jambani, who had been always a subject of Delhi, had rebelled and fortified himself. The imperial army invested the city, but as provisions and forage became excessively scarce, and the rains had set in with great violence, Ferose was obliged to raise the siege, and march to Guzerat. He there spent the season in hunting, and, after the rains, he conferred the government of Guzerat upon Ziffer, and returned again to Tatta. which he reduces. Jambani capitulated, and delivered himself up to Ferose, who carried him, and the principals of his faction, to Delhi; but, after some time, he took him again into favour, and sent him to resume his former government.

The vizier and prince royal, die, In the year 774, Jehan, the vizier, died, and his son was honoured with his titles. Nothing remarkable happened till two years after, when the Emperor was plunged into affliction, by the death of his favourite son Fatte, a prince of great expectations. Ferose, in the year 778, was informed, that the revenues of Guzerat were greatly deficient of the collections. This induced him to listen to the proposals of Wamaghani, who offered to give one hundred elephants, forty lacks of rupees, four hundred Abassinian slaves, and forty Arabian horses, every year, over and above the present payment, should he be appointed to that government. The Emperor replied, that if the present viceroy, the successor of Ziffer, who was dead, would consent

to

to give as much, he ſhould be continued. But to this the viceroy would not agree, and therefore the imperial mandates were granted to Wamaghani, and he forthwith ſet out for Guzerat. Not being able the next year to perform his promiſe, he withheld the revenue, and rebelled, which was a juſt puniſhment upon Feroſe for his folly and avarice. The rebel, however, having greatly oppreſſed the people of his province, a conſpiracy was formed againſt him, and, by the aſſiſtance of the Mogul mercenaries, who were ſettled in that country, they ſeized him, and ſent his head to Delhi. This was the only rebellion which happened during this emperor's reign. The government of Guzerat was conferred upon Muſirra, with the title of Firhit ul Muluck.

A. D. 1379. Hig. 781.

There was a petty inſurrection among the zemindars of Atava, in the year 779. It was however ſoon cruſhed, and the inſurgents brought to puniſhment, while forts were built to keep them in proper ſubjection. In the year 781, Feroſe marched towards Samana, Amballa, and Shawabad, as far as the foot of the mountains of Saitoor, and, after demanding his tribute from the princes of the hills, which they paid him, he returned to his capital.

An inſurrection at Atava.

Much about this time, information was brought to the Emperor, that the zemindar of Kitter, whoſe name was Kirgu, had invited Mahommed, governor of Budaoon, and a number of his family, to his houſe, where he baſely aſſaſſinated them. The Emperor, enraged at this villany, marched immediately that way, and took ſevere vengeance upon the aſſociates and kindred of the aſſaſſin, putting them without diſtinction to the ſword, and levelling their houſes with the ground. The murderer himſelf made his eſcape to the mountains of Cumaoon, and was protected by the

Seid Mahommed's death revenged.

A. D. 1385. Hig. 787. the Indian princes of thofe parts. Ferofe ordered a adetachment of his army againft them. They brought back near thirty thoufand of thofe unhappy mountaineers, who were all condemned to flavery. The Emperor's juftice, in this cafe, degenerated into extreme feverity. Neither did the misfortunes brought upon thofe miferable captives fatisfy his thirft for revenge. He returned, every year, under pretence of hunting, to that unhappy country; but the people, and not the beafts of the foreft, were his prey. He by degrees cut off all the inhabitants, and converted whole provinces into a wildernefs.

The Emperor becomes aged and infirm.

Age and infirmity began, in the year 787, to prefs hard upon Ferofe. Jehan the vizier, having the fole management of affairs, became very powerful in the empire. The Emperor was fo much under his direction in all things, that he had the effrontery falfely to accufe Mahommed, the King's fon, of a defign againft his father's life, in conjunction with feveral Omrahs. He brought the old man firmly to credit this accufation, and obtained his authority to fecure the fuppofed confpirators. Ziffer was accordingly recalled from his government of Mahoba, and confined.

The prince's contrivance to undeceive the King.

A party was fent to feize the prince, who, having previous intelligence of the defign againft him, began to provide for his fecurity, placing guards, and fortifying himfelf in his own palace. In this fituation he remained fhut up for fome days; and at laft, having obtained leave for his wife to vifit the King's Zinnana, he put on his armour, went into the clofe chair, and was carried into the Seraglio. When he difcovered himfelf in that drefs, the frightened women ran fcreaming into the Emperor's apartment, and told him, that the prince had come in armour with

with a treaſonable deſign. The prince having followed them, preſented himſelf to his father, and falling at his feet, told him with great emotion, "That the ſuſpicions he had entertained of him were worſe than death itſelf. That he came therefore to receive it from his own hands. But firſt he begged leave to inform him, that he was perfectly innocent of the villanous charge which the vizier had purpoſely contrived to pave his own way to the throne."

A. D. 1387. Hig. 789.

The vizier puniſhed.

Feroſe, ſenſible of his ſon's ſincerity, claſped him in his arms, and weeping, told him, he had been deceived; and therefore deſired him to proceed, as his judgment ſhould direct him, againſt the traitor. Mahommed upon this went out from the preſence, and ordered twelve thouſand horſe to be in readineſs. With this body he ſurrounded the vizier's houſe that night, who, upon hearing of the prince's approach, put Ziffer to death, and collecting his friends, came out to engage him in the ſtreet. Upon the firſt onſet, the traitor was wounded, and drew back to his houſe. He fled immediately towards Mewat, and the prince ſeized all his wealth, and cut off his adherents.

Feroſe reſigns the crown to his ſon.

Feroſe, immediately after theſe tranſactions, reſigned the reins of government into the hands of his ſon, and abdicated the throne. The prince, aſſuming the name of Mahommed *, aſcended the throne in the month of Shaban 689; and immediately ordered the Chutba to be read in his own and his father's name. He ſettled the offices of ſtate, and diſtributed honorary dreſſes among the Omrahs. Facoob, an Omrah in great repute, was promoted to the government of Guzerat, with the title of Secunder Chan.

* His titles were, Nazir ul dien, ul Dunia.

Secunder

A. D. 1387. Hig. 789. The vizier delivered up and ſlain

Secunder having arrived at Mewat, upon his way to his government, Goga, with whom Jehan, the vizier, had taken refuge, fearing the new Emperor's reſentment, ſeized him, and ſent him bound to Secunder, who cut off his head, and ſent it to Delhi. Mahommed went with his army, in the year 790, towards the mountains of Sirmore, to hunt, according to the cuſtom of ſovereigns. When he was employed in the diverſion of the chace, advices were received, that Muſirra, governor of Guzerat, at the head of the Mogul mercenaries ſettled in that country, had riſen in rebellion, defeated, and ſlain Secunder, who had been appointed to ſucceed him. The Emperor haſtened to Delhi; but, as if all at once infatuated, he gave himſelf up entirely to pleaſure, and ſeemed to be inſenſible of the loſs which he had ſuſtained, and of the dangers in which his conduct had involved him. When his old Omrahs attempted to rouſe him from his lethargy, he turned them from his preſence, and filled their offices with pimps and court flatterers.

Baha conſpires againſt the Emperor.

The Emperor's nephew, Baha, reſolved to ruſh upon him in the midſt of his dream of pleaſure. He, for this purpoſe, conſpired with the diſgraced Omrahs, and arming one hundred thouſand ſlaves, erected the ſtandard of rebellion. Mahommed immediately diſpatched Malleck Lahori, to treat with the rebels. When he came to their camp, which was pitched without the city, the mob pelted him with ſtones, and obliged him to retire, very much bruiſed and wounded. Mahommed, ſeeing no hopes of a peaceable accommodation, began, at length, to beſtir himſelf, and advanced with his army againſt the conſpirators, and, after a bloody conteſt, drove them into the city. They immediately

A dreadful maſſacre in the city.

poſſeſſed themſelves of the palace, and again renewed the fight. The city became now a horrid ſcene

scene of slaughter and confusion. During the space of two days and two nights, there was nothing but death in every street: friends and foes, victors and vanquished, were jumbled together without any possibility of distinction. A. D. 1387. Hig. 789.

The old King placed between the combatants.

The slaves, upon the third day, brought out the old King, in his palakie, and set him down in the street between the combatants. When Mahommed's troops saw their former master, their affection returned, and, imagining that this was a voluntary deed of his, they at once deserted the prince, and crouded with shouts of joy to Ferose. Mahommed fled instantly, with a small retinue, to the mountains of Sirmore. Both parties looking up to the aged monarch, settled themselves into peace in his presence. Ferose, unable to govern on account of the infirmities of age, placed, by advice of the Omrahs, Tuglick, the son of his eldest son prince Fatte, upon the throne. The slaves, in the mean time, assassinated Hassen, the Emperor's son-in-law, for having endeavoured to support Mahommed: and even the first orders issued by Tuglick, when he mounted the imperial throne, was to kill all the adherents of Mahommed, wherever they should be found.

Ferose dies. His character.

Ferose, who had arrived at the age of ninety, died in the year 790. Though no great warrior in the field, he was, by his excellent qualities, well calculated for a reign of peace. His severity to the inhabitants of Cumaoon, for the assassination of the governor of Samana, is a great blot in his reputation. But to this he, perhaps, was prompted by a religious zeal and enthusiasm: for the persons murdered were seids or descendants of the prophet. He reigned thirty-eight years and nine months, and left many memorials of his magnificence in the land. He built fifty great sluices, forty mosques, thirty schools, twen-

ty

A. D. 1388. Hig. 790. ty caravanferas, an hundred palaces, five hofpitals, an hundred tombs, ten baths, ten fpires, one hundred and fifty wells, one hundred bridges; and the pleafure gardens he made were without number.

State of Afia. The Empire of Perfia continued under petty princes till Timur-Bec, commonly called Tamerlane in Europe, mounted the throne of the kingdoms of Zagatay, which comprehended all Maver-ul-nere or Tranfoxiana, and the provinces of Cabul, Zabuliftan, and others towards the Indus. After the conqueft of the northern Tartary, he turned his arms againft Perfia, and entered Chorafian, feven years before the death of Ferofe, the Patan Emperor of Hindoftan. He completed the conqueft of Perfia in lefs than five years, and when Ferofe died, Timur was employed in the reduction of the provinces upon the Euphrates.

TUGLICK * having mounted the throne in the palace of Ferofeabad, ordered, according to cuftom, the Chutba to be read, and the currency to be ftruck in his own name. He appointed Ferofe Ali his vizier, by the title of Jehan, and confirmed Mufirra, the rebellious governor, in his command of Guzerat. He foon after fent an army under the vizier, to expel his uncle Mahommed from Sirmore, and that prince, upon the approach of the imperial army, fled to the mountains. He there took poffeffion of a ftrong poft, and fecuring the wives and children of his adherents, waited to give the imperialifts battle. He was however beat from poft to poft till he arrived at Nagracut, and fhut himfelf up in that place. That fortrefs being very ftrong, his enemies did not think proper to befiege it, and therefore returned to Delhi. A.D. 1388. Hig. 790. Tuglick mounts the throne.

Tuglick giving reins to his youthful paffions, and neglecting the affairs of ftate, vice, luxury, and oppreffion began to rife up on every fide. He was not blind to thofe misfortunes, but he miftook the caufe, and admitted jealoufy and miftruft within his mind. He confined, and treated cruelly, his own brother, Sallar: and his coufin Abu Bicker, having reafon to dread the Emperor's refentment, fled the court, and, to fecure himfelf, ftirred up a faction againft Tuglick. The confpirators confifted of Rukun, the vizier's deputy, and feveral other Omrahs of Mal-adminiftration of the Emperor. A confpiracy.

* His titles were Yeas-ul-Dien.

high

A.D. 1389. Hig. 791. high repute, with all the imperial ſlaves, many of whom were in the higheſt offices at court.

Matters being ripe for execution, the conſpirators ruſhed into the Divan, and aſſaſſinated Mubarick, the captain general of the forces. Tuglick being thus ſurprized, fled by the Jumna gate. Rukun purſued him, and having taken him and Jehan the vizier, they were immediately put to death. This event happened on the twenty first of Siffer, in the 791; Tuglick, after a reign of five months and a few days, having fallen by the effects of the folly of youth.

He is ſlain.

THE conspirators having assassinated the King, raised Abu Bicker, the grandson of the Emperor Ferose, by his third son, to the empire. Rukun, being appointed vizier, took the reins of government in his own hands. But his ambition was not satisfied with that high employ. He formed schemes to cut off the new King, and to usurp the throne. Abu Bicker, having timely information of his intentions, was before-hand with him, and ordered him and many of the principal slaves concerned in the conspiracy to be put to death.

A. D. 1389. Hig. 791. Abu Bicker mounts the throne.

In the mean time, the Mogul chiefs of Samana assassinated the viceroy, Sultan, the fast friend of the reigning Emperor, and sent his head to the prince Mahommed, at Nagracut. They earnestly solicited him to come and assert his right to the empire. Mahommed accordingly, having collected his friends, advanced by the way of Jallendar to Samana, and proclaiming himself King at that place, advanced with a great army towards Delhi. After some repulses, Mahommed, as we shall see in the sequel, proved victorious, and sent Abu Bicker to his grave upon the twentieth of Zihige, in the year 792, when he had reigned one year and six months.

Mahommed enters Delhi.

MAHOMMED IV.

A. D. 1389. Hig. 792. Mahommed

MAHOMMED *, as we have already ſeen, mounted the throne in his father's life-time, in the 789. How he was depoſed and expelled by Baha, and the other Omrahs, in confederacy with the Mogul mercenaries of Guzerat, and the ſlaves of the houſehold, and his tranſactions, till he ſhut himſelf up in the fort of Nagracut, has been alſo related. When the chiefs of the Moguls had aſſaſſinated the governor of Samana, Mahommed, according to their invitation, marched with great expedition from Nagracut, calling all his friends from Delhi. He ſoon found himſelf at the head of twenty thouſand horſe, with which he advanced towards the capital. Upon the fifth of the firſt Ribbi, in the year 792,

enters Delhi

he entered Delhi, and lighted at the palace of Jehan. The Emperor, Abu Bicker, in the other quarter of the city, called Feroſeabad, prepared himſelf for battle; and on the ſecond of the firſt Jemmad, the two armies engaged in the ſtreets of Feroſeabad. In the mean time Nahir, with a ſtrong reinforcement, arrived, and joining Abu

Is driven from the city with great ſlaughter.

Bicker; they marched out of Feroſeabad next morning, and drove Mahommed, with great ſlaughter, quite out of Delhi.

* Naſir ul dunia ul dien, Mahommed Shaw.

Mahommed retreated with two thousand horse only, over the Jumna; and immediately dispatched Humaioon his son, and several Omrahs, to Samana to recruit his army. He himself, in the mean time, remained in the town of Tillasar upon the banks of the Ganges. Having experienced from first to last, that the slaves of Ferose were his declared enemies, he gave orders to plunder all their estates in the neighbouring country, and to slay them wherever they should be found. The zemindars fell upon some thousands, who had possessions in other parts of the empire, and massacred them; while the farmers in general, disgusted with Abu Bicker's government, which had been very oppressive, withheld their rents, and listed themselves under Mahommed. A. D. 1389. Hig. 792. He send to raise forces.

In the mean time, the viceroy of Moultan, and many Omrahs of note, having joined Mahommed with their forces, he collected, in a few days, an army of fifty thousand horse, made the usual appointments in the empire to please his friends, and advanced a second time towards Delhi. Abu Bicker had remained inactive in that city, ever since his late victory; he, however drew out his army at a village called Hindali, to oppose Mahommed, and was so fortunate as to come off victorious once more. He drove Mahommed towards Tillasar, but contented himself with pursuing him three crores, and with taking his baggage, and then returned to his capital. Is again overthrown

Humaioon, the son of Mahommed, not many days after the battle of Hindali, with the troops he had raised at Samana, made another attempt upon the capital, but succeeded no better than his father, being defeated at Paniput, and obliged to retreat towards Samana. But after all these successes, Abu Bicker thought it unsafe to His son defeated.

A. D. 1390. Hig. 793. leave the capital, being ſuſpicious of a faction in the city in favour of Mahommed. Having at length puniſhed ſome of the moſt diſaffected, he ventured to march about forty miles towards Tillaſar, where Mahommed was again collecting an army. The latter having, by this time, concerted meaſures with his faction in the city, left the body of his army, with all his baggage, at Tillaſar, and advanced, with four thouſand choſen horſe, towards Abu Bicker. When Abu Bicker had drawn up his army, Mahommed made a quick motion to the left, and paſſing the enemy's line, puſhed forward to the capital. He there engaged the troops of Abu Bicker who guarded the walls, and having ſet fire to the Budaoon gate, forced his way into the city. He immediately entered the imperial palace, whither the citizens flocked to pay him their reſpects. But Abu Bicker, having cloſely purſued Mahommed, arrived the ſame day before the city; and having forced the guards which Mahommed had placed at the gates, advanced to the palace, and drove that prince, whoſe troops had diſperſed themſelves, quite out of the city. He was obliged to retreat again to Tillaſar, where he joined his army, having loſt the major part of his detachment in the action.

Mahommed by a forced march, enters Delhi

Is again driven out by Abu Bicker.

Some time having thus paſſed without any deciſive action, Hagib, chief of the imperial ſlaves, known by the title of Iſlam, diſguſted with Abu Bicker, wrote to Mahommed, that if he would make another attempt upon the city, he would ſupport him with the greateſt part of the ſlaves who were under his direction. Abu Bicker hearing that Mahommed was again in motion, and having alſo diſcovered the diſaffection of the ſlaves and others in his army, ſhamefully abandoned the capital, and fled with a ſmall retinue. Mahommed,

Abu Bicker abandons Delhi.

hommed, in the month of Ramzan, entered Delhi, and aſcended the imperial throne. He gave the office of vizier to Iſlam, to whom he principally owed his reſtoration. When he found himſelf firmly eſtabliſhed, he ordered all the elephants which belonged to the ſlaves of Feroſe, to be taken from them, and converted to his own uſe. The ſlaves, enraged at this injuſtice, fled the city that night, and haſtened to join Abu Bicker. Mahommed, upon this deſertion, turned out a few who remained, and ordered them, upon pain of death, never to appear in the city, where they had acquired ſuch dangerous influence. Notwithſtanding this decree, many ſlaves, unwilling to leave Delhi, concealed themſelves: a ſearch was ordered to be made, and ſuch as were found were maſſacred. Some of thoſe poor wretches, upon this occaſion, cried out for mercy, affirming that they were originally Tartars. They were, upon this, ordered to pronounce the word Gurragurri, by which they were immediately diſtinguiſhed. All who ſounded it with the accent of Hindoſtan were put to death.

A. D. 1390. Hig. 793.

Mahommed, after having expelled the ſlaves, began to recruit his army, and ſent Humaioon his ſon, with a conſiderable force, againſt the Emperor Abu Bicker. When this army arrived at Kotluh, Abu Bicker, by advice of Nahir, ſurprized Humaioon in his camp. The prince, however, exerted his utmoſt efforts in oppoſing the enemy, being gallantly ſupported by the vizier, drove Abu Bicker, after a brave reſiſtance, quite off the field. Mahommed marched at the ſame time, with great expedition, towards Mewat, where Abu Bicker, ſeeing no hopes left, ſurrendered himſelf, and was ſent priſoner to the fort

Humaioon, marching againſt Abu Bicker.

Abu Bicker ſurrenders himſelf.

A.D. 1390. Hig. 793.

fort of Merat, where he died ſome years after.

Rebellion in Guzerat.

Mahommed returning to Delhi, received advices that Muſirra governor of Guzerat, rebelled. Ziffer was immediately diſpatched with an army to ſuppreſs the rebellion; but for the particulars of this expedition, we muſt refer the reader to the hiſtory of the province of Guzerat.* In the year 794, intelligence was brought to Delhi, that the prince Nirſingh, Sirvadon chief of the Mahrattors, and Bireban of Beſſu, chiefs of the Hindoos, had roſe in arms againſt the empire. Mahommed ordered the vizier, with a conſiderable force, againſt Narſingh, the moſt powerful of the inſurgents. Narſingh was defeated, made peace, and attended the conqueror to Delhi. The other two chiefs were ſubjugated at the ſame time. The zemindars of Attava, upon account of ſome grievance, roſe in arms, and ravaged Bittaram and the adjacent diſtricts. Mahommed marched againſt them in perſon, and chaſtiſed them. The fort of Attava was levelled with the ground, and the Emperor took the rout of Kinnoge and Tillaſar, in the laſt of which cities he built a fort, which, from his own name, he called Mahommed-abad.

The vizier falſely accuſed of treaſon.

Advice came to the Emperor from Delhi, that the vizier was preparing to fly to Lahore and Moultan, to kindle in thoſe provinces the flames of rebellion. Mahommed haſtened to the capital, and charged him with his treaſonable intentions. The vizier abſolutely denied the fact, but Jaju, a Hindoo and his own nephew, ſwore

* Our author's ſecond volume, in the original Perſian, treats of the particular hiſtory of all the provinces in Hindoſtan.

falſely

falsely against him. Mahommed, being either convinced of his vizier's guilt, or instigated by a jealousy of his power, condemned him to die. Jehan, who was perhaps a no small promoter of the vizier's fall, was advanced to his office. Muckurrib, who made a figure in the next reign, was, at the same time, appointed governor of Mahommed-abad. A.D. 1391, Hig. 794. Is put to death.

In the year 795, Sirvadon chief of the Mahrattors, and Bireban of Bessu, appeared in arms; and Muckurrib was ordered, with the troops at Mahommed-abad, against them. The Emperor, about this time, marched to Mewat, to quell some disturbances in that place. Upon his return to Mahommed-abad, he was taken ill of a dangerous fever, which rendered him delirious for some days. When he was in this condition, news was brought, that Nahir * had plundered the country to the gates of Delhi. The Emperor, though far from being recovered of his illness, hastened to Mewat. Nahir, who headed the rebels, drew up his army at Kottilab, and gave Mahommed battle; but he was defeated, and fled to Jidger. Mahommed falls sick.

Mahommed, after this victory, returned to Mahommed-abad, and, in the month of Ribbi the second of the year 796, sent his son Humaioon, to crush the prince of the Gickers, who had rebelled, and possessed himself of Lahore. But before the prince had left Delhi, news was brought to him of his father's decease; for the Emperor, having relapsed into his former disorder, expired on the 17th of Ribbi the second, at Mahommed-abad. He reigned about six years His death.

* An adherent of Abu Bicker.

and

A. D. 1392. Hig. 793. and ſeven months, and his body was depoſited at Delhi, with his fathers.

Humaioon aſcends the throne.

Mahommed being mixed with the dead, his ſon Humaioon aſcended the throne, by the name of Secunder. He continued or confirmed all his father's officers; but being in a few days taken with a violent diſorder, he went the way of his fathers, after a reign of forty-five days.

Dies.

MAMOOD

MAMOOD III.

WHEN Humaioon yielded to the power of his fate, violent diſputes aroſe among the nobles about the ſucceſſion. They at laſt fixed upon Mamood *, an infant ſon of the Emperor Mahommed, whom they placed upon the throne, by the name of Mamood Shaw; while Jehan remained in the office of vizier, and abſolute government of the ſtate. Muckirrib, governor of Mahommed-abad, was made captain-general of the forces. Sadit was appointed lord of the audience, Saring Chan governor of Debalpoor, and Dowlat nominated to the office of chief ſecretary of the empire.

A. D. 1393
Hig. 796.
Mamood, an infant, placed on the throne.

Promotions at court.

The apparent debility of the empire, ariſing from the King's minority, and diſſentions of the Omrahs, encouraged all the Hindoos around to kindle the flames of rebellion; particularly thoſe of the eaſtern provinces. Jehan, the vizier, upon this occaſion, aſſumed the title of King of the Eaſt, and proceeded towards Behar, with a great army. He ſoon reduced that coun-

Diſtractions in the empire.

* Naſir ul dien, Mamood Shaw.

A. D. 1393. Hig. 796. try to obedience, and having at the ſame time forced the Prince of Bengal to pay him the cuſtomary tribute, he returned, and fixed his reſidence at Jionpoor. While Jehan thus eſtabliſhed himſelf, in oppoſition to his maſter, in the Eaſt, Saring, governor of the provinces near the Indus, began to form an independency in the Weſt. Having, as ſuba of Debalpoor, collected the troops of the province of Moultan, and the north-weſt diviſion of the empire, he advanced againſt the Gickers, who waited for him at Adjodin, about twenty-four miles from Lahore. A battle immediately enſued, and the Gickers, being defeated, were obliged to take refuge among the mountains of Jimbo. Saring, after this victory, left his brother Adil in the government of Lahore, and returned himſelf to Debalpoor.

Mamood marched to Biana and Gualier. Mamood this year, having left Delhi in charge of Muckirrib the captain-general, marched towards Gualier and Biana, accompanied by Sadit and many of the chief Omrahs. When the King had arrived in the neighbourhood of Gualier, Mubarick, Eckbal the brother of Saring, and Alla, conſpired againſt the life of Sadit. But Sadit, having timely information of the plot, ſlew Mubarick and Alla, while Eckbal eſcaped to Delhi. Though the conſpiracy was thus quaſhed, the confuſions which were the conſequences of it, obliged the Emperor to return to the capital, without proſecuting the ſcheme of reducing thoſe territories to obedience.

The gates of Delhi ſhut againſt him. The diſtractions in the empire began now to multiply exceedingly. Mamood arriving in the neighbourhood of Delhi, Muckirrib, the captain-general, came out to pay his reſpects. But having on his way underſtood that Sadit had ſworn vengeance againſt him, for affording protection

to

to Eckbal, he fled back to the city, and, ſhutting the gates againſt the Prince, prepared to make a reſolute defence. The city in ſhort was beſieged for three months, till the King being aſſured that the war was commenced, and continued on account of Sadit, accommodated matters with Muckirrib, and in the month of Mohirrim 797, was admitted into Delhi.

A. D. 1394. Hig. 797.

Muckirrib, encouraged by the coming over of this Prince, marched the next day out of the city, with all his force, againſt Sadit; but he was beat back with great loſs. The rains had now come on, and it being impoſſible for Sadit to keep the field, he ſtruck his tents, and marched into Feroſeabad. He immediately ſent for Nuſerit, the ſon of the prince Fatte, the eldeſt ſon of the Emperor Feroſe, from Mewat, and ſet him up in oppoſition to Mamood, by the title of Nuſerit Shaw. Under the name of this Prince, Sadit began to manage the affairs of that part of the empire which adhered to Nuſerit. But a new faction breaking out in his government, diſconcerted his meaſures. The ſlaves of the Emperor Feroſe, diſguſted with his behaviour towards them, prevailed upon the keepers of the elephants to join them. They forcibly placed Nuſerit upon an elephant, advanced againſt Sadit, and drove him quite out of the city of Feroſeabad, before he had time to prepare for his own defence. To avoid one danger, the unfortunate Sadit fell into another; for having ſought protection under Muckirrib, the captain-general, he was by him put to death.

Another Emperor ſet up by Sadit.

He is ſlain.

The misfortunes of the ſtate daily encreaſed. The Omrahs of Feroſeabad, and ſome of the provinces, eſpouſed the cauſe of Nuſerit. Thoſe of Delhi, and others, ſupported the title of Mamood.

The uncommon misfortunes of the empire.

A. D. 1394 Hig. 797. Mamood. The whole empire fell into a ſtate of anarchy, confuſion, and diſtraction. A civil war was kindled in every corner, and, a thing unheard of before, two Kings, in arms againſt one another, reſided in one capital. Things however remained in this unfortunate ſituation for three years, with a ſurprizing equality on both ſides; for if one monarch's party had at any time a ſuperiority over the other, it was in ſingularity of misfortunes. It was not a ſtate of war, but a continued battle between the two cities: Thouſands were killed almoſt every day, and the place of the ſlain was conſtantly ſupplied by reinforcements from different parts of the empire. Some of the ſubas of the provinces took no part in this civil war. They hoped to ſee the empire ſo weakened by public calamities, that they themſelves might become independant; and to lay a foundation for their future power, they withheld the cuſtomary revenues.

Tranſactions in the north-weſt provinces.

In the year 798, Saring, the brother of the famous Eckbal, the governor of Debalpoor, having ſome differences with Chizer, governor of Moultan, made war upon him. After ſeveral engagements with various ſucceſs, victory declared for Saring. He immediately ſeized Moultan, became very powerful, and, in the year following, advanced with a great army to Samana, which he reduced to his obedience. Nuſerit diſpatched Tatar, ſuba of Panniput, and Almaſs, with an army, againſt him. They engaged Saring on the firſt of Mohirrim, in the year 799, gave him a ſignal overthrow, and obliged him to fly to Moultan.

The grandſon of Timur paſſes the Indus,

Saring received, in that city, intelligence, that the prince Mahommed Jehangire, the grandſon

ſon of Timur *, had built a bridge over the Indus, and that, having croſſed that river, he inveſted Outch. Saring immediately diſpatched his deputy, with other Omrahs, and the beſt part of his army, to reinforce Ali, the deputy of the governor of Outch. Mahommed, hearing of this army, advanced to the Bea, fell upon them by ſurprize juſt as they had croſſed that river, defeated, and drove them back into the ſtream; ſo that more were drowned than fell by the ſword. A few of the diſcomfited army made the beſt of their way to Moultan. Mahommed kept cloſe at the heels of the runaways, and obliged Saring to ſhut himſelf up in Moultan. After a ſiege of ſix months he was obliged, for want of proviſions, to ſurrender at diſcretion; and being impriſoned, with all his army, Mahommed took poſſeſſion of the city. Saring, in a few days, found means to eſcape: but the country remained in ſubjection to the Moguls.

A.D. 1397. Hig. 799.

Takes Moultan.

But to return to the tranſactions at Delhi. Eckbal, being diſguſted with the Emperor Mamood, deſerted him. He ſent a meſſage to Nuſerit, to deſire leave to join him with his party. This offer was very readily accepted; they met, went to the palace of Seri, and, upon the Koran, ſwore mutual friendſhip, at the tomb of Chaja Kaki. During theſe tranſactions, Mamood, with Muckirrib the captain-general of his forces, remained in the old city. The perfidious Eckbal, about three days after his deſertion, quarrelled with Nuſerit, and not regarding his oath, began to form a con-

Tranſactions at Delhi.

* Tamerlane.

ſpiracy

A. D. 1397. Hig. 799. Eckbal Chan's perfidy.

ſpiracy againſt him. Nuſerit, being informed of the plot, found himſelf conſtrained to quit the palace of Seri. The traitor fell upon him in his retreat, and took all his elephants, treaſure and baggage. The unfortunate prince, being in no condition to keep the field, fled to his vizier at Panniput.

A treaty between him and Sultan Mamood.

Eckbal took immediately poſſeſſion of Feroſeabad. His power daily increaſed, and he now employed it to expel the Emperor Mamood and Muckirrib from the old city. At length, by the mediation of ſome nobles, peace was concluded between the parties. But Eckbal, peculiarly perfidious, broke through all the ſacred ties of the treaty; and ſetting upon Muckirrib in his own houſe, by ſurprize, ſlew him. He immediately ſeized Mamood, and left him nothing but his life and the name of Emperor. Eckbal, in the ſame year, marched from Delhi with Mamood, againſt Nuſerit, and Tatar at Panniput. Tatar, leaving his elephants and baggage in the fort, paſſed, by forced marches, the army of Eckbal, arrived before Delhi, and inveſted it. Eckbal, truſting to the ſtrength he left in Delhi, advanced and attacked Panniput, and took it the third day, by eſcalade. He then haſtened back to Delhi, and Tatar having failed in his attempt upon that place, fled to his father in Guzerat. Eckbal entering the city, began to regulate the government, which had fallen into the utmoſt confuſion. In the mean time, to complete the miſeries of the unhappy city and empire, news arrived, that Timur had croſſed the Indus, with an intention to conquer Hindoſtan.

From

From the year 790 to the preſent year, Timur extended his conqueſt over all the weſtern Aſia, reduced the northern Tartary, and ſpread his ravages into Ruſſia, as far as the Arctic Circle. A. D. 1398. Hig. 800. State of Aſia.

END OF THE FIRST VOLUME.